THE 20TH CENTURY LEGAL PHILOSOPHY SERIES

VII

LAW AND MORALITY: LEON PETRAZYCKI

20TH CENTURY LEGAL PHILOSOPHY SERIES: VOL. VII

Law and Morality: Leon Petrażycki

TRANSLATED BY

HUGH W. BABB

WITH AN INTRODUCTION BY

NICHOLAS S. TIMASHEFF

CAMBRIDGE, MASSACHUSETTS
HARVARD UNIVERSITY PRESS
1955

Distributed in Great Britain by

GEOFFREY CUMBERLEGE

OXFORD UNIVERSITY PRESS

LONDON

LIBRARY OF CONGRESS CATALOG NUMBER 54-9329

PRINTED IN THE UNITED STATES OF AMERICA

GENERAL INTRODUCTION TO THE SERIES

BY THE EDITORIAL COMMITTEE

THIS book is one of the 20TH CENTURY LEGAL PHILOSOPHY SERIES, published under the auspices of the Association of American Law Schools. At its annual meeting in December, 1939, the Association authorized the creation of a special committee "for the purpose of preparing and securing the publication of translations on the same general lines as the Modern Legal Philosophy Series, sponsored by this association at the annual meeting thirty years ago . . . the materials to represent as nearly as possible the progress of Continental Legal thought in all aspects of Philosophy and Jurisprudence in the last fifty years."

Whereas the earlier Series was a very daring venture, coming, as it did, at the beginning of the century when only a few legal scholars were much interested in legal philosophy, the present Series could be undertaken with considerable assurance. In 1909 only a few of the leading law schools in this country included Jurisprudence in their curricula, and it was usually restricted to the Analytical School. By 1939 Jurisprudence was being taught in many law schools, and the courses had been broadened to include not only Analytical Jurisprudence, but also the Philosophy and the Sociology of Law. The progress in logical theory, in ethics, and in social science between 1909 and 1939 was without doubt an important factor in the expansion of Jurisprudence. In 1939 there was not only the successful precedent of the earlier Series, now completely out of print, but also the known rise of a very substantial body of interested readers, including students and practicing lawyers as well as professional scholars. This thoroughly admirable change, especially in the English-speaking countries, has been widely recognized as productive of a great enrichment of Anglo-American law. The Modern Legal Philosophy Series has been justly credited with a major part of that influence by making readily available the Continental jurisprudence of the last century.

The primary task of the legal philosopher is to reveal and to maintain the dominant long-run influence of ideas over events, of the general over the particular. In discharging this task he may help his generation to understand the basic trends of the law from one generation to the next, and the common cultural ties of seemingly disparate national legal systems. He may, again, create from these common ideal goods of the world's culture general theories, beliefs, and insights that will be accepted and used as guides by coming generations. The works of great legal philosophers serve not only the needs of the practitioner and other utilitarian ends; they also contribute abundantly to our theoretical knowledge. Indeed, in a deeper sense, we have come to understand the superficiality of setting utility against theory. The day is past when jurisprudence can defensibly be regarded as a curious hobby or as "merely cultural" in the sense that the fine arts contribute to the rounded education of a gentleman at the Bar. The issues are now correctly formulated in terms of whether one wishes to be a highly competent lawyer or a technician. Since the question, thus put, is obviously rhetorical, it is but another mode of asserting the considered judgment of those best qualified to pass on such matters, that the science and philosophy of law deal with the chief ideas that are common to the rules and methods of all positive law, and that a full understanding of any legal order therefore eludes those whose confining specialties keep them from these important disciplines.

The recent revival of interest in American history also reminds us emphatically that the great Fathers of the Republic, many of them lawyers, were men of universal intellectual outlook. They were as thoroughly grounded in French thought as in English. Grotius and Pufendorf were almost as widely read as the treatises on common law. Indeed, Jefferson and Wilson, to select two of the many great lawyers who come to mind, were able philosophers and social scientists. They apparently regarded it as essential to the best conduct of their professional careers to study philosophy and, especially, jurisprudence, Jefferson remarking that they are "as necessary as law to form an accomplished lawyer." The current movements in politics and economics have raised innumerable problems which, just as in the formative era of the Republic, require for their solution the sort of knowledge and skills that transcend specialization and technical proficiency. They call for a competence that is grounded in a wide perspective, one that represents an integration of the practitioner's technical skills with a knowledge of the various disciplines that bear directly on the wise solution of the present-day problems; and these are by no means confined to public affairs — they equally concern the daily practice of the private practitioner. With many such legal problems, with methods relevant to sound solutions, with the basic ideas and values involved, the eminent legal philosophers whose principal works appear in this Series have been particularly concerned. If it seems to some that the literature of jurisprudence is rather remote from the immediate practical problems that occupy the attention of most lawyers, it is necessary to reassert our primary dependence for the solution of all such problems upon theory — a truth that has been demonstrated many times in the physical sciences but which holds, also, in the realm of social problems. The publication of such a Series as this rests on the premise that it is possible to discover better answers than are now given many problems, that a closer approximation to truth and a greater measure of justice are attainable by lawyers, and that in part, at least, this can be brought about through their greater sensitivity to the relevant ideals of justice and through a broader vision of the jurisprudential fundamentals.

In the General Introduction to the first Series, it was noted that "The value of the study of comparative law has only in recent years come to be recognized by us. Our juristic methods are still primitive, in that we seek to know only by our own experience, and pay no heed to the experience of others." As the nations are drawn closer together by forces not wholly in human control, it is inevitable that they should come to understand each other more fully. The legal institutions of any country are no less significant than its language, political ideals, and social organization. The two great legal systems of the world, the civilian and the common law, have for some years been moving toward what may become, in various fields of law, a common ground. The civilian system has come more and more to recognize actually, if not avowedly, the importance of case-law, whereas the common law system has been exhibiting an increasing reliance on legislation and even on codes. In a number of fields, e.g., commercial law, wills, and criminal law, there is such an agreement of substantive principles as to make uniformity a very practical objective. While economic interests will undoubtedly provide the chief stimulus to that end, in the long-range view the possibility of focusing the energies of leading scholars and lawyers, the whole world over, on the same problems is the most inviting ideal of all. The problems of terminology, legal methods, the role of precedent, statutory interpretation, underlying rationale, the use of different types of authority, the efficacy of various controls and their operation in diverse factual conditions, the basic issues concerning the values that are implemented — these and innumerable other fundamental problems of legal science and philosophy may and should receive collaboration on a scale never before attainable. The road to the attainment of these objectives is not an easy one, but if any such avenue exists it is surely that indicated by the best literature in jurisprudence.

These fundamentals are also invaluable aids to better understanding of one's own law. On the side of insight into legal methods and substantive doctrines alone, the gain is immeasurably great. The common lawyer, at least until very recent times, was wont to accept a rigorous adherence to the rule of precedent as axiomatic in any modern system. He was apt to regard the common law through Blackstonian eyes; and he can hardly be said to have been even initiated into the criticism of statutes from other perspectives than those required by an unquestioning acceptance of the primacy of case-law. The gains should be no less great as regards organization of the substantive law. A century and a quarter ago John Austin remarked that the common law was a "mess." Although much progress in systematization has been made since that time, we still have a great deal to learn from our civilian friends — particularly from those who have attained wide recognition for their jurisprudential analyses of the common problems of modern legal systems. In addition, there is that vast illumination to be had from the discovery that other advanced legal systems, representing cultures of high achievement, sometimes apply to the solution of many problems different rules of law and even different basic doctrines than does our own. What better avenue to sound criticism of our legal system, what easier road to its early enrichment than by way of intimate knowledge of the innumerable ideas, some identical with our own but otherwise enunciated, some slightly divergent, others directly opposite, that are supplied so generously in the works of legal philosophers!

With the above objectives in view, the Editorial Committee, appointed early in 1940, immediately took up its task. For almost an entire year it engaged in active correspondence with practically all the legal philosophers in the United States, with many European, including English, legal philosophers; and, later on, when the Committee decided to include in the Series a volume devoted to Latin-American jurisprudence, there was much correspondence with legal philosophers of the various countries of Latin America. In addition, like activities centered on the engagement of translators qualified to translate correctly great works of jurisprudence into readable English. Anyone who has undertaken such translation will realize the difficulties involved, and the very high competence that is required. The Committee was able to set very rigorous standards in this regard because of the presence in the United States of an exceptionally able group of European legal scholars, some of whom had for many years been well versed in the English language.

In making its selection of works for inclusion in this Series, the Editorial Committee has been guided in part by the originality and intrinsic merit of the works chosen and in part by their being representative of leading schools of thought. The first Series, the Modern Legal Philosophy Series, had made available some of the work of nineteenth-century European legal philosophers — including Jhering, Stammler, del Vecchio, Korkunov, Kohler, and Gény. That Series and other publications had brought Duguit to the English-reading public. In 1936 the Harvard University Press published a translation of Ehrlich's *Fundamental Principles of the Sociology of Law.* The present century has also seen the rise of a number of brilliant legal philosophers who have attained very wide recognition. Among those whose inclusion in this Series was clearly called for were Max Weber, Kelsen, Petrazycki, Radbruch, the French Institutionalists, chiefly Hauriou and Renard, the Interests-Jurisprudence School centering around Heck, and some others. The opinion of the Committee as to these men was abundantly confirmed by the numerous communications received from legal philosophers of many countries, and the chief problem was to decide which of their works should be translated. But distinction in jurisprudence is not confined to a few writers, and any choice solely on the basis of scholarly merit would be enormously difficult, if not impossible. The Committee, like its predecessors, sought "to present to Anglo-American readers, the views of the best modern representative writers in jurisprudence . . . but the selection has not centered on the notion of giving equal recognition to all countries. Primarily, the design has been to represent the various schools of thought." (General Introduction to the Modern Legal Philosophy Series.) Some schools of thought have been much more productive than others; especially has this been true of those of Legal Positivism and Sociology of Law, which number many very able representatives. Without further presentation of the numerous phases of this problem, it may be stated that the Committee, whose members represent various legal philosophies, has endeavored to make the best selection possible under the conditions of its appointment, the objectives set before it, and the rigorous restriction resulting from the size of the Series.

The success of such a project as this required considerable assistance of many kinds, and the Committee is pleased to acknowledge the abundant aid extended to it. Our greatest debt is to the late John H. Wigmore, whose broad experience as Chairman of the Editorial Committee of the Modern Legal Philosophy Series was placed at our disposal, and who advised us frequently on many problems that arose in the initial stages of the work. As Honorary Chairman of this Committee until his death on April 20, 1943, he participated in many of its conferences and took an active and highly important part in launching the project and assuring its success. It was Mr. Wigmore who, in the early uncertain days of the enterprise, interested his former student, a Trustee of Northwestern University, Mr. Bertram J. Cahn, and Mrs. Cahn to contribute a substantial sum to defray the expenses of translation. The publication of the Series involved the expenditure of a considerable sum of money, and would have been impossible had not the Committee received a very substantial subsidy from Harvard Law School. No less a debt does the Committee acknowledge to the authors who contributed their work and, in some instances, their close personal collaboration. The translators have earned the Committee's admiration for their splendid achievements in the face of serious obstacles and with very little financial assistance to ease their task. We of the Committee wish, also, to give our very hearty thanks to the many legal philosophers, American, Continental, English, and Latin-American, who made many valuable suggestions and encouraged us greatly by their interest in the project. They are far too numerous to be named, as are those many persons in various positions, some of them rather humble ones, who lightened our tasks by their kindly aid. Finally the Committee acknowledges the special help given by Harvard Law School, the University of San Francisco Law School, Columbia University Law School, and Indiana University Law School. Each of the first two schools provided at its own cost a member of its faculty to serve as a translator, as well as stenographic assistance, and the other schools provided considerable stenographic, clerical, and other help. To each of the above persons and institutions the Committee gives its grateful thanks for assistance, without which the publication of this Series would not have been possible.

Special Acknowledgment

The Committee acknowledge with thanks that the publication of this volume of the Series was greatly aided by a substantial grant from the Humanities Fund, Inc.

The Committee also wish to express their appreciation of the very important contribution of Professor N. S. Timasheff who assisted in the selection of the materials for publication, in reading the proofs, compiling the Index, and in other ways.

CONTENTS

INTRODUCTION

By Nicholas S. Timasheff *

I. Russian Jurisprudence before Petrazhitsky †

Leo J. Petrazhitsky was the most eminent of the Russian legal philosophers of the early twentieth century. At that time, Russian legal philosophy, although less than a hundred years old, was definitely going through a period of flowering characterized by the diversity of schools and the presence, in most of them, of outstanding jurists. But the schools reflected similar schools in German and French jurisprudence and legal philosophy, and the debate between them was conducted with great courtesy, by an exchange of arguments implying that, whereas the opponent was wrong, he still was contributing something of importance to the understanding of the elusive phenomenon which is law.

The situation changed entirely when Petrazhitsky joined the debate. He bluntly told his students and colleagues that all the existing theories on the nature and properties of law were essentially wrong because they ignored the nature of its reality. What they considered to be real were mere phantasmata, and what is real in the law — they did not even suspect.

Of course, this was a tremendous exaggeration, but an exaggeration which, as known from the history of science, often occurs when a truly creative mind achieves every scholar's dream — a novel and promising solution of a difficult problem. Petrazhitsky had that creative ability and actually offered a solution of the basic problems of legal philosophy along paths not yet tried.

The novelty of his approach could be only relative: it is common knowledge that every invention, technological or cultural, depends on the "cultural base," that is, on existing knowledge, and incorporates a number of suggestions made by the inventor's predecessors. To understand the sources of Petrazhitsky's inspiration, as well as the reaction met by his work, a brief survey of the state of Russian legal philosophy and jurisprudence, as of 1900, is necessary.[1]

* Professor of Sociology, Fordham University.

† Although the Polish spelling has been used in the title (see Translator's Note, p. xxxix), we have used the transliteration "Petrazhitsky" throughout the rest of the book as it most clearly indicates the pronunciation. Publisher's Note.

[1] On the history of Russian legal philosophy see articles by Novgorodtseff, Gurvitch, and others in 2 Philosophie und Recht (1922); and Laserson, *Russische*

As elsewhere in continental Europe, Russia's legal philosophy was divided between legal idealism and legal positivism. The idealists tried to locate the law in the world of ideas and took it for granted that, in one way or another, law as idea is reflected in the world of human actions. The positivists were further divided between sociological positivism emphasizing the place of the law among social phenomena, and legal positivism in the narrow meaning considering that law was a self-sufficient system of norms to be studied from within, not from "above" as alleged by the idealists, nor from "without" as done by the sociological jurists.

Historically, in Russia, idealism was older than positivism. It was expressed in the earliest work in Russian on the subject — *Natural Law* by Professor A. V. Kunitsin (1783–1841), a work in two volumes (1818–1820), well-written along the lines of Kantian philosophy. Later on, Russian philosophy received a more conservative Hegelian flavor. The first and, for quite a time, the most prominent among the Russian Hegelians in legal philosophy was K. N. Nevolin (1806–1855). His *opus magnum* was *Legal Encyclopedia* (2 vols., 1838–1840). The title reflected the official program of the Russian universities which required that first-year law students be given a survey (encyclopedia) of the main branches of positive law (civil, criminal, procedural, commercial, constitutional), preceded by brief discussions of law in general. But, instead of a dull encyclopedia, Nevolin offered a brilliant course of lectures on legal philosophy. This is to be noted because, many years later, Petrazhitsky used the same method.

Since the seventies, idealism had begun to recede before the vogue of positivism. Nevertheless, works of the idealistic type continued to appear, and the very end of the century saw the emergence of a new and brilliant idealistic school. One of its most renowned members was B. Chicherin (1828–1902) whose major works were *A History of Political Theories* (5 vols., 1877–1902) and *Legal Philosophy* (1902). Chicherin, a follower of Hegel, believed that the denial of metaphysics, common among the positivists, was tantamount to the denial of law. But, despite his Hegelianism, Chicherin was not inclined to grant to the state the top rank among the social values. In his view, the state must be subservient to the law, since it is an instrument for the materialization of the latter. Aversion to the state was typical of Russia's

---

Rechtsphilosophie, 26 ARCHIV FÜR RECHTS-UND WIRTSCHFTSPHILOSOPHIE (1933). The present writer wishes hereby to acknowledge his indebtedness to the above authors as regards the first section of this Introduction.

social thought of the time; we shall meet it in Petrazhitsky's work, and shall also meet Chicherin among Petrazhitsky's critics.

Another late-nineteenth-century idealist, V. Soloviev (1853–1900), was a far more original thinker than Chicherin, and embodied in his work much of true Russian mysticism. Setting aside the rather theological aspects of his doctrine, his teaching on law, especially as expressed in his mature work, *The Vindication of Goodness* (1895), can be summarized as follows:

The central problem of the philosophy of law is that of the relationship of law and morals. The two cannot be separated. Law is a value because it makes possible the realization of the moral ideal. Between ideal goodness and the actuality of evil, law occupies an intermediate position, helping to actualize goodness and placing limits on evil. However, law and morals are not identical. The main difference revolves around the fact that morals are in the realm of freedom while law accepts coercion, although it does not demand it. At the same time, law is actually based on morals and is a "minimum" of morality. In its totality, morality is oriented towards an absolute object which is love. This is another important point to be remembered when studying the theories of Petrazhitsky.

The majority of the Russian idealists of the time were, however, neo-Kantians. Most prominent among them were P. I. Novgorodtseff (1868–1924), and Kistiakovsky (1920). Novgorodtseff was the first among Russian legal philosophers to advocate the revival of natural law. He proposed and defended this thesis in a series of works, among them *The Historical School in Jurisprudence* (1896) and the brilliant monograph on *Kant and Hegel* (1901). Kistiakovsky went much further along the lines of neo-Kantianism than did Novgorodtseff, as may be seen in his numerous articles collected under the title *The Social Sciences and the Law* (1916). We shall meet Novgorodtseff and Kistiakovsky as participants in the debate provoked by Petrazhitsky's revolution in legal philosophy.

Let us now turn to the positivist trends in Russian jurisprudence and legal philosophy. The rise of sociological positivism can be traced to one of Russia's greatest legal historians, V. I. Sergueyevich (1841–1910). In 1868, he published a work entitled *The Tasks and Methods of Political Science* which was conspicuously influenced by Comte, J. S. Mill, and Spencer. He denied as nonscientific the purely dogmatic study of law, and advocated the use of a positive or empiric method. Law should not be treated as a system of norms of a somewhat mysterious nature, but as part of social reality. Consequently, jurisprudence should be coördinated with sociology which is the general science of social phenomena. Sergueyevich's emphasis on law as reality (and not a system of ideas) obviously influenced Petrazhitsky; but, when the latter's works appeared, nobody was so bitterly critical as Sergueyevich.

In general, the writings of Sergueyevich exerted a profound influence on many Russian jurists of the day. Two of them, S. Muromtseff (1850–1910) and N. Korkunoff (1833–1902), combined the sociological heritage of Comte and Spencer with the teaching of R. Jhering. They fully accepted that part of Jhering's theory which functionally connected law with interests, but tried to liberate law from reference to the state, an institution which, as has already been said, was greatly disliked by most Russian thinkers.

There never was any tangible mental interaction between Muromtseff and Petrazhitsky; but one of Korkunoff's ideas has become a source of inspiration in Petrazhitsky's creative work. Korkunoff is best known as the author of *Lectures on the General Theory of Law* (1888, English translation, by W. S. Hastings, Boston 1909). But, in this context, Korkunoff's *Russian Constitutional Law* (2 vols., 1883–1886) is more important. There, Korkunoff denied the reality of "the will of the state" which had been a basic assumption made by all his German and Russian contemporaries. Instead, he proclaimed the existence of a force engendered by the consciousness of dependency (subordination) on the part of the citizens or subjects. Thus, the state was asserted to be a psychological phenomenon, an important point to be kept in mind when considering the theory of law held by Petrazhitsky.

To a certain extent, Korkunoff's psychologism could be traced back to the work of K. D. Kavelin (1818–1885) who combined positivism with certain elements of idealism. His writings on law were strongly influenced by the subjective school in Russian sociology which emphasized the role of the individual in society, the duty of improving one's moral character, and the duty of promoting social progress. Petrazhitsky never made any statement which would classify him among the members of the school; but it is very probable that his endeavor to discover the reality of law on the level of psychology depended on his acquaintance with the doctrine of the "subjective" school in sociology.

Legal positivism in the narrow meaning of the word, a precursor of H. Kelsen's "pure theory of law," was well represented in the Russia of Petrazhitsky's days. The first representative of the trend in Russia was S. V. Pakhman (1825–1910) who, in a work entitled *The Modern Movement in the Science of Law* (1882), developed the idea that jurisprudence was an autonomous, formal, logical science to be unfolded independently of philosophical or sociological considerations. A large number of Russian jurists, especially those teaching civil law, accepted Pakhman's lead. Among them one finds two outstanding jurists, G. F. Shershenevich (1863–1912) and D. D. Grimm, both bitter opponents of Petrazhitsky's novel views.

II. Petrazhitsky: The Man and His Work

Such was the situation in Russian legal philosophy when, around 1900, Leo J. Petrazhitsky engaged in his turbulent, almost revolutionary, activity with respect to the science of law.

Petrazhitsky was born in 1867 in the province of Vitebsk which formed the northeastern corner of the territory annexed by Russia from Poland in 1772. He belonged to the local gentry which in Vitebsk was predominantly Polish in its culture in contrast to the predominantly White Russian culture of the "people" of the province. The fact that he was of Polish ancestry and that he belonged to the nobility seemed to have had some bearing on the formation of Petrazhitsky's personality. He had to teach in Russian, but his accent was definitely Polish. In the beginning of his academic career this fact seems to have caused him some embarrassment, but in later years, after he had achieved fame, this was no longer important. The majority of his earlier works were published in German and signed "von" Petrazhitsky. In his Russian works, however, this prefix did not appear, because no article of nobility corresponding to the German "von" or the French "de" exists in the Russian language.

Leo Petrazhitsky studied at the University of Kiev where he was first enrolled in the School of Medicine. After two years, however, he transferred to the Law School, choosing Roman and civil law as his field of specialized study. As there was no good Russian textbook on Roman law, he translated, while still a student, Baron's famous *Pandects*, a work which was widely used for many years as a text in Russian law schools.

This unusual feat of having published a book while still a student, in combination with Petrazhitsky's brilliant performance in courses and his thesis (to graduate from a Russian University with a "first class diploma" one had to write a thesis approximately of the rank of an American Master's thesis), was the starting point of his academic career. The faculty of the Law School gave young Petrazhitsky the position of a "professorial aspirant," a high honor granted to only a few outstanding students. The "professorial aspirants" were required to take two to three years of postgraduate study under the supervision of three professors, pass a very difficult comprehensive examination, and publish a substantial monograph which had to be defended at a public meeting of the faculty. On successful completion of this program, the "professorial aspirant" received a "Magister's degree"; however, in order to receive the Doctor's degree one had to publish another monograph and, in turn, defend this work successfully before another public meeting of the faculty of the school.

Petrazhitsky had the good fortune to start his preparation for the professorship at a time when the Ministry of Education, aware of the shortcomings of Russian legal science, created in Berlin a special seminar for Russian "professorial aspirants," headed by Professor Dernburg, at that time the greatest living expert in Roman law. Petrazhitsky was chosen to participate in this seminar.

Contact with Dernburg and other German scholars gave a new depth to Petrazhitsky's command of the field. However, his life work was probably determined and more deeply influenced by another event that coincided with his studies in Berlin. At this time German jurisprudence had been given the most important task of helping to draft a new Civil Code. Thus, young Petrazhitsky was directly immersed in the problem of scientifically treating law in-the-making. The German jurists sought to accomplish this task on the basis of the doctrines of the historical and legal positivistic schools. This precluded the use of philosophical, sociological, or psychological points of view and caused the draftsmen to concentrate on the technical perfection of their product.

Petrazhitsky was by no means pleased or impressed by the performance of the German scholars and came to the conclusion that to provide a scientific background for legislation a new science, that of legal policy, was necessary. This was the turning point in his scientific development. In addition to becoming an excellent "dogmatic" jurist, able to interpret the most complicated legal texts, he developed an empirical theory of law reflecting many elements then present in both Russian and German jurisprudence, but in its main aspect quite original, testifying to his superlative creative ability.

At this point a parallel may be drawn with Comte (with whose work Petrazhitsky was familiar). Comte was striving to place social reform on a scientific foundation. Being aware that no empiric science of society existed, he decided to create one. Similarly, Petrazhitsky concluded that improvement of the law required, first, an applied science, namely, legal policy; and second, as its foundation, a theoretical, empiric-causal science of law which, he asserted, was conspicuous by its absence. Meditating on the empiric nature of law, he came to the conclusion that its reality was psychological. This idea had been anticipated by Bierling and Jellinek, Kavelin and Korkunoff, but it had never received adequate development. Petrazhitsky turned for assistance to psychology, but the psychology of his day was inadequate for the construction of the theory he needed. Boldly, he decided to create a new psychology, and in large measure he repeated the achievement of Spencer who, without previous training in psychology, wrote a remarkable treatise on the subject. While working on both his legal theory and his new psychology, Petrazhitsky saw that the teachings of contemporary logicians as to the formation and definition of concepts were insufficient, and he thereupon decided, also, to construct a new logic, at least with regard to concepts. This he succeeded in doing.

Of course, Petrazhitsky did not decide to take the steps outlined above at any one specific time. These ideas and plans developed gradually. When still studying in Berlin, he published two works primarily devoted to the dogmatic interpretation of civil law according to the best German models, namely, *Fruchtverteilung beim Wechsel des Nutzungsberechtigten* (1892) and *Die Lehre vom Einkommen* (2 vols., 1893–1895). The second of these contained an Appendix entitled "Civil Policy and Political Economy." It is in this Appendix that one finds the germ of Petrazhitsky's ideas on legal policy, especially, the principle of "active love." According to Petrazhitsky, "active love" must guide the efforts of the legislator in his search for better law. This was a truly Russian version of the doctrine of progress, as well as an original expression of the then incipient movement aiming at the revival of natural law. Strangely enough, it was so uniquely Russian that Novgorodtseff, himself an enthusiastic adept of the natural law movement, called Petrazhitsky's version fantastic, sentimental, and almost unintelligible to a Westerner.[2]

In a revised and expanded form Petrazhitsky published the Appendix in Russian under the title *Introduction to the Science of Legal Policy* (1896–97). For this work he was granted the Magister's degree and on the publication of his next monograph, *The Joint Stock Company* (in Russian, 1898), he received the Doctor's degree and the Chair of Legal Encyclopedia at the University of St. Petersburg. It was indeed fortunate that Petrazhitsky received this position rather than the Chair of Roman or civil law to which he was equally entitled. For had he been appointed to either the Roman or civil law posts, he could easily have developed

[2] *Über die eigentümlichen Elemente der russischen Rechtsphilosophie*, 2 PHILOSOPHIE UND RECHT 61.

into a typical *Gelehrter* of the German type and put aside the ambitious plan he had conceived in Berlin. However, as a professor of legal encyclopedia he followed the example of Nevolin and presented a course of lectures in legal philosophy.

When Petrazhitsky began his lectures at the University of St. Petersburg, he had not yet published any work on the general theory of law. His *Introduction to Legal Policy* was an outline of an applied science in the realm of jurisprudence. But from the very beginning the content of his lectures was quite at variance with what students of law heard in their other courses. Petrazhitsky bluntly asserted that, until his day, jurisprudence had been in a pre-scientific state, and that with his work it was ascending to the level of science. Petrazhitsky offered his students a novel theory couched in a system of new concepts. In his lectures, differences with previous theories were accentuated and these other theories were thoroughly demolished. But demolition was not an end in itself. From the ruins of these destroyed theories, a scientific edifice, beautiful in consistency and dramatic expression, emerged. Only a few could understand the more subtle aspects of the new doctrine. The majority were simply fascinated; some expressed admiration and agreement because Petrazhitsky was fast becoming the fashion among students of the University. This was true not only among students in the Law School, but also among those in science and the humanities who attended his lectures in large numbers.

Gradually the content of his lectures began to appear in print. The quintessence of the psychological theory of law was expressed in Part One (first 43 pages) of his *Essays on Legal Philosophy*, published in 1900. (Part Two of this same text, 95 pages, was devoted to a survey and criticism of the most important legal theories of Petrazhitsky's time.) Part One of his *Essays* contained these basic propositions:

(1) Law is part of reality, but its reality is psychological; in other words, it can be observed only in the content of mental processes.

(2) Legal experience is primarily the consciousness of will being bound by duty.

(3) Since this trait obtains also in moral experience, a *differentia specifica* must be found. It consists of a trait present in legal, but absent from moral, experience, to wit: the experience in law that a duty which is binding upon a first person, "A," is also indestructibly tied to a right or claim against "A" which is attributed to a second person "B"; this is not the case with regard to morals. In other words, morality is merely imperative, while law is attributive-imperative.

Petrazhitsky's *Essays*, positivistic in their aim and presentation, could not but provoke a negative reaction on the part of the leaders of idealism. Chicherin and E. Troubetskoy subjected the ideas of their young colleague to sharp, but kindly criticism. Chicherin denied the very possibility of thinking of law otherwise than in terms of norms which, for Petrazhitsky, were mere "phantasmata" (see below). The norm, according to Chicherin, is not an individual experience, but a principle obligatory for all. Positive law takes law out of the realm of thought where freedom reigns, and places it in the realm of an actuality which imposes itself on the individual. Troubetskoy reproached Petrazhitsky for confusing the psychological and ethical points of view, and for including sheer phantasies in the realm of law. He asserted that the nature of law could be cognized only on the philosophical level, by reference to natural law.

Petrazhitsky did not reply to these criticisms, for he understood very well that the psychological theory of law, as stated in his *Essays*, was far from definitive. As has already been said, neither the scattered statements of jurists asserting that law was somehow related to psychology, nor academic psychology, could help him. Hence, he embarked on the most daring enterprise of his life, the creation of a new psychology. The result of his studies appeared in a monograph entitled *On the Motives of Human Conduct* (1904), incorporated with some changes in the works translated (in abridged form) in this volume.

The psychology of Petrazhitsky's day was mainly analytical. The content of the mental process was divided into three compartments, cognitive, emotional, and volitional. Their synthesis into a total mental process was conspicuous by its absence, until the rise of the *Gestalt* school. Correctly observing that there were concrete mental processes combining passive (cognitive and emotional) and active (volitional) elements, Petrazhitsky suggested, in addition to the three traditional components, a fourth, concerning "bilateral experiences." These included not only such experiences as hunger or sex, but also the experience of duty.

The discovery of the complex, or bilateral, experiences was a decisive step in the development of Petrazhitsky's theory, since both law and morals or, more exactly, both legal and moral experiences belonged to this class. The bilateral experiences are, however, most diversified; hence a theory of law in terms of mental experience could be formulated only on the basis of a classification of these experiences. At this point, Petrazhitsky made another discovery, resembling the almost simultaneous discovery of conditioned reflexes by the Russian physiologist,

Ivan Pavlov. According to Petrazhitsky, in some bilateral experiences such as hunger or sex the active ingredient is completely predetermined by the passive ingredient. In other bilateral experiences, for instance, those caused by commands, or connected with aesthetic urges, or the sentiment of duty, the active ingredient is determined by the mental image of virtual action experienced simultaneously with the passive ingredient. The second type of bilateral experiences he called "abstract," while those of the first type he called "special." In terms of contemporary psychology, Petrazhitsky's "special" experiences of the bilateral type approximately correspond to unconditioned reflexes (instincts), while his "abstract" experiences correspond to conditioned reflexes in which the passive element (stimulus) brings about the active element (response) according to definite laws of learning.

Legal and moral experiences, according to Petrazhitsky, belonged to the class of abstract bilateral experiences. However, Petrazhitsky knew that this was not enough to identify them precisely. Instead, a complex classification was necessary, which he painstakingly provided. After doing this, he concluded that the *differentia specifica* of ethical experience (a term covering both legal and moral experiences) was to be found in the specific character of the mental images perceived simultaneously with the bilateral experiences. This was positive or negative evaluation of a virtual action *in se*, independent of considerations of utility or beauty.

Law and morals, for Petrazhitsky, together formed the class of ethics. In this regard he sided with V. Soloviev and, of course, with many other philosophers as against Chicherin and other Hegelians who were inclined to accentuate the differences between the two. It is noteworthy that, at about the same time in the United States, William G. Sumner, in his famous Preface to *Folkways* (1906), deplored the fact that modern nations had lost the Greek idea of ethos, the sum total of the standards of right.

In this way, the problems left unanswered in *Essays* seemed to be solved. The psychological nature of legal and moral experience in which, according to Petrazhitsky, the reality of law and morals consisted, was solidly intrenched in his new theory. From that foundation Petrazhitsky's *opus magnum* emerged, consisting of two closely related works, *Introduction to the Study of Law and Morals* (1905) and *Theory of Law and the State in Connection with a Theory of Morals* (2 vols., 1907). These works speak for themselves, and what follows is merely an indication of the *leitmotifs* of Petrazhitsky's system.

According to Petrazhitsky, the reality of law and morals is tantamount to the experience, by individuals, of mental processes, bilateral and abstract, containing (1) images of virtual actions, and (2) their evaluation not as means to an end, but in themselves. What it really means, can be demonstrated on these simple instances. Assume that A has borrowed from B $100, and the day stipulated for payment has arrived. What is happening in the real world? — asks Petrazhitsky. In the minds of A, B, and probably many bystanders, the image of a virtual action, payment by A to B, emerges. This image is combined with a positive evaluation: the action is good in itself, independently of any consideration of utility. Occurring in the mind of A, the image and the evaluation put in motion the ethical impulsion, or the impulsion of duty. This impulsion is a bilateral experience: the passive (cognitive) part is awareness of the situation (implying the image of the virtual action); its active part is action itself; the latter is committed, insofar as the ethical impulsion is not overcome by other, stronger, nonethical impulsions. Or let us think of a situation when a bank clerk is in the position of committing an embezzlement, with little chance of detection. But the image of the virtual action is combined with a negative evaluation. The ethical impulsion of duty works with the same intensity as in the former case; more often than not, its presence results in the omission of the anticipated action; but, time and again, an ethical impulsion may be overcome by stronger nonethical impulsions. The ethical impulsions, combined with images of anticipated actions and their evaluations, and not rights, duties, or norms, form the real *substratum* of the law. The law is therefore to be found in the minds of those who have the corresponding experiences, and nowhere else.

Emphasis on the presence or absence of specified ideas does not however make Petrazhitsky's legal philosophy idealistic. For him, not ideas themselves, but the actual experience of ideas, whether they are valid or not, whether they are shared by other individuals or not, is all that matters. It is, of course, common for individuals to share their legal or moral ideas. This usual sharing is explained by Petrazhitsky as the result of subconscious mass adaptation fostered by the necessities of survival. This idea is akin to Sumner's view that the most fitting folkways are selected by a process of trial-and-error.

Real, in Petrazhitsky's system, is the very mental process with legal or moral content. He designated as mere phantasies those things which are commonly considered by jurists to be real, for example, statutes, judicial precedents, customs, and the like. According to Petrazhitsky, the mental phenomena which form the reality of law, such as states of human minds ascribing rights and duties, possess the property of being projected onto the persons and things they concern; this property they share with many other phenomena. In other words, "real" is the mental fact of ascribing a right or a duty to oneself or another; this ascription always depends on the acceptance of normative judgment of norms. The latter are also merely states of mind, but are also projected into reality, in other words, ascribed reality. Men naturally behave as if the projections were real, while in actuality they are not; and on these projections the jurists found their theories.

Petrazhitsky understood how very different his concept of law was from the traditional ones. But, after scrutinizing the legal theories of his time one by one, he asserted that none of them contained a scientifically valid "class concept," nor did they explain the reality of law. He firmly believed that his solution was scientifically the only tenable one.

To a certain extent, however, Petrazhitsky was willing to reconcile his revolutionary views with common opinion. He divided law and morals into two types, positive and intuitive. The *differentia specifica* was the presence in positive law or morals of reference to "normative facts" from which the individuals derive their judgments on rights and duties, while in intuitive law such reference is conspicuous by its absence. Among the normative facts one could find not only statutes, customs, and judicial practices, but also *communis opinio doctorum*, contract, and so on. Petrazhitsky, further, divided law into official and unofficial. Official law was that used by courts and other state institutions, while law not used by such institutions he termed unofficial law.

The two classifications are independent of one another so that, according to Petrazhitsky, law may be (1) positive and official; (2) positive and unofficial; (3) intuitive and official; and (4) intuitive and unofficial. He conceded that official positive law, as defined by him, was very similar to law in the conventional meaning (not covering, however, international law).

The meaning of the classifications above may be best demonstrated by the following examples: (1) When a court renders a decision and refers to Article X of the Civil Code, or to a precedent, this is positive law (because of the reference to a normative fact) and simultaneously official law (because of the character of the agency). (2) When a freely chosen arbitrator solves an industrial conflict by reference to a well-established practice, this is positive law (because of the reference to a normative fact) and simultaneously unofficial law (because of the character of the agency). (3) When an Anglo-Saxon court decides a case on the foundation of equity, or a Swiss judge decides a case on the basis of a norm which he would have enacted if he were the legislator, this is intuitive law (because of the lack of reference to a normative fact), but official law (because of the character of the agency). (4) When, in a frontier situation, men take the law in their hands and hang a "bad man" because "he deserves it," this is intuitive law (because of the lack of reference to a normative fact) and unofficial law (because of the absence of an official agency).

It is obvious that a large number of norms commonly held non-legal must, according to Petrazhitsky, be classified as norms of unofficial law. Such are, for instance, numerous rules of politeness. These rules are attributive-imperative, in that they not only impose duties on certain individuals, but grant other individuals correlative rights. Thus, in polite society one must greet an acquaintance when meeting him, and the latter has a claim on that greeting, so that its omission would be felt as an insult. Most by-standers would agree with such qualifications of the reciprocal actions; *ergo,* they comply with Petrazhitsky's definition of law and fall into the class of unofficial law. Other classes of unofficial law may be found, such as nursery law (attributive-imperative impulsions among children), the law of various games, the law of criminal gangs, and so on.

Particularistic or even purely individual experiences of the attributive-imperative type are also legal, according to Petrazhitsky. When, before the Russian revolution, many peasants ascribed to themselves the right to own land, at the exclusion of landlords; or when workers ascribe to themselves the exclusive right to work in a factory where they have been employed for a certain time, and, in consequence, the right to use violence against strike breakers, these experiences are legal, though on the level of intuitive law. And if a person considers that he has sold his soul to the devil and ascribes him rights, and himself duties, the experience is also legal.

Petrazhitsky's theory in its developed form provoked a storm of indignation. A number of outstanding Russian jurists published articles and pamphlets, or included in their texts and monographs sections of criticism of the psychological theory of law. Representatives of all the trends joined in that criticism: Sergueyevich, the sociological positivist, Shershenevich, the legal positivist, Novgorodtseff and Kistiakovsky, the neo-Kantians, to mention only a few. Most vicious and implacable was the criticism by Sergueyevich.

This time Petrazhitsky decided to reply to his critics. In answer to his principal opponent, Sergueyevich, he published two articles and then expanded them into a small book entitled *The New Doctrine of Law and Its Criticism by Sergueyevich* (1910).

Of the other criticisms leveled against him, Petrazhitsky chose to answer that of Novgorodtseff.[3] He said that the great legal philosopher was more hostile to the psychological theory of law than he had been previously. Whereas, in an earlier paper published in 1902, Novgorodtseff recognized the desirability and even the necessity of studying law on the level of individual experience, in later articles he denied that Petrazhitsky was on the right track. Nor would he admit that Petrazhitsky's investigations had anything to do with the revival of natural law, which was a thesis close to the hearts of both men.

Petrazhitsky used this opportunity to restate his views on that subject, first expressed in his German works. He asserted that he did believe that natural law ought to be revived, but not in the form of rigid precepts formulated by philosophical abstraction. Natural law should be identified with a new empiric science, legal policy, to be built on the foundations of an empiric and causal theory of law which, in turn, must be based on psychology. Novgorodtseff replied by asserting that the science of law was not, nor could it be for him, a causal science.[4]

Petrazhitsky's article, in answer to the criticism of Novgorodtseff, contains much more than polemics. From the very start, he said, he had posed the problem of constructing a science of legal policy on the basis of an empiric study of law as a psychological phenomenon. The first task was to define the end of the law. Somewhat modifying his earlier view, Petrazhitsky now asserted that the end of law was man and social solidarity. Law had always moved towards this end, but in an unconscious manner. Now the time had come to make the movement a conscious one. However, since human beings are not ready to achieve this goal completely, law must strive, as an intermediary, to educate men in the spirit of love for their neighbors.

Between the publication of his *opus magnum* and the outbreak of the First World War, Petrazhitsky's attention was largely absorbed in this great controversy. He had first intended to summarize his answers to the critics in an appendix to his *Theory of Law and the State*, but later changed his mind and decided to devote a special volume to the controversy. Political events, however, did not allow him any opportunity to carry out this plan.

The lack of major contributions during this period does not mean, however, that Petrazhitsky limited himself to the struggle against the adversaries of his ideas. He published a number of excellent articles in

[3] *The Social Ideal and Natural Law*, 1 YURIDICHESKI VESTNIK (1913).

[4] *The Psychological Theory of Law and the Philosophy of Natural Law*, 1 YURIDICHESKI VESTNIK.

the weekly *Pravo* (The Law), of which he was one of the editors. In these papers he criticized the unfortunate tendency of Russian intellectuals to neglect the legal phase of social life and to strive for its improvement by revolutionary means. He also published during this period a book entitled *University and Science*, comparable in value to Max Weber's *Wissenschaft als Beruf* which appeared fourteen years later.

After the democratic revolution of March 1917, the Provisional Government appointed Petrazhitsky to the Senate, Russia's Supreme Court. Pessimistic, however, about the outcome of the revolution, he did not attend the Senate's sessions. When, after the peace treaty of Riga (1921), persons of Polish descent were granted the option of staying in the Soviet state or emigrating to Poland, Petrazhitsky chose the latter course. He was appointed Professor at the University of Warsaw and awarded the degree of Doctor of Laws *honoris causa* by the University of Wilno. His teaching was as brilliant then as it had been in Russia. A liberal, and deeply disturbed by the reactionary *coup d'état* of Marshal Pilsudski in 1926, he nevertheless contributed wholeheartedly to the project of unifying the civil law of the revived Polish state, which at that time was expressed in four different codes: Russian, German, Austrian, and a modified version of the *Code Napoléon*. He completed a number of manuscripts on various topics, but he published little. The pessimism engendered in him by Russian and Polish experiences deepened to such a degree that on May 15, 1931 he put an end to his life.

III. The Significance of Petrazhitsky's Work for Legal Philosophy

Despite his colleagues' resistance to Petrazhitsky's psychological theory of law, the theory began to have a strong influence on the thought of the rising generation of Russian jurists. One of his students, A. Kruglevsky based his monograph, *The Criminal Attempt,* on that theory. He submitted it to the University of St. Petersburg Law School as a Magister's thesis only to see it rejected because of the negative attitude of the majority of professors toward Petrazhitsky's ideas.

Nevertheless, two outstanding neo-Kantians, B. Kistiakovsky and V. Taranovsky, though critical of the psychological theory of law, incorporated a psychological element into their pluralistic theory on the nature of law. Kistiakovsky even wrote a few sentences stressing the merits of Petrazhitsky's work. "The idea of looking at the law as a psychological phenomenon has proven to be fruitful. Many of Petrazhitsky's pages on legal mentality can be considered classic. Very interesting are his statements about the actualization of the prescriptions of law and morals, on the violation of these prescriptions, on the reaction provoked by such violations, and on the tendency of the law to unify the views of parties confronting each other." [5] He concluded, however, that the advantages of Petrazhitsky's theory went just that far, but no farther and that the theory did not explain the reality of law as a universal phenomenon.

On the other hand, M. Reisner, a Marxian, attempted to combine Petrazhitsky with Marx. Marx had held that law was part of the ideology, which was itself part of the social superstructure; but neither Marx nor any one of his followers ever elaborated on these generalizations. Hence, Reisner reasoned, why not use Petrazhitsky's theory to explain ideologies in a realistic manner.[6]

After the Communist Revolution, Reisner was appointed Vice-Commissar of Justice. He used this opportunity to persuade his superior, the Commissar of Justice, that it was possible to abrogate *uno actu* the legislation of the Tsarist regime and of the Provisional Government since a substitute already existed in the form of the intuitive law of the workers' class. Reisner's advice was embodied in the decree *On Courts* (November 30, 1918), according to which the new courts had to render decisions on the basis of the enactments of the "Workers' and Peasants' Government" and of the revolutionary consciousness of the judges which was supposed to coincide with the ideas on justice held by the workingmen. Since, at that time, the enactments of the new government were scarce and unsystematic, the other source, revolutionary consciousness, had to prevail. As was later acknowledged by the Soviets, the result was legal chaos; [7] in consequence, in 1921–1923 a series of "codes" were promulgated, and Reisner's views fell into oblivion.

Later on, Petrazhitsky's name became taboo in the Soviet Union. He was classified among the idealists (which he certainly was not), while Soviet law and jurisprudence turned to legal positivism in its extreme form identifying the law with norms enforced by the state. Of course, the Soviet definition of law goes further and insists that the will of the state is tantamount to the will and interests of the dominant

[5] Social Sciences and Law (in Russian, 1916).

[6] Reisner's paper on the subject, published in 1908, appears in the volume on *Soviet Legal Philosophy* (1951, pp. 71–80), forming vol. v of the present series.

[7] Cf. N. S. Timasheff, "The Impact of the Penal Law of Imperial Russia on Soviet Penal Law," *American Slavic and East European Review* (1953), p. 445.

class.[8] This identification is, however, taken for granted, as a kind of *praesumptio juris and de jure*. Nothing could be more removed from Petrazhitsky's views.

Russian scholars who emigrated to other countries have contributed to the propagation of Petrazhitsky's ideas and to their amalgamation with the cultural heritage of the West. Pitirim A. Sorokin, a student of Petrazhitsky in Russia, has taken over several of Petrazhitsky's concepts, namely, that ethics is divided into law and morals, and Petrazhitsky's *differentia specifica*. In the *Social and Cultural Dynamics* (1937–1941) and *Society, Culture and Personality* (1947), Sorokin considers ethics as one of the five great systems which make up the super-system of total culture. He also treats law as almost coincident with the total social order, which accords with Petrazhitsky's theory.

Another jurist and sociologist of Russian origin, G. D. Gurvitch, has also maintained that the *differentia specifica* of law is its attributive-imperative character. However, he corrected Petrazhitsky's principal shortcoming, namely, the treatment of law as a phenomenon of individual consciousness, and dealt with it as the convergent recognition of values by group members.[9]

Very little has been done until recently to give American jurisprudence the opportunity of becoming familiar with the thought of the great Russo-Polish master. The short article on him which appeared in *Modern Theories of Law* (Oxford, 1933) is pitifully inadequate. In 1937–38 Professor Hugh W. Babb of Boston University published two important articles, one concerning Petrazhitsky's views on legal policy, the other, on his empiric theory of law.[10] Professor Roscoe Pound in 1938 called the attention of his colleagues to the theories of Petrazhitsky.[11] In 1947, in *Interpretations of Modern Legal Philosophy* published in honor of Pound's seventy-fifth anniversary, three articles appeared by Max Laserson, Pitirim Sorokin, and the present writer interpreting Petrazhitsky's contribution to the philosophy and science of law.

Petrazhitsky, himself, was much interested in making Americans familiar with his work. Thus, in a letter written shortly before his death he asked his former student, Professor G. C. Guins, then of the Law School at Harbin, Manchuria, now at the University of California in

[8] Cf. Vyshinsky's definition in the volume cited in n. 6, p. 336.

[9] Cf. his Sociology of Law (1942) 52–60.

[10] 17 Boston University Law Review (1937) 793–829, and 18 B.U.L. Rev. (1938) 511–578.

[11] 51 Harvard Law Review (1938) 809.

Berkeley, to emphasize "the empirical character of his theory based on observation of corresponding real phenomena, as distinguished from earlier theories having to do with unreal objects." [12]

There has never been much contact between Russian and American legal science, but, early in the twentieth century, there was a vivid exchange of views between scholars of Russia and of Western Europe, especially Germany. Unfortunately, however, Petrazhitsky's views on legal policy were available in German only in the rudimentary form presented in *Die Lehre vom Einkommen.* In 1907 a German translation of his pamphlet *On the Motives of Human Conduct* did appear, but this was only a fragment of his great work and, at that, the most questionable part of it. Shortly before the First World War, a complete German translation of Petrazhitsky's *opus magnum* was contemplated, but did not materialize. Only Rudolph Stammler found Petrazhitsky's ideas congenial, and in the twenties, A. Baumgarten and M. Rümelin barely mentioned him; later on, they were joined by W. Sauer.[13]

In Poland, a group of enthusiasts formed a Leo Petrazhitsky association which collected and classified all the manuscripts left by the master. A few articles appeared about him written by his students, among them J. Finkelkraut, President of the Petrazhitsky Association.[14] After Petrazhitsky's death, a few commentaries were written in French, Spanish, Italian, and Dutch,[15] and part of his *Introduction to the Study of Law and Morals,* again unfortunately devoted mainly to logical and psychological considerations, appeared in a German translation published in Paris.

It is noteworthy that, during the past two decades, there has arisen, in the Scandinavian countries, a new school of the sociology of law, the so-called Uppsala school whose members have posed the same problem as Petrazhitsky, the problem of a realistic interpretation of law on a psychological basis.[16] They try to replace the objective "ought to be"

[12] Communicated by Babb, 18 B.U.L. Rev. 574, n. 250.

[13] Baumgarten, Die Wissenschaft vom Recht (1920); Rümelin, Rechtsgefühl und Rechtsbewusstsein (1925); Sauer, Rechts- und Wirtschaftsphilosophie (1936).

[14] Communicated by Babb, 17 B.U.L. Rev. 796–797.

[15] Gurvitch, *Une philosophie intuitioniste du droit,* Archives de philosophie de droit et de sociologie juridique (1931) 403 ff.; Cornil, *A-propos d'un livre posthume de L. Petrazhitsky,* Archives de philosophie de droit et de sociologie juridique (1934) 59–101; Pietka, *Leone Petrazycky,* 12 Rivista di Filosofia del Diritto (1932) 109 ff.; Haskin, *Leo von Petrazycki,* 164 Rivista General de Legislacíon y Jurisprudencia (1934) 299 ff.; Verwey, *Een Paladijn der Rechtwetenshap,* 52 Rechtsgeleerd Magazijn (1933) 233 ff.

[16] The major representatives of the school are A. Hägerström whose contributions

(belonging to the realm of ideas) with the subjective experience of right and duty. This is very close to Petrazhitsky's theory; but, contrary to Petrazhitsky, the Scandinavians are not inclined to expand the concept of law to cover what the latter called intuitive law and unofficial law. The partial coincidence of views is an example of the familiar phenomenon of converging development in science; in any case, the members of the Uppsala school did not have direct access to Petrazhitsky's work. This did not prevent one of them, Karl Olivecrona, from writing a lengthy criticism of the theories of the Russo-Polish master.[17]

One may conjecture that, had it not been for the First World War and the Communist Revolution in Russia, Petrazhitsky's impact on legal philosophy would have been very great. In Russia, as has already been said, a number of young scholars were deeply impressed by Petrazhitsky and would probably have developed and modified his theories in their work. Had there been no war, a German translation of Petrazhitsky's complete works would undoubtedly have provoked interest and discussion among continental jurists. After World War I new problems, more practical than theoretical, arose. In general, the universality of science, especially the tendency to consider the contributions of scholars of all countries as contributions to a common treasury, was seriously curtailed.

For these reasons, Petrazhitsky's theory did not receive the attention it deserved, and did not fructify jurisprudence and legal philosophy to the full extent of its potentialities. The times are now more favorable for the revival of his theory — although not, of course, in its entirety. Petrazhitsky was a man of his time, a thinker marked by the early twentieth century. He shared the prevalent optimistic views on evolution as conducive to unlimited progress. His psychological theories only partly anticipated the revolution in that discipline effected by Pavlov. He could not be influenced by sociological jurisprudence and the sociology of law since he wrote his major works before these disciplines came into existence. Nor could he become familiar with the work of the American neo-realists which, in many regards, was congenial to his own. Petrazhitsky would have incorporated into his theory some of their findings, but he probably would have pointed out that the neo-realistic approach is a narrow one since law is not confined to court action, but permeates all of social life.

---

to the subject have been collected and edited by K. Olivecrona in a volume entitled INQUIRIES INTO THE NATURE OF LAW AND MORALS (1953); K. OLIVECRONA, LAW AS A FACT (1939); ALF ROSS, TOWARD A REALISTIC JURISPRUDENCE (1946); and T. GEIGER, VORSTUDIEN ZU EINER SOZIOLOGIE DES RECHTS (1947).

[17] 14 THEORIA (1948) 168–181.

There are in Petrazhitsky's theory numerous elements which are essentially sound and which, after modifications necessitated by scientific advances, could and should be incorporated into legal philosophy. Certainly, Petrazhitsky was the first legal philosopher who went beyond programmatic statements about the necessity of treating law as part of reality and beyond merely speculating that this reality was sociological or psychological. His theory, despite its limitations, was a complete and consistent theory of the reality of law.

Fifty years after the publication of his work, we are better able to judge what was sound and what was questionable in it. Emphasis on the psychological nature of legal reality was clearly very significant. Law is part of culture, and culture includes the "mental stuff" of its bearers. Even material objects, the so-called artifacts, have no meaning in themselves, but receive it only through mental processes of the men using them. Petrazhitsky was also on firm ground when he explained the reality of law and morals in terms of bilateral, passive-active, mental experience. However, one must reject Petrazhitsky's belief that these concatenations of stimuli-responses are stereotypes created through an evolutionary process and that such stereotypes include specific "ethical impulsions." Today, we know that there are no such biologically inheritable stereotypes. Learned behavior-tendencies do exist, but they are comprised of differentiated stimuli and responses to them. Behavior-tendencies are acquired by everyone through experience mainly on the basis of repetition and imitation reinforced by rewards for adequate responses, and penalization for inadequate ones. The reality of law and morals, as is true of many other parts of culture, consists in the fixation of identical or similar behavior-tendencies in the members of definite social groups. As part of culture, law consists of norms (which, contrary to Petrazhitsky's thesis, possess specific reality). Through learning, these norms are internalized in the personalities of the group members. Since the older generation strongly affects the learning process of the younger one, the content of learned behavior-tendencies is at least partly inherited, not however in a biological sense, but rather culturally. Though Petrazhitsky's interpretation was faulty in this respect, much of it can easily be restated in terms of modern psychology and sociology. This would undoubtedly provide important insights into the mechanisms of controlling human conduct by law and morals.

Second, Petrazhitsky's methodological innovations are in conformity with modern views on the subject, for example, the "class concepts." But the test of adequacy, or of the possibility of formulating a number of theorems in which the concept of law would be the subject, indicates the need for a narrower concept of law than the one formed by Petrazhitsky. Of course, Petrazhitsky was right when asserting that the concatenation of rights and duties (attributive-imperative experience, in his terminology) transcends the province of what he called positive official law. Since the middle thirties, this fact has been more and more perceived in sociology; now, the concepts of social position, status, and role play an important part in it, and status is commonly defined as the sum total of rights and duties attached to the social position occupied by an individual. There is however no cogent reason to consider legal all social phenomena in which rights and duties are involved. In advanced society, numerous and complicated techniques have evolved to create, ascertain, and actualize specified rights and enforce the correlated duties. The presence or absence of these techniques makes a great difference. Therefore the concept of law, contrary to Petrazhitsky's view, should emphasize enforcement by politically organized society or, as suggested by the present writer, by social power.[18] In this manner purely individual or particularistic experiences of the attributive-imperative type could be eliminated from the province of law.

Third, Petrazhitsky's treatise opens new horizons for the scientific interpretation of justice. In an illuminating section (32), he identifies justice with "intuitive law." Instead of the loose and vague terms in which justice is commonly discussed, Petrazhitsky formulates a system of propositions based on "intuitive law" and couched in terms analogous to those applicable to positive law. For one who does not accept Petrazhitsky's broad concept of law, justice or "intuitive law" forms a cluster of peripheral phenomena located around the nucleus of the law; they must be interpreted as an area of culture premeated by legal considerations without actually being part of the law. But one has to concede that scientific analysis of this area of culture is a prerequisite to the discovery of uniformities in the process of legal change, prediction of the probable consequences of enactment or repeal of a statute, better understanding of the process through which judicial decisions are arrived at, and the solution of many other important problems. In these regards, Petrazhitsky's work is full of stimulating ideas which merit systematic development.

Fourth, Petrazhitsky made an important contribution to jurisprudence by introducing the concept of "normative facts." According to Petrazhitsky, normative facts are those elements of legal (eventually moral) experience which point to the very foundations of the experience of

[18] Timasheff, Introduction to the Sociology of Law (1939), 12–17 and 263–267.

being "bound by duty." His discussion of normative facts (sections 35–38) is an excellent instance of a theory based on the class concept of law, and not on law as it appears in a concrete legal system. The theory of normative facts could and should be correlated with Petrazhitsky's psychological theory restated in terms of modern psychology. The experience of normative facts operative in a given culture would then appear as a stimulus-situation, the response to which would be the formation of new learned behavior-tendencies with legal (eventually moral) content. This could give new impetus to the theory of the internalization of law, which concerns the relationship between legal norms and individual legal consciousness.

Fifth, Petrazhitsky offered stimulating studies of the social functions of law, especially of positive official law. Two of these functions have received his special attention, the organizational and the educational. The organizational function of law, according to Petrazhitsky, molds the motives conducive to human actions, coördinates the very actions and thus creates social order. The educational function modifies the behavior tendencies of human beings, eradicating the anti-social and fostering the social elements. Thus, for instance, the civil law of liberal society has greatly developed thrift, the spirit of enterprise, and love of work, whereas the different types of constitutional law have differently molded the political mentality of the corresponding nations, inducing the members of some to independence, consciousness of rights and the tendency to fight for them, while the members of other nations have been taught to display obedience and acceptance of oppression and egocentrism on the part of those in power.

Both in his *opus magnum* and in several articles (partly referred to in Section II of this Introduction) Petrazhitsky exhorted the legislator to be conscious of the educative potentialities of official law and thus prepared a solid foundation for the conception of law as "social engineering."

The normal impact of Petrazhitsky's great contributions was cut short by an unfavorable tragic turn of history. This makes it even more incumbent upon Americans and English-speaking scholars, in general, to become familiar with the salient parts of Petrazhitsky's theory so that a constructive and original contribution will not have been made in vain.

TRANSLATOR'S NOTE

THE translation of this text for the 20th Century Legal Philosophy Series was begun in 1940. As published in St. Petersburg, The Introduction (to the Study of Law and Morality: the Foundations of Emotional Psychology) comprised 311 pages and The Theory (of Law and State, in Connection with a Theory of Morality) 758 pages. Some of the material was to be omitted from the translation, as important only at a particular time (forty or more years ago) or in a European context, or because its interest was solely polemical. Professor Timasheff (now of Fordham University, formerly a colleague of the author at the University of St. Petersburg) was to prepare a synopsis of Chapter III of the Introduction (now Section 4 *infra*): The Formation of General Concepts and Theories. Three complete drafts of the residue were made, the last being nearly 1,000 (typewritten) pages in length. In the result, there were certain defects from the viewpoint of an English reader. (a) Not merely is the original not particularly good or typical Russian (certainly not comparable with the luminous clarity of such contemporary texts as those of Novgorodtsev or I. A. Pokrovsky), but the almost incredibly repetitious prolixity (which I conceived that the faithful translator had no choice but to reproduce) would be repellent to a "Western" reader. (b) Still more formidable was the author's arbitrary use of terms (generally of Latin etymology) with a meaning (not suggested or found in any dictionary) which they did not bear in current Russian: thus aktsiiâ does *not* mean action or share (but response), kontrol' does *not* mean control (but verification), pritiâzatel'niĭ does *not* mean exigent (but attributive), psikhika does *not* mean psyche (but mentality), emotsiiâ does *not* mean emotion (but impulsion), and so forth. Most generously and unselfishly Professor Timasheff undertook the herculean task of removing these defects which disfigure a philosophical work of the very first importance, and carried through magnificently the complicated and delicate operation of excision and correction without sacrificing anything of substantial scientific significance. Responsibility for the text — and for any infelicities of form or substance therein — is, of course exclusively mine.

It is not for the translator to decide either the title of the work (Law and Morality would suffice, in his opinion) or the form of the author's name — whether Leon Petrażycki (which would seem desirable since he was born and died a Pole) or one of the two or three transliterations of the Russianized version.

Acknowledgment is due, and is gratefully tendered, to Professor Jerome Hall (long-suffering Chairman of the Editorial Committee), The American Council of Learned Societies (Mortimer Graves, Executive Director, and W. Chapin Huntington, Editor of the Russian Translation Project), The Kosciuszko Foundation (Professor Stephen Mizwa, President), and Philo C. Calhoun, Esq., for generous support and counsel; to my wife (who has devotedly read through the entire text no less than three times while I followed in the original); and to Barbara Worthevn, my secretary (who was able to decipher correctly and to transcribe coherently my hieroglyphics superimposed upon those of Professor Timasheff, from paper which was practically disintegrating at the outset).

H. W. B.

Watertown, February 27, 1954

COMPARATIVE TABLE

Translation *Section*	Russian Original (A) *Section*
1	1
2	2
3	3
4	4–6
5	7
	Russian Original (B)
5–20	1–16
21	22
22	23
23	24
24	25–28
25	29, 30
26–39	31–34
40	46
41	49
42	50
43, 44	51

(A) *Introduction to the Study of Law and Morality* (2nd ed., 1907).
(B) *Theory of Law and the State* (2nd ed., 1910).

NOTE ON OMISSIONS AND CONDENSATIONS

In this translation, certain parts of Petrazhitsky's treatise have been omitted: (1) the detailed exposition of his new psychological theory (*Introduction*, section 7 *ad fin.* to 19) as repeated in abridged form in section 1 of the *Theory* (section 5 of the translation); (2) the survey of the theories on the nature of law (*Theory*, sections 17–21); (3) the survey of the content of Russia's official law (*Theory*, section 45); the survey of the theories on public and private law (*Theory*, sections 46 *ad fin*, and 47, 48); (5) many paragraphs printed, in Russian, in single space indicating that the corresponding statements were not of primary importance; and (6) most of the footnotes which are of a predominantly polemical character.

The theory of logic (107 pages in the *Introduction*) has been condensed to a short section of four pages. The discussion of the various theories of legal relationships, rights, duties, and subjects of rights and duties (sections 25–32 of the *Theory*) has been significantly condensed.

In many places, repetitious statements have been omitted.

BIBLIOGRAPHY

(1) *Principal Russian and German Works of Petrazhitsky*

Baron: *System of Roman Civil Law*, translated into Russian by Petrazhitsky (1st ed. 1883; 2nd ed. 1899–1908; 3rd ed. 1908–1910).

Die Fruchtverteilung beim Wechsel des Nutzgungsberechtigten. Drei civilrechtliche Abhandlungen (1892).

Die Lehre vom Einkommen. Vom Standpunkt des gemeinen Civilrechts, u. s. w. Vol. 1. Grundbegriffe (1893); vol. 2 (1895–96) Einkommensersatz (1) Grundlegung (1–120), (2) Zinsen (123–333), (3) Arbeitseinkommen, Honorar, Unternehmergewinn (333–433). Anhang: Entwurf (II) Civilpolitik und politische Oekonomie (437–628).

Introduction to the Science of Legal Policy. Kiev. Univ. Isvest. 1896 (numbers 8, 10) and 1897 (number 9) pages I-CCL (See 17 B.U.L. Rev. 793) (1895).

The Stock Company (Russian): St. Petersburg (1898).

What is Law (1899) Viestnik Prava (1) 1. (Russian).

Administrative Law: (1899) Pravo 9-. (Russian).

Papers on Custom: (1899) Pravo 65-, 209-, 319-, 377-, 426-, 599-, 901-. (Russian).

The Exile of Criminals: (1899) Pravo 599-, 1001-, 1072-. (Russian).

The Part Played by Statutes in Civil Law: (1899) Pravo 809-. (Russian).

Suits for Unjust Enrichment: (1900) Viestnik Prava. (1) 1, (2) 131, (3) 192, (4) 50. (Russian).

Essays on Legal Philosophy: (St. Petersburg, 1900) (Russian).

Reform of University Teaching: (1901) Pravo 1163-, 1203-, 1251-, 1291-, 1325-, 1363-. (Russian).

The Law and the Court: (1901) Pravo 1-, 117-, 311-. (Russian).

The Renascence of Natural Law: (1902) Pravo 1793-, 1841-, 1915-. (apropos of Novgorodtsev: Kant and Hegel) (Russian).

Bona Fides in Civil Law (Russian): 2nd ed. 1903, St. Petersburg.

The Motives of Human Conduct (Russian): St. Petersburg, 1904.

Introduction to the Study of Law and Morality: The Bases of Emotional Psychology: (1st ed. 1905, 2nd ed. 1907, 3rd ed. 1908) (Russian).

Aktienwesen und Spekulation. Eine ökonomische und rechtspsychologische Untersuchung (translated from Russian into German): 1906.

The University and Science (Russian): (1907).

Theory of Law and State in Connection with a Theory of Morality: (two volumes: 1st ed. 1907; 2nd ed. 1909–10) (Russian).

Ueber die Motive des Handelns und über das Wesen der Moral und des Rechts (translated from Russian into German): 1907.

The Critique of My Introduction: (1909) Zhur. Min. Yust (9) 152 (Russian).
The New Doctrine of Law and Morality and the Critique of Sergeyevich: St. Petersburg (1910) 134 pages. (Russian).
Rejoinder to Sergeyevich: (1910) Pravo 1927-, 1980-. (Russian).
Papers on Private International Law: (1911) Pravo 2609-, 2694-, 2767-, 2851-, 2906-, 2974-. (Russian).
Ritual Murders: (1913) Pravo 2403-, 2423-. (Russian).
The Social Ideal and Natural Law: (1913) Yur. Viest. (2) 5. (Russian).
Methodologie der Theorien des Rechts und der Moral (translated from Russian into German); Paris, 1933.

(2) *Principal Commentators on Petrazhitsky's Theory of Law*

*Alexeyev (N. N.): *Fundamental Philosophical Postulates of the Psychological Theory.* (1913) Yur. Viest. (4) 5.
Babb: *Petrazhitskii: Science of Legal Policy and Theory of Law:* 17–18 Boston University Law Review (1937–38), 795 ff., 511 ff.
*Chicherin: *The Psychological Theory of Law*, 55 Voprosy Phil. i Psikh. 365 (1900).
Cornil: *A-propos d'un livre posthume de Petrazhitsky*, Archives de philosophie de droit et de sociologie juridique (1931) 403 ff.
*Gintsberg: *Petrazhitsky's Theory of Law and Its Premises:* 97 Voprosy Phil. i Psikh. 204 (April 1909).
*Gogel: (1898) *Zhur. Min. Yust.* (10) 282.
*Gredeskyl: *Petrazhitsky and His Policy of Law:* (1899) Zap. Imp. Khark. Univ. (3) 19.
*Grouber: *Une théorie psychologique du droit:* (1912) Rev. Trimestrielle de droit civil 531.
*Guins: *Characterization of the Scientific Creativeness of Petrazhitsky:* (1931) Isv. Yur. Fac. v. Kharbinie 5.
Guins: *Petrazhitsky:* (Harbin, 1931).
*Gurvich: *Petrazhitsky:* 47 Sovr. Zap. 480 (1931).
Gurvich: *Une philosophie intuitiviste du droit:* (1931) Archiv. de Phil. de droit, etc. 403.
Haskin: *Leo von Petrazycki:* 164 Rivista general de Legislacíon y Jurisprudencia (1934) 299 ff.
*IAshchenko: *Theory of Federalism:* Yuriev (1912).
*Ivanov: *The New Theory of Law and Morality* (St. Petersburg, 1910).
Ivanov: *The Psychological Theory of Law in Critical Literature* (St. Petersburg, 1913).
Khvostov: *Studies in Contemporary Ethics: Petrazhitsky's Doctrine of Law and Morality* (Moscow, 1908).
Kistiakovsky: *The Reality of Objective Law:* (1910) Logos II, 193.
Kistiakovsky: *Crisis of Jurisprudence:* (1914) Yur. Viest. (1) 70.
*Kistiakovsky: *Social Sciences and the Law* (Moscow, 1916).

*Kokoshkin: *Lectures on General Constitutional Law* (Moscow, 1912).
Kovalevsky: *Morality and Law:* (1907) Russkiya Viedomosti, No. 235.
*Krolik: *Ideas of Legislative Creativeness, etc.* (St. Petersburg, 1913).
Landau: *Die Voraussetzungen des psychologischen Rechtslehre L. v. Petrazickis:* (1922) *Philosophie und Recht, Sonderheft: Russische Rechtsphilosophie*, 102.
Laserson: *General Theory of Law* (Riga, 1930).
*Laserson: *Russische Rechtsphilosophie:* (1933) 26 Archiv. für Rechts- und Wirtschaftsphilosophie 289, 324 ff.
Laserson: *Positive and natural law and their correlation:* P. Sayre (editor), Interpretations of modern legal philosophy (1947), 434 ff.
Meyendorff: *The Theory of Petrazhitsky:* in Modern Theories of Law (Oxford, 1933).
Meyendorff: The Tragedy of Modern Jurisprudence, in P. Sayre (*op. cit. supra*), 521 ff.
*Mikhailov: *The Psychological Theory of Law, etc.* (1910) Pravo 719-, 1842.
Mikhailov: *The Psychological Theory of Law Before the Court of Russian Jurisprudence* (St. Petersburg, 1910).
Mikhailov: *The New Doctrine of Private and Public Law* (1912) Yur. Zap. Demidov. Yur. Lits. (iv) 567.
*Mikhailov: *The Reality of Law:* (1914) Yur. Viest. (1) 5.
*Nechaev: *The Juridic Messenger and Nineteenth Century Jurisprudence:* (1899) Zhur. Min. Yust. (3) 309.
*Novgorodtsev: *Contemporary Problems of Natural Law:* (1913) Yur. Viestnik (1) 18.
*Novgorodtsev: *The Psychological Theory of Law and the Philosophy of Natural Law:* (1913) Yur. Viestnik (3) 5.
Olivecrona: *Is a sociological explanation of law possible:* Theoria, 14 (1948), 167 ff.
*Orzhenskiĭ: 92 Voprosy Phil. i Psikh. 111 (1908).
Palienko: *The New Psychological Theory of Law and the Idea of Law:* 82 Vremen. Demid. Yur. Lits. (1901).
Palienko: *The Normative Character of Law* (1905).
*Palienko: *Doctrine of the Essence of Law etc.* (Kharkov, 1908).
Pietka: *Leone Petrazhitsky*, 12 Rivista di Filosofia di diritto (1932) 109 ff.
Poppe: *Critique of Methodological Bases of the Theories of Law and Morality of Prof. Petrazhitsky.*
*Reisner: *The Theory of Petrazhitsky: Marxism and Social Ideology* (1908). English translation in Soviet Legal Philosophy (1951) 71–82.
Sauer: *Rechts und Staatsphilosophie* (1936) 116.
*Savalsky: *Foundations of Legal Philosophy in Scientific Idealism* 33 Uchen. Zap. Imp. Mos. Univ. Yur. Fac. 273 (1909).
*Sergeyevich: *New Doctrine of Law and Morality:* (1909) Zhur. Min. Yust. (2) 1.
*Sergeyevich: *Answer to Petrazhitsky:* (1910) do. (2) 101.

*Shershenevich: *General Doctrine of Law and State* (Moscow, 1911).
*Shershenevich: *General Theory of Law* (Moscow, 1912).
Sirinov: *Theoretical Political Economy as a Science.*
Sorokin: *Contemporary Sociological Theories* (1928).
Sorokin: *The Organized Group and Law Norms*, in P. Sayre (*op. cit. supra*) 668 ff.
*Spektorsky: *Philosophy and Jurisprudence:* (1913) Yur. Viest. (2) 60.
*Spektorsky: *The Dispute About the Reality of Law:* (1914) Yur. Viest. (1) 53.
*Taranovsky: *Entsiklopediia Prava* (Yuriev, 1917; Berlin, 1923).
Timasheff: *Petrazhitsky's Philosophy of Law*, in P. Sayre (*op. cit. supra*) 736 ff.
Trubetzkoi: *The Legal Philosophy of Professor Petrazhitsky:* 57 Voprosy Phil. i. Psikh 9 (1901).
Verwey: *Een Paladijn der Rechtswetenshep:* 52 Rechtsgeleerd Magazijn (1933) 233 ff.
Vinogradoff: (1908) *Kriticheskoe Obozrienie* (III).
An important practical interpretation of Petrazhitsky's theory is to be found in *Guins: *New Ideas in Law* (654 pages); Harbin, 1931, 1932.

* The Russian volumes checked* are in the Library of Congress.

LAW AND MORALITY

CHAPTER I

THE PREMISES OF A SCIENTIFIC THEORY OF LAW AND MORALITY

SECTION I. *The Prerequisites of a Scientific Methodology for Jurisprudence*

The great philosopher Kant poked fun at the jurisprudence of his time as still not knowing how to define law: "jurists are still searching for a definition of their concept of law," he remarked ironically. He himself worked — but without success — to find a solution of the problem, and since his time many outstanding thinkers, philosophers, and jurists have worked in the same field of investigation. Even now, however, "jurists are still seeking a definition for their concept of law." The fact that the enormous amount of labor expended in this direction, and the great number of more or less ingenious and profound attempts to define the essential nature of law that have accumulated in the course of time, have thus far failed has even given rise to doubt, recently, that the problem can actually be solved.

It would, however, be utterly wrong to suppose that a science of law can be constructed, and the various problems related thereto scientifically solved, if the questions: what is law? what phenomena are to be deemed legal phenomena? and how are legal phenomena to be distinguished from other phenomena? are left unanswered. Above all, the establishment of a scientific concept of law is a condition precedent to the scientific formation of all the other concepts of jurisprudence. These concepts may be divided into two categories.

(1) To the first category belong concepts of various species, subspecies, and further subdivisions of law: customary law, statutory law, public, international, constitutional, criminal, and civil law, and so forth; concepts of the law of obligations, domestic relations, and inheritance as varieties of civil law, and the like.

The concept of a species is the concept of the genus whereof the species is a component part plus the *differentia* of that species; consequently a species concept postulates, first of all, the presence of the appropriate (and indispensable) genus concept. Thus, the concept "international law" is the concept of law plus the *differentia specifica* distinguishing *international* law from other species of law; and there can be no scientific concept of international law so long as there is no scientific concept of law.

The concept of a subspecies, or variety, of any given species (such as the concept of a law of obligations, or of domestic relations, as species of civil law) presupposes a scientific concept of the species; and since, prior to the establishment of a scientific concept of the genus "law," there can be no scientific concepts of species of law, so there cannot in such case be proper concepts of subspecies of law.

(2) The second category of legal concepts consists of those which embrace not law or its varieties, but other objects, in the sense that appropriate designations of these objects as within or outside a given concept depend on their definite relationship to the law. Such, for example, is the concept of a violation of law; violations of law are not law, or varieties of law: they are phenomena absolutely distinct from law. The designation of certain phenomena as violations of law depends, however, upon the relationship between them and law, upon their violating the law and upon the law prohibiting them. Concepts of a legal act — of a will or international compact, or of criminal conduct — connote certain human actions from the point of view that law — or, specifically, civil law, international law, or criminal law — associate with them definite consequences.

We may call such concepts relatively-legal concepts, to distinguish them from the supreme concept of law and concepts (subordinate thereto) of various species and varieties of law, which may be called absolutely-legal concepts.

Every relatively-juridic concept necessarily comprises, as a component part, the concept of a certain relationship of certain objects to law, or to some branch of law; consequently, *every relatively-legal concept must inevitably contain one of the absolutely-legal concepts as an element*: either the supreme concept of law (as in the concept: violation of law, legal transaction, and the like), or the concept of one of the species of law (such as criminal conduct) or the concept of some further subdivision of law ("binding contract," in the sense of obligatory civil law, and the like).

With reference to all absolutely-legal concepts, we have already shown that they cannot be scientific if there is no scientific concept of law. Hence it follows that no relatively-legal concepts can be admitted as proper scientific concepts until a scientific concept of law has been created. If our division of legal concepts is acknowledged to be complete and exhaustive, the conclusion must then be that not a single legal concept — not a single one of a multitude of ideas referring to the province of jurisprudence — can be scientific until a scientific concept of law has been created.

By forming general concepts, science attains orientation in the world of phenomena and converts the chaotic and boundless diversity of utterly heterogeneous and concrete objects and events into an ordered system, consisting of categories, genera, species, and varieties. Proper systematization is thus accomplished. Human knowledge is reduced to order. The proper arrangement and bearing of knowledge within the individual sciences is achieved, as well as the arrangement *inter se* of the different disciplines as branches and heads of a single Science: a single system of human knowledge.

Our purpose has been to make clear the importance of the scientific concept of law to the end that an entire system of subordinate concepts may properly be formed within the boundaries of jurisprudence. However, law is itself a species among the species and genera of world phenomena; while jurisprudence is one of the headings of Science in general.

From the viewpoint of Science in general and general scientific education, as well as from that of jurisprudence and specifically legal education, it is essential to know the corresponding relationships — in particular, to get clearly in mind the higher and more general class of phenomena to which law is related, the other species within the same genus, the sciences to which jurisprudence stands in logical proximity (and the boundaries between them). However, only on the basis of a scientific solution of the problem as to the concept of law can a definite scientific answer to all these and allied questions be given.

To an understanding of the significance of the scientific concept of law, and of scientific concepts in general, certain considerations are essential.

1. Proper concepts of different classes of objects are most important not only for orientation in the world of phenomena and proper systematization of the knowledge gained, but also for the very acquisition of knowledge. A scientifically-methodological and systematic study of a certain category of phenomena presupposes the presence of a scientific concept of the corresponding class of phenomena.

The scientific formulation of propositions as to a certain class of phenomena on the basis of the corresponding facts presupposes, above all, the selection and examination of facts related to the class under study, and the elimination of facts extraneous thereto. Upon the correctness with which the data are chosen depends the accuracy of the inferences therefrom. If these are to be trustworthy, all confusion and misunderstanding in choosing the data must be avoided: thus, in studying morality, a phenomenon bearing in fact no relation thereto must not have been so taken as relating to morality, since no inferences as to morality can properly be based thereon; but so long as there is no scientific concept of the corresponding class of phenomena there is neither any criterion for the proper choice and selection of factual material nor any guaranty against confusion; and until there is a scientific concept of law there can be no scientific acquisition of any truths whatsoever concerning law — still less is it possible to formulate a system of these truths which shall deserve the name of science.

If the nature of a certain category of phenomena is correctly defined, science cannot merely gain knowledge about these objects by studying the appropriate concrete facts, but also — through use of the deductive method — reveal truths about them not yet acquired by observation of them. Knowing the basic property of the phenomena of a given class, science can explain deductively further characteristics of the given province of being (associated with this basic property) as natural or necessary consequences of the basic property, or even foresee facts that have, in general, not yet been noted, or may have escaped notice. However, this second possible source of scientific knowledge is closed to legal science so long as there is no concept of law: no knowledge of the nature of the phenomena to be studied by that science.

2. Even if the necessity of observing scientific methods for the acquisition of scientific propositions be not conceded, and assertions without such foundation be accepted as scientific, propositions as to this or that category of objects, lacking a definite concept of this class of objects, must still be unscientific: they would be judgments formed in ignorance of what specifically was the point at issue and the greater the confidence with which such assertions (concerning a subject unknown) were expressed, the more monstrous they would be from the standpoint of science. In the same way, all judgments about law are — so long as there is no definite concept of law — judgments and assertions about an object unknown and indefinite.

The foregoing demonstrates how cardinal are the misunderstandings at the foundation of the view (explicit or implicit) that scientific investigations into the more particular questions of legal science — without spending time to decide: "what is law" — can, and even should, be pursued.

The problem of the concept of law is by no means one of a multitude of problems of jurisprudence. It is, purely and simply, *the* problem of the science of law in general: a fundamental problem upon whose solution depends the very possibility of legal science, as distinguished from a collection of opinions, assertions, and propositions which cannot pretend to rank as scientific in respect either of their origin or of their content. On the other hand, statements, or even confident assertions, that the problem is beyond solution since attempts to solve it hitherto have failed are equally without scientific foundation.[1]

A sound and scientifically correct hypothesis is entirely different: it must be assumed that the methods hitherto applied to the study of legal phenomena, and to the formation of appropriate concepts, have failed, and those methods must be reëxamined critically and in detail, and appropriate and scientific methods — which can bring us to the goal — worked out.

This view is sustained by the condition of the other basic concepts and problems of contemporary legal science — a condition just as cheerless as that of the problem of legal science, and entailing consequences just as negative within their spheres of action as were pointed out *supra* with reference to the failure to ascertain the nature of the law in general.

The "search for a definition" (and the successive failures of attempts to find one) is a phenomenon repeated as regards other general (absolutely-legal and relatively-legal) concepts: until the problem of the supreme concept — the concept of law as such — has been solved there cannot be proper scientific concepts. However — precisely because there is no supreme scientific concept — the defects of subordinate legal concepts ordinarily escape attention, and the term, "law" or some similarly indistinct notion operates as if it were a scientific concept of law, while the formation of subordinate concepts proceeds as if "law" were a known and scientifically defined quantity. Nonetheless, there are countless difficulties and dissensions with regard to these concepts, extending — as time goes on — even to the general concepts which theretofore aroused no doubt and seemed finally established and completely satisfactory.

This scientific ailment is noted in a particularly sharp and striking form in the sphere of the general theory of law, the so-called *Allgemeine Rechtslehre*, but there is likewise utter chaos in the conceptual schemes of particular legal disciplines — of the sciences of private and public law, and especially of constitutional law.

In general, the amazingly deplorable and chaotic condition of legal science is beyond question — and particularly the failure of innumerable attempts to solve its fundamental and elementary problems — and this makes it of primary and insistent importance to proceed with the task of verifying critically the means and methods hitherto employed to gain knowledge of law and to build a consciously-scientific epistemology and methodology thereof. Even if it were not for the specific symptoms *supra* of the failure in fact of the ordinary means and methods of in-

[1] This is so also with regard to the concept of morals.

vestigation, this task would still loom as one of the basic and most important confronting legal science: the fundamental postulate of every sort of *scientific* knowledge is a consciously-critical application of scientific means and methods of cognition, scientifically verified and proven.

The means and methods of solving problems of legal science that were formerly — and are still being — employed are based on tradition and habit, and not on the propositions of the appropriate consciously-scientific methodology: no such methodology exists, for the time being, in the science either of law or of morality.

SECTION 2. *The Sphere Where Legal Phenomena and Their Elements Are Found*

The fundamental method of studying and gaining knowledge of objects and of phenomena is observation. In studying the objects and phenomena of the physical and material world, observation consists in perception with the aid of "the external senses" (sight, hearing, smell, taste, and touch), and is termed external observation. In studying phenomena of the spiritual world — psychic phenomena — observation consists in internal perception of what is taking place within one's own mind,[1] and is termed internal observation: self-observation or introspection.

In certain spheres of cognition — as where extremely small objects, imperceptible to ordinary vision, or extremely remote objects, are under study — observation must, in order to be successful, employ special technical means and methods: the microscope and the telescope are great technical discoveries which broadened the province of human observation and cognition very subtantially. As will be explained elsewhere, there are also certain categories of psychic phenomena — including essential elements of moral and legal phenomena — which cannot, under ordinary conditions, be perceived by inward observation, so that here, also, special means and methods for achieving successful observation and cognition must be worked out and applied.

There are fields of cognition, where the application of observation and the success of cognition are obstructed by misunderstanding as to the actual sphere where the corresponding real phenomena are. We shall deal *infra* with a special class of psychic processes which have the peculiar property that external objects seem (to persons experiencing these

[1] It has been decided, after some hesitation, to use the English word "mind" for the Russian word (*psykhika*) employed by the author: cf. 17 BOSTON UNIVERSITY LAW REVIEW 806 (note).

processes) to possess particular attributes (not actually existent) or to exist in the external world (where they do not so exist at all).

In the corresponding fields of cognition, we must avoid the error of accepting as real that which seems to exist in a world external to the person experiencing such processes, and keep in mind that the corresponding real phenomena are to be found in the mind — and only in the mind — of that person. It would be naive to suppose that an epithet "nice" or "dear" as applied to another connotes any peculiar qualities of the person to whom such attributes are ascribed: however closely we study that person — examining him from head to foot, and seeking otherwise to find something corresponding to the epithet "dear" — our search will fail, and the meaning of the word "dear" will remain hidden from us. Only when we turn to a study of the psychic experiences of the persons using these terms can that meaning be explained.

Misunderstandings of this sort are possible — and in fact play a great part — in the sphere of phenomena of moral life. The statement that so-and-so is under such-and-such a moral obligation ordinarily presupposes, as the expression itself shows, that "moral obligation" is a real phenomenon, found where the man is found to whom that obligation is ascribed. In reality, however, the real phenomenon corresponding to the expression "moral obligation" is found in an entirely different sphere: in the mind of him who finds that another is under a moral obligation.

This must be kept in mind also in the field of law and the study of law. Suppose we are concerned with this judgment: "Squire A has a right to obtain from lessee B, 5,000 rubles rent"; or "lessee B is bound to pay to Squire A the 5,000 rubles stipulated in the lease." According to legal terminology, there is — as between A and B — the legal relationship of lessor-lessee. Here a legal phenomenon confronts us: Where is it? Where can it be found for purposes of study?

It would be a mistake to suppose that it is to be found somewhere in space between A and B, or that — if A and B are in a certain province — the legal phenomenon is somewhere in that province, or to suppose that the legal obligation ascribed to lessee B in the judgment aforesaid is something found in him, and that the right to obtain 5,000 rubles is something present — and to be found — in Squire A, in his hands, or in his spirit, or anywhere at all around or in him.

The scientific and critical answer to this question can and should be simply this: the legal phenomenon is in the mind of the third person C, who supposes that A has a right to receive — and that B is bound to pay — 5,000 rubles.

In precisely the same way, if a learned jurist experiences the judgment: "lessees are bound to pay lessors the agreed rent upon the expiration of the period of occupancy," we have before us a legal phenomenon; and the learned jurist may take advantage of its presence to observe, study, and analyze it. He would, however, be acting under a misapprehension if he sought the corresponding legal phenomenon somewhere in space above or between people, in the "social milieu," or the like: it occurs within himself — in his own mind — and only there.

Legal phenomena consist of unique psychic processes (to be further studied, analyzed, and defined *infra*) expressed, incidentally, in the unique form of ascribing to different beings (not only to people, but to beings of various other classes, conceived of in the mind), or to certain classes of such beings, "duties" and "rights"; so that these beings, so conceived of, are seemingly found in certain peculiar conditions of being bound or of possessing special objects ("rights"), and the like.

The science of law (and the science of morality where moral obligations, norms, and the like are under study) is therefore influenced by the misunderstanding which came to light in our survey of persons as "nice" or "dear" in order to find in them corresponding attributes. The content of traditional legal science is tantamount to an optical illusion: it does not see legal phenomena where they actually occur, but discerns them where there is absolutely naught of them — where they cannot be found, observed, or known — that is to say, in a world external to the subject who is experiencing the legal phenomena. We shall see *infra* that this optical illusion has its natural psychological causes, precisely as the optical illusion (in the literal sense of the word) is perfectly natural, when people ignorant of astronomy suppose (as the science of astronomy itself did down to Copernicus) that the sun "rises" in the morning and revolves around us.

The corresponding concepts and beliefs of jurisprudence are no less completely mistaken than were those of primeval astronomy. Moreover, modern legal science may be said to be based upon a misunderstanding far more fundamental than that which formerly prevented the successful development of astronomy. Even ancient astronomy was concerned with real objects: the earth, the sun, and other heavenly bodies. It could observe them and acquire genuine knowledge of them, falling into error only as regards the true relationship of such objects to each other. On the other hand, the error wherein legal science is found is such as altogether to conceal from the view of science what actually is and to prevent the very possibility of observing and knowing it, while at the same time compelling science to expend time and energy — utterly in vain and fruitlessly — on searches and investigations in a sphere where the object of the quest cannot be found or examined and so to resort to fanciful and arbitrary speculation regarding that which has in reality no existence whatsoever.

Such pursuit of phantoms, and more or less ingenious and abstruse speculation as to things which do not exist still make up the theories of the jurists and legal philosophers, and as time goes on these theories become not only more controversial, but increasingly obscure, subtle, and unnatural.

As legal theory is formulated at present, the character of its problems — and of the appropriate solutions — is threefold. The general type of these problems and solutions may be best conceived of if we assume that a student of logic (or grammar) is given the problem of making a logical (or grammatical) analysis of the following three judgments or propositions: (1) the servant is in the anteroom, (2) Zeus is the king of the Olympian gods, and (3) the treasury has extensive property; and that our supposed student solves this problem as follows: to find the logical subject of the first judgment (or the grammatical subject of the first proposition) he sets out for the anteroom, is happy to find the servant there, brings him to the person awaiting the conclusion, and declares triumphantly, "Here is the subject of the first judgment (the subject of the first proposition)!" Nor does he encounter any difficulty as to the subject of the second judgment (or the subject of the second proposition): he is no pagan, and has too good an education to believe in the existence of Zeus, wherefore he spends neither time nor money on a trip to Greece in order to inspect the clouds on Olympus, but asserts confidently that there is no subject in this case and that there can be no judgment (or proposition) without a subject.

However, the subject of the third judgment seems to him to present a highly complicated and subtle problem: he proceeds to construct extremely profound hypotheses as to what exactly is the subject here, and advances some such belief as that there is here some special and enormous organism — something supra-animal, with a whole system of organs. All these conclusions, manifestly, are based on a misunderstanding as to where subjects are found and how they should be sought out: they are, of course, found in the judgments themselves (in the consciousness of those who experience these judgments) as constituent parts thereof, and nowhere at all in space outside the judgments — either in the anteroom, or in the clouds of Olympus, or anything of that sort.

This fundamental and general misunderstanding is responsible for three types of mistaken solutions: (1) The first consists in mistakenly accepting an actually existing object (the servant) found in an improper sphere (the anteroom) as the object which is being sought for, whereas in fact what is sought has an entirely different nature, and is to be found in an entirely different sphere, that is to say, in the judgment itself; this may be termed a naïve-realistic solution. (2) The second consists in mistakenly denying the existence of a subject (which undoubtedly exists and can be readily found in the subject's very judgment) and therefore the existence of the judgment itself, because of disbelief in the existence of an irrelevant object in an improper sphere (the living Zeus in the clouds of Olympus); this may be termed a naïve-nihilistic conclusion. (3) Finally, the third consists in conjectures as to the existence and nature of irrelevant objects in an improper sphere of investigation, followed by speculation more or less profound or fantastic; these we will term naïve-speculative theories.

We shall have later to be concerned with a section of legal science entirely similar in nature to the logical doctrines concerned with the elements of judgments (subjects, predicates) and the doctrines of grammar as to subjects, predicates, objects — particularly with problems and doctrines concerning subjects (to which legal rights or duties are ascribed); and we shall find that the relevant doctrines of modern legal science copy exactly the models cited of the definition of logical or grammatical subjects. We shall, in particular, become more closely acquainted with the (mistakenly) realistic doctrine of "physical" subjects of law ("living human individuals"); with nihilistic theories concerning other categories of subjects of rights; with disbelief in the existence of many subjects of rights and duties which undoubtedly have existed and do exist; and with a whole series of fantastic and speculative theories as to the treasury and similar subjects.

Modern jurisprudence also contains other doctrines, not concerned with "subjects" as such or consisting in seeking — or in devising and constructing different living creatures within the realm of the earth's fauna — but resting on the same fundamental misunderstanding and reducible to the same three types of theory: realistic, nihilistic, and speculative. Thus the common theory which makes legal norms mere commands (orders and prohibitions by some persons to others) is naïve-realistic insofar as the search for real events of this sort (commands) may succeed in certain cases: that is to say, insofar as the persons experiencing legal judgments are referred to the corresponding commands issued by people such as monarchs. Yet people have, in history, been frequently referred — and are even now being referred — to commands of gods which are more authoritative for them than the commands of men. Unlike medieval jurisprudence which included precise and orderly theories of divine law, modern legal theory believes only in the existence of law enacted by human beings (which is no less fallaciously nihilistic than disbelief in the capacity of gods to be subjects of law). In the field of so-called customary law, where — when rights and obligations are ascribed to oneself or to others — people are not referred to anyone's commands but to the fact that "such was the conduct of our forefathers" and the like, modern legal science is nevertheless occupied with the effort to work out nonexistent commands under the heading: "general will of the people," and similar fantastic speculations. In the field of legislation, also, some investigators not only confuse norms of law with the human conduct termed "commands," but — with the aid of deep argumentation and sundry fictions — devise the presence of general consent; they postulate acknowledgment of these commands by all citizens, although it is absurd to talk of knowledge — to say nothing of acknowledgment — of all laws on the part of all citizens.

The same difficulties and mistakes are repeated with reference to the doctrine concerning obligations, rights, and so forth.

Such legal judgments, therefore, as: "The treasury has a property right in such and such a forest in such and such a province; all persons are bound to refrain from willfully felling wood . . . " constitute for modern legal science a combination of a whole series of head-splitting problems, and furnish the arena for a whole series of misunderstandings. (1) The subject of this property right must be identified or imagined; (2) this subject must be examined so as to find out exactly what he has — what precisely is meant by his right of property; (3) the subjects of the corresponding obligations must be identified or imagined — perhaps they are all mankind in the anthropological sense, since the prohibition against encroachment upon the object of the property right is addressed to all of them. In this way, millions of different events occur in connection with the purchase of every trifle — a pen or a pin — in the modern legal theory's world of phantasy.

All these peculiar and fantastic speculations collapse *per se*, and all the millions of imaginary phenomena disappear, if we rid ourselves of the optical delusion *supra*. When a right of property is ascribed to the treasury, and a corresponding duty is ascribed to "all," there is nothing whatsoever such as is found or devised by jurisprudence. There is a single legal phenomenon: in the consciousness of the person who ascribes to the treasury the right of property in the forest and to "all" a duty to refrain from felling timber. There is a perfectly real subject of the right: that conceived by the person thinking about "the treasury"; there is a subject of the obligation: "all," "everyone" — that is to say, the concept which is expressed by the pronouns "all" and "everyone." There is a single subject, found in the consciousness of the person experiencing the legal judgment — not a multitude of subjects, dispersed over the whole earth.

SECTION 3. *The Scientific Method of Studying Legal Phenomena and Their Elements*

Observation is the fundamental method of studying phenomena — whether of the physical world or of the spiritual world. It is clear from what has already been set out, that legal phenomena occur — and can be found for purposes of observation — not where optical illusion leads us to suppose they are but much nearer: here, within us; in our consciousness; in the consciousness of him who is experiencing rights and duties at that given second. To be freed from this optical illusion means the elimination of a vast province where legal phenomena are (supposedly) found and can (supposedly) be investigated, as well as of a vast quantity of (supposedly) legal phenomena and their elements. Even with the number of legal phenomena, and of the spheres of their being, thus significantly smaller than those contemplated by the prevailing theory, their number is still not small, even from our point of view: the number of the spheres where legal phenomena are is the same as the number of living creatuers capable of experiencing — and in fact experiencing — the corresponding mental states, while the number of legal phenomena is equal to the number of these experiences.

Of all the extremely numerous species of beings endowed with psychic life on earth (animals), only one — Homo sapiens — is distinguished by the capacity to experience the complicated psychic processes which constitute legal phenomena. Within the boundaries of this species, the capacity to experience psychic processes of the legal type — and consequently legal phenomena — emerged only with the attainment of a certain level of culture (extremely high in comparison with the condition of other animals), and in particular the attainment of a certain progress in language. Even now by no means all persons possess, as such, capacity for legal experiences: only those who have attained a certain age, and been subjected to certain educative influences, have that capacity. On the other hand, all persons under no specific bodily or psychic defect (such as deaf-mutes or idiots), who are being educated in the everyday conditions of human life (even though in definitely criminal surroundings), acquire that capacity fairly early — long before they legally come of age.

The quantity of genuine legal phenomena actually existing — which will prove to be extremely great — must be enormously reduced if we are concerned with the direct and reliable cognition and study of them through observation (and not with their existence, as such) since we are utterly unable to see, or otherwise to observe, that which takes place in another's mind, and all the spheres where legal phenomena — and all psychic phenomena in general — exist are therefore absolutely closed and inaccessible to our observation with a single exception: our own mind — the consciousness of our ego.

The proper, and the only possible, method of observing legal phenomena must, therefore, be the method of self-observation: the introspective method. Introspection in the general sense is (a) the directing of inward attention to the psychic phenomenon to be studied during the time when it is being experienced — self-observation in the narrow sense, such as the observation of hunger, thirst, or toothache, and the like — and (b) the inward observation of ideas — of "images" — of previously experienced acts of a given class (such as recollections of last night's toothache).

Every sort of observation, including introspective observation, may be either simple or experimental. The experimental method means observation complicated by designedly influencing the phenomena to be observed — that is to say, by applying special means to evoke, to change, or to terminate them. If this is done relative to phenomena which are to be observed inwardly, this is the introspective-experimental method.

Application of the experimental method must not be thought to be impossible without special laboratories, machines, or other instruments specially fashioned for scientific investigation. We are concerned with the experimental method of studying psychic phenomena if — in order to study certain pain phenomena — one pricks himself with a pin so as to cause pain, or remains without food so as to study hunger, or gives himself over to the reading of a novel which compels him to await the outcome with intense curiosity so as to study that state of mind, or asks someone to provoke him on purpose — taking him unawares at some moment and then immediately to remind him that it is in fulfillment of his request — so that he may study anger.

This method does not even presuppose the necessity of any external action or influence: one can lie motionless on a sofa with closed eyes and produce within himself series after series of psychological experiments in the course of introspective-experimental investigations. A suitable means for studying shame, pride, ambition, gratitude, injured self-love, jealousy, and the like may be afforded by experiments consisting in the creation, within our imagination, of vivid pictures of particular combinations of circumstances capable of evoking corresponding emotions. All these varieties of the introspective method are entirely applicable to the study of legal phenomena.

In everyday cases, legal phenomena, as psychic experiences, are not of great intensity: they pass by unnoted, or at least it is only with difficulty that they yield to observation. The nature of law, the character of its attributes, and the manner and the reason of its influence upon conduct cannot be known without cognizance of the psychic background of legal phenomena; hence it is highly important to raise the intensity of these experiences to the degree that they become noted and yield to study. Here particularly the experimental method — including experiments similar to the examples above — can render valuable services: reading stories, novels, newspaper reports, and the like containing vivid portrayals of "shockingly" arbitrary conduct, clear and "sacred" rights trampled under foot, utterly just demands repudiated, and the like; the vivid image of one's own self under strong temptation to deny and to dispute — or otherwise to "trample upon" — the clear and "sacred" right of another, or as a victim of the shockingly arbitrary conduct and violation of law; the services of friends in bringing us (for purposes of the experiment) to the point of legal enthusiasm, or "boiling" and indignation, and so forth; all such experimental means may enable us to observe and to study the relevant psychic experiences particularly characteristic of law, in various forms and degress of intensity, up to and including tempestous emotion.

The same experiments enable us also to become acquainted with similar experiences which characterize morality, and — by putting together the results of these and other experiments — we can come to know the (hitherto uncomprehended) difference between morality and law.

The introspective method — simple and experimental "self-knowledge" — is the sole means of observation, *and of the immediate and reliable* cognition and study, of legal and moral phenomena. Without it there is *no possibility whatsoever of any knowledge of them at all.*

In general, the only categories of psychic phenomena accessible to our cognition are those known to us from the history of our ego — with them we are acquainted because we have ourselves experienced them. The other categories of psychic phenomena are absolutely inaccessible to our cognition. One who did not, through his own psychic experience, know of hunger, thirst, anger, joy, and the like would, in general, be incapable of knowing these psychic phenomena, although others know and experience them; hence he could not understand the corresponding behavior, bodily movements, or speeches of others, and so forth. The same is true as to legal phenomena. A man suffering from absolute legal idiotism — that is to say, complete inability to have legal experiences — could not possibly know what law is or understand the human conduct evoked thereby. Having heard the word "law," and seen that much in human society is done with reference to "law," he would perhaps fashion his own special interpretation of these expressions and of this conduct: he might suppose that it was a matter of commands laid by the powerful in their own interests upon the weak and defenseless, with appropriate threats in case of disobedience, and that these threatening orders were carried out by the weak for reasons of expediency. This, however, would have absolutely nothing in common with the knowledge of what law actually is.

There may be a similar ignorance or mistaken interpretation of the nature of various categories of psychic processes — and a like failure to understand the significance and motives of the corresponding human behavior — on the part of those who are not suffering from any psychic shortcoming, and even on the part of eminent thinkers and scholars. This is possible in cases of ignorance as to where and how one may find phenomena of a given class and of the application of an improper method, or of the arbitrary fashioning of formulae and theories outside of any scientific methods of investigation whatsoever. But if we have employed proper methods — that is to say, simple or experimental introspection — in attaining knowledge of psychic experiences of a certain class, we have then the means of acquiring information (indirect, and more or less hypothetical, however) as to phenomena of the same class in the minds of others: another's mind ceases to represent for us herein an utterly impenetrable secret.

The point is that our inward, psychic acts — such as anger or joy — cause various movements of the body which may be observed externally, and this is particularly so as to the bodily movements we produce in order to communicate to others some psychic condition or process (gesticulation, or the pronouncing and writing of words, and so forth). When we observe the same actions on the part of others, we can by analogy suppose — with more or less probability — that they are based on the same psychic experiences.

How far such assumptions — based on "inference by analogy" — are likely to prove true depends upon various circumstances: whether or not we are concerned with a truthful man or with one prone to pretense and falsehood; whether or not the case under consideration affords any special cause to assume untruthfulness (as on the part of a criminal in court); whether or not the given movements of the body — including words — ordinarily correspond to a single defined type of psychic processes, or are homogeneous external manifestations of heterogeneous inward experiences; and so on.

A scientific investigation of psychic experiences of others presupposes, therefore, not merely scientific knowledge of the same experiences in oneself, but also a scientific criticism of the suitability of the bodily movements of others (including oral or written communications) as factual data for assuming psychic processes of a given sort.

Available records (such as annals, biographies, and records of travelers) regarding actions which they have seen, speeches of others which they have heard, are a more or less suitable substitute for our own observations of the bodily movements of others as we study their psychic processes. The scientific employment of such data ("tradition" as a substitute for direct observation) manifestly presupposes that they be critically examined: (a) as already pointed out; and (b) as to the reliability of the observations themselves; and if the communications are received at second hand from another, the probability of mistake is obviously still greater.

In sum, then, introspective cognition of experiences of the same sort on the part of the investigator himself, together with knowledge as to external manifestations of experiences of this class, is a condition precedent to comprehension of the psychic experiences of others. The corresponding scientific methods of cognition may therefore be called the joint method of inward and outward observation. No particular elucidation is required to show that external observation — as an element of this method — may, like inward observation, be either simple or experimental.

What we have said concerning the joint method is entirely applicable in the study of legal or moral phenomena as well. In particular, a genuinely scientific study of legal phenomena is the study — as elaborate as possible — of different classes of external manifestations of legal experiences and of the differences between these experiences and the manifestation of related psychic processes (especially moral processes). Thus a scientific basis for studying the legal experiences of others (particularly of people of earlier time, of lower grades of cultural development, and the like) can be obtained. To the study of law, the experimental method is to be applied precisely as in other fields where the psychic experiences of others are under scientific study. If, for example, we take a plaything from a child and insist that it is ours and that we will not return it; or if we agree with the child that if he does certain work for us he shall receive so much candy, and then refuse to carry out the agreement after he has done the work; or if we make an agreement with the child that — after we have performed — he must perform what will require from him more or less serious sacrifice (such as doing without a favorite toy, or going without food for a long time) — such experiments and observation of their external effects enable us, on the basis of proper knowledge of the nature and attributes of legal phenomena, to determine with scientific reliability whether or not the child is capable of experiencing legal psychic processes, how vivid and intense are his experiences of them in general, and their motivation force, as compared, for example, with hunger — appetite. Furthermore, the same experimental method enables us to examine the legal mind of the child and to explore whether or not there are also present therein the attributes of various particular species of legal phenomena — such as the law of property, the law of contracts, the law of domestic relations, and so on. The same experiments with idiots or deaf-mutes may lead to interesting discoveries as to the conditions essential to the development of law.

The foregoing is a complete enumeration of the scientific methods of studying legal phenomena as real phenomena. The very nature of legal phenomena as psychic processes of a particular class precludes the possibility of employing for their scientific study methods other than (a) the introspective method (simple or experimental) as the fundamental and indispensable manner of acquiring knowledge of the nature of legal phenomena, and (b) the joint method of inward and outward observation (simple or experimental).

SECTION 4. *Class Concepts and Adequate Theories*

The misunderstanding as to the whereabouts of legal phenomena, set out above, is not the only obstacle to the formulation of a scientific theory of law: another — even more formidable — is that in jurisprudence (as in the social sciences and the humanities) there is no correct doctrine as to the formation of general concepts.

It is commonly assumed that, in order to form the concept "law," one should make a survey of legal phenomena, compare them with one another and then with kindred phenomena, and finally select *the* attributes which are common to the law and distinguish law from other phenomena. This is, however, impossible: such surveys and comparisons presuppose knowledge of what are — and what are not — legal phenomena. The proper procedure is to formulate class concepts correctly.

A general or class concept is the *idea* of objects which possess certain attributes or traits. A class consists of all the objects having these traits. Thus the *idea* of white things is a *class concept*, and the *things themselves* comprise the corresponding *class*. Class concepts are by no means limited to things which actually exist: there are class concepts of things entirely imaginary, such as those in geometry, and even class concepts meant to cover real things are not limited to those actually existent but include as well things of the past and of the future possessing the relevant attributes.

The accepted methods of forming class concepts are either by reasoning in a circle or by slavishly accepting established terminologies. Thus when jurists try to formulate the concept "law," they make a comparative survey of objects commonly called law. Manifestly, however, the term "law," and such related concepts as "right," are found (a) in everyday speech (when the content is very broad), and (b) as used by professional men and the lawyers (when the content is far more restricted). "Law" and "right" are used when people are playing cards, or arranging social parties, or discussing relations between friends, lovers, and so on. Sometimes the expression is "moral right," which combines law and morals. There is no reason to hold that either of the usages is better, or more correct, than the other: and it is not impossible that each is, scientifically, indefensible.

The ultimate purpose in formulating a system of the basic concepts of a science (such as of law) is to select (out of the many which are possible) those concepts which, as logical subjects of scientifically relevant propositions, would facilitate the proper arrangement of those propositions into a system. It may be asserted *a-priori* that neither everyday usage nor professional usage can yield scientifically adequate concepts in this regard. In professional or occupational usage, the prevailing concepts are those that unify objects possessing the same (or a similar) value from the point of view of the practical activities of those engaging in a particular occupation: while a cook may properly call certain objects "vegetables" or "game," it would go ill with a botanist or zoologist who set out to formulate scientific theories with these concepts as logical subjects. That lawyers occupy so high a place among the professions militates strongly against overcoming the professional terminology and reaching concepts of law which are truly scientific. Nevertheless, this must be done.

The obstacles of reasoning in a circle, or reiterating the inconsistencies of everyday or professional word-usage, disappear when one understands the real nature of class concepts: he chooses a certain number of traits or attributes and — by juxtaposition thereof — forms a class concept. Schematically, he announces that all the objects possessing traits *A.B.C.* . . . . *N* make up class *X*, and the idea of those objects the class concept *X*. He thus accomplishes two results: (1) no object whose component traits are different appears in the class, and (2) all the objects comprising the relevant traits are included.

Obviously, while innumerable class concepts can thus be formed, only a few possess scientific value, which is judged by the possibility of formulating adequate scientific theories with respect to them. Scientific theories are those having a sound methodological and systematic basis, while adequate scientific theories are those which satisfy this very definite prerequisite: what is predicated must be precisely true of the class of objects with respect to which it is predicated.

Many theories, comprising no fallacy, are yet inadequate: one may form the concept of "a cigar weighing five ounces," predicate about that class everything known about material things in general (about solid bodies in general, the chemical properties of the ingredients of these cigars, the influence of smoking them on health, and so on); these "theories" — while perfectly correct — are manifestly inadequate since what is predicated with respect to "cigars weighing five ounces" is also true of innumerable objects which do not belong to that class, such as cigars in general.

A theory may be inadequate either (1) because the predicates are related to classes which are too narrow (as was the case with the theory in the preceding paragraph) or (2) because the predicate is related to a class which is too broad (such as various sociological theories which attribute "everything" to the influence of one factor which in fact plays a much more modest part). Inadequate theories of the former type may be said to "limp"; those of the latter to "jump." There may, of course, be absolutely inadequate theories, which predicate something not true of any class at all. Science should admit adequate theories only: scrutinizing every statement, which is tentatively introduced as a scientific theory, for the possible presence of these errors. Often something predicated of a narrow class turns out to be true of a broader class: the theory then "limps," and we must refashion it by selecting the concept of a genus — not of a species, as has been done tentatively — as the logical subject. It may be stated, incidentally, that, if a genus consists of n species relative to the class corresponding to the generic concept, $n + 1$ adequate theories can be constructed: one concerning each of the species, and in addition one concerning the genus. If it turns out that the theory "jumps," we must cut it down by selecting a class concept —

appearing as a species of the one we have already tried — as the logical subject.

Two fundamental procedures are conducive to the formation and testing of classes and class concepts: (1) to start from some theory already existing and — on the basis of theoretical statements (predicates) — determine the adequate logical subject, eventually correcting the existing theory if it appears to "limp" or to "jump"; or (2) to form a class concept by trial and error — or even by guess — and thereafter to formulate theories which are adequate with respect thereto.

In reaching a conclusion that a theory is — or is not — adequate we must bear in mind that theoretical truths — that is to say, truths predicated of classes in the above sense — are not of such a character as to be discoverable in every individual instance by means of observation: many theoretical truths have been brought to light in the physical sciences. In no instance, however, do real processes go in precise accordance with the corresponding propositions, and this is so *a fortiori* as to truths established by the social sciences (and particularly economics): that which is asserted by the so-called laws of nature never takes place in nature, yet these "laws" are valuable as explaining and predicting facts. Actually they tell what would happen were there no complications, which in fact there always are. In most cases, however, their impact is infinitesimal: if we know the few determining factors, we can explain the facts and predict the future developments: while observation alone would show only chaos and change, theory reveals the interaction of a few constant tendencies (the proper expression, rather than "laws of nature").

Formulation of a scientific theory requires more than knowledge about something which frequently occurs, viz., the establishment of a logical nexus or causal tendency between a specified attribute (of a specified class of objects), appearing as the theoretical subject of the proposition, and something else. On this basis, the following propositions about the adequacy of theories can be formulated. If it has been established that, between attribute *a* of class *A* and something else (*b*), there exists either a necessary logical nexus or a constant causal tendency, this proves that the theory does not "limp" — in other words, it may be taken for granted that all objects — past, present, or future — covered by the class concept *A* possess attribute *b*. This is the only guaranty against this type of error. But this is no guaranty against the error of proposing a theory which "jumps." Two types of class attributes must be distinguished: those which are common to all the objects of a given class (but not to them exclusively) and those which are common to such objects exclusively and are the *differentia specifica* of the class. Theories which predicate something about attributes of the former type are, of necessity, theories which "jump," and must be corrected by being restated with reference to a more comprehensive class, while those which predicate something about attributes of the second type do not "jump" and are therefore adequate.

From these propositions it is manifest that the *differentia specifica* of a class constitutes the scientific foundation of all theories. The content of a scientific theory must be that it predicates what is logically or causally connected with the *differentia specifica* of the class under study and furnishes explanations and proofs of these connections.

Political science, jurisprudence, and the science of morals contain many theories which are inadequate because no valid class concepts exist in these sciences. Lay efforts have, however, assembled a large number of truths which may be employed to form adequate theories, but relative to class concepts still to be constructed.

CHAPTER II

THE NATURE OF LAW AND MORALITY

SECTION 5. *The Dependency of Legal and Moral Science upon Psychology*

The principal — though not the only — obstacle to the construction and successful development of the sciences of law and morality is the lack of proper scientific methodology, and the application of methods of thinking and of investigation which are unsuited to scientific ends. In order to study successfully psychic phenomena of a complex nature we must have an appropriate scientific basis in the shape of a system of general class concepts regarding psychic processes in general — their elements, their causal relations and attributes, and their influence on conduct. To the development of this knowledge psychology — the theory of psychic phenomena — is dedicated; but the traditional and prevailing teachings of psychology are disfigured by such fundamental faults that it is impossible to build a scientific theory of law and morality on the foundation of psychology in its present shape. The elements of psychic life known to contemporary psychology are divided (by it) into three categories: (1) cognition (sensations and ideas); (2) feelings (pleasures and sufferings); and (3) will (aspirations, active experiences).

This classification cannot be deemed satisfactory. Cognitive experiences (of sight, hearing, taste, smell, touch, temperature and other sensations) and corresponding ideas and perceptions possess a unilateral-passive nature in the general sense: they are passive (*pati*) experiences. Feelings in the technical sense (pleasures and sufferings) likewise possess a unilateral-passive nature: they are passive experiences of the pleasant and the unpleasant. Will experiences — such as the will to continue work regardless of fatigue — are unilateral-active experiences. Proper self-observation can reveal the existence of experiences in our psychic life not fitting within any one of the three categories, but possessing a bilateral, passive-active nature — containing passive experiences which are distinct from those of cognition and of feeling, as well as specific active experiences (appetences). These impulse-stimuli — such as experiences of hunger (appetite), thirst, and sex excitation — we may term passive-active, bilateral experiences. The essence of the psychic phenomenon termed hunger or appetite consists in specific passive experiences and — at the same time — a specific urge or appetence, an inward incitement, an aspiration (*ad-petitus*). The passive side of hunger-appetite is not to be confused with the feeling of suffering — a feeling of the unpleasant. The suffering observed in certain conditions together with hunger is a concomitant phenomenon unrelated to the psychological structure of hunger as such but having special causes of a pathological character. Normal, moderate, and healthy hunger is more frequently accompanied by feelings of satisfaction than by those of suffering. The traditional theory — which regards hunger as a negative feeling or suffering — at once ignores the active side of the phenomenon and confuses the passive experience which is experienced in hunger-appetite (and is distinct from feeling in the sense of traditional psychology) with the phenomena which may accompany hunger but are not essential thereto. Passive-active experiences — though with a different specific character — are likewise to be observed with reference to thirst and sex excitation. Through self-observation the same may be shown as to the nature of fear and of different types of aversions (as when taking into the mouth, and trying to chew and swallow, different objects — such as rotted objects unsuitable for food, or when coming into contact with spiders and certain insects, reptiles, and the like). As motor stimuli which repel, these and similar experiences are to be distinguished from appetite, thirst, and the like (which are appulsive). *We unite into a special class all the phenomena of the human and animal mind which possess this bilateral passive-active nature and term them impulsions.*[1]

For the traditional threefold division of the elements of mental life which constitutes the very foundation of psychology (and of the other sciences which deal with phenomena of the mind) we must substitute a division into (1) bilateral, passive-active experiences (impulsions) and (2) unilateral experiences, falling into (a) unilateral-passive (cognitive and feeling) experiences, and (b) unilateral-active (will) experiences.

In the life of animals and of man, impulsions act as the principal and directing psychic factors of adaptation to the conditions of life; other (unilateral) elements of psychic life play an ancillary, subordinate, and subservient part. Impulsions perform the function of stimulating external movements of the body and other actions — such as intellectual work

[1] The Russian original says "impulses or emotions," but there is persuasive authority for the view that the author did not employ the Russian word (*emotsiya*) in our English sense of "emotion" (an agitated or excited state of mind) — indeed.

and other inward actions — and evoke directly the appropriate physiological and psychic processes. The enormous majority of impulsions — all except a very few indeed which attain such a degree of intensity and such trenchant expression as to catch the attention of those experiencing them — pass by unnoted. Every day we experience many thousands of them. They govern our body and our mind. They evoke the bodily movements which we make, the thoughts and the decisions which appear in our consciousness, and various other physical and psychic processes. Ruling our psychic life, these factors themselves remain, with rare exceptions, unnoted, and we are conscious only of deviations from their normal course: when either the waves of impulsions run extraordinarily high or they sink extraordinarily low; in the latter case, the peculiar, oppressive condition of boredom or apathy is noted.

Since ordinarily impulsions are neither perceptible nor discernible, a question of the greatest significance for psychology and other sciences — including the sciences of legal and of moral phenomena — arises: are experimental ways and means to distinguish, and more or less clearly to observe, the ordinarily unnoted and undiscerned impulsions discoverable?

The characteristics of impulsions include extremely high sensitivity and elasticity: they may — according to circumstances — be subject to great variations of intensity, and when specified conditions are present, impulsions which are relatively weak — and therefore unnoted and undiscerned — in the ordinary way attain an extraordinarily powerful uplift of intensity and become thereupon noted and accessible to observation and study. Through study of the laws governing the variations of this intensity — and particularly, by gaining knowledge of the conditions whereby impulsions are brought to the highest degrees of intensity — we may acquire technical means which (like magnifying glasses, microscopes, and the like in other fields of science) would enable us to discover and to observe the corresponding phenomena, which are not accessible to our cognition in ordinary conditions.

If their realization and satisfaction are obstructed, and their demands not complied with, the force of impulsions tends to increase. Those of appetite and thirst thus attain great force — and even become tempestuous and passionate — if we hold back from satisfying their demands. Various repulsions as to harmful substances unsuitable for food attain great force if there are attempts to violate their prohibitions by taking these into the mouth — still more so if they are chewed and swallowed. *The appropriate experimental method of discovering and discerning impulsions may be termed the method of counteraction.* If the obstacles to the satisfaction of an impulsion seem capable of being overcome but attempts in that regard do not in fact succeed completely — and especially if such approximations to success and temporary failures recur several times — the impulsion (such as appetite, thirst, sex excitation, or curiosity) attains an extraordinarily high degree of intensity. *This experimental method of diagnostics may be termed the method of provocation.* The methods of counteraction and provocation are applicable not only in the form of external experiments, but also in that of internal experiment carried through in the imagination by means of the corresponding ideas: by vividly imagining one's self on the edge of a precipice, or as having in his mouth something loathsome, the corresponding repulsive and restraining impulsions can thus be evoked.

In order to establish a scientific theory of conduct, we must distinguish two classes of impulsions.

(A) Certain impulsions tend to evoke definite and specific conduct especially associated with them by nature; and since we term the systems of body movements and other physiological and psychological processes evoked by impulsions the responses[8] thereto we may characterize the first class of impulsions as impulsions with predetermined and specific responses. Thus hunger-appetite has its own definite and specifically characteristic response, whose constituent elements include: (a) the appearance of ideas and thoughts as to food and eating — the stronger the hunger, the more vivid the form (attaining sometimes the stage of delirium and hallucination); (b) the displacement of other intellectual — as well as impulsional and will — processes; (c) the awakening, and the intensified action (at the sight or the idea of food), of the salivary and other glands ancillary to nourishment, of nerves of taste and smell and other nerves important in nourishment, and of the muscles ancillary to nourishment — including the muscles of the tongue (which attains convulsive movement at the sight of food where there is strong appetite, as in cases of animals licking their mouths), lips (which are thrust forward and smacked), cheeks, and those active in the seizing of food, and so forth.

Another special response is associated with food repulsions — such as impulsions aroused by the sight, smell, taste, or idea of decayed meat. This response consists, not in eating and the subsidiary processes, but in the opposite processes: those directed at not admitting the object into the cavity of mouth or stomach, or of removing it and cleansing the mouth and stomach.

In precisely the same way there are special responses characteristic of thirst, sex excitation, curiosity, fear, shame and countless other impulsions — some of them having special names in language and some not.

As a general formula defining the operation of impulsion with special

[8] There is persuasive authority for the view that Petrazhitsky here employs the Russian word (*Aktsiya*) in the sense of "response," and not in our English sense of "action."

responses (succinctly termed special impulsions) the following proposition may be established: special impulsions tend to turn the organism — the individual psycho-physical apparatus suited, in general, to the production of many and extremely diverse actions — into an apparatus especially adapted for the time being to the fulfillment of a definite biological function; that is to say, they tend to evoke corresponding movements (muscular contractions) and countless auxiliary physiological and psychic processes.

This formula does not purport to assert either that the responses to special impulsions are absolutely predetermined and uniform like the movements of machines, or that the same identical movements are repeated without change whenever a certain special impulsion is present. The predetermination of responses to special impulsions is relative, not absolute; different elements thereof — in particular, bodily movements — may, within certain limits, be adapted to specific circumstances and change accordingly. Thus, the bodily movements of eating — as elements of the response to hunger-appetite — are not always repeated in absolutely identical form; they are adapted to the properties of the objects being eaten and change in conformity with what is indicated by the corresponding sensations. The responses to special impulsions, are, in general, more strictly and exactly predetermined in the lower than in the higher animals; in man the responses to special impulsions are generally freer and more subject to change than are those of other higher animals. In the very same animals, responses to some impulsions are more mechanical, and to others more flexible and free. In men, certain impulsions are of so free and changeable a character that their predetermination is limited to the general direction of conduct. This is especially so as to the elements of man's mind which are most important from the point of view of social life, such as the impulsions whose responses consist of benevolent conduct toward others. This may be expressed in the most diverse forms: Love in the sense of cordial devotion toward another — being nothing but a propensity or disposition to experience caritative impulsions as to that other — is manifested in thousands of different benevolent actions and abstentions, and the same is true of love in the evangelical sense — a general trait of character — a propensity to experience caritative impulsion — as regards others in general. Opposed to these caritative impulsions are impulsions of malice or hatred directed at causing evil and endowed, in their turn, with extremely free responses which change in concrete cases. Thousands of diverse actions manifest hatred. Responses to impulsions of ambition and vanity and to many other impulsions are, in the same way, extremely free and subject to variation.

(B) Besides the very numerous impulsions to which there are definite responses (though sometimes these are definite only in general character and direction), there are others which play an extremely important part in life. *Per se* the latter predetermine neither the details, nor even the general character and direction, of the actions — they can serve as stimuli to any conduct whatever: they incite specifically those responses whose ideas are experienced in association with them. *These we will term "abstract" or "blanket" impul-*

sions. They include the impulsions aroused by commands or prohibitions addressed to us. Appropriate experiments and self-observation will demonstrate that commands and prohibitions — especially if they are sudden, short, and sharp, such as "quiet!" "back!" "don't touch!" and are stated in a properly impressive and stern tone and with properly imperative gestures — act like an electric current in evoking instantly in the mind specified processes conducive to conduct in conformity with the content of the command or prohibition. Positive commands arouse impulsions which incite to corresponding action; negative commands (prohibitions) arouse restraining impulsions — that is to say, repulsions — with reference to the movements or other actions inhibited. Requests, prayers, and advice operate similarly upon the mind, arousing impulsions in favor of, or against, certain conduct. The difference between impulsions aroused by commands or prohibitions, and those aroused by requests and advice, is *inter alia* that the former have the character of rigid and coercive inward incitements, whereas the latter have a gentle, compliant, and yielding character; the former are experienced as constraint and an inward curbing of freedom, the latter as free stimuli. Through impulsions aroused by such means of governing the conduct of others as commands, requests, and advice, it is possible to evoke any bodily movement or other action insofar as there are no peculiar physical obstacles, or more powerful counteracting psychic factors. It will be shown *infra* that the impulsions *which make up the essential elements of moral and legal experiences and evoke moral and legal conduct belong to the class of blanket impulsions.*

The stimuli of our behavior are, in general, either special impulsions (in which case, our conduct has the character of the specific action historically associated with the given impulsion), or blanket (abstract) impulsions (in which case the content of the idea of the conduct associated with the impulsion — of the action idea — defines the character and direction of our conduct). Pleasures and sufferings, on the contrary, have no part whatever in the process of motivation if — as happens every so often — they do not bring us to the awakening of an impulsion: if, in other words, we remain indifferent (apathetic) with regard to them. In the other cases — that is to say, when these experiences are present and do excite impulsions — stimuli to actions or to abstentions do arise, but they consist of the impulsions which emerge and operate in these cases, and not at all in positive or negative feelings, pleasures, or sufferings as such. Ordinarily, pleasures evoke attractive impulsions while sufferings evoke repulsions; and to this extent there are impulsions operating in aid of pleasures and against sufferings. But the converse also occurs: sometimes satisfactions arouse repulsions by reason of the education and character of the person concerned or his psychic condition at the particular time (for example, after the death of one who is dear), and in these cases there is antihedonistic conduct directed against pleasure. Similarly, sufferings sometimes arouse attractive impulsions, and are accompanied likewise by antihedonistic conduct.

Those motivational processes wherein pleasure and suffering act as the stimuli of impulsions may be called sense-impulsive motivation. Those motivational processes wherein notions, ideas, or other intellectual processes act as the stimuli of impulsions — inciting to this conduct or that — may be termed intellectual-impulsive motivation. That species of intellectual-impulsive motivation which contains ideas of the effects to be attained by means of certain actions or abstentions may be called purposive or teleological motivations; the ideas of the effects to be realized we may term purposive or teleological ideas; and the imagined effect we may term the purpose — a positive purpose if it is a matter of attaining some change in an existing situation, or a negative purpose if it is a matter of averting a change in an existing situation.

By no means must images of possible pleasures or sufferings be deemed the only ideas capable of acting as purposive ideas: the capacity to arouse impulsions — attractive and otherwise — belongs as well to various other conceptions of the possible effects of our behavior. This is so particularly as to various ideas of advantage and disadvantage — utilitarian ideas — which must be carefully distinguished from hedonistic ideas and comprise various ideas of purely objective effects (such as technical or scientific effects) with no idea of satisfaction or advantage to anyone at all.

It must, however, be noted with regard to all ideas as to the possible effects of conduct, that these have no monopoly in respect of evoking impulsions and defining our behavior: many other ideas act in precisely the same way and there are as well various other classes of intellectual-impulsion motivation (aside from various species of teleological motivation). It has often been assumed by philosophers, psychologists, jurists, moralists, economists, and others — and accepted as a self-evident truth — that all human behavior has a certain purpose, as if action without purpose were absurd and impossible. This is a cardinal error, due chiefly to a failure to distinguish between the practical and the theoretical viewpoints, and an acceptance of the opinion that the irrationality of anything proves that it is in fact impossible and nonexistent. The very great majority of human and animal actions are non-purposive in character and are based on other than purposive motivation.

(A) First, actions based on specific reasoning — actions "because" — are to be contrasted with actions "in order that" (actions taken for the sake of accomplishing a particular purpose). Ideas concerning the past (such as ideas of an affront put upon us) are no less capable of arousing impulsions than are ideas as to what is possible in the future, and — once present — an impulsion seeks to evoke the corresponding response without asking whether or not a certain end must be accomplished. Thus, if the behavior of another arouses in the mind of the subject indignation, contempt, enthusiasm, or the like, the corresponding impulsions then flare (manifest their responses) in the form of words (abuse, contemptuous expressions, or enthusiastic praise) or other actions (such as striking the insulting person, applauding, embracing, or kissing) without (ordinarily) the slightest reasoning or any idea of the purpose of the corresponding bodily movements. Thus if one bursts into abuse — or expresses "noble indignation," enthusiasm, and the like — "in order that," this may be said to be a comedy or a pretense, and not a genuine expression of anger, indignation, or enthusiasm. Many species of human conduct inevitably presuppose a motivation whose origin is in the past and are, by their very nature, incompatible with purposive motivation concerned with the future.

Motivation of the type portrayed we will term *fundamental motivation*; ideas (of something that has occurred or is present) acting as cognitive factors which arouse impulsions and directly cause the corresponding responses we will term *basic ideas*; and the corresponding phenomena present in consciousness — the actions of others and the like — we will term the *bases of conduct*.

(B) A second species of intellectual-impulsive motivation (to which purposive calculations and ideas are completely alien) is a motivational process consisting in the fact that perceptions of certain objects (such as bread perceived by a hungry person, or water by a thirsty person, or mice by a cat, or a cat by mice) evoke in the mind of the percipient impulsions — attractive or otherwise — with reference to those objects and (with no considerations of purpose whatsoever) evoke bodily movements directed toward grasping the object or drawing nearer to it (in case of attractive impulsions) or withdrawing from or thrusting away the object (such as an annoying insect, or a disgusting substance which has fallen into one's mouth), or withdrawing oneself therefrom (as in the case of flight from an animal arousing fear). This class of motivation we will term *objective motivation*. This is the most ordinary and widespread species of motivation in human — and *a fortiori* in animal — life. Upon it are built feeding (including the bodily movements of eating, drinking, and hunting, and other actions directed at gaining possession of objects of nourishment), sex life, bodily movements of preservation from threatening enemies and from other harmful and dangerous influences, and the like, in the animal kingdom. Even in human life, and when one has achieved the lofty intellectual culture of an adult (as distinguished from savages or children), purposive motivation is a rare exception as compared with objective motivation. A scientific diagnosis of the motivation at the foundation of the thousands of bodily movements we make every day — from the time we put on our clothes in the morning, wash, breakfast, smoke, and so forth, to our final movements and ending as we are preparing for sleep — will demonstrate that there are hundreds of cases of objective motivation to each single case of purposive motivation.

(C) Finally, mention must be made of still another species of intellectual-impulsive motivation, which plays an important part in certain fields of human conduct (including moral and legal behavior): those motivational processes wherein *the images of conduct themselves act as their cognitive components* — which arouse the impulsions evoking various positive and negative actions (abstentions). These may be succinctly termed *action ideas.*

In an honorable man, invited to commit (for money or other advantage) deceit, perjury, defamation, homicide by poisoning, or the like, the very idea of such "foul" and "wicked" conduct will evoke impulsions which reject these acts; moreover that rejection will be so powerful as not to permit the attractive impulsions (with reference to the promised advantages) and the corresponding purposive motivation to arise, or to crush such motives if they do appear. Other action ideas — such as ideas of behavior termed "good" or "sympathetic" — evoke, on the contrary, attractive impulsions with reference to such behavior (which is the very reason for their being called "good").

Motivation wherein action ideas operate — arousing impulsions for or against corresponding conduct — may be termed *self-sufficing motivation* (self-sufficing in the sense that here no extraneous — purposive or other — cognitive processes are needed: the idea of the conduct is itself sufficient to evoke the impulsions in favor of or against it).

The existence and operation, in our mind, of immediate combinations of action ideas and impulsions (rejecting or encouraging corresponding conduct), may be manifested in the form of judgments rejecting or encouraging certain conduct *per se* — and not as a means to a certain end: "a lie is shameful"; "one should not lie"; "one should speak the truth"; and so forth. Judgments based on such combinations of action ideas with repulsions or attractions we term *normative judgments*; and their content we term principles of conduct — or norms.

The classes of the motivational processes established *supra* are all complex psychic processes composed of feeling and intellectual processes together with impulsions. However, from the point of view of the basic propositions of the psychological theory proposed *supra*, simpler motivational processes — consisting solely of impulsions evoking corresponding actions — exist as well.

Impulsions can, and often do, arise without the participation of any psychic processes (feelings, sensations, ideas, or the like) whatsoever under the influence of physiological processes and conditions. Thus, after the organism's strength has been restored by sufficiently long sleep, impulsions stimulate us to get up. In the converse case — where the organism requires sleep to restore strength — impulsions to sleep constrain us with increasing insistence to lean against something or to lie down, to close our eyes, and so forth. Where the refuse products of organic life have accumulated and require removal, impulsions more and more forcibly stimulate us to the appropriate actions. Insofar as the responses to these and similar special impulsions — whose emergence presupposes no other psychic processes — can be realized without the participation of any psychic process whatsoever, we are dealing with motivational processes and actions comprising, from the psychological point of view, nothing whatsoever except impulsions; more specifically neither purposive (or analogous) ideas — nor even sensations — are present.

Contrasting the propositions set out *supra* with reference to the motives of conduct with the theory obtaining in contemporary psychology, we must note that (1) the prevailing psychological doctrine reduces all conduct to a single motivational pattern, which (2) is a pattern of hedonism and egoism. From the standpoint of the theory set out *supra*, no such single pattern does or can exist: there is, on the contrary, a great multitude of diverse species and varieties of motivational processes which is increased by the participation of other psychic factors in evoking impulsions. Irrespective, therefore, of the diversity of impulsions, there are different species and varieties of motivational processes: the simplest or purely impulsive motivation, the various species and varieties of complex sense-impulsive and intellectual-impulsive motivation, various species of purposive motivation, objective motivation, and so forth.

SECTION 6. *The Fundamental Propositions of the Psychological Theory of Aesthetic and Ethical Phenomena*

The general psychological propositions set out *supra* make it possible to find a solution for problems concerning the nature of morality and law hitherto unsolved by science and impossible of solution on the basis of traditional psychological theories. In order to explain the nature of these phenomena we must return to self-sufficing motivation and normative judgments.

In different cases, the structure of normative judgments and motivational processes comprises different impulsions which — in conformity with their specific nature — communicate to the various provinces of mental life and conduct diverse qualities and special characteristics. It is possible and desirable, therefore, to form different classes of normative experience.

Certain normative experiences comprise specific positive or negative impulsions — we will term them aesthetic impulsions — which are frequently experienced by us, with reference not only to different human conduct but also to various other phenomena and objects termed in such cases pretty or beautiful (if the aesthetic impulsion is positive) or ill-formed, ugly, or foul (if the aesthetic impulsion is negative). It is upon combinations of different action ideas with these impulsions that the so-called rules of decorum — rules of *savoir vivre,* of good form, of social usage, of elegance — rest. Among persons who are "well brought up," ideas of such actions as using one's fingers or the tablecloth or the napkins instead of a pocket handkerchief, using "unseemly" words in society — especially in the society of ladies — and the like are combined with negative aesthetic impulsions. Appropriate experiments employing the method of counteraction enable us to become familiar with the character of these impulsions and the sometimes invincible force of the pressure they exert upon conduct. Other action ideas — ideas of actions required by "decorum," related to "good form," or "elegant" — are combined with positive aesthetic impulsions. The same impulsions rebel against slips in grammar, syntax, and the like, and are the basis of rules of grammar, style, and rhetoric — thus playing an important part in the field of language and its development, literature, and so forth. All the corresponding aesthetic (positive or negative) impulsions comprising action ideas of this content or that, and directed against or in aid of the corresponding actions, we will term aesthetic normative experiences; the corresponding norms — aesthetic norms; and the corresponding motivation and the conduct resting thereon — aesthetic motivation and aesthetic actions.

Over and above action ideas, the structure of aesthetic normative experiences (particularly of judgments) often comprises ideas of a different intellectual content: this is so as to ideas of circumstances where aesthetically the corresponding action is required (or not permitted) if those circumstances are present — such as the ideas corresponding to the words "in society," "in the society of ladies," "on the occasion of the first visit," and the like. These ideas may be termed aesthetic conditions; and the circumstances themselves aesthetically-relevant facts. Aesthetic judgments, convictions, and norms (not themselves containing indications of conditions and relevant facts) unconditionally ordaining or rejecting specified conduct may be termed categorical or unconditional aesthetic judgments, convictions, and norms. In hypothetical aesthetic judgments we may distinguish two parts: the hypothesis (indicating the conditions), and the disposition (the other elements); in unconditional aesthetic norms and judgments, there is only the second part — the disposition.

Furthermore, the structure of aesthetic normative complexes often includes ideas of individuals, or classes or people (such as "children," "cavaliers," "women," and the like) or of other beings (such as states — for which there are rules of international decorum, of international aesthetics of conduct and the like — corporations, institutions, and the like): in general, of subjects from whom certain conduct is aesthetically required (subject ideas: ideas of aesthetic subjects).

In certain fields of the aesthetic normative mentality one finds, in addition, ideas of facts — such as the existence of an ancient custom or a "new style," actions of a local leader who "sets the tone" in the matter of elegance, admonitions of parents as to indecorum, the ugliness of certain conduct and the like — which define the content, and condition the "obligation," of the aesthetic disposition: that one should do (or it is seemly to do) so and so because so it was from time immemorial, or that such is the custom, or that everyone behaves so, or that such is the style, or that this is the way the Prince of Wales dresses; or that one is not supposed to act so because mother said it was not proper, or because that is what is said in the book of decorum — in the book on *savoir vivre*. Such constituent parts of the (normative) experiences we may term ideas of norm establishing, or normative, facts. Aesthetic normative experiences and aesthetic norms comprising such ideas we shall term heteronomous or positive, and the others autonomous or intuitive.

Thus, if one experiences an aesthetic judgment (or has an aesthetic conviction) that it is unseemly — bad form — to blow one's nose on one's fingers, without the idea of any normative facts whatever (such as admonitions of a nurse) in support of this but in the exercise of his own judgment, the corresponding norm is then an autonomous, intuitive norm. However, in the case of the child whose attitude to such actions is that they are unseemly — bad form, and to be avoided — "because the nurse said so," or "because elders don't do it," the corresponding norm is a positive or heteronomous norm. In the period of patriarchal life — and in general in the lower stages of culture — popular aesthetics had, and still has, for the most part, the character of positive aesthetics; at all events, positive aesthetics had far greater importance in national life — and intuitive aesthetics far less — than is the case now among civilized nations. Qua ideas of normative facts, those of the corresponding mass behavior of ancestors — of their customs, of ancient customs — were of principal and controlling importance; as regards manners, dress, the building, arrangement and adornment of dwellings and temples, ceremonies, and so on, that which corresponded with old customs and with tradition seemed fine and decorous, whereas any individual and independent deviations and novelties excited sharp aesthetic censure as ugly and unseemly. In our time, intuitive autonomous aesthetics — side by side with positive aesthetics — is extremely important and widely applicable, while in the province of positive aesthetics (except for certain more conservative spheres of spiritual life — chiefly religion and the religious cult), it is not old customs but the fashion or the mode — the new mass conduct — which here sets the tone.

As we have already seen, aesthetic impulsions (positive and negative) are experienced by us not only in connection with various action ideas and with reference to corresponding phenomena (bodily movements and other actions), but also in connection with ideas (and perceptions) of various other phenomena and objects. If we go for a walk and have on one side a square with piles of refuse, and on the other a garden with green lawns and flower beds, we shall unfailingly turn toward the garden under the influence of the negative aesthetic impulsions aroused by the refuse, and the attractive aesthetic impulsions aroused by the flower beds and the lawns. Negative aesthetic impulsions incite us, in general, to turn away — to depart — and to avoid what arouses them, while positive aesthetic impulsions incite us to turn toward the object arousing them, to draw near it, to examine it attentively, and to remain near or among such objects.

According to the general law of impulsive experiences the realization (the satisfaction) of impulsive demands tends to arouse feelings of contentment, while the opposite phenomena — actions running counter to impulsive demands (such as the removal of an object of a positive impulsion, or the approach to an object provoking a negative impulsion) tend to elicit the opposite feelings: dissatisfaction. Accordingly, the approach to an object evoking aesthetic repulsion — to what is "plain," "ugly," or "foul" — the contemplation of that object, the necessity of being among such objects, and so forth are all unpleasant and evoke negative feelings; whereas the approach to an object evoking aesthetic attraction — to what is "pretty," "comely," "beautiful," "magnificent" — the contemplation of that object, being among such objects and in such a locality, and the like, is pleasant and evokes positive feelings.

All modern aesthetics — the science concerned with aesthetic phenomena — revolves around the fact that the contemplation of certain objects or phenomena is pleasant and furnishes satisfaction — enjoyment — that is to say, around one of the particular manifestations of (positive) aesthetic impulsions which are unknown to modern psychology in general, and to the science of aesthetic phenomena in particular. These manifestations represent, however, nothing peculiar or specifically characteristic of the province of aesthetics, but according to the general law of impulsions are repeated in thousands of other impulsions. Aesthetic phenomena are identified with "aesthetic enjoyment," and various more or less profound and contradictory theories are put forward as to its nature: the nature of that, contemplation whereof furnishes "aesthetic enjoyment," and so forth. Only the study of impulsions and their attributes, in general, and cognition of their positive and negative species in particular, can furnish the foundation for the successful development of the science of aesthetics in harmony with the essence of the matter.

Moral and legal experiences are further species of normative impulsive-intellectual complexes in which we are particularly interested. The corresponding moral and legal impulsions (positive and negative) have — besides various attributes (to be examined *infra*) distinguishing them from each other — certain common attributes which furnish a basis for the formation of a single higher class of impulsions, which we will term experiences of duty — of obligation: *ethical impulsions*. The corresponding normative impulsive-intellectual complexes we term consciousness of duty — of obligation: ethical experiences, ethical consciousness.

Ethical impulsions are experienced by us, and rule our conduct, with very great frequency — especially as regards our relations toward those near us. Like many other impulsions, however, they are ordinarily unnoted by the subject: they cannot be differentiated and observed — at all events, they cannot be clearly and distinctly known — wherefore their existence, nature, and attributes are still unascertained (in science, as well as in life). For this reason — if there were no other — knowledge of the nature of morality and law is conspicuously absent.

In order to discover the existence, and to know the nature, of the impulsions in the field of duty consciousness in which we are interested, we must make introspective investigations into cases — actual, or imagined for experimental purposes — when more or less powerful "temptations" to act otherwise oppose and counteract the consciousness of duty — that is to say, when the experience and action of different impulsions, which impel divergent conduct, operate against the realization of ethical impulsions. Ethical impulsions — like other impulsions — are characterized by great variations of intensity which — if there are obstacles, counteraction, and provocation — becomes so great that the impulsions become distinct and yield to study.

Especially powerful onsets of ethical impulsions experienced in general — in intermittent onsets or waves, appearing and rising, and then abating and disappearing — occur during the period of indecision: in the course of the struggle between these and other conflicting, "tempting" impulsions. Even after the struggle has been decided for or against the ethical impulsion and the corresponding action has begun, certain conditions cause recurrent attacks of powerful ethical excitation. If an impulsion opposed to duty is victorious and the corresponding action starts — thus if a child, under the influence of the appetitive excitation evoked by the appearance of another's candy, decides (in the absence of the owner) to snatch one or more pieces from the basket (notwithstanding his consciousness that he is bound not to encroach upon another's goods) and stretches out his hand to fulfill his "criminal" purpose — then it comes to pass that the formerly weakened and vanquished ethical impulsions reappear and resume the attack so strongly as sometimes to compel fulfillment of the action opposed to them to be broken off for a time or altogether: movement of the hand toward another's property is momentarily halted so as to proceed with the theft only after the attack by the protesting ethical impulsion shall have subsided. If the ethical impulsion prevails and the corresponding conduct begins — if the child or other subject (notwithstanding the powerful impulsions aroused by the appearance of another's property which can be secretly made off with) withdraws from the object of the appetitive impulsion in obedience to the more powerful impulsion of duty, then the formerly weakened and vanquished "temptation" impulsions sometimes — after the weakening of the ethical impulsion because of the elimination of counteraction — reappear in the shape of recurrent attacks more or less powerful; so that, for example, the subject who is going away from the other's property halts and looks around — or even turns and begins again to draw near the tempting object — and these processes, like counteraction, evoke in their turn the recurring manifestation and increase of intensive ethical impulsions. Even after the duty has been finally and irrevocably breached — even if the child has secretly snatched and eaten another's candy — there are recurrent attacks (sometimes over a very long time: months or years) of the corresponding duty consciousness, protesting against what has been done. In such cases, however, complicating processes prevent the clear and distinct cognition of ethical impulsions: in accordance with the general law that phenomena opposed to impulsive demands evoke negative feelings, dissatisfactions, and sufferings, the presence of ethical impulsions and the concomitant consciousness that the fulfillment of their demand is no longer possible causes more or less strong sufferings (compare the expression "the gnawing of conscience"). This complication hampers the acquisition of clear and distinct knowledge of ethical impulsions, and may even result in a failure to differentiate these from essentially distinct and purely passive processes: those commonly called sufferings.

Ethical impulsions may also attain great intensity and be noted in cases when it is not a matter of the subject's own but of another's behavior provided there is counteraction or provocation. Thus if we try, under the influence of our ethical experiences, to persuade a brother, friend, or acquaintance not to do something — for instance, not to affront an innocent man or not to violate the peace of another's family, and he resists and quarrels and refuses to recognize the obligation (or first assents and yields, and then returns once more to the purpose which is ethically disturbing to us), this counteraction and provocation may bring our ethical impulsions to the pitch of powerful and marked agitation. The reading of stories, tales, dramas, tragedies, and the like — vividly portraying events whose ideas are able to arouse the reader's ethical impulsions and bring them to great intensity through imaginary counteraction and provocation — or attendance at corresponding theatrical exhibitions may likewise serve as an excellent means of studying ethical impulsions experimentally.

Study of such experiences through self-observation induces the conviction that specific passive-active experiences (impulsions) are a constituent element of ethical experiences, and are distinguished by two characteristic qualities: (1) the stimuli and incitements involved possess a unique character of mystic authority, and (2) such impulsions are experienced as an inward impediment to freedom.

(1) The stimuli and incitements now under study are of a unique mystic-authoritative character: they stand opposed to our emotional propensities and appetences as impulsions with the loftiest aureole and

authority, proceeding as from a source unknown and mysterious, and extraneous to our prosaic ego, and possessing a mystic coloration not without a tinge of fear. This character of ethical impulsions finds expression in popular speech, poetry, mythology, religion, and similar creations of the human spirit in the form of fantastic ideas, and particularly in the idea that in such cases some being other than our ego is also present opposing our ego and inciting it to certain conduct: some mysterious voice addressing us and talking to us. This is responsible for the word conscience (con-scio) indicating the presence of another being as well as for various verbal collocations such as "the voice of conscience." Religion, proverbs, poetry, and so forth ascribe this voice to mystic beings: to the revered spirits of ancestors, to various deities, or to God in monotheistic religions (the voice of God). These impersonations, this belief in the divine origin of the voice of conscience, and such expressions as "listening to conscience," "fear of conscience," and the like, reflect this character of the loftiest authoritativeness — and a tinge of the celestial — characteristic of ethical impulsions. These special characteristics of ethical impulsions exert pressure also on the thinking of philosophers and scholars, and define the character and the direction of their intellectual labor in the field of ethics. Socrates, the founder of moral philosophy, spoke of the higher spirit (*daemon*) which suggested to him how he ought to act. Kant founded his theory of morality on the hypothetical existence of a special, metaphysical ego — a double of our empirical ego — which gives directions to the latter. In other philosophical theories diverse metaphysical beings play the same part: "nature" conceived as the supreme being, world "reason," the "objective spirit," and the like. Even the theories of law and morality propounded by scholars of a positive and skeptical turn of mind, who strive to remain aloof from all mysticism, show a tendency toward various mystic impersonations: such are the ideas of the historical school of jurists, and of various contemporary jurists and moralists as to a "national spirit," a "general will," a *gens* instinct, and the like — where the "national spirit" or the "general will," or the *gens* are represented as endowed with higher authority and standing above the individual and his individual will.

(2) The class of impulsions with which we are concerned is characterized further by the quality that they are experienced as an inward impediment to freedom — as a particular obstacle to the free exercise of a preference and the free selection and free following of our propensities, appetences, and purposes — and as a strong and undeviating pressure toward the conduct with whose idea the corresponding impulsions

are combined. In this regard, ethical impulsions are similar to the imperative impulsions aroused by commands or prohibitions addressed to us.

This quality of ethical impulsions is reflected in language and other products of the human spirit in the form of two categories of fantastic ideas.

(a) On the one hand, the corresponding principles of conduct — the norms — are termed "laws," "commands," and "prohibitions." In conformity with the character of lofty mystic authority possessed by ethical impulsions, these seem supreme laws which govern persons (and even gods). Insofar as we have in view more picturesque and personal ideas of mystical beings entering into relations with our ego (or with persons in general), these beings — or the corresponding mysterious "voice" — address us, not with requests or advice, but with commands. "Conscience" does not ask, it "commands." Moral and legal principles are laws, commands, prohibitions, and so forth, established by deities. The same ideas prevail in philosophy and in the legal and moral sciences: the corresponding principles are regarded as "commands" and "prohibitions" — as imperatives. According to Kant, the metaphysical double addresses our ego with "a categorical imperative," and the like. Associated with this idea is the importance of the word "will" in legal, political, and other sciences: in the abstract form of reducing law to "will," of discerning the essence of law in will, or in the more specific forms of various fictions of a "general will," the "will of the state," and the like. It must be borne in mind that the word "will" is ambiguous: it has a psychological meaning as designating a special class of psychic processes which precede bodily or mental action, but it also has another and essentially distinct meaning not uncommonly associated with the word "will" in popular speech, where not infrequently it signifies commands, orders, and prohibitions addressed by some to others. The servant or other subordinate carries out "the will of the master," "the will of the chief," and the like (will in the sense of scientific psychology is, of course, "carried out" by the organism of the subject himself and not by any other subject). Similarly jurists, political scientists, moralists, and even some psychologists — with no suspicion that the word "will" is thus ambiguous — fail to distinguish between demands (commands addressed to others) and will in the psychological sense, and so conceive of the norms of law and morality as the commands of someone and fashion theories of law and morality as theories of will: theories of the relationships of the will of some to the will of others, theories of "general will" and "joint will," and the like.

(b) On the other hand, the subject to whom the supposed (fantastic) commands and prohibitions — the imperatives, the fictitious "will," and the like — are addressed appears as being found in the special condition of being unfree: of being bound (and hence the expression "obligation"). Following one's appetences despite the "demands of duty" appears as the breach or disruption of a bond — as the destruction or overstepping of a barrier (and hence the expressions "breach of duty" and "transgression"). Jurists and moralists interpret moral and legal obligations as subordination to commands and prohibitions, or to a "will" conjured up for the purpose. In the literature concerning the nature of law, the matter is not infrequently put thus: commands or prohibitions of every kind have behind them the threat of disadvantageous consequences in case of breach, hence the necessity of subordination.

To make clear the actual nature of ethical (moral and legal) norms and obligations we must have in view the following considerations. Stimuli aroused in us by various objects (by perceptions or ideas of them), or experienced with reference to them, communicate to the corresponding perceptions or ideas a particular coloration so that the objects themselves appear to us as if they objectively possessed the relevant qualities. Thus, if a certain object such as a roast (the perception, appearance, sight, smell, and so forth of the roast) arouses appetite in us, it then acquires in our eyes a particular aspect, and we ascribe particular qualities to it and speak of it as appetizing, as having an appetizing appearance, and the like. If the same object (the physiological condition of our organism being different) or another object offered to us as food awakens in us the contrary (negative) impulsion instead of appetite, we then — if this (negative) impulsion is relatively weak — ascribe to the object the quality of being unappetizing, whereas if stimulus is more intense, we endow the object with the quality of "loathsomeness." If the perception of any object or phenomenon awakens in us impulsions termed fear, fright, terror, or horror, we then call this object or phenomenon fearful, threatening, or horrible: a hissing goose or a barking dog has an extremely threatening and fearful aspect — and are terrifying animals — to a child, while to an adult or to a bold child they are not fearful animals, and their aspect inspires no fear at all. A, for whom B experiences the impulsion of love, seems, to B "amiable" or "dear," but if love disappears and is replaced by a propensity to repulsive experiences, the "amiable" person becomes "hateful" or even "foul and disgusting." The epithets sympathetic, comely, antipathetic, marvelous, and interesting (as in the case of a story), comic and touching (as in a comic, touching scene), or vile and shocking (as in the case of conduct) further illustrate the same psychic phenomenon.

This phenomenon — which may also be found in fields of impulsive life where no special names exist in our language for the imaginary qualities of the material objects — we will term an impulsive projection or phantasy; that which under the influence of impulsive phantasy seems to us objectively existing we will term impulsive phantasmata or projected ideological entities; and the corresponding viewpoint of the subject — his attitude to impulsive phantasmata, or ideological entities as something real and actually existing in the place to which he refers or projects it — we will term the projection or ideological point of view.

The impulsive phantasy creates not only various qualities and attributes for objects and phenomena to which various adjectives correspond in language, but also other categories of diverse entities which do not in fact exist — including various nonexistent objects, situations, and conditions of objects, processes, and events concerning them to which sundry nouns, verbs, and adverbs correspond in popular speech. Thus in the field of the aesthetic mentality (where, in general, impulsive projection plays no small part) not only are fantastic ideological attributes ascribed to objects and phenomena but there are fantastic processes in operation: confused ideas of some demanding and obtaining of certain conduct from subjects, or of not permitting — and of rejecting for some reason — certain behavior. These processes and ideas are produced by impulsive projection.

If the subject experiences positive or negative aesthetic impulsions as to an object or phenomenon of a nature perceived or imagined by him, an ensuing impulsive projection endows these objects or phenomena with qualities and attributes corresponding to the specific character of the aesthetic impulsions. To this psychic process various adjectival epithets correspond: "ill-favored," "ugly," "deformed," "disgusting," and "repulsive" (to negative aesthetic repulsions), and "pretty," "beautiful," "comely," "charming," "splendid," and the like to positive aesthetic impulsions. The noun "beauty" designates the corresponding impulsive-fantastic quality. The same projections occur also with relation to movements of the human body and to other human actions, with corresponding epithets indicating the action of aesthetic impulsions — negative ("unlovely conduct," "unlovely motion," "ugly," "unseemly," "foul," "vulgar," "trivial," "impudent," and the like) and positive ("pretty," "elegant," "stately," "refined," and the like).

Bodily movements or other actions are endowed with aesthetic qualities (by way of projection) chiefly when the subject perceives (sees or imagines) a bodily movement as something which has been — or is being — accomplished: when the concern is, in general, with movement of the body or other conduct as a fact and with the designation or labeling of that fact. If, however, one thinks of a certain action as something which may (or may not) be accomplished by him — and especially if it comes to the choice of this conduct or that — and a negative aesthetic impulsion against certain conduct arises in his mind, or a positive aesthetic impulsion operates in aid of certain conduct — the corresponding quality is then projected, not upon the conduct itself, but upon the positive (or negative) requirement that this course of action be (or be not) taken. Such judgments as that it is, in this case becoming — proper or decorous — to act thus, to make such and such a visit, and the like merely manifest in words an impulsive projection. If there is in our consciousness the idea of a certain subject or subjects with whose behavior we are concerned, the processes of imposing demands seem as if they were taking place between the subject and the conduct: they seem to be addressed to the subject and to induce him to accomplish (or not to accomplish) a certain action. Judgments of the class: it is seemly or proper or becoming for him to act so and so — or it is not becoming, proper, or decorous to act thus, and the like — correspond to these projection processes. Moreover, the phrase "it is proper," or the expression "he should" or "he should not," is applied not only in the field of aesthetic appulsions and repulsions but also in that of various other impulsions with reference to anticipated actions.

Those categorical commands with higher authority, which in case of ethical experiences appear objectively existing and addressed to subjects — as well as the particular state of being bound (obligated), or being unfree and subordinate, ascribed to the subjects to whom ethical laws command or forbid certain conduct — are thus nothing but products of impulsive projection: impulsive phantasmata.

Only ethical impulsions — in association with ideas of certain conduct (such as lying) and certain other ideas (of subjects with whose conduct we are concerned and so forth) — really and truly exist; but the impulsive projection makes it seem to one experiencing such processes that somewhere — in a higher space, as it were, above mankind — a corresponding categorical and strict imperative or prohibition exists and holds sway (for example, a prohibition against lying), and those to whom such commands and prohibitions seem addressed are in a peculiar condition of being bound or obligated.

In the domain of ethics it is generally true that mankind inclines — as in habits of thought, terminology, and speech — to the projection viewpoint, broadly speaking, and — ignoring the actual psychic processes — stubbornly assumes that prohibitions, commands, and obligations (corresponding to the impulsive projections) really exist. There has been such complete adjustment to this point of view that to start an examination of problems of ethics from the teaching of scientific psychology (that these are phantasmata which do not exist, and that the only real existence is that of the peculiar impulsions in the mind of the person attributing the obligations in connection with certain intellectual processes) is to raise difficulties of thinking and of language and in substance to talk an unknown language. When, therefore, many of the problems of the general theory of ethical phenomena are under consideration, it is more convenient — for simplicity of exposition — to keep to the traditional and customary projection point of view, and speak of obligations and of their content, of kinds of obligations, and the like, as if they actually existed, bearing constantly and clearly in mind we are actually concerned with impulsive phantasmata to which known emotional and intellectual processes correspond as real facts. There is nothing unscientific about this critical point of view as distinguished from the everyday and uncritical naïve-projection point of view: it does not start from — or lead others into — a fallacy. It is merely an expedient form of exposition.

In this sense — and for the purpose of this exposition — we may accept the terminology which assigns the designations "commands" and "prohibitions" to ethical (legal and moral) norms — or better (in order to avoid confusion with regard to genuine commands and prohibitions — that is to say, with a special class of actions or behavior) imperatives: imperative norms. The expressions "imperatives" and "imperative norms" in our sense do not at all signify that anyone issues orders to anyone else about anything, or that any "will" addresses another "will": they designate the projections founded upon the impulsions characterized *supra* (and similar to the impulsions evoked by commands and prohibitions addressed to us). They may be termed imperative impulsions.

All imperative impulsions are abstract impulsions. They do not *per se* predetermine our conduct, but operate like the impulsions aroused by requests, commands, and so forth for or against the conduct whose idea is experienced in a particular case in association with imperative (positive or negative) impulsion. Hence with the aid of ethical imperative impulsions the most diverse behavior may be evoked including acts directly opposed to each other in their trend: in general, any conduct at will, conduct of any kind, the idea whereof is brought into association with the imperative impulsion. On the other hand, ethical impulsions are without specific response and would, therefore, evoke no conduct of any sort in the absence of action ideas: they would have neither motivation significance nor meaning. Dissociated from action ideas of every sort, they would manifestly not be experienced. The minimal psychological structure of ethical experiences is an action idea — the idea of some external or internal conduct — plus a positive or negative ethical impulsion (whether weak and unnoted, or powerful and noted); frequently, however, these experiences comprise still other cognitive elements of the same categories as those mentioned *supra* with regard to the structure of aesthetic normative complexes.

(1) Ideas of the circumstances or of the conditions, upon whose presence the obligation of certain conduct depends: for example *"if anyone shall strike you upon the right cheek*, turn to him the other also"; on *Sabbath* "thou shalt. . . " are ideas of ethical conditions or of ethically relevant facts. Ethical judgments, convictions, obligations, or norms comprising no conditions of any sort (such as "thou shalt not kill") we shall call categorical or unconditional; the others we shall call hypothetical or conditional — distinguishing, in the field of the latter, ethical hypotheses and dispositions; thus, "in God's temple" (if we are in the temple: the hypothesis) "we must conduct ourselves so and so" (the disposition).

(2) Ideas of individuals or classes of people (such as subjects, monarchs, parents, or children) or of other beings (such as gods, states with regard to so-called international and other obligations, land committees or cities) from which certain conduct is ethically required are subject ideas: ideas of the subjects of a duty (an obligation).

(3) As we have seen in the domain of aesthetics, the structure of certain ethical experiences comprises ideas of norm-establishing or normative facts: thus "we must act thus *because it is so written in the New Testament, or in the Koran, or in the Code of Laws, or "because our fathers and grandfathers acted so*," or "because the assembly of the people has so ordained." Ethical ideas comprising ideas of these and similar normative facts and the corresponding obligations and norms we shall call heteronomous (or positive); and the others autonomous (or intuitive). Thus, if anyone ascribes to himself an obligation to help those in need, to pay his workers the agreed wage punctually, or the like independently of any outside authority whatsoever, the corresponding judgments, convictions, obligations, and norms are then autonomous (intuitive) ethical judgments; whereas if he considers it his duty to help the needy "because this was the teaching of our Saviour," or to pay his

workers punctually "because it is so stated in the statutes," the corresponding ethical experiences and their projections (obligations and norms) are then positive (heteronomous).

SECTION 7. *Two Kinds of Ethical Obligations and Norms*

We must distinguish two varieties of ethical impulsions, and so two kinds of ethical, impulsive-intellectual complexes and projections thereof: obligations and norms. In order to explain the relevant differences, it is more convenient to take up first the diverse character of the projections in different cases of ethical consciousness.

In some cases what we deem ourselves obligated to do seems to us something owed to another — something due to him, something which he ought to have from us — so that he can assert a claim that we appropriately fulfill our part. Such fulfillment by us (paying the agreed wages to a worker or servant) appears only as the rendering to him of what was his due — the receipt by him of what is "his," and not as causing any peculiar good — and not as a benefit or benefaction to him; and nonfulfillment seems to cause harm to another in that he is deprived of that which he could claim as his due.

In other cases of ethical consciousness — as where we consider ourselves bound to render pecuniary assistance to the needy, to give alms and the like — that to which we consider ourselves obligated does not then seem to us something owing to another or due to *him*, or as something which he ought to have from us. A corresponding claim or demand on his part would seem to us inappropriate and unfounded. Our furnishing of the corresponding object — such as alms — to another, and his obtaining the same, seem not the furnishing to him of that which is his due and the receipt by him of that which is his, but the causing of good which is dependent upon our own benevolence; while our not furnishing the corresponding object (as where we change our original intention to help the one asking alms because we meet someone else in greater need) seems not at all an inadmissible encroachment, or the causing of harm, or a refusal to satisfy a well-founded claim.

In cases of the first sort our duty seems an obligation with regard to another made secure in his behalf as his property: an asset belonging to him (earned or otherwise acquired by him). In cases of the second class, our duty comprises no obligation with regard to others: it seems free with reference to them and not made secure in their behalf.

Obligations conceived of as free with reference to others — obligations as to which nothing appertains or is due from obligors — we will term *moral obligations*.

Obligations which are felt as unfree with reference to others — as made secure in their behalf — we shall term *legal obligations*. The relationships between the two sides — the bonds between them, consisting in the duties resting upon the one side and made secure in behalf of the other — we will call *legal relationships* or *legal bonds*. Legal obligations — the duties of some made secure in behalf of others — regarded from the point of view of the side to which the duty belongs we will call *rights*. Our rights are others' duties, secured in our behalf and belonging to us as our assets. In this sense rights and legal relationships are not anything separate or distinct from legal obligations: that which, from the point of view of the burden — the liability — of one side, is termed legal obligation is, from the point of view of the asset belonging to the other side, termed the right of the latter and, from the neutral point of view, is termed the legal relationship between the two sides.

Two varieties of ethical norms (imperatives) correspond to the two kinds of obligations characterized above.

Certain norms establish obligations free in respect to others: these authoritatively prescribe certain conduct for us but give others no claim or rights of any kind to fulfillment by us. These are unilateral, binding, non-exigent, purely imperative norms — such as the norms corresponding to certain passages in the New Testament: "But I say unto you: resist not evil. Whosoever shall smite thee on thy right cheek, turn to him the other also; and if any man will sue thee at law and take away thy shirt, let him have thy cloak also," and the like. In the consciousness of persons who have advocated and experienced — or are now experiencing — such ethical judgments, the underlying norms do not, of course, mean that corresponding claims in behalf of the offenders have been established: that they have been endowed with the right to demand that the other cheek be proffered to be struck, or that — as a reward — there was deemed to be due to the person who had taken the shirt (or that he ought rightly to get) the outer garment of the injured party as well. The same is true as to other norms of genuine Christian ethics. For the spirit of this system of ethics — radically differing in this regard from the ethics of the Old Testament — is that people are bound to a very great deal with regard to their neighbors which it is extremely difficult to fulfill, but the neighbors neither have — nor should have — claims to the fulfillment thereof. Christian ethics are entirely non-exigent, and if — in the Middle Ages and recently — from various sides there have been (and are being) deduced various rights and claims (of an ecclesiastical or social character and the like), this is due to a complete failure to understand the very essence of the entire doctrine.

Other norms — establishing obligations for some — make these obligations secure in behalf of others: give the latter rights — claims — so that, in accordance with these norms, that to which some are bound is due to others as something authoritatively granted to them and made secure in their behalf: these are binding-exigent, imperative-attributive norms.

Norms of the first class — unilaterally binding, non-exigent and purely imperative — we will term *moral norms*; norms of the second class — bindingly-exigent and imperative-attributive — we will call *legal norms.*

The dual, imperative-attributive character of legal norms is reflected sometimes in legal language in an extremely graphic and striking form, in that the content of the relevant norm is communicated by means of two propositions: one indicating the obligation of one side, and the other the claim or right of the other side. This form of expressing legal norms — pointing out both the passive element (the obligation of the one side) and the active element (the right of the other side: that the debt due from the one side is made secure in behalf of the other side) — may be termed the imperative-attributive (or the complete and adequate) formulation of legal norms.

In the domain of morality, the unilateral-obligatory, unilateral-imperative formulation is complete and adequate: we are bound to do this, we are bound not to do the other, and the like.

Apart from the complete imperative-attributive formulation in the province of law, there are three abbreviated forms of expression which are perfectly admissible (insofar as hearers or readers are not thereby brought into misunderstanding) and are in fact so applied. (1) The abbreviated attributive formulation: this points out only the legal asset — the claim of the one side — without indicating the obligation of the other; for example, "if the obligation is not performed within the time limited, the creditor may demand compensation for his injuries," and the like. Here it is understood that the other side (the debtor or his heirs) is bound to corresponding conduct, to furnish the corresponding object and the like. (2) The abbreviated imperative, obligatory formulation: this points out only the legal debit — the obligation of one side — without indicating the right of the other; for example "if the obligation is not performed within the time limited, the debtor must make compensation for the injury"; here it is understood that the other side (the creditor or his heir) has a right to corresponding action in his behalf, to obtain the corresponding object, and the like. (3) A doubly abbreviated, neutral form: this points out impersonally what should occur without indicating the obligation of the one side or the right of the other; for example, "if the obligation is not performed within the time limited, damages are payable" . . . "the sum total of the duty is augmented by the amount of the injury caused," and the like. Here it is understood that one side is bound to corresponding action for the benefit of the other, and that the latter has a corresponding right with regard to the former.

For an exact and complete ascertainment of the meaning of legal norms, these three abbreviated formulations must be replaced by complete formulations through proper interpretation. In the case of the first, it is necessary to define who is the obligor and to what he is obligated; in case of the second, who is the obligee in the given case and to what he has a right; and in case of the third, interpretative amplification in each direction is required. Sometimes such interpretative amplification — the establishment of the complete imperative-attributive meaning of the expression — is a difficult task, or at least one which presupposes certain supplementary historical or other information. Thus ancient sources of law often say that in case of such and such a crime — robbery, for instance — such and such an amount of money is to be paid. A modern reader, who is not familiar with the law of that time, would be inclined — if the problem of defining the corresponding norm and expressing it in a complete imperative-attributive form were put to him — to say that the meaning was simply that one who had perpetrated the crime is bound to pay, and the one who had suffered from the crime has a right to receive,. the corresponding sum of money. Such interpretation would often be wrong. In antiquity, responsibility for a crime which had been committed often rested on others — the inhabitants of the same village — as well as on those who were guilty; and the right to receive the sum of money established was possessed by princes — or the kin of the injured party had the right to one part of the fine and the prince had a right to the rest.

In the sphere of morality — in accordance with its unilaterally binding, nonattributive nature — the form of expressing norms and their interpretation are much simpler. Here we are concerned only with obligors and their obligations; it is inappropriate to talk of obligees and of claims granted to them: there is, therefore, neither imperative-attributive nor abbreviated attributive formulation. Only unilateral imperative formulation as the full form and neutral formulation as the unilateral abbreviated form of stating an obligation are conceivable (as, for example, in the expressions in the Sermon on the Mount in the New Testament).

SECTION 8. *Moral and Legal Impulsions*

The difference between the two kinds of obligations and norms — between unilateral-imperative and imperative-attributive obligations and norms — is based upon a distinction in the corresponding ethical impulsions.

To reveal the fact that peculiar impulsions are at the foundation of ethical experiences in general, and to gain familiarity with the character of these impulsions — as well as to discover the existence of the two varieties of ethical impulsions and to become familiar with the specific and peculiar characteristics of each — requires that the proper technique of investigation and cognition be consciously and methodically applied: (1) through appropriate experimental means (the methods of counteraction and provocation) such intensity of the impulsions of both kinds must be attained as to make possible their psychological study and comparison (or at least the searching out and selection of intensive experiences of the same type, evoked not by experimental actions but by the circumstances of life), and (2) the relevant (moral and legal) impulsions must be introspectively studied and compared according to their bilateral nature.

To the study of moral and legal impulsions the general directions given in Section 6 are applicable; they may be supplemented by special directions as to the method of studying legal impulsions.

(A) Strong legal impulsions — subject to immediate or reminiscent observation and study — occur when a struggle goes on in our mind between (a) consciousness of our legal duty with regard to another (of the right of the other as regards us), and (b) temptations (other impulsions) which would lead us to violate the duty — to trample under foot the rights of that other. This is particularly the case if our legal duty with reference to the other (the right of that other in reference to us) seems to us "indubitable and sacred," and if non-satisfaction of the right would seriously and irreparably injure that other. In that event there is a vigorous excitation of the legal conscience if temptations correspondingly strong and capable of serious conflict with that ethical consciousness are present, and extremely intensive and marked (though intermittent) fluctuations of legal impulsions are manifested. If other impulsions have already prevailed, and the right of the other person has already been trampled under foot, powerful legal impulsions, in connection with corresponding negative feelings — sufferings (gnawings of the legal conscience) — recur at the thought of that other, of his right, and of the evil caused to him. For real events of this class (or recollections thereof), vivid images of oneself as ready to trample (or as trampling) upon important and sacred rights of others may be substituted (for experimental purposes). In addition to the counteraction and provocation of legal impulsions whose origin is in psychic processes, we may mention external impediments to the satisfaction of another's right as factors which can heighten the intensity of legal impulsions: these may evoke rather powerful legal impulsions — particularly if they are intermittent, with resulting provocation. Through previous arrangement with a third person, who pretends to place obstacles in the way of our fulfilling our legal duty with reference to some other person when we have forgotten about the arrangement or when it does not occur to us that this is an experimental "comedy," experiments may be carried out along this line.

(B) Further factual material for gaining familiarity with the specific nature of legal impulsions is provided by cases (actual, or vividly imagined for experimental purposes) where there is consciousness of our right with reference to another — of the legal duty of another in reference to us — and the corresponding impulsions are provoked because he disputes our right — his own legal obligation — or at one time expresses readiness to acknowledge and satisfy that right and at another refuses so to do or otherwise encroaches upon our "indubitable" — or even "sacred" — right. There is no difficulty in arranging experiments along these lines. Very powerful legal impulsions sometimes develop in persons who are defending their right by protracted proceedings passing through various courts with varying success, so that powerful dispositions to corresponding legal experiences develop and take root and actual legal impulsions of a passionate and tempestuous character appear. The action of the rest of the controlling and restraining apparatus in the mind ("reason" or "common sense," so-called) is then stifled and destroyed, and the subject, "blinded" by legal passion prolongs the proceedings instead of yielding, and does things which seen abnormal and senseless to the quiet observer: acts of a madman or of a psychopath, bringing ruin upon himself and his family.

(C) The third and last category of factual material for the study of legal impulsions is afforded by cases where our legal consciousness consists in vividly conceiving some legal duty — a legal right — as present between third persons (as when we ascribe to someone a certain legal duty with reference to a third person), and our legal impulsions are intensified because the corresponding duty — the corresponding right of the third person which we conceive of as "indubitable" and "sacred" — is contested or trampled under foot. Powerful legal impulsions of this character were experienced by thousands at the time of the Dreyfus affair, the facts of which were such as to provoke extremely strong legal impulsions in persons with a sensitive legal conscience, who followed the developments closely.

Legal impulsions with reference to another yield particularly readily to experimental study. Besides there is abundant experimental material in experiments appropriately designed, the reading of tales, dramas, and descriptions of legal proceedings, and attending theatrical performances or court sessions, whose content can evoke legal impulsions and subject them to provocation.

Introspective study of the psychological material of the categories *supra* — from both the passive and the active sides — will demonstrate that impulsions, as we have analyzed them, are the foundation of our ascription to ourselves or to others of rights (legal obligations) and we shall then know the character of these impulsions. Parallel introspective study of corresponding nonattributive moral experiences (comprising impulsions made powerful by counteraction and provocation), and a comparison of these and other impulsions with each other, warrant the statement that the general attributes — the class attributes — of ethical impulsions are present in them, and make it possible to discover the existence of an important distinction between the two.

Some of the impulsions we encounter have the peculiar character of seeming to be attractions from without and to originate in something perceived or imagined, rather than urges which act within and upon us. Thus, if someone calls us (by name, with the appropriate intonation, or with suitable gestures), we experience peculiar impulsions which seem to originate in the place where he who summoned us is perceived or imagined — particularly if the intonation and gesticulation are properly expressive. In cases of hunger, appetite, thirst, the hunting stimulus, or the like, impulsions with reference to the relevant object (food, water, or game) have the character of a longing actuating us toward the object. However, in the province of impulsions aroused by another's calling, beckoning, or waving his hand to us in a manner suggestive of seizing us and drawing us to himself, the very character of the impulsion itself suggests that we are being subjected to an attraction issuing out of the summoner. In precisely the same way, if a person begs anything of us — some object, for example — with proper intonation and gesticulation, this evokes peculiar impulsions which have the character (originating in the suppliant) of attracting, drawing out, acquiring something from us. The impulsions are similar if someone seeks in an imperious tone which peremptorily asserts a claim — to get something from us for himself. It is only precatory impulsions that have a soft, flexible, and free character: whereas exigent impulsions have a rigid coercive, and unfree character. Those impulsions which have the character of originating in some (perceived or imagined) attraction or extraction, or the acquisition of something from us, may be called attraction impulsions, extraction impulsions, or acquisition impulsions.

Similarly there may be distinguished among negative impulsions (a) those having the character of impulsions acting within and upon us and holding us back from something — rising up against our proximity to something, and (b) those having the character of forces as from without — issuing from some object perceived or imagined — thrusting us away, putting us aside, or not admitting us. Impulsions of shame or shyness illustrate impulsions of the first sort: these may be called restraining impulsions in the narrow sense. Impulsions arising from entering raw and dark caves, or in drawing near fire or anything giving a repulsive odor and the like, are examples of the second sort; these may be called repelling or deflectant impulsions in the narrow sense.

In general, we may distinguish among the impulsions of various classes (a) those which seem to our consciousness to be processes within us, acting with reference to something or issuing from us — "inner" impulsions or impulsions "from within," and (b) those which seem to our consciousness to be processes originating *ab extra* and acting upon us — "external" impulsions or impulsions "from without." The impulsions at the foundation of the consciousness of our legal obligations with regard to others belong to the category of external impulsions. If we ascribe to ourselves an obligation to furnish something — such as a certain sum of money — to another as something due to him from us, the corresponding impulsions are experienced as impulsions "from without." In general, even in those cases when we ascribe a legal duty to another, the relevant impulsions seem to our consciousness as processes "from without" with reference to the obligor. The expressions A "is entitled to receive" from B, or A "ought" to receive from B, or such and such a "claim" — a "demand" (right) as regards B — belongs to A and the like, verbally reflect and portray this character of legal impulsions: in accordance with the general nature of ethical impulsions, they possess an imperative, binding, coercive character and are similar — in this regard also — to the impulsions which are operative when one is addressed in a mandatory tone. This accounts for rights being called "demands" or "claims," and for the imputation by jurists of a corresponding "will" to those to whom we ascribe rights. This, of course, fails to distinguish commands and demands from will.

In accordance with the general character of lofty and mystic authoritativeness which ethical impulsions possess, the corresponding taking of something from one in behalf of another appears as an authoritative furnishing of the relevant benefit to that other. This defines and explains the character of the norms and obligations which are projected outward: (a) somewhere in the higher spheres there are authoritative laws holding sway over persons (or even over persons and gods) — which burden some in favor of others — which command some and demand from some, and endow others and bestow upon others; and (b) under the aegis of their higher directive authority, some persons and other beings are subjected to these authoritative demands for various objects in behalf of others and under a duty to obey these demands submissively and to furnish to such others what is owed to them. The duties — the obligations — of the former are authoritatively granted and given over to the latter: are made secure for them as their assets. They are duties resting upon some and belonging to others, and may be referred to as dual bonds — legal relations between the parties: legal claims of obligees and legal duties of obligors.

Because of the mystic-authoritative character of ethical impulsions in general, the popular mind tends to ascribe to beings of a higher order the ethical commands and prohibitions projected outward, and with reference to the particular species of ethical impulsions now under consideration this is manifested in a peculiar way: such beings seem not only to be commanding and forbidding — to be establishing obligations — but at the same time to be endowing others with corresponding rights.

The impulsions which make up the structure of moral experiences possess a specific character which is different from that possessed by legal impulsions. If we ascribe to ourselves an obligation to certain conduct as such — and not as furnishing to others that which is due them or as satisfying their claims — the relevant impulsions are then inward authoritative incitements to the corresponding actions (without an attributive character as regards anyone) and are not authoritative extractive or abstractive impulsions acting from without. This conforms with the specific character of moral projections and expresses that character: the relevant obligations are not claims of others — they are not made secure in behalf of others as their assets: they are obligations which are free in respect to others, and the relevant norms are unilateral commands and prohibitions binding and burdening some, but in no way endowing others.

The ethical projections of this second class — as well as the impulsions themselves and the psychic experiences in general on which they are based — we may characterize as purely or unilaterally imperative, thus distinguishing them from imperative-attributive projections and impulsions of the first class.

A caveat is essential if misunderstanding with regard to these expressions is to be avoided: they must by no means be understood to import that imperativeness and attributiveness are two separate and independent properties of legal impulsions and of legal phenomena in general. The actual relationship between the imperativeness of legal phenomena and their attributiveness is that the imperativeness is merely a reflex of the attributive nature of the relevant impulsions and possesses no independent character. The *adtractio* in behalf of the one is *extractio* as regards the other. The authoritative acquisition — the demand — in behalf of the one (*attributio*) is the authoritative acquisition — the demand — from the other (the imperative). That the imperativeness of legal impulsions is thus derivative is manifest from the fact that, as regards the intellectual structure of legal experiences, ideas of the positive effects and benefits enuring to obligees — from their obtaining what is owed to them — plays an important part along with ideas of the actions required from obligors. What is important and decisive from the point of view of the legal mentality is not the accomplishment, as such, of the relevant action by the obligor, but the obligee's obtaining what is owed to him. Thus, if what is owed to the obligee is furnished to him by others (and not by the obligor), as where the amount due to the creditor is paid to him not by the debtor but by his kinsman or acquaintance, all is then well from the point of view of the law and the proper performance has been rendered.

The imperativeness of moral impulsions is of a different character — independent and not derivative — with reference to the attributive. The comparative study of legal impulsions in different cases of legal experiences will demonstrate, however, that the character of these impulsions varies in accordance with the actions required of obligors in behalf of obligees and the character of the positive effects owed to the latter. Three species of furnishing-receiving, and three varieties of legal impulsions, must be carefully distinguished.

(1) That which obligors are required to do or to furnish may consist in doing something for the behoof of the other side: paying a certain sum of money, or furnishing other objects, or performing certain work,

or rendering other positive services. These are positive actions and positive furnishings: doings and furnishings in the narrow sense (*facere*). The corresponding positive receipts — receipts in the narrow sense (*accipere*) — are owed to the obligees. The impulsions specifically experienced in these cases must be characterized as authoritatively abstractive or extractive. The relevant legal impulsions and the corresponding legal experiences in general — as well as their projections (norms and legal relationships, legal obligations, and legal rights) — we shall call positive-attributive, or attributive in the narrow sense. Positive-attributive rights may be called positive legal claims, or legal claims in the narrow sense of the word.

(2) That which obligors are, in a general sense, to do or to furnish may further consist in not doing something, in refraining from something (as from encroaching on the life, health, honor, of the other side, and the like): negative actions, negative furnishings, restraints (*non-facere*). In these cases the receiving, in the general sense of the positive effects owed to the obligees, consists in not undergoing — in freedom from — the corresponding effects. These may be termed "negative freedoms," "immunities," "safeguardings" (*non-pati*). In the corresponding fields of the legal mentality the attributive impulsions are repellent, deflectent stimuli which authoritatively safeguard the obligee: authoritatively diverting encroachments upon the corresponding goods of the obligee as if they were something turned over to him by higher authority and kept sacrosanct and inviolate for him. The relevant legal impulsions and the corresponding legal experiences in general — as well as their projections (norms and legal relationships, legal obligations, and legal rights) — we will term safeguarding or negative-attributive, and rights of this character may be termed negative rights. In the corresponding fields of the moral mentality — in the province of those moral experiences where the concern is with the not doing of something (*non-facere*), such as refraining from profligacy, lying, and the like — the relevant impulsions have the character of repulses, restraining in the narrow sense of the word — authoritatively rejecting and disapproving the corresponding conduct *per se* and not as an encroachment upon something authoritatively turned over to or kept safe for the other side.

(3) Finally, that which obligors are, in a general sense, to do or to furnish may consist in tolerating or suffering certain actions of the obligees: uncomplainingly enduring certain unpleasant conduct originating with the obligees and taking effect upon the obligors (such as reproofs or physical punishment); in tolerating oral or printed communications and support by the obligee of religious, political, and other

opinions, the organization of public assemblies, meetings, and so forth (*pati*). Here that which is received, in the general sense of the positive effects which are due to the obligees, consist in the corresponding actions endured by the obligors — in the corresponding freedoms of action: positive freedoms (*facere*). In the corresponding provinces of the legal mentality, attributive impulsions have the character of a loftier sanction with reference to the relevant actions of one side, and of an authoritative demand from the other side of a submissively respectful attitude toward the actions as being sustained by a higher sanction and a higher authority in their behalf. The relevant legal impulsions, and the corresponding legal experiences in general (as well as their projections: norms and legal relationships, legal obligations, and legal rights) we will call empowering. Rights of this character — such as the right of punishing, the right of freedom of speech, of the press and of assembly, and the like — may be called legal powers. In the corresponding provinces of the moral mentality — as regards those moral experiences where it is a matter of suffering anything (*pati*): such as affronts by neighbors, persecutions for faith and the like — the relevant impulsions have the character of inner authoritative incitements to endure quietly the malicious and unjustified actions: to endurance as such, and not because that endurance is called for by action (of the other party) conceived of as endowed with a higher sanction.

Each of the three kinds of legal impulsions — the positive-attributive, the safeguarding, and the empowering — is, as regards obligors, an impulsion "from without" — the furnishing, with a higher authority, a certain plus to the other side — and addressed to the obligors as an authoritative pressure toward the corresponding conduct. This character is altogether foreign to moral impulsions — to those which operate in favor of positive actions or tolerances, and to those which restrain from actions: as regards obligors, they are inner, authoritative stimuli toward certain conduct as such, and not as a method and means of conforming with anything attributed to another.

What has been already set out as to ethical experiences in general is certainly referable to the *intellectual* structure of moral and legal experiences. Specifically, psychological analysis demonstrates that there are certain categories of ideas which are component parts of the structure of moral and legal experiences alike. (1) *Action ideas*: in the province of morality we shall call them moral actions or objects of moral obligations, and in the province of law we shall call them legal actions or objects of legal obligations; (2) *subject ideas*: ideas of subjects of moral obligations and subjects of legal obligations; and (3) *ideas of relevant facts*: of conditions (in hypothetical moral and legal experiences). The relevant parts of moral experiences and norms (such as "if one strikes you upon the right cheek") we shall call moral hypotheses; and the other parts (such as "turn to him the left cheek also") we shall call moral dispositions; and the corresponding facts (the blow or the insult) *morally relevant* — or, more briefly, *moral* — *facts*. The corresponding terms in the province of law are legal hypotheses, legal dispositions, and legal facts: thus in the legal experience "if a crime causes property damage, the offender must make compensation and the injured party has the right of compensation for his loss," the first part (the condition) is the legal hypothesis, the second part is the legal disposition, and the loss caused is a legal fact. Finally, there are (4) ideas of *normative facts*: moral experiences comprising ideas of normative facts — we should forgive insult because *this is the teaching of Christ*, or because *it is so written in the New Testament* we shall call positive moral experiences or positive morality, and the others (which include no references to external authorities) we shall call intuitive moral experiences or intuitive morality. Legal experiences comprising ideas of normative facts we shall call positive legal experiences or positive law; those legal experiences which contain no references to outside authorities and are independent thereof we shall call intuitive legal experiences or intuitive law. In everyday life, we ascribe to ourselves and to others various rights at every step and act in conformity therewith — not at all because it is so stated in the Code or the like, but simply because our independent conviction is that it should be so. Statutes recognize no obligation to pay the winner what one has lost at cards, but all respectable people (including as well those who know that — so far as any statute is concerned — they may refuse to pay) acknowledge, respect, and promptly satisfy the corresponding rights in accordance with intuitive law. Present legal theory acknowledges only the existence of positive law. It neither knows nor acknowledges any other.

Only with respect to morality, however, and not with respect to law, does the foregoing pattern of categories of intellectual elements seem complete and exhaustive since, in conformity with the attributive-imperative nature of legal impulsions there are — along with ideas touching the imperative side (obligors, and that to which they are bound) — ideas touching the attributive side of the matter (obligees and that which is owing to them) which play an important part.

We have already seen that in legal experiences ideas of the positive effect for obligees — of what they are to obtain and what is owing to them — are no less important than ideas of the actions — the furnishings

— required of obligors. In the domain of morality — in conformity with the purely imperative nature of the relevant impulsion — we do not and cannot speak of any acquisitions whatever as owed or due to anyone. These acquisitions (owed to obligees in the domain of law) have been termed objects of rights — attributive objects — as distinct from actions required of obligors — objects of obligations or imperative objects. The intellectual structure of the legal mentality may then be said to possess the special characteristic that ideas of objects of rights (attributive objects) take part also, along with ideas of objects of obligations (imperative objects). The same is true of subject ideas: whereas in morality the concern is solely with imperative subjects (subjects of obligations), subjects of rights stand in law opposed to subjects of obligations. There are two sides or pairs of subjects.

The above enumeration is, therefore, exhaustive as regards the intellectual structure of moral experiences — ideas of (1) objects of obligations, (2) subjects of obligations, (3) relevant facts, and (4) normative facts (in the province of positive ethics) — but must in the province of law be supplemented by adding ideas of objects and subjects of rights. The intellectual structure of legal experiences comprises, accordingly,

(1) Object ideas — ideas: (a) of objects of obligations (of obligatory actions) and (b) of objects of rights (of acquisitions which are due and owing);

(2) Subject ideas — ideas: (a) of subjects of obligations, and (b) of subjects of rights;

(3) Ideas of relevant legal facts; and

(4) Ideas of normative facts.

This scheme of the intellectual structure of law is complete and exhaustive: within these headings may be brought all the intellectual components of legal experiences.

It may be that not all of these categories are to be found in an actual legal experience: not only are ideas of normative facts absent from the field of intuitive law and ideas of legal facts from categorical legal experiences, but it is by no means true that ideas of subjects of obligations, of subjects of rights, of objects of obligations, and of objects of rights are present in every particular legal experience.

From the point of view of jurisprudence it is essential in each individual case to know — and to be able to answer — the questions: (1) who is bound (the subject of the obligation)? (2) to what action or actions is he bound (the object of the obligation)? (3) who is the subject of the relevant right? and (4) to what does he have a right — what is due to him (the object of the right)? Actual legal experiences are, however, very far from always meeting this requirement.

As we look at concrete psychic experiences, and consider particularly how the attention of the individual experiencing psychic processes of the legal type is being directed, either the imperative side (ideas of obligors and of that to which they are bound) or the attributive side (ideas of obligees and of that to which they have a right) comes unilaterally into the foreground as a rule, while the other side fades out and is effaced and the corresponding ideas are of a confused and indistinct character if, indeed, they are present at all.

It might seem at first sight that such legal experiences with a unilateral (imperative or attributive) intellectual content were logically impossible and contrary to the very nature of law, which requires the presence of two subjects — one from whom, and one to whom, something is due. How can there be imperative-*attributive* consciousness if the idea of a subject to whom something is owed is not present in consciousness? Or an *imperative*-attributive consciousness if the idea of a subject from whom something is required is not present in consciousness? Does not the very nature of imperative-attributive impulsions necessarily connote complementary ideas of two parties: obligor and obligee?

The answer is that we can — and frequently do — experience imperative-attributive acts of consciousness without imperative-intellectual (or without attributive-intellectual) supplements, as in judgments comprising absolutely no idea of obligors and of that to which they are bound ("an owner has the right to enjoy his property as he will," or "every citizen has a right to bodily inviolability") and importing that all persons are bound to tolerate the relevant actions of the owner. Actually we have here imperative-attributive, legal judgments: the relevant impulsions have an imperative character — although not with reference to a definite person, and the imperative — the demand of conformity with the relevant right — is directed, so to speak, into space. In precisely the same way, judgments in which there is absolutely no idea of the subjects of corresponding claims, or of anything due to them ("land owners are bound to pay land taxes," or "lodgers must be careful with fire") may be imperative-attributive, legal judgments: the relevant impulsions have an attributive character, although there is no idea of a person from whom the claim issues, or to whom the relevant receipt is due.

Moreover, imperative-attributive (legal) experiences can and do occur wherein there are neither ideas of subjects bound nor of subjects empowered: subjectless, impersonal legal experiences. In persons normally brought up in respect to law and possessed of a properly developed legal mentality, many action ideas (such as ideas of theft, robbery, defamation, or insult) as such — that is to say, independently of other ideas — are associated with imperative-attributive impulsions so that where such ideas appear in consciousness, the corresponding impulsions tend to appear likewise, whether or not subject ideas are present. Appropriate experimental methods — such as the attempt secretly to pick and appropriate a rose in a public garden — will readily demonstrate that this is so.

There is no difference whatsoever as regards *intellectual* content between legal experiences — which are without any attributive intellectual content, having no ideas of subjects of a right and of that which is due to them — and moral experiences. The sole difference lies in the character of the impulsions: in the attributive nature of the impulsion which is experienced. Thus, the intellectual content of such expressions and judgments as "one should not steal," "one should not defame," "one should not address a servant coarsely," or "parents should be concerned about the upbringing of their children," does not enable us to say whether they are concerned with legal or with moral phenomena: they may be (and are) sometimes legal and sometimes moral, or they may be experienced at first as moral judgments, and a few seconds later as legal judgments — or vice versa. If a purely imperative impulsion is united with the idea of larceny, defamation, coarse treatment of a servant, and the like, rejection of the relevant actions *per se* and as something not good (but not as an encroachment upon something attributed to others) is a moral phenomenon, whereas rejection of them because they are deemed an encroachment upon something attributed to others is a legal phenomenon.

Moreover, it cannot be asserted, on the basis of their intellectual content, that these aphorisms and judgments are either moral or legal: they may be neither of these, but related to other categories of psychic processes — and not to the class of ethical phenomena at all. They may, for example, be aesthetic experiences. If larceny, defamation, or coarse treatment of a servant is rejected as uncomely, ugly, or inelegant — if, in other words, the relevant impulsion is a negative aesthetic impulsion — the judgments are then neither moral nor legal: they are aesthetic experiences. The same aphorisms may in general be based on judgments of opportunism or expediency, and not on judgments of principle. If a person, making such a statement as "one should not steal," contemplated merely that the relevant conduct might entail a term in prison, punishment in the life to come, or the like, and solely by reason thereof the judgment ("one should not steal") is associated in his mind — as regards larceny — neither with an ethical (legal or moral) nor with an aesthetic impulsion, but with the repulsion of fear which generally accompanies the idea of a term in prison or tortures in Hades and is here extended to larceny, his judgment ("one should not steal") is then an opportunist and teleological experience — a judgment of worldly prudence and calculation — and not an experience of principle at all.

The specific nature of phenomena of law, morality and aesthetics, and their differences (each from the other and from other experiences) have their roots in the sphere of their impulsive content (in our sense), and not in that of their intellectual content.

It has already been demonstrated that it is the imperative-attributive nature of legal impulsions which defines and explains the specific character of legal projections — and, in particular, the special characteristics of legal obligations (as distinguished from moral obligations) that they seem made secure in behalf of others and appear as rights of those others. Norms of law appear not only as imperatives addressed to some but as authoritatively attributing the corresponding goods to others. The sphere wherein these norms are dominant — that of the projection of obligations and rights in actual cases — is defined and explained by the intellectual content of legal experiences: if there are no limitations in respect of the intellectual content, the relevant norms then appear eternal and universal — obligatory always, everywhere and upon all, and attributing rights to all (for example, the right of life and so forth).

However, projections of legal norms, obligations, and rights do not always accompany legal experiences. This is far from being the case, particularly where impersonal, subjectless legal experiences provide no adequate material for projections of the duties burdening some and enuring to others. Persons who are tempted to commit an act which is contrary to their legal (imperative-attributive) convictions, or are suffering the pangs of conscience because they have already committed it, frequently experience ideas of the relevant behavior in connection with imperative-attributive impulsions (for example, ideas of insulting another, in connection with legal repulsion, without the projection of norms, obligations, and rights). The same is true, *mutatis mutandis,* of moral experiences.

Whether legal experiences are or are not accompanied by projections of the corresponding norms and the ascription of obligations to some subjects and of rights to others, it is at all events specifically these experiences — combinations of imperative-attributive impulsions with the intellectual elements indicated *supra* — and not the norms (appearing to the subject to be found somewhere in the higher spheres) that are here the real phenomena. However strenuously we sought for something real, physical or psychic, corresponding to these projections — however hard we tried to find in the persons to whom we ascribe rights something corresponding which is real — our efforts would inevitably be in vain, and to be occupied with such searches would be naïve — just as naïve as to investigate that to which the epithets "amiable" or "dear" are ascribed for something real which corresponds to these epithets. In each case it is a matter of impulsive phantasmata. The corresponding real phenomena must be sought in a wholly different sphere, and not at all where (from the naïve-projection point of view) they are apparently present. Precisely as there are no special physical or psychic attributes of the person to whom the epithets "amiable" or "dear" are ascribed, so there are no special realities in the various subjects which correspond to their legal obligations and rights: the real phenomena are the special processes in the mind of the person who ascribes obligations or rights to these subjects, that is to say, the combination of imperative-attributive impulsions with the idea of these subjects and of the actions rejected or required.

Accordingly: *law* — in the sense of a special class of real phenomena — *is to be understood as those ethical experiences whose impulsions have an attributive character. All other ethical experiences — those connected with purely imperative impulsions — we shall call moral phenomena.*

SECTION 9. *The Scope of Law as Attributive Ethical Experience*

The concept of law established by the foregoing analysis is in no sense a definition of that which jurists call law.

First of all, the terminology of jurists and their ideas of law rest upon a naïve-projection point of view which accepts as real legal phenomena impulsion phantasmata: norms ("commands" and "prohibitions") addressed to persons subject to the law and the legal relations between individuals (their obligations and their rights). This raises a whole series of essentially insoluble problems as to the nature of the corresponding realities, and recourse is had to fictions and to arbitrary and fanciful speculation (the acceptance of sundry nonexistent "wills," a "general will," a "single will" of the state, or general acknowledgment). Norms of law ("the totality of norms of law") are termed by European jurists "objective law" or "law in the objective sense." Legal relations between subjects, their obligations and their rights (taken to be three different things) they call "subjective law" or law "in the subjective sense." The result is two species of law; theorists should obviously seek for a single definition of law: that is to say, of the nature of the class which embraces both objective and subjective law. This, however, is not done; there is an established tradition of identifying the problem of defining law with that of defining the nature of objective law (that is to say, the norms of law) and the result is that "subjective law" becomes, as it were, appended to "objective law."

Our concept of law — and, in general, the doctrine of law herein set out — starts from a wholly different point of view, which in terms denies the real existence of what is held by jurists really to exist in the legal field, and reveals real legal phenomena as a special class of complex psychic processes in a wholly different sphere: that is to say, in the mind of the individual who accomplishes the projections aforesaid.

Another radical distinction between what jurists call law and strive to define, and the class formed and defined *supra* under the name of law, is this: if — in order to obtain a standard whereby to measure and to compare that which is understood as law by the definition proposed *supra,* on the one hand, and that which jurists call law and strive to define as such, on the other — we consider law from the projection point of view as the class and the class concept: "all imperative-attributive norms"; or if — distinguishing according to tradition "objective" law and "subjective" law, we establish the corresponding two concepts: (1) all imperative-attributive norms (projection "objective" law), and (2) all duties of some actively made secure in behalf of others (legal obligations — legal relationships — rights, projection "subjective" law), and then compare these classes with what jurists acknowledge as law in the objective or in the subjective sense, we shall note an enormous difference in the content of the relevant classes. Ours are much broader — and our class concepts embrace far more — than what jurists acknowledge as law.

The concepts of law in the realistic-psychological sense and in the projection sense established *supra* include all imperative-attributive experiences and all the corresponding projections without exception or limitation of any kind. From the point of view of these concepts it is immaterial — as is already obvious from the division of law into intuitive law and positive law — whether or not the corresponding norms, obligations, and rights are founded on anyone's commands, custom or on other normative facts, on the one hand, or whether it is a matter of imperative-attributive experiences and norms, obligations and so forth independent of such facts and having nothing to do with them, on the other. It is equally immaterial whether or not the corresponding norms, obligations, and rights are acknowledged by the organs of state authority — the courts, the administration and the like — or in general by the organs or other members of any community whatsoever.

Within the area of problems of conduct which are foreseen and decided in this or that sense by statutes or other forms of positive law — for example, in the field of the relationship to the life or property of another, in the field of the business turnover of property or of buying and selling or of hiring a lodging or a servant or of entering into loan contracts or other credit arrangements and so forth — in all these cases people do in fact ascribe to themselves or to others at every step various obligations of a legal type and legal rights, and do fulfill these obligations and effectuate these rights because such is the prompting of their intuitive-law conscience, and not at all because it is so written in the Civil Code or the like. Ordinarily they do not even know what the paragraphs of the civil — or other — code prescribe in the relevant case, or even think of the existence of these articles and codes. Only in certain cases — chiefly of differences of opinion and disputes, and only then when the differences and disputes are particularly serious and incapable of being resolved without resort to the statutes, the courts and the like — do people inform themselves as to the articles of statutes, and pass from the ground of intuitive law to that of positive law — asserting claims of the same content as before (or slightly different) but citing what is required by the statute and the like. Similarly, all the innumerable imperative-attributive experiences which lack a positive character (whether they coincide or diverge in their content as regards positive experiences) come completely within the concept of law in the sense established *supra,* and are embraced by the general theory of law developed herein.

Furthermore, this concept and theory embrace all the still more numerous imperative-attributive experiences and norms, obligations and so forth (of an intuitive and of a positive character) which are concerned with life and conduct outside the sphere where statutes, courts, and other official institutions and authorities have jurisdiction and operate. These may be divided into three categories.

(1) There are many occupations and relationships which have no serious business character or significance. Rules of games (such as games of cards, checkers, chess, dominoes, lotto, forfeits, bowls, billiards, and cricket) which define who can and should, in what order and how, accomplish the various actions involved therein (the deal of the cards,

the making of certain declarations and "leads," the play of the cards, what cards can take others, and so forth) and state the general principles regarding the obligation to observe special preliminary arrangements and payment of what has been lost, all represent, from our point of view, legal norms. They are of an imperative-attributive character: the obligations of some appear as the claims of others and not as "free" obligations, and imperative-attributive, normative complexes are the basis of the corresponding projections. Moreover the corresponding imperative-attributive dispositions are distinguished by great force and strength as the experimental method will readily demonstrate if provocation is applied in the form of contesting the corresponding rights: powerful imperative-attributive impulsions will flare up, and there will be strong legal indignation accompanied by corresponding external manifestations which are typical. Further confirmation is found in the fact that refusal to yield to the corresponding motivation — a conscious breach of the relevant norms, obligations, and rights — is an extremely rare and exceptional phenomenon, and is recognized as particularly foul and revolting conduct. Everyone except sharpers and those whose legal mentality is unusually atrophied as regards play always recognizes and satisfies without cavil the corresponding rights of others in a manner seldom observed in other domains of the legal mentality.

Imperative-attributive experiences are, to a considerable degree, the basis of the so-called rules of courtesy and etiquette (*savoir vivre*) and are, from the point of view of the established concept of law, nothing but legal norms. Hosts owe guests various signs of attention and courtesy: places of honor at the table and being served with food before others (to say nothing of the right, in general, of admission to the table and of receiving the food provided, a breach of which would be a most serious and unheard of "crime"), as well as swift and zealous fulfillment of their requests and wishes, and so forth.

Similar preferential rights (privileges) are ascribed to the old and the honored as regards the young, to adults as regards children, to "ladies" as regards "gentlemen," to those standing higher in social position as regards those standing lower, and the like. Rights in the nature of privileges in these fields include not only various preferential claims of right, but also innumerable preferential legal powers. Thus certain persons are privileged with regard to others — elders with regard to children, "masters" with regard to servants, and the like. To the former is ascribed the right to speak familiarly, to reprimand and to instruct, to clap the others on the shoulder, and to permit themselves various jokes and other familiarities whereas the latter enjoy no like privilege as regards them. In the reverse direction it is assumed with imperative-attributive force that the mode of address must be formal, and there are sometimes further requirements, such as titles and the like, a tone of respect, an appropriate attitude, refraining from bodily contact and other familiarities.

Investigation of the history of these fields of the legal mentality would demonstrate that there are definitive historical "laws" (tendencies of development): privileged positions tend generally to decline, and there are also special tendencies (differing in particulars) in various special fields of the privileged position. Preferential rights associated with social position (according to caste, feudal orders, classes, professions, and so forth) become weaker and die out otherwise than do those depending on birth, sex, and the like. On the basis of historical material (and deductive considerations resting on examination of the role and the significance of the relevant branches of law in human life) it may be asserted that privileges dependent upon social position are doomed to complete extinction whereas the importance of those associated with age is less transitory (although they have a gentler character, and become definitely weaker, with the disappearance of so-called patriarchal mode of life).

Besides the norms which establish different preferential rights in favor of some at the expense of others, there are innumerable imperative-attributive rules which give rise to legal powers and claims in the field of courtesy and etiquette. Some of them are binding upon everyone everywhere, while others are binding only in defined situations or for defined categories of persons — such as persons who know each other, or who are not acquainted, or males as between themselves, or ladies, or companions in school or in service, or students, or officers.

Further imperative-attributive norms define the consequences of what has occurred in case preferential or other rights of courtesy are violated. In civilized society, the most widespread of the relevant psychic phenomena is in the imperative-attributive consciousness that the wrongdoer owes the person who has suffered the wrong an acknowledgment of his guilt and an expression of regret therefor — together with a request for forgiveness: one side is obligated to apologize for himself, and the other has a claim to the appropriate declaration. In addition — especially in the less advanced stages of development and in (culturally) lower strata of society — the injured parties are recognized as possessing in such cases various other rights: especially the right actively to punish the wrongdoer with words (of censure or abuse) or actions (a blow or a beating). In cases of very serious breaches, the primitive legal mind ascribes to the party wronged even the right to kill the wrongdoer on the spot. A related legal phenomenon (a survival of the barbarian legal mind) is to ascribe to the person wronged the right to call out the wrongdoer to a duel, and to the latter an obligation of satisfaction in this form. In spheres where the law of duels flourishes, there are more or less complex and detailed positive legal norms (based on customs or written dueling "codes") defining the order of proceeding and the mutual rights and duties of the parties and their seconds. To these general rules concrete norms (in their turn legal from our point of view) are added through an agreement concluded by the seconds as to the specific concrete duel, which is thus regulated by combination of unwritten customary law and written or contractual law.

(2) The province of intimate relationships between persons close to each other — united by ties of sex or otherwise (fraternity, love, friendship, or joint family life, and so forth). In general this sphere of life and conduct is outside the area of regulation and intervention on the part of statutes, courts, and so forth, but from the point of view of the psychological theory of law this province, too, is subject to legal regulation. Thus, mutual rights are recognized in the domain of amatory relationships — rights to fidelity, love, and frankness; to defense in case of malicious gossip or other attack by third persons, to support in case of need, and to thousands of other sorts of assistance and service. From the moment love is declared on the one side and accepted on the other, the legal relationships of the parties are fundamentally revolutionized and various legal barriers drop. The one who has proposed acquires various rights which he did not theretofore possess, and there are various further facts which are now legally relevant evoking in their turn more or less essential revolutions in the minds of both sides, making legal bonds closer, and creating new rights and obligations.

Law partly coinciding in content with "love law," and partly differing therefrom, operates in the province of friendship, of love between brothers, sisters, and the like. To the pact of love (the proposal and the acceptance) corresponds the pact of friendship, which has its juridic symbology (the offering of one's hand, or striking hands). In antiquity, the pact of friendship or of brotherhood imposed on the parties extremely serious legal obligations involving risk to one's life — particularly the obligation to go forth shoulder to shoulder against enemies, of blood vengeance in the event that the other were murdered, and so forth. The symbol of blood was employed in various forms to signify that the serious obligations contained in the pact were actively made secure in behalf of others.

In certain fields of the relations between people who are close — as in that of the relationships between husband and wife and parents and children — there are statutory directives regarding mutual rights and obligations. These, however, are extremely meager, and take on practical importance only in extremely rare cases — chiefly where relationships of closeness are absent in fact and those of enmity and sharp conflicts are present. Hence jurists traditionally say that relationships between husband and wife — and between parents and children — are regulated chiefly by morality and not by law. However, from the point of view of the psychological theory of law as imperative-attributive experiences, family and intimate domestic life (regardless of whether or not there are between those participants any bonds officially recognized) is a broad and peculiar legal world which is awaiting investigation: a legal world with innumerable legal norms, obligations, and rights independent of what is written in the statutes, and solving thousands of questions unforeseen therein. While there are some features of the content, and of the trend of the historical development, that are common to all systems of the law governing domestic relations, there are also many variants and great differences of a more or less common origin and a common significance. They may be connected with the class structure of a population — the typical domestic law prevailing in the well-to-do and rich strata is distinguished from the same law in the spheres of those who are not well-to-do and of proletarians, while the typical domestic law of the peasants is different from that of the businessman and the aristocrat. But they are, in part, of an individual character: each family is a unique legal world, and each of those taking part in the domestic life (including aunts, grandmothers, poor kinsfolk in remote degree, or friends received into the house and into the family, hangers-on, adopted and foster children, and the like) has his own particular position in the legal mentality which prevails in that family — the right to enjoy one's room and certain other objects alone and to take part in enjoying other parts of the dwelling and objects, the right to take part in common meals and pleasures and in family celebrations and the like, the right of a decisive or advisory voice in certain matters of domestic life (economic and personal), the right to certain degrees of civility, love, and gratitude and to appropriate behavior in different cases, and so forth.

(3) The foregoing observations had in view various spheres of the law of adults. Imperative-attributive experiences and projections characteristic of childhood — the law which guides children in the field of their amusements, their childish pacts and other conduct (child law, the legal mentality of the child) — deserve particularly serious scientific

attention and study: those are domains of law (in the sense established *supra*) which from the point of view of statutes, courts, and so forth are not referred to law. Legal science would be enriched by interesting and important factual data and theoretical propositions with reference to the nature and development of law in general if psychic phenomena of this class were included in the sphere of scientific attention and study.

Thus in the child's room one can observe and study experimentally the development and action of the psychological background of the law of property and reactions to various violations of this law (as by attempts to dispute it through removal and appropriation of a toy or the like). Here the mentality of contract law is created and in operation, various contracts of exchange and grant are concluded and carried out — contracts of gratuitous bailment, of deposit (handing over a thing for preservation with obligation to return it), of partnership, and sometimes of a "criminal" character (for example, one is bound to steal some forbidden thing, while another stands on guard, each having a right to an equal share of the booty). Well brought up children, with a sensitive legal conscience, know — and sometimes very zealously carry out — even so-called delictual obligations (obligations arising out of violations of law) — thus in case of culpable or even accidental injury of another's toy, they willingly submit to the injured party's claim to be compensated for the harm done (as for example, to have the plaything of the wrongdoer handed over in place of that which has been destroyed).

In relationships between children of the same age and friends, laws of equality and obligation of solidarity operate as regards strangers and elders. In particular, the mutual obligation not to be a talebearer is serious and important and a breach thereof is a most serious criminal offense, giving the injured parties the right to inflict cruel retribution and, at the least — to refuse association with the wrongdoer and to express contempt for him.

In relationships between children of different ages, various rights of seniority prevail: privileges, and sometimes rights, of authority and of issuing commands and orders. The mentality of the law of guardianship may develop here, with corresponding rights and obligations as regards the ward and the representatives of superior fiduciary supervision (the mother or the father). Rights with reference to a ward and, in general, rights of older children as regards younger children, include both disciplinary and criminal law. Moreover, the law of punishment which operates is far more civilized than that in effect as between children of the same age: the latter has the character of the primitive law of vengeance, and the principle of the *lex talionis* (that is to say, the law of causing the same evil as the guilty party has inflicted) is not infrequently applied.

In general, the child's legal mind discloses in various relations a kinship with the legal mind of the less advanced peoples or the (culturally) lower strata and classes of society. However, the content of the law by which the conduct of children is defined is extremely changeable and diverse — depending upon the regulations, directions, and arrangements of parents, and the other conditions of life which prevail in the home and the education of the particular child.

In the legal life of the child — and especially in the first stages of the development of his legal mind — the law in operation is, for the most part, positive rather than intuitive law; no system of stable, independent, intuitive, legal convictions has been developed therein to the slightest degree. Such convictions develop slowly and gradually. There is great scope here for suggestion and for the decisive and uncontrolled action of sundry positive legal experiences undergone with reference to various external authorities. First, the directions of elders — which have for children the same significance as the commands of absolute monarchs or the orders of the legislature in the life of the state — play an important part as normative facts. At every step small children ascribe to themselves with reference to other children, servants, and so forth — and to others in reference to themselves — various rights with regard to what "father directed," or "mother said," or the "nurse allowed," or "aunt decided," and the like (statute law). Thereafter, arrangements established in the house, customs (customary law), court decisions of elders where children have quarreled (with each other or with a servant), the matter is handed over to the judgment of domestic authorities, and certain other facts possess juridically normative significance for children.

In conformity with the character, content, and direction of the positive law suggested to children — and with other educative influences — the legal mentality which develops on this ground may take on a direction more or less abnormal and harmful from the point of view of the conditions of social life. If, for example, legal chaos and arbitrary willfulness prevail in the family — and particularly if no one and nothing suggests to the child definite and stable legal principles — there is then no ground for the development of the normal intuitive-law mentality and a condition more or less close to legal idiotism follows (and, in the remote future, a criminal mind and the conduct appropriate thereto).

If in the home the attitude to the child is that everything is permitted to the child with regard to others, and the child's demands of every kind are carried out unquestioningly, the result is an anomalous legal mind which may be characterized as a hypertrophy of the active legal mentality: the subject becomes possessed of a propensity to ascribe to himself with reference to others innumerable unreasoning and inordinate legal powers and legal claims, while at the same time acknowledging no such rights in behalf of others. The abnormally developed legal mind elevates the child into a sort of being privileged among mortals. If, on the contrary, the child is neglected as regards the law — if no rights of any kind (not even the most modest) are acknowledged in his behalf and no active law sphere of any sort is assigned to him — the reverse psychic anomaly then ensues: underdevelopment of the active law mentality.

In what follows it will be manifest that the state of one's legal mind exerts enormous influence not only on his conduct but on the development of the various sides and elements of his character. In particular, an appropriate legal education in childhood (in the family, in school, and so forth) is of vital importance for the attainment of a normal and socially useful direction of life, and the development of a healthy and efficient character. In view of this, the study of the child's legal mind and of the conditions and factors of its normal and pathological development would have important practical — as well as theoretical — significance and constitute a valuable contribution to science.

The foregoing neither purports nor can be said to exhaust all the fields of life outside the sphere of state intervention and official regulation which are yet within the domain of the action of law in the sense of the imperative-attributive ethics. *The number of everyday cases and problems of conduct contemplated and determined by official regulation, as compared with the immense quantity thereof anticipated by law (in the sense herein established) is infinitesimal.* Particularly in all the innumerable and manifold cases and areas of conduct, which neither are nor can be provided for by official codes of any kind, there is ordinarily some imperative-attributive indication in our legal consciousness — where it is a matter of causing any kind of good or evil to another (even though it be a small satisfaction or a trifling unpleasantness) — as to what is due and owing to others from us, or to us from others, or to others from a third person; or that we have a right to do — and that others should endure — it, or the reverse. This includes such elements of conduct as words addressed to others (their content, the means of pronouncing them, the intonation, the gestures, and the pose) or judgments expressed about third persons (of their content and their shades of meaning). If, in their content or in the tone in which they are pronounced, words addressed to others contain anything pleasant or unpleasant for them (as where it is a matter of expressing sympathy, respect, gratitude, and the like — or reproaches on some score, censure, irony, or derision — or of using a "dry" and "cold" tone of scorn in speaking or a contemptuous smile), the legal conscience holds court and adjudges whether or not such conduct is in conformity with the deserts of the other: whether or not the reproach is well founded and merited (so that the person making the reproach had a right to do so) or without foundation (so that the person who suffered it had a right that the former refrain from it, and now has a right that it be recognized as without foundation and retracted). If judgments concerning third persons (orally expressed in conversation with anyone, or stated in writing) contain something apparently causing good or evil to the one to whom the language refers (as where the judgments include praise, encouragement, a recognition of merits and good qualities of character and the like — or censure, condemnation, a denial of merits and good qualities of character, suspicion, and the like), these actions, too, then appear — from the point of view of the developed legal conscience — as corresponding to the deserts of the person concerning whom the remarks were made and not as matters of indifference. Accordingly, even artistic, scientific, technical, or other criticism of the product of another's creative or other labor is subjected to legal regulations in our sense since it is in the sphere within which law, as attributive ethical experience, operates. When malevolence (personal, national, party, or other), envy, and the like lead a critic to deny recognition to the merits of something created by another or the deserts of the creator, or to endeavor to minimize them, to hunt out and to ascribe to them reprehensible qualities and the like (which do not exist), he finds himself in conflict with the law: he discovers that he is acting contrary not only to his own legal conscience (if this is normally developed) and its intimation that the injured party has a right to a different attitude — that a different appraisal of his labor is his due — but also to the same sort of directions and demands of the legal conscience of others.

Furthermore, law in the sense herein established includes not only much that is outside the cognizance of the state and does not enjoy positive official recognition and protection, but also much that encounters an attitude of outright hostility on the part of the state and is to be hunted out and eradicated as contrary and antagonistic to the law officially recognized by the state. Some of these categories of phenomena are of special interest and merit particular attention.

(1) The law of criminal organizations. In these (robber bands,

pirates, gangs of thieves, and the like), entire systems of imperative-attributive norms (or more or less complexity) have been worked out and are carried out with unhesitating precision; they define the organization of the gang, distribute obligations and functions among the members, and endow them with corresponding rights (in particular, to a definite share of the booty, and otherwise). Ordinarily the right to obedience on the part of the other members and to exercise authority over them is secured in favor of their leader. This right is sometimes unconditional and unlimited (as in absolute monarchies), and sometimes limited, in respect of certain particularly important matters and decisions, by the prerequisite of consent on the part of a council of members of the gang (as in limited monarchies). Sometimes the legal organization of the gangs is of a republican character, with all members having an equal right to participate in the government and in decisions as to general affairs, and temporary chiefs and leaders for separate expeditions elected or designated by turn or by lot. Sometimes older and younger confederates — with or without complete rights — are found in the midst of the gang, and matters are decided by the advice of those with full rights (an aristocratic or oligarchic organization). All members of the gang are ordinarily bound by a mutual obligation of solidarity (which is extremely strict) and are bound not to reveal information to the authorities: if this obligation is broken the law of vengeance comes into merciless operation. Other delinquencies — such as disobedience to the order of the leader, failure to comply with a collective decision, or the concealment and appropriation without right of part of the booty — cause a law of disciplinary and other punishments to be applied by the leader, or the delinquents are dealt with otherwise (sometimes after preliminary trial and sentence).

Insofar as contracts establish actual rights and obligations in criminal organizations of long standing — and likewise as to those formed for a short time or to perpetuate one or more specific crimes, and based entirely on contracts — the contract rights and obligations (those concerned with helping to commit the crime and being paid a reward therefor, and the like) are ordinarily observed strictly and "honorably," and the same is true as to contracts concluded by criminal gangs or individual criminals with outsiders. Thus if the leader or other authorized representatives of the gang undertook for a certain remuneration to spare, or even to safeguard, the other contracting party, or for a specified sum (paid in advance) to set free a traveler who had been taken captive, or to return stolen horses or the like, or if a professional bribe-taker, or a go-between in bribery, undertook to carry through some business of that sort (and to return the money in case of failure), the party of the second part can ordinarily be confident that the obligation accepted by the gang (or by the professional criminals individually) would be fulfilled. In any event, such obligations, while entirely without official protection through the courts, are carried out with greater punctiliousness and honor than is true of some obligations which the courts do recognize and enforce, such as the duty to return money borrowed from an acquaintance, or to pay when due the purchase price of things that have been bought.

(2) Law which continues to exist and to operate in the minds of certain strata of the population — certain classes of society, or religious or tribal groups which are component parts of the state — notwithstanding the fact that not merely are the corresponding imperative-attributive norms not acknowledged as law from the official point of view: they are eradicated, more or less inexorably, as inadmissible, barbarian, anti-cultural and the like. Thus modern cultural states — having colonies and other possessions inhabited by "savages," or in general by tribes whose legal culture is lower — carry on a struggle against various "barbarous customs" of these tribes, although these are nothing but legal customs which these tribes sometimes hold in the highest degree sacred: such are the right of blood-vengeance; the right of heads of clans or of families and like persons to subject women, children, and others to the punishment of death; and the right that their wives, surviving them, follow them into the life beyond the grave.

Notwithstanding the hostile competition of another law (supported by the authority of the state and the force at its disposal), the tribal mind holds tenaciously to certain elements of ancient law, so that — for centuries, sometimes — a dual system of law continues to exist, with resulting conflicts and occasional tragedies, and the imposition of more or less cruel punishments (from organs of official power which follow the official law, and consider it alone "law") upon persons acting in accordance with the directions of their legal conscience in effectuating rights sacred in their opinion or in fulfilling a sacred legal duty.

No significance of any kind attaches either to recognition and protection by the state, or to any acknowledgment of whatsoever sort by anyone at all, as regards the concept of law herein established and its extension to the corresponding psychic phenomena. From the point of view of this concept, the countless imperative-attributive experiences and the projections thereof are none the less law, legal judgments, and so forth because they are present in the mind of but one individual and are unknown to anyone else in the world. In general, every kind of law and all legal phenomena — including such legal judgments as meet with assent and encouragement from others — represent purely and exclusively individual phenomena from our point of view, and the eventual consent and encouragement on the part of others are irrelevant from the point of view of defining and studying the nature of legal phenomena. This is a necessary conclusion from the psychological theory of law. Every sort of psychic phenomenon appears in the mind of one individual and only there: its nature does not change as something else does, or does not, appear somewhere — between individuals or above them or in the minds of others. Imperative-attributive experiences and the projection thereof (norms and so forth) which are present in an individual who is completely outside all community with others (living on an uninhabited island cut off from all the rest of the world, or the sole human being surviving on earth, or on the planet Mars) would come completely and perfectly within the concept of law herein established, precisely as his joys, griefs, and thoughts are none the less joys, griefs, and thoughts because of his solitude and the absence of human society.

Furthermore, for the concept of law herein established, and for bringing the corresponding psychic phenomena thereunder, it is of no significance whatsoever whether the imperative-attributive judgments, norms, and the like are rational in content, or irrational, absurd, superstitious, pathological, or even the ravings of a madman. If a superstitious man, because of a vision or under an illusion or hallucination, is convinced that he has concluded an agreement with the devil and is thereupon obligated to turn over to him his soul, the corresponding imperative-attributive experiences and the projections thereof, the right of the devil and so forth, come perfectly within the concept of law herein established. From the point of view of the psychological theory of law, the different legal superstitions widespread among the different nations — "superstition law" — represent (like child law, crime law, and so forth) a field for descriptive, historical, and theoretical investigation and study which is deserving of attention and interest. In the same way, if an insane man thinks he is an emperor and claims obedience from his supposed subjects, and is indignant and impatient because they do not obey, this phenomenon and countless other similar *idées fixes* come completely within the concept of law herein established, and may likewise provide a special object of study as pathological law or legal pathology.

The same is true — *mutatis mutandis* — as to the concept of morality which we have established. If a superstitious man experiences a purely imperative judgment of such content that he is bound to do obeisance to the devil and to do the devil's pleasure in every way — if a man mentally ill considers it his duty to murder and to exterminate people wherever he can find them — then from the point of view of the concept of morality proposed *supra,* the relevant, purely imperative experiences are referable to morality, and represent moral phenomena, even though they seem to every person of common sense absurd, shocking, or the like (superstitions, pathological morality) — and although moralists and the public have been accustomed to call moral, and to refer to morality, only that which they encourage or consider useful and good from the point of view of the general welfare, or the like. Such a view of law and morality, and the inclusion of what seems to us criminal, superstitious, or delirious in these — so to say — undiscriminate concepts of ethical phenomena is a necessary consequence of the relevant *theoretical* formulation of the doctrine and its insistence upon clearly distinguishing the theoretical from the practical viewpoint. In the domain of the theoretical sciences, phenomena which are homogeneous in their material or psychic nature must be assigned to a single class, whether or not they please us or are desired by us.

The concept of law herein established does not in general comprise any limitations whatsoever as regards the content of legal experiences — of the ideas which (side by side with imperative-attributive impulses) are components of legal experiences (object ideas, subject ideas, ideas of relevant facts, and ideas of normative facts). From the point of view of this theory the specific nature of ethical phenomena in general has its roots in impulsions; accordingly ethical phenomena include only those normative experiences whose impulsions have an imperative (whether purely imperative, or imperative-attributive) character. *All* such experiences are, however, included, and the content of the object, subject, and other ideas which make them up is immaterial. Morality includes only those ethical experiences — but all of them — whose impulsions have a purely imperative character, while law includes only those ethical experiences — but all of them — whose impulsions have an imperative-attributive character, irrespective of the content of the ideas entering into a given impulsive-intellectual complex, the actions appearing as required (obligatory), the beings appearing as subjects of obligations or subjects of rights, and the facts appearing as relevant or normative. Some special observations are in order at this point.

(1) Imperative-attributive impulsions — like purely imperative impulsions — are abstract and capable of being combined with all possible action ideas (including ideas of various purely inward or mental actions). Comprising in general no limitations of any sort as to the content of

action ideas, the established concept of law embraces as well all possible (real and imaginary) imperative-attributive experiences and norms which "prescribe" any purely inward conduct — that is to say, whose action ideas are ideas of psychic phenomena. Thus in the field of the intimate relationships between near persons, the latter ascribe to themselves and to the other party the right to love, respect, friendship, and the like. Here the object of obligations and rights is emotional relationship. Emotional relationships are subject to legal regulation in other provinces of life as well — this is true principally as to those emotions and emotional dispositions whose existence in the mind of another seems good or evil for him with reference to whom they exist, and particularly as to the caritative and benevolent — and to the hateful and malevolent — emotional relationships. A right to sympathy, love, and the like from others is ascribed to persons recognized as good or fine. Such rights in the minds of others are, on the contrary, not ascribed in behalf of persons recognized as evil: they "do not deserve" this attitude, or they even "deserve the contrary" (antipathy, enmity, and so forth). With reference to persons whose life and conduct suggest respect there is not only respect in fact but also a recognized right thereto. Conversely, such a right is not ascribed in behalf of those whose conduct is unseemly and others even consider themselves sometimes entitled to be contemptuous of them in thought or even in external conduct. Moreover, in the popular mentality, rights to respect, and rights to disrespect and contempt, are distributed not only in accordance with individual merits but also in conformity with an individual's legal and social position: masters as compared with the servants, or representatives of the higher orders and classes — "honorables" and the like — as compared with those of the lower, occupy in the popular mind positions essentially different as regards the rights to respect and to contempt. As the cultural process attains a higher level, a gradual democratization or leveling takes place here as elsewhere, and those of a loftier legal culture have the legal conviction that every human being, even an outcast, has a right to a certain degree of respect as a human personality.

One of the most widespread phenomena of the legal mentality — characteristic alike of nations in the lower stages of culture and of legally underdeveloped individuals — is the imperative-attributive consciousness that one who has experienced a benefit from another (some good to which he had no claim and that is not legally obligatory) is bound to be grateful to the latter: the benefactor has a right (a legal claim) to gratitude from the beneficiary.

Such legal phenomena (chiefly of the intuitive law) as consciousness of a right to respect, to gratitude, and the like must in no wise be confused with consciousness of a right to external acts: to outward signs of respect, gratitude, and the like. In the different peoples, strata of society and spheres of life, differing norms of positive (chiefly of customary) law are applied, and as against others various categories of persons are endowed with claims to external signs of respect (such as doffing the cap, or falling on one's face and the like): in behalf of those who have done something in aid of others, claims are established to various substantial returns (such as gifts or entertainment) or to external signs of gratitude (words or acts plainly demonstrative thereof). In the former area of legal consciousness self-observation will demonstrate that it is not a matter of any outward manifestation of respect or gratitude, but specifically of respect itself — of gratitude itself as such — as inward conditions: the content of the corresponding ideas is purely psychological and there is no image whatsoever of any bodily movements. In the second area of legal consciousness, on the contrary, definite external actions — body movements as such — are specifically the objects of action ideas, so that the presence of genuine respect, actual gratitude, and so forth is not required.

Various intellectual processes which are combined with impulsive processes are likewise subjected to legal regulation: thoughts, convictions, and beliefs in particular. It is manifest, from self-observation, that if certain unexpressed judgments — such as inward accusations or suspicions of something foul with reference to persons we love and honor — seem to us without sufficient foundation, they evoke protests of the legal conscience, repentance of the legal type, and consciousness that we have caused unmerited insult, and that the other deserves — and may claim — a different attitude on our part: we ascribe to persons of irreproachable veracity the "right" to have their words believed, and so forth. In the sphere of religion, legal claims that others adhere to certain convictions and beliefs — and do not believe in false doctrines, heresies, and the like — expand greatly at certain stages of development and assume broad practical significance. A related phenomenon is the claim to commendable political thinking.

(2) Imperative-attributive impulsions — like purely imperative impulsions — can further merge with ideas of all possible beings (and not merely of human beings) as subject ideas (that is, ideas of subjects of obligations, or of subjects of rights). Comprising in general no limitations as to the content of the subject ideas, the concept of law herein established embraces as well all imperative-attributive experiences and norms "imposing obligations" on all possible non-human beings, or

"endowing with rights" non-human beings. Three of these — the subject ideas of which are unrelated to the world of mankind — require particular treatment.

(a) Imperative-attributive experiences with ideas of animals as subjects of obligations or subjects of rights. First of all, the introspective method furnishes evidence that such legal phenomena exist. If we are dealing with animals — with dogs, for example, requiring of them certain actions or abstentions and punishing them for disobedience — we not infrequently experience imperative-attributive processes with regard to them wherein they figure as subjects of obligations.

The joint method of external and internal observation demonstrates that legal obligations of animals are extremely common, and play a particularly important part, in the province of child law, as well as in that of culturally underdeveloped nations. In certain stages of the development of the legal mind there are — among other positive norms of law extending to animals as subjects of obligations — peculiar norms of criminal law which prescribe various punishments (including death, and so forth) for serious violations of law (such as killing a man) by animals. Where one's property has been invaded, and injury done, by the animal of another not himself culpable, it was as if the violation of law had been by a slave of the latter, or by a wife subject to his authority or by his unemancipated son, and the injured party had a right to have the offending animal handed over to him to be dealt with. If there were in addition fault on the part of the owner of the animal both law-breakers were subject to legal responsibility. Thus according to ancient Hebrew law, if a man were killed by an animal and the owner of the animal were also at fault, both animal and owner were liable to the death penalty.

In precisely the same way — through observation and the joint method — it may be established that moral norms and obligations extend to animals — especially in child morality and that of primitive nations, but also occasionally among adult and civilized people. To modern moralists and jurists, who start from the position that morality and law "address," and "can address," only "the free will of man," moral and legal obligations of animals seem impossible, absurd and, of course, nonexistent. This is but one of the manifestations of the methodological fault running like a scarlet thread throughout the system of the present moral and legal science, and is manifested also in the treatment of a host of other questions. It consists in a failure to distinguish between the theoretical and the practical points of view. What for some reason the author thinks irrational is treated as nonexistent because of his subjective disapproval. If we shake off this methodological error, and take our stand on scientific psychology, the inclusion of animals in the number of subjects of moral and legal obligations can arouse neither doubt nor difficulty of any sort. It has already been pointed out that there are in our minds associations of action ideas as such — such as ideas of killing a man and the like — with ethical impulsions, and that actual perceptions or ideas of corresponding actions tend — according to the general law of associations — to evoke the corresponding impulsions irrespective of who appears to be the actor and where and when the action appears to be occurring. It is, then, neither strange nor incredible that moral and legal obligations be extended to animals: it is a natural development from general psychological tendencies.

In precisely the same way it is to be expected *a priori,* from the point of view of the general law of associations, that animals should figure also as *subjects of rights*: as obligees possessing just claims, and so forth. Imperative-attributive impulsions and ideas are associated in our minds with the idea of certain facts and in appropriate cases something is owed — a certain right is ascribed, and so forth — to him who was the cause of these facts. For example, with the idea of saving the life of another — or of other benefits and services with respect to him — there is associated in our minds the idea that one who has saved life or rendered the other services has a right to gratitude and so forth. If an animal was effective in saving a person's life or rendering some other benefit to him, the one whose life the animal saved, or to whom the animal caused such other benefit, would not be expected to repay the animal with evil for good, but would be likely to experience legal states of mind wherein gratitude would be deemed to be due to the animal from him for saving his life. And in reality scientific investigation of the facts — and particularly resort to recollective or other introspection — will readily demonstrate that, in our dealings with animals, we not infrequently ascribe to them various rights, powers, and claims of right, and in general experience states of legal consciousness wherein these beings figure as subjects of rights. While we claim obedience and other actions from our dog in hunting (that is to say, while we are related to the dog as to a subject of legal obligations) or are impatient and punish the dog for delinquencies, we consider it our duty, in case of proper services by our setter in the hunting field (and *a fortiori* if the services were outstanding) to adopt a corresponding attitude toward the setter, to reward it with a good meal after hunting, and the like. Our ethical consciousness tells us that the dog has deserved this — that the reward was due to the dog. In those types of hunting where it is the accepted practice to reward dogs that have contributed to the success — with certain parts of the slain game, for example — hunters consider to which of the dogs the reward is due, and disputes of a legal character arise: that is to say, a legal mentality is at their basis. If the owner of an old horse, that has served him faithfully and truly when it was younger, nonchalantly let it starve, people with a more subtle ethical (and particularly a more subtle legal) conscience would disapprove and even be indignant over the injustice.

The introspective method — simple or experimental — will demonstrate that legal relationships are not merely possible but exist in fact wherein both subjects — the subject of the right, and the subject of the obligation — are animals. We can readily become familiar with legal experiences wherein both subject ideas are ideas of the animals by experiments with two or more dogs, consisting in giving them food, dainty bits and the like either equally or upon other principles (according to their deserts, after hunting, for example); if one dog encroaches on what has been given to the other, we have the same legal phenomena as are experienced in seeing or imagining like encroachments as between persons, children, and the like: specifically, imperative-attributive experiences wherein one animal appears the subject of a right to exclusive enjoyment of what is given it, while the other is the subject of an obligation not to touch that object but to respect the right of the former.

Further factual material for becoming acquainted with the rights of animals with regard to people and to other animals may be found in historical data and in contemporary literature where animals came forth as *dramatis personae* (as heroes of stories, legends and tales), or the concern is with the relations of people to animals (such as the Buddhist legendary and ethical literature, the literature of cruel treatment of animals, vivisection, vegetarian literature, and the like). Psychological study of these manifestations of the human mind (by the joint method of inward and outward observation) demonstrates that at the basis of these historical or literary data are experiences of the legal type with projections of the different rights upon animals (such as the right of life, the right to good — and not harsh — treatment, and so forth).

From the point of view of contemporary legal science, the rights of animals — the inclusion of animals in the category of subjects of rights, and so forth — are, of course, a completely inadmissible scientific heresy: a strange and incoherent fallacy. In setting out the traditional axiomatic assertions that law exists only for people and to safeguard human interests, and regulates only the relationships between human beings, modern literature reiterates the trite doctrine that even if law does sometimes touch animals — forbid cruelty to them and the like — it must by no means be supposed that this is done in the interests of the animals: the only concern is with the interests and the rights of people — to safeguard people from the unpleasant sight of the purposeless torture of animals, and so forth. Judging by the ideas and opinions obtaining in this field of contemporary jurisprudence, one would suppose that *homo sapiens* is a breed created by nature solely to exploit, with complete and utter egoism, all the other creatures that live and suffer on earth, and that people are not — at least from the point of view of jurists — reasonably bound to think and act otherwise. To the honor of *homo sapiens,* jurists are undoubtedly wrong. In the earlier savage and crudely barbaric time, people were not inclined to ascribe and to respect the rights (most elementary from our point of view) of the vast majority of other people — slaves, persons of another race or tribe, and so forth — to say nothing of animals. However, the cultural process gradually but undeviatingly changes the human mind substantially for the better. And in the best part of contemporary cultural mankind, not only is it true already that there is "neither Greek nor Jew," but more and more the moral and the legal conscience — even with regard to other non-human living beings — is being awakened and developing in strength, and it may be hoped that certain moral and legal obligations with reference to animals will become the common ethical property of all mankind, as is suggested by the abundant and animated literature in defense of animals.

(b) It is characteristic of the human mind to tend to ascribe to objects and phenomena of nature spiritual powers and attributes which are familiar to the individual in his own spiritual life, insofar as there are similarities between the relevant phenomena of nature on the one hand and human actions or other manifestations of human spiritual life on the other. This tendency finds especially broad application, and operates with peculiar force, among primitive peoples and children. In view of this — and in connection with what has already been pointed out with reference to ascribing moral and legal obligations and rights to animals — it can and should be deductively anticipated, from the point of view of the psychological theory of law that moral and legal obligations and rights are to be ascribed not only to animals but also to inanimate objects, such as trees and stones, insofar as there is basis therefor in the law of association according to likeness. Thus where any evil (pain, a wound, death, and the like) is caused by the movements of inanimate objects (stones, beams, and the like), and particularly if these movements seem spontaneous, it may be predicted *a priori* that ethical reactions — flashes of purely imperative moral or imperative-attributive impulsions with reference to these objects — should occur in the childish or other less developed mind, and punishments and so forth be applied to them there. Experiments — and particularly the study (through observation and experiment) of child reactions in these cases — demonstrate that these propositions are correct. In history (in the history of Greece, for example) are known cases where stones which had killed a person, and the like, were prosecuted and punished as criminals. Doubtless the Persian king punished the sea for disobedience under the influence of similar legal mentality.

(c) Furthermore, from the point of view of the psychological theory of morality and law herein set out, we should *a priori* anticipate the existence of moral and legal experiences wherein various incorporeal spirits and other imagined beings — with which the anthropomorphic phantasy of man populates the world, the earth, the forests, the streams, the mountains, the sky, Hades, and the like — come forward as subjects of moral and legal obligations and rights. In particular, the spirits of the departed — and, in general, the dead (not always imagined as disembodied spirits) — play an extremely important part in the legal life of mankind as legal subjects.

Even in the contemporary ethical life of cultured nations, the introspective method and the joint method of inward and outward observation reveal not a few categories and examples of legal experiences with ideas of the dead as subjects of rights. Thus the preservation of graves of the deceased and of various gifts brought to them (flowers, wreaths, monuments, clothes, precious ornaments, rings, bracelets, and the like), the safeguarding of the honor and good name of the deceased, and the unquestioning effectuation of their dispositions of property and other substance before their death (especially dispositions of a beneficent character, and dispositions for their own advantage: such as those relating to yearly payment by the heir of a certain sum for prayers for their souls) are very frequently promoted — and to an important degree — by imperative-attributive experiences with reference to the deceased as subjects to whom the corresponding conduct is owed from the living as obligors. In scientific, literary, artistic, and other criticism of the products of the creativeness of scholars now dead, of poets, and so forth, and in the historical appraisal of the merits of historical personalities, the legal mentality, which indicates to critics the degree of recognition of the merits, respect, and so forth which is owed to the deceased, plays an extremely essential and positive part in contributing to the correctness and impartiality of the criticism.

In the legal mentality and social life of our forebears during the long periods of their cultural development — as well as of contemporary peoples in the lower stages of culture — the rights of the dead are broader and richer, and sometimes entail extremely serious sacrifices and self-restraint on the part of the living — indeed they may be a more serious economic burden upon the living than the taxes paid to the state and to other social organizations. The dead have, and preserve over a long period after death, the right to be supplied with food, drink, and various other objects. They retain a right of property over arms, horses, and various other things which must therefore be buried in the grave or burned so that they may follow in incorporeal form into the owner's life beyond the grave. Among certain nations, the dead not only preserve rights of property to the dwellings in which they lived and the appurtenant parcels of land but do not allow the living to participate in the enjoyment of these objects: the latter must leave the dwelling and land for the benefit of the deceased and move to another place, build a new dwelling, and so forth. The preservation after death of the rights of a master's authority over slaves, of marriage rights with regard to wives, and so forth, requires that the slaves and wives be interred in the grave or burned, so that they may follow their lord and master and serve him further in the life beyond the grave. . .

Moral and legal obligations are also ascribed to the dead with reference to the living who, furnishing the souls of the departed with food and other benefits, have in their turn rights to various services from the dead — particularly to defense and protection, or at least that the dead refrain from causing evil or persecution.

Rights of vengeance and punishment with reference to the law-breakers are ascribed to the dead if their rights are violated, while if the spirits of the dead do not fulfill their obligations with reference to the living — if, for example, the living suffer misfortunes and failures which, according to the interpretation of the adepts, have their origin in the spirits of the deceased — those who have thus suffered sometimes ascribe to themselves a right of vengeance and punishment (such as the right to deprive the deceased of the feeding due to them where their conduct is proper, and the like). Attempts to furnish satisfaction to the spirit of a slain animal — the conclusion of a peace compact with it, the ceremony of punishment for killing and the like — are manifestations of the legal mentality, with ideas of the spirits of the slain animals as subjects of rights.

The extension of the authority of ethical (moral and legal) norms to superhuman or divine beings corresponds, as we have seen, to the character of higher mystic authoritativeness peculiar to ethical impulsions:

even these beings must submit to the higher authority of ethical laws and observe their commands. They, too, are subjects of moral and legal obligations. On the other hand, above these beings — themselves distinguished by peculiar might and the source of various benefits and favors for human beings — is the higher authority of legal norms which endow them with various benefits. They, too, appear as subjects of legal powers and legal claims.

The realm of deities in man's religious mentality is extremely broad, including the space beneath the earth and the heavens, the moon, the sun, and the star: in general, world space *ad infinitum*. Accordingly the sphere of action of the religious law touching the gods embraces world spaces which are infinitely vast; the earthly surface on which people live is only a small part of the expanse wherein this law operates. The population of this world of subjects of moral and legal obligations and rights is extremely abundant and diverse — sometimes altogether fantastic in forms and character — corresponding to the tremendous productivity of human phantasy and the diversity and whimsicality of what it produces in the various stages of its development and in different races and nations.

Moreover, besides a great host of beings created by popular phantasy — corporeal and incorporeal, and those which are partly material and partly spiritual — there is in the world of divine subjects of obligations and rights an incalculable number of real phenomena and objects of nature and of human manufacture, conceived of as spiritual beings — as incarnations of divine spirits: the sky, the sun, the moon, the stars, sky-glow, the earth, the winds, mountains, streams, stones, various plants (chiefly trees such as oaks), groves, various animals, representations of the manlike or other beings (including animals) made out of stone, wood, clay, and the like (idols), and various other things great and small seem spiritual and divine beings in different nations. And in different stages of culture the spirits of the deceased — for example, of the ancestors and the leaders — play an important part as deities, and even living people — Chinese emperors, Pharaohs and the like — become deities or repositories of the divine spirit. A great wealth of appropriate religious law — that is to say, of law establishing obligations and rights for divine beings with reference to people — corresponds to the rich diversity of the subjects of this class.

The legal claims of deities to be furnished with food and drink are important among the rights of gods with reference to people, especially in the lower stages of the development of religious law. Sometimes the obligor is required to feed the deities directly — for example, to smear the lips of the idol punctually with food; sometimes to furnish provisions for the deity to his servants and representatives, or to the priests; sometimes to grant objects of nourishment to the deities through popular abstention from consumption of these objects as reserved for the deity, or through granting to the exclusive use of the deities certain parcels of earth with their products: berries, game, and so forth. Sometimes the objects of nourishment are furnished in the same shape as that in which they are consumed by people, but sometimes in the form of gases or "spirits" of burned substances, animals, and the like. Legal claims of gods to human sacrifices are found in the epoch of cannibalism.

Besides rights to nourishment, rights of gods to divers other offerings in kind or in money develop. Sometimes there are complicated systems of direct taxes (tithes of various kinds and the like) and of indirect taxes in favor of the deity or deities, collected by representatives, priests, state officers, or the like. Sometimes gods have a property right in great stretches of earth, in various regalia, in monopolies, and so forth. Rights of gods further include: claims to different signs of reverence and service — for example, one day of the week of the laboring man is reserved in their behalf, as well as various other days or longer intervals of time during the year; and claims to obedience and to the patient acceptance of misfortune and punishment from above.

A particularly important and highly beneficial part in the social life and the cultural education of mankind is played by rights of gods to claim that people behave in a certain way with respect to others: that they do not kill, rob, steal, or cause various other evils to their fellow citizens; that they observe contracts which have been made; and that they speak the truth where the gods have been called to witness the correctness of their statements. Other examples may be seen in claims that parents duly educate their children, that the latter obey and honor their parents, that monarchs and other officials exercise their authority for the good of the people, that citizens obey the monarch and other established authorities, and that wives obey their husbands and observe conjugal fidelity. The result is thus that there are two systems of behavior required by law and coincident in content: (a) the law as between men, establishing for human obligations with respect to others as obligees; and (b) religious law, establishing for the same persons obligations which require the same conduct, with ideas of deities as the subjects of the claim thereto. He who murders or steals breaks human law — and at the same time divine law (the legal claim of the deity that he abstain from such conduct). Of course, this substantially intensifies the motivation pressure toward the required conduct: one who — influenced by evil impulsions — would perhaps lightly break the law of man will not so readily decide upon such a deed when the corresponding religious legal experience appears and he realizes that the relevant conduct would at the same time encroach upon the rights of the deity.

Rights of punishing law breakers are ascribed to the gods where their rights are not satisfied. In the earlier stages of the development of religious law, this punitive law has a character of a cruel and pitiless right of vengeance in the shape of causing death, diseases, and other misfortunes in the life here (as distinguished from the life to come) without examination of the matter in court, and extending not only to the person of the wrongdoer but to his entire *gens* or even to still wider groups: his tribe or his nation. In general, the principles characteristic of primitive criminal law as between men are applied. The subsequent development of religious punitive law corresponds in general to the development of criminal law as between men, and the idea of court proceedings appears; punishments are, however, deferred to the life beyond the grave.

Legal relationships between persons and gods have a mutual character — that is to say, legal obligations of deities with reference to people and rights of people with reference to deities — correspond to the rights of the deity with reference to people and to the obligations of people. Legal obligations of gods with reference to people — where the latter conduct themselves properly: that is to say, observe the rights of the gods precisely and honorably — consist in abstaining from causing evil, and in various positive services: aid in hunting and war, taking vengeance on third persons for violations of law, and general defense and protection in the most diverse forms. If the gods fail to fulfill their obligations with reference to persons, they are — among primitive races — subjected to various punishments, including the loss of food and other offerings arranged for, bodily punishments, beating with sticks, and the like. Sometimes the matter even goes to the point of "punishment by death" through beating the idol with stones or otherwise destroying it, and so forth.

In addition to those referable to stable and settled principles of religious law, fortuitous and temporary rights and obligations are frequently established between people and deities through legal agreements: thus contracts of barter are often concluded with deities — in order to obtain various special services (great and small) on their part — whereby they are bound to render the required service in return for a certain quantity of food, sacrifices, and the like. Consent to the arrangement on the part of the deities is defined by the contracting parties themselves — or by the intermediaries at the concluding of the contract (priests) — by means of various signs, with the help of sundry divinations, and the like. Likewise various gratuitous arrangements in favor of the gods are extremely frequent — gifts, wills, and so forth. As was to be expected from the psychological point of view, gods may occupy legal relationships to other beings — and not to persons alone: an animal which has defiled the dwelling of a deity (the temple) or killed a man is a criminal and subject to punishment at the instance of the affronted deity. Even in the life beyond the grave the spirits of deceased persons that have violated the religious law are subject to responsibility before the gods for what has been done, hence expiatory sacrifices and so forth are offered in their behalf and in their names.

In the religious law of polytheistic peoples, law between gods — law in which gods are both subjects of obligations and subjects of right — has developed extensively: Zeus was a king, possessing the right of royal power with reference to the other Greek gods, rights of marital authority with regard to Hera, rights of paternal authority with regard to the gods who were his children, and so forth. To subordinate the gods to law, and to endow them with rights and legal obligations with regard to people and to other beings, is a phenomenon particularly natural and psychologically inevitable under the dominance of polytheism — and, in general, in the lower stages of religious development — when ideas of deities are highly anthropomorphic and there is no sharp distinction between gods and human beings (and the former do not stand much higher than the latter). A different situation would obviously be expected in the monotheistic religions, yet, even in those of so lofty a type as the Hebrew and the Mohammedan, the Deity appears subordinate to law: bound by various legal obligations and endowed with rights with regard to persons — a particularly striking confirmation of the foregoing proposition as to the character of higher mystic aureole and authority typical of the legal species of ethical impulsions.

The teaching of the New Testament comprises a radical reform of the relationships between man and the Deity, and in general an essential change of the character of religious ethics: moral, purely imperative ethics take the place of legal imperative-attributive ethics. Later, however, in the Middle Ages, even the Christian religious mind was penetrated by a multitude of legal elements, and medieval — and to some extent modern Christian — ethics reflect once more an important metamorphosis into legal ethics, with the various attributes characteristic thereof (exact definiteness of the objects of obligations, casuistry, and so forth).

CHAPTER III

PROPERTIES AND TENDENCIES OF LAW AND MORALITY

SECTION 10. *The Scientific Significance of the Division of Ethics into Law and Morality*

The foregoing division of ethical phenomena into two species and definition of the concept of law constitute an independent classification of phenomena which bears no relation to the usage accepted in juridic spheres and differs radically therefrom. It is far nearer to the subconscious classification found in the everyday language of common people, which — as distinguished from the professional language of jurists — may be said broadly to manifest a tendency to apply the word "law" to cases where there is an imperative-attributive consciousness (legal consciousness in our sense). In the language of the people, accordingly, "law" has a vastly wider meaning than when it is used by professional jurists. Moreover, a closer investigation of the scope of the words "law," "morality," "moral," and so forth, as applied by the common people would reveal instances where there was no such coincidence with the terminology proposed above — chiefly in respect of innumerable ethical experiences (which according to our terminology are referable to intuitive law) where everyday speech applies indiscriminately the words "law" and "moral," or uses the expressions "I have a moral right," "he has no moral right," and the like. In this respect — that is to say, insofar as the word moral is also applied in these cases — everyday speech is nearer to the customary views of jurists, who refer to morality that which is by our terminology referable to intuitive law; insofar, however, as everyday language does, at all events, apply also the word "law" in these cases, this is in accord with our terminology. However, neither the coincidence in general of our terminology with the everyday usage of the words nor the cases (which have been pointed out and others which are possible) where there is no such coincidence have the slightest importance from the point of view of scientific classification. That the class formed and the class concept defined coincided completely with any professional or everyday usage would by no means signify that the classification was scientific or even in fact successful, nor would the fact that there was no such coincidence prove anything against the classification. The consciously scientific formation of classes and class concepts must conform, not with what is indicated by this language or that (that is to say, with habits of nomenclature which took historical form subconsciously), but with the problems of knowing and explaining phenomena, and particularly of forming adequate scientific theories. To this purpose the foregoing formation of a higher class of ethical phenomena, and the division of this class according to the character of the ethical impulsions into two subclasses: (1) imperative-attributive ethical phenomena ("law"), and (2) purely imperative ethical phenomena ("morality") were specifically adapted. The concepts which have been established are completely free from the character (inherent in other attempts to define "law" and "morality") of being mere interpretations of words; they do not purport to define what is meant or what is embraced by these terms in any particular habit of speech. This means that there can be no serious or scientific ground for objecting to the proposed classes and class concepts because different terminology is, in practice, applied (by the objector or by anyone else) to these or other objects of the classes we have formed — such as calling various imperative-attributive phenomena something other than law ("morality," "mores," "religious commandments," and so forth). The same is true of objections that certain phenomena which we relate to law are "undoubtedly not law" but "moral norms" or "rules of behavior in society," or that the concept of law we have proposed thus comprises a mixture of law with morality, mores, and so forth. Such objections would not correspond to the nature and sense of the disputed definitions or to the problems and meaning of scientific classification; they would express only a naïve faith that words and habits of calling (or not calling) certain objects by a certain term define the nature of the relevant objects, so that a different term would be contrary to their nature. To the same category should be assigned doubts and objections on the ground that the proposed concepts do not comprise in themselves indications of the *distinctive attributes* of law (since certain phenomena related to morality or to mores likewise possess an imperative-attributive nature, and so forth). From the point of view of the classification we have established, the answer to these and similar objections is simple: everything possessing an imperative-attributive nature must of course be referred to the corresponding class, for that is precisely what scientific classification (as distinguished from verbal definitions) means. There can, in general, be no question or doubt as to whether or not the attributes of the classes and class concepts which we have established are general and distinguishing: *only* that which possesses the relevant attributes is referable to the corresponding classes according to the meaning of scientific classification. All the relevant objects must inevitably possess the relevant attributes, and these are inevitably general. On the other hand, *everything* possessing these attributes is related to these classes; consequently only that which is distinct from objects of the given class remains beyond the bounds of the class and the class concept. The established attributes are inevitably differentiating attributes.

Words — existing habits of nomenclature — may play a part as regards fashioning or searching for convenient names for classes which have been formed, but not where classes and class concepts are being formed (and justified or challenged). Instead of inventing new terms for the two classes of ethical impulsions which we have formed, we preferred to borrow words ("law" and "morality") which exist also in the general language of the people and are so applied that there is approximate coincidence. If one does not agree with the choice of these words as terms, and considers others more suitable, that problem may then be considered, it being always understood that what is involved is terminology alone and not the essence of the matter — which is the scientific propriety and vindication of the formation of the corresponding classes and concepts: these may, without changing the substance, be given any names one likes or be represented by letters, or symbols, or remain without any particular designation at all.

A scientific appraisal of the division of ethical experiences into two classes according to the character of the ethical impulsions — of accepting the attributive nature of the relevant impulsions as the distinguishing attribute (*differentia specifica*) of one class (law), and the purely imperative nature of the relevant impulsions as the distinguishing attribute of the other class (morality) — should be concerned with the suitability of this division as a means and a foundation for gaining scientific light: for the correct cognition and explanation of the phenomena. If any further special characteristics of the classes thus formed are associated with the proposed classificatory attributes and are explained by reference to them — if any laws (tendencies) especially referable (and adequate) to the classes formed can be established — the division is scientifically vindicated then; the greater the scientific light it sheds, the higher is its scientific value.

From what has already been set out, it is clear that the differences in the intellectual content of legal and moral experiences and of their projections are associated with — and explained by — the attributive nature of legal impulsions on the one hand and the purely imperative nature of moral impulsions on the other. In the field of law there is a complication of the intellectual content (corresponding to the imperative-attributive nature of legal impulsions) consisting in the duality of the subject ideas (subjects of the obligation — subjects of the rights) and of the object ideas (objects of obligation — objects of right), as contradistinguished from morality, whose intellectual content is poorer and simpler in this regard and has no dual character. In precisely the same way, impulsive phantasmata and projections related to law possess a different and likewise dual character, as distinguished from unilateral moral phantasmata and projections. Norms of law appear as burdening on the one hand, and as endowing on the other. Norms of morality are burdening norms only. In morality there are only unilateral obligations. In law there are dual bonds between the two sides: the duties of some actively made secure in behalf of others, and legal relationships representing obligations for some and rights for others. The corresponding differences in external forms of reflecting and expressing legal and moral experiences and in the structure of the corresponding expressions of popular language, the form of setting out corresponding documents, and so forth are associated with — and further explained by — these distinctions in the intellectual content and in the character of the projection. The making secure of the duty of one in behalf of another clarifies and explains the phenomena which are characteristic of legal symbolism (and are uncomprehended by modern jurisprudence): the symbol of binding hands — of holding or giving the hand and other lengthy objects, the symbols of blood, breathing, delivering a document, and so forth. Incidentally, the very phenomenon of establishing obligations by contract — of an act consisting of offer and acceptance — represents a phenomenon characteristic of law (but foreign to morality) which is explained by the attributive nature of that species of ethics. It represents on the one side the act of proposing a duty for confirmation, and on the other the act of making secure in one's behalf that which is offered. The same is true as to various other acts directed at some change of legal relationships, to legal transactions, to assigning one's rights (that is to say, the duties of others) to third persons (with or without consideration), and to other acts of disposing of the obligations of another (which is unthinkable in morality), and so forth.

Since these characteristics of the intellectual content and projections of law — as distinguished from morals — are associated with the attributive nature of the relevant impulsions, the corresponding general propositions must be referred specifically to the class of ethical experiences which are based on imperative-attributive impulsions — this class alone is adequate and scientifically appropriate. To refer them to another class would be to form theories scientifically misshapen: theories which "limp" or "jump" or are utterly false (compare Section 4 *supra*).

The prevailing opinion reduces law to commands (positive orders and prohibitions) addressed to citizens by others; and the controversy is as to the attributes which distinguish these from other commands. Is it that they are coercive? Is it that they originate in (or are recognized by) the state? With the nature of law so defined, the origin of the intellectual content of legal phenomena and the source of legal relationships and the rights of the obligees (as contrasted to the obligors) and so forth defy explanation. In general, to refer law as demonstrated herein (imperative-attributive ethical experiences) to any commands whatsoever — from whomsoever issuing — would be to form theories that are absolutely false. Even if our concept of imperative-attributive ethical experiences were substituted for commands — if the propositions herein established as to the intellectual content, projections, and so forth were referred especially to law in the sense in which the word is used by jurists — the result would be theories that "limp" (since they are related to a class which is too narrow) and are therefore scientifically indefensible.

In addition to the characteristics differentiating law and morality, already indicated, there is a multitude of other attributes and tendencies (differing for these two branches of ethics) which are associated with the attributive nature of law on the one hand and the purely imperative nature of morality on the other, and the proposed classification consequently represents a basis for creating two broad systems of adequate theories (two theoretical sciences).

SECTION 11. *The Motivational and Educative Effects of Moral and Legal Experiences*

The essential significance in human life of ethical experiences of both the moral and of the legal type is that they: (a) operate as motives of conduct and stimulate to the accomplishment of some actions and to abstention from others (the motivational effect of ethical experiences), and (b) produce certain changes in the mind of individuals and masses, developing and intensifying some habits and propensities and weakening and eradicating others (the pedagogical or educational effect of ethical experiences). Since they are abstract, moral and legal impulsions do not *per se* predetermine the character and direction of conduct and can (having regard to the content of the action and other ideas connected with them) serve as stimuli to the most diverse conduct (including conduct which is socially harmful) and exert an educative influence in the most diverse directions (including directions socially harmful). By virtue, however, of the action of those socialpsychic processes which evoke the appearance — and define the direction of the development — of ethical impulsive-intellectual complexes, the latter, speaking generally, receive such a content — as regards motivation and education — as corresponds with the welfare of society. They act in general in favor of conduct socially desirable and against conduct socially harmful, and educate in the direction of developing and intensifying socially desirable habits and propensities, and of weakening and eradicating those which are socially harmful.

In accordance with its imperative-attributive nature, however, the action of law upon human behavior and the development of the human mind differs from that of morality (purely imperative ethics) in two important respects.

(1) The attributive nature of the consciousness of legal duty — the consciousness that here is not merely a simple deontological concept of what is due (an obligation which is free in regard to others), but a duty of such a character that the obligation to which we are bound is at the same time owed to another as his due — gives this consciousness a special motivational force, and creates an additional pressure toward the corresponding conduct, not found in morality (where we do not consider as owing from us to others the obligation to which we are bound). *Ceteris paribus,* the attributive or legal consciousness of duty exerts upon conduct a pressure more powerful, and evokes conduct more consistently compliant, than does the purely imperative consciousness of duty (the consciousness of a purely moral duty where there is no right in any other person). Fulfillment with reference to others of what is owing to them is a normal, common, and perfectly obvious phenomenon. Even to suffer blows without repining, indignation, or resistance to bodily punishment is deemed a matter of course by persons (slaves, children, and wives — at a certain stage of culture) who ascribe to others the corresponding right (the master of the house). On the other hand the performance, in relation to one's fellow men, of morally recommended actions (to which they cannot, according to existing ethical views, assert a claim) generally seems a special merit (and neither obvious nor commonplace), and observance of such a moral commandment as turning the left cheek to one who strikes you on the right seems ethical heroism and presupposes extraordinary Christian enthusiasm.

That the legal imperative-attributive mentality can evoke relatively general and constant observance of the corresponding rules of social conduct must be recognized as a great advantage of this branch of ethics over the purely imperative morality which has no such motivational force. If the idea of certain conduct as socially desirable was originally united with purely imperative impulsions (consciousness that so to act was good and proper, but not that the opposite conduct would be depriving the other party of that which was due), its subsequent conversion into legal consciousness (its association with imperative-attributive impulsions) is an important step forward. This is social progress: socially desirable conduct, observed formerly in particular instances only and by persons ethically outstanding, now prevails in the community and is converted into a common social phenomenon. There are many examples of such development in the history of the legal consciousness and social life of modern European nations. The sublime ethics of Christianity — which are purely imperative — comprised (and still comprise) rich source material for the formation of the corresponding imperative-attributive principles of conduct, and not a few of the principles of conduct with reference to fellow creatures (in the narrow sense, or in the broad sense as inclusive of nations and persons of alien extraction) which originated in the general principles of Christian morals gradually ceased, by reason of the action of many centuries of the cultural-educative process, to be purely imperative (as they had originally been) and became stable imperative-attributive psychic crystallizations. Undoubtedly development in the same direction will take place in the future as well: individuals and nations will be furnished by other individuals — and as a matter of right — with what now (notwithstanding the presence of corresponding moral principles) they enjoy either not at all or only as special favors and benefactions in isolated instances. Law, more successfully and constantly than morality, confirms socially desirable habits and propensities and eradicates the opposite elements of character by exerting a more powerful and decisive pressure upon conduct, by evoking that which is socially desirable, and by not admitting that which is malicious and antisocial; and so exerts a more consistent and powerful educative influence on human minds than does morality.

(2) The imperative-attributive consciousness exerts specific and immediate influence upon our conduct — not only when we experience it as consciousness of our being obligated (of the right of another) but also where we experience it as consciousness of the duty of another with regard to us (of our being endowed with a right as regards that other). Here the urge provoked by the imperative-attributive impulsion has

the character of an impelling and authoritatively sanctioning stimulus to conduct which corresponds with the content of our right: the corresponding conduct appears to us sanctioned by the higher authority of the attributive norm. And the more intensive the corresponding impulsion, the more powerful the mystic-authoritative character of the attribution, and the more "sacred" and indubitable our right seems to us, the more powerful is this motivation and the more lively, assured, and decisive is our action.

This proposition is confirmed at every step by self-observation and observation of the conduct of others: the specific influence of the corresponding impulsions on deportment, gait, voice, and facial expression may be noted (erect deportment, raised head, a resolute tone of voice, and so forth), and it may be assumed that the action of the heart and lungs is heightened, the pulse strengthened, the flow of blood livelier, the breathing deeper, and so forth. A more detailed investigation of the physiological actions of active legal experiences (including the aid of laboratory experiments) is one of the interesting problems of the future psychological theory of law.

Motivation originating in consciousness of our right and another's duty we may call active legal motivation, to distinguish it from that originating in consciousness of our legal and moral duty, which we may call passive ethical (legal and moral) motivation. Active ethical motivation manifestly does not exist in the province of morality: it is peculiar to the law in the sense herein established.

Active legal motivation is extremely important where the law is concerned with legal powers in the sense we have established (rights to do something plus the obligations of others to permit the corresponding actions) for here the chief actor is the subject of the right — the obligee. But it is by no means negligible in the field of positive and negative legal claims, where the chief actors in the effectuation of rights are subjects of duty who are bound to do something or to refrain from something in behalf of the obligees. Here the motivation consists, first and foremost, in the encouragement and ethical sanctioning of quiet and confident (though passive) utilization of the corresponding positive services and other actions and abstentions of others as owed to us — as distinguished from special favors and benefactions bestowed in accordance with purely moral or other stimuli. Thereafter, insofar as the realization of claims requires certain positive actions on the part of the obligee — such as appearing before the obligor in order to receive what is due, to remind him thereof, and so forth — active motivation consists in the encouraging and sanctioning of these actions.

In general, active legal motivation — side by side with passive motivation — is an essential and necessary factor of social life and social order: without it the latter could not exist as it does now. The present distribution of property, and the corresponding economic order and economic life, are created not only on the basis that members of society respect and observe property rights of others, but also that those others ascribe to themselves corresponding rights and act in conformity therewith. Formerly, in the epoch of slavery, people ascribed to themselves rights to possess, use, and dispose of other persons — slaves — as objects of property and economic exploitation. This right was deemed altogether natural and sacred — established by the gods themselves. Now, however, the reëstablishment of slavery, serfdom, and the like would be unthinkable, not merely because it would be impossible to achieve the corresponding passive legal motivation on the part of those held to be subordinate, but also because the masters would not be conscious of the rectitude of their position and of the active ethical motivation of slave-possessing conduct. In precisely the same way, the existing state order — indeed every sort of state order — is built on the subordination of some to the legal injunctions of others *plus* the ascription to themselves by those others of the right to command, to manage common affairs, and so forth and action by them accordingly.

In certain instances and areas of legal life active legal motivation completely defines the realization of a right: the corresponding passive legal motivation is nonexistent. This is so in cases where only beings that are imaginary (such as deities) are on the passive side or to whom knowledge and consciousness of law are alien (such as animals and infants) and provided, of course, the obligors are not represented by others. In precisely the same way there are instances and areas wherein only passive legal consciousness and passive motivation operate, but in general the basis of the legal order is the correspondence or coördination of passive and active legal motivation with the two corresponding classes of conduct. Even where the subjects of obligations or rights are beings incapable of taking an active part in legal life, the coördination of passive and active legal behavior is commonly achieved by means of representation, the relevant acts being done by others in behalf of the incompetents.

Active legal consciousness — in the same way as passive legal consciousness — has important educative significance as well as motivational significance.

To some extent the direction in which active legal consciousness influences the development of habits and propensities depends upon the special character and content of the rights being conceived of and carried into effect; however, in its influence upon the development of individual and mass character there are elements which are common to different manifestations of that consciousness irrespective of their special content.

Consciousness of one's right puts one in that particular respect on an equality with — or even higher than — persons who in other respects seem to him to stand higher than himself. The law "does not regard the person": it raises "the little people" to the elevation of "the great ones" of this world. Consequently a healthy and adequately intense consciousness of one's rights exerts an important educative influence upon one. It makes him "a citizen" in character and conscious of his own dignity. It saves him from faults of character and conduct which develop when there is no proper consciousness of one's own dignity and self-respect and are traditionally associated with such terms as "slavish" or "servile" spirit. These expressions are, in a way, eloquent historical documents. Slavery is distinguished from other phenomena which might seem at first glance to resemble it (subordination in the family or in the *gens* — *patria postestas* and *manus mariti* — which were formerly of an altogether unlimited character and included the right of life and death) by the special characteristic that slaves possessed no rights, wherefore the slave mentality was altogether peculiar and unlike that of citizens possessing full rights (including even those who were subject to the absolutely unlimited power of the Roman *patres familias*). "Civis Romanus sum" (*civitas* designating the completeness of legal rights) indicates a special type of character and a well-established *habitus* of conduct. The character of a "slavish soul" (*anima servilis*) was the opposite. The preservation of these expressions from the history of slavery down to the present time to signify a particular group of gloomy traits shows how harmful for the education of character is the absence of consciousness of one's rights, and how important it is for the healthy development of character that such consciousness be present and operate.

Parents and educators should devote serious attention to the development of strong and vivid legal consciousness in children and be concerned to impress upon them law, and not morality only. Moreover, it is important to develop both sides of law, suggesting not only the rights of others (and their sanctity and strong respect for them) but also the individual pupil's rights (and respect for them) in precisely the same way. The proper development of consciousness of, and respect for, the rights of others affords firm support for the proper relationship toward others (and for the proper respect of their individuality): the relationship of rendering what is due. The development of consciousness of his own rights communicates to the pupil proper personal dignity and the traits of character associated therewith (frankness, directness, and so forth). The consequence of education "without law" is that there is neither firm ethical ground nor assurance against the temptations of life; and with special reference to the relationship to human personality — the personality of others and one's own — such upbringing naturally produces a "slavish spirit" and a lack of respect for another's personality: despotism and stupid willfulness.

The development of the proper active legal consciousness (consciousness of one's own rights) is further important in pedagogy from the point of view of the development of occupational and economic efficiency. It communicates the firmness and the confidence, the energy and the initiative, essential for life. A child brought up in an atmosphere of arbitrary caprice (however beneficent and gracious), with no definite assignment to him of a particular sphere of rights (although of a modest and childish character), will not be trained to construct and carry out the plans of life with assurance. In the economic field, particularly, he will be deficient in confidence, boldness, and initiative: he will be apathetic, act at random, and procrastinate in the hope of favorable "chances," help from another, alms, gifts, and the like.

What has been said about bringing up children is applicable as well to the education of the nation, and to legal policy which is a powerful means of achieving that education. The evolution, in the masses, of a "citizen" type of a special and ideal character — possessing economic efficiency, energy, and initiative — depends upon the structure of the law and the direction of legal policy, and in particular and especially upon developing the principle of legality and a system of subjective rights which are strong, stable, and guaranteed against arbitrary conduct (instead of hanging upon the exercise of a gracious discretion). To suppose that the economic debility or prosperity of a country turns on a particular direction of "protectionist" or other economic policy would be in the highest degree superficial and unscientific. Economic debility and prosperity depend upon the character of the millions of subjects of economic activity, and upon the type of "owners" — upon their energy, their initiative, and their *savoir faire* in the bold and confident conception and execution of economic plans, and their reliance upon themselves rather than upon chance. Legality is a condition essential to the inculcation of these traits of character and the impregnation of all spheres of social life (including the economic sphere) with *law*.

The purely moral, nonattributive mentality is exceedingly lofty and ideal, but normal and healthy development of character requires the attributive legal mentality as well. Without such a complement — or, more accurately, without this imperative-attributive foundation — healthy ethics are lacking, and character is disfigured by deformities, some of which are repulsive.

SECTION 12. *Fulfillment of the Requirements of Law and Morality*

In conformity with the attributive nature of law, the impulsion toward the fulfillment of a legal duty has the character of pressure in the direction of furnishing the other side (the obligee) with that which is due to him, while the conduct of the obligor is important, not in and of itself, but as the method and the means whereby that result is attained for the obligee. Conversely, moral impulsion has the character of immediate pressure toward definite conduct as such, and not as a means of satisfying the right of the other party.

In the field of morals, the imperative function — the only one existing there — is of independent and exclusively decisive significance. In the province of the law, on the other hand, the attributive function is chiefly and predominantly important, while the imperative function has only subordinate and derivative significance. What is paramount from the point of view of the law is that there be furnished to the obligee the appropriate gain (*accipere*) which is the object of the right — that his right (the attributive side of the legal relationship) be satisfied, and the attributive function carried into effect. As to the imperative function on the other hand — consciousness of the obligation taking effect upon the conduct of the obligor, effectuation of the object of the imperative (*facere*) and fulfillment of his duty by the obligor — this aspect is important only as a means (and not the only possible means) of actually bringing about the attributive effect.

This explains the various phenomena which are typical in the province of the law, and the special characteristics of law with reference to morality — phenomena which seem incomprehensible from the point of view of the prevailing legal theory of "imperatives" (and nothing more) in the sense of commands addressed by states or other communities to citizens, and the like. We now proceed to set out the most important of these special characteristics of law as compared with morality.

(1) *The relationship of law and morality toward the fulfillment of obligations by third parties rather than by the obligors themselves.*

The fulfillment of legal obligations is possible without participation, and without any sacrifice, by the obligor — provided what is due to the obligee is furnished by someone. For example, a nephew has run up debts; the creditor turns to the uncle and the uncle pays the debts. The requirements of the norm of law are thus satisfied: the legal obligations of the nephew are fulfilled. From the psychological point of view (as distinguished from the projection point of view) the formulation and explanation of this phenomenon should be that, conformably with their attributive nature, the legal impulsions (in the minds of the obligor, the obligee, and third persons) are satisfied by the furnishing to the obligee of that which is due to him (in the same way that impulsions of hunger and thirst are satisfied if the organism is appropriately supplied) even though it was not the subject of the obligation that performed the corresponding action. The fulfillment of legal obligations by third parties, rather than by the obligor, can of course occur only in those cases where, and to the extent that, the obligee is thereby furnished with that which is owing to him — to the proper satisfaction of his right — and insofar as action by the obligor himself is not requisite therefore. Many legal obligations — such as those due from one spouse to the other, or from children with regard to their parents — can be carried out only by the obligor himself *since the corresponding actions of third parties would not be a proper satisfaction of the rights of the other side.*

In the province of morality obligations cannot in general be fulfilled by someone else's doing for us that which we ought to do, although those for whose benefit this is done are entirely indifferent as to who does it. Moral impulsions — as purely imperative impulsions — are satisfied only by conduct corresponding to the duty of the obligor.

(2) *The relationship of law and morality to representation.*

If, in view of the decisive significance of the attributive function of law, legal obligations can be carried out by third persons acting in the name and for the account of the obligor (insofar as that which is owing to the obligee is furnished thereby), it is understandable and natural that these obligations can be fulfilled (upon the same condition that proper satisfaction be furnished to the obligee) through representatives — third persons acting by virtue of special legal relationships to the obligor in his name and for his account — as in the case of guardians managing the property of the obligor.

Even in the fulfillment of our moral obligations we may, of course, avail ourselves of the help of others — our action in aiding a neighbor in the name of a moral duty does not lose its moral character and its moral value by reason of the fact that the gift was sent by post or by a messenger, and not presented by the donor in person: the messenger is merely instrumental in carrying out our decision — precisely as our hand would be — and the action physically carried out by others is psychologically our action and produced by our decision. Representation in the technical sense is of a different character: it consists in the independent actions of another in the fulfillment of the representative's own decisions while the legal consequences of those actions are attributed to his principal. If, therefore, the representative of the obligor (even without the knowledge and wish of the latter) furnishes in his name satisfaction to the obligee, the obligor has then concededly fulfilled his obligation (through the representative) and has completely satisfied the requirements of law.

Besides representation of the imperative side (of the obligor), there may also be legal representation of the attributive side (of the obligee); performance may be legally demanded and accepted in the name of the obligee; and representation is likewise admissible as regards contractual and other formal acts whereby legal duties and rights (which are associated with the attributive nature of law and do not exist in the province of morality) are created, assigned, discharged, and so forth. Legal obligations and other legal acts may thus be carried out through the appropriate actions of representatives without any sort of participation in fact by the parties themselves: a contract may create obligations between two new-born infants, these obligations may be carried out, and so forth. On the other hand, moral obligations cannot be fulfilled by other persons without the participation of the obligor (even though the action may have been in the name of the obligor): in the field of morality there is in general no place for representation.

(3) *The relationship of law and morality to coercive fulfillment.*

Conformably with the purely imperative nature of morality, the fulfillment of moral obligations cannot be other than voluntary. If the obligor is not doing the bidding of the moral imperative, but is subjected to physical force which leads to the same outward result as if he had fulfilled his obligation — as where what he should have given voluntarily is taken from him by force — this does not constitute a realization of the imperative function (the only function which exists in morality) and there is no fulfillment of a moral obligation. In the law, however, the attributive function is effectuated if satisfaction is furnished, in whatever manner, to the obligee. If by means of violence, as frequently happens in lower states of legal culture, the obligee (by himself, with his kinsmen, or the like) secures from the obligor (who does not wish voluntarily to carry out his duty) that which it is his due to obtain, or if the organs of authority (such as the bailiff or the police) forcibly take from the obligor and turn over to the obligee the object of his right, the law regards and recognizes this as a realization of its demands and the fulfillment of the legal obligation. But coercive fulfillment should not be deemed possible in all the fields of law: its admissibility results from the attributive nature of law only where, and insofar as, that which is owing to the obligee (his proper satisfaction) is thereby furnished. Where rights are directed specifically at the voluntary fulfillment of something on behalf of the obligor, the attainment of the appropriate external effect through constraint is not the furnishing of what is due — is not the proper satisfaction — and of this character are the rights of parents and superiors to obedience, a respectful attitude, and so forth from children and subordinates. It must, moreover, be borne in mind that even in those fields of law where the element of voluntariness is not an integral part of the object of the claim, laws of nature make the coercive fulfillment of a host of obligations impossible in fact. Manifestly claims whose realization requires the performance of certain intellectual labors on the part of the obligor — such as the claims of the state or other subjects upon judges that they judge in accordance with conscience, or with regard to administrative organs, teachers, and tutors, that they govern, teach and tutor properly — exclude the possibility of any coercive fulfillment since the appropriate intellectual activity cannot be evoked by physical force. The same is true as to many claims directed at external acts — at physical actions by obligors (such as the uttering of certain words and the accomplishment of more or less complicated manual labors and so forth).

(4) *The relationship of law and morality to the intentions of obligors in the sphere of the fulfillment of obligations.*

If the law can be satisfied by the action of a third party in place of the obligor, or by the coercive procurement of what is required for the obligee, inasmuch as the attributive function is thereby satisfied, then *a fortiori* it is understandable and natural that the legal consciousness should be satisfied where the same condition obtains — that is, satisfaction is furnished to the obligee — through the accomplishment of what is required on the part of the obligor even though this occurred fortuitously without the wish and intent of the obligor, as where he acted absent-mindedly or mechanically, or otherwise independently of intent.

The relationship of morality — of purely imperative ethics — to this phase of the matter of fulfilling obligations is different. One cannot speak of the action and the realization of the imperative function (the only function in the province of morals), or of conduct in accord with morality or moral conduct, where the obligor neither wished nor intended to carry out what was required, and it was mere chance that the same result came about as if he had intentionally acted.

It should not, however, be supposed that law is altogether indifferent to the presence or absence (and to the content) of the intentions in the minds of those who act. As regards violations of law and other actions juridically relevant as entailing definite legal consequences, contracts, and so forth, the intention of the actors is not without significance — even in law. Thus, according to the law of cultural nations, the accidental causing of harm, without design or fault of any kind, does not entail the punishment that would be imposed if the actor had been at fault. Causing harm carelessly entails other and less severe consequences than does causation accompanied by positive intent, and so forth. In contracts and other legal acts intent is taken into account although it was not directly expressed, and so forth.

(5) *The relationship of law and morality to the motives of fulfillment.*

That the law is indifferent to the motives of fulfillment is to be anticipated or explained (by deduction) from the same point of view: that of the attributive nature of the law, and of the decisive significance of furnishing satisfaction to the obligee. If the obligor has furnished to the obligee that which is due to him, all is well from the point of view of the law, even though the action of the obligor was evoked by extraneous motives entirely unrelated to law (such as egoistic motives, a desire to attain some advantage for himself, or fear of disadvantage) or even by evil motives (such as the wish to compromise the obligee).

It is otherwise as to the motives underlying the accomplishment of that which is required in the field of morality, for the reason that morality is of a purely imperative nature: we cannot speak of the influence and realization of morality with reference to conduct guided by motives of gain or by other motives unrelated to morality. The satisfaction of the moral duties requires the presence of moral motives.

Certain considerations must be borne in mind in order to avoid misunderstanding. (a) It must not be supposed that the motives of actions are a matter of indifference to law in general — that is to say, in all fields. Thus, in the criminal law of cultured nations, the motives for the commission of a criminal deed are important in the determination of the punishment. In other fields of law — the law of wills, for example — the motives underlying the accomplishment of actions are also taken into account. (b) Nor must it be supposed that the law regulates only external conduct — bodily movements — or is satisfied with purely external conduct, holding a certain external effect to be adequate for fulfillment without reference to the phenomena of the inner world. Aside from what has already been said, there are various fields of law (as jurists use the word) where specific inward actions are required of obligors in addition to external conduct. A guardian, a state officer, one in charge of the affairs of others, and the like is bound — in cases where the decision of any question depends on his discretion — to exercise careful discretion in good faith, and to this the obligee (the ward, the state, the principal, and so forth) has a claim: the exercise of discretion and decision in good faith are specifically required by law, irrespective of the benefit or harm resulting from the exercise of that discretion to act or not to act. Even in these cases, the law is satisfied with effectuation of the attributive function regardless of the motives arousing the obligor to the careful exercise of discretion — consciousness of duty or personal interest, a desire to merit approbation, to obtain a decoration or other reward, and so forth; but the claim of the obligee is directed at inward conduct, and not to purely external acts. In general there must be a clear distinction between two completely different questions: (i) as to what is required from the obligor for the obligee, and (ii) as to the significance of motives in accordance with which what is required is accomplished.

The foregoing propositions purport to set out the difference between the relationship of morality and the relationship of law to the imperative side of the matter (to the obligor and his conduct) and not the distinction between the internal world and conduct and the external world and conduct. It is clear from what has been said that the law does not require (over and above definite motives of action) that there be action by the obligor in person: it is satisfied if the obligee is furnished with what is due to him by any means whatsoever (as, for example, by the action of a third party).

All these propositions are psychological laws (tendencies) associated with the specific differences of law and morality and with the division of ethics in our sense into imperative-attributive and purely imperative ethics. They relate to law in our broad sense and to morality in our sense. Referring them to other groups of phenomena — as, for example, referring the corresponding propositions to law in the sense in which jurists use the word — would signify the formation of inadequate ("limping") theories.

SECTION 13. *Nonfulfillment of Moral and Legal Obligations*

In order to obtain further knowledge of the attributes and causal tendencies which characterize law and morals, it is important to study the psychic processes evoked by the violation of legal and moral obligations in the minds of the violator and of those around him.

In accordance with generic attributes found in all ethical experiences (whether legal or moral), certain consequences of a breach of duty are common to law and morality alike: thus where persons act because of impulsions ("temptations") more powerful at a particular moment than are the ethical (legal or moral) impulsions, so that their behavior is contrary to "the voice of conscience," they experience inward conflicts, paroxysms and intense ethical impulsions authoritatively condemning the conduct pursued, and corresponding inward disquiet and (negative) suffering. These, depending upon their force, paralyze or poison the pleasure afforded by the satisfaction of the "temptation." Nor does satisfaction of the impulsions which have served to tempt eliminate the reappearance thereafter — on the ground of the corresponding associations — of the same authoritatively condemnatory ethical experiences regarding what has been done, with the result of further inner disquiet and corresponding sufferings (the "gnawings of conscience") which take on a sharper and more morbid character for the reason that the impulsions (formerly acting and now satisfied) and the pleasures associated with their satisfaction are absent and no longer "stifle the voice of conscience." Sometimes, as where images of what has been done, the sufferings of the victim, and so forth are powerfully impressed on the memory, such relapses of ethical experiences and the sufferings incidental thereto torment the wrongdoer for many years or all the rest of his life: indeed the manifestations and actions sometimes attain such force and tenacity, and entail such suffering, that the organism is completely exhausted and health and life are shattered, or the subject commits suicide in despair.

To the extent that the breach of duty is such that what has been done can be undone and the consequences eliminated — as where something that has been taken can be returned — repeated onsets of the corresponding ethical experiences stimulate thereto and evoke a corresponding repetition of the struggle of impulsions; this struggle may end either in a fresh victory for the impulsions formerly victorious (those of gain, for example) or, if these have been weakened and defeated, in "repentance" — a reversal of the earlier conduct.

Insofar as the corresponding ethical impulsions are associated, in the minds of those around, with the idea of the conduct under consideration, the individual perception or knowledge of the breach evokes in those minds as well impulsions authoritatively condemnatory of the breach and the corresponding negative feelings (dissatisfactions). All this is reflected in words of censure which have a color of authority, in facial expression, and so forth. By association this attitude, authoritatively condemnatory of the breach, is extended to the personality of the transgressor, lessens respect for him in general, and so forth. To the extent that what has been done can be corrected, corresponding ethical experiences appear in the minds of those around, and there are appropriate admonitions and the like if personal relationships making this permissible exist.

Subsequently, however, in conformity with the specific distinction between legal and moral experiences, there are also specific differences relative to reactions to a breach. Differences of this sort are particularly important for general cognitive orientation in the world of law and morality. They concern the minds of persons around, and preëminently the minds of those who are opposed to the obligors: the subjects of the relevant rights in the field of law, or the recipients of the corresponding conduct in the field of morality. Here there are two tendencies (psychological laws) especially characteristic of law as distinguished from morality.

(1) *Eagerness to attain the effectuation of a right is independent of the desire of the obligor.*

By reason of the attributive nature of legal impulsions, that to which one side is bound is recognized as attributed to the other side; as something due to the other side and to be furnished whatever be the good will and the judgment of the obligor. Free discretion to fulfill or not to fulfill is, accordingly, not recognized in behalf of the obligor: it appears intolerably and inadmissibly arbitrary with regard to the other side — which *should* be furnished with what is due to it — if the obligor does not wish to submit. The demand is recognized, and a desire arises either to compel the obligor to submit or to cause the right to be effectuated independently of him. This property of the law is manifested in various forms in the external conduct of obligees and of other persons and is reflected in the very content of law in the standardizing of the corresponding behavior. A number of specific phenomena may be cited as relevant.

(a) Verbally urging and constraining obligors to furnish that which is due, and verbal or written communications to them of an authoritative-imperative character, on the part of the obligee. Persons possessing a right do not beg: they demand that which is "theirs." They assert claims. Rights in general, or certain species thereof, are termed "claims" or "demands." Legislative and other legal expressions recite that one "may demand" or "has a right to demand" (or, having a negative right, "may prohibit" and the like), instead of saying that he has a right to so and so or to obtain so and so. Although it is very common, even in the most modern codes, such language distorts — or at all events fails to express correctly — the essence of the matter: the gist of the right of the creditor and obligation of the debtor is the creditor's right to be furnished what is due without any urgings whatsoever, and not his right to address corresponding verbal urgings to the debtor and the obligation of the latter to tolerate such actions. However, consciousness of the principal rights (to obtain something, and so forth) is commonly supplemented by consciousness — as of an ancillary or collateral right — of the right to demand fulfillment and of the obligation of the other side to tolerate such communications (and "to respond to" the demands rather than to ignore them).

(b) If the demands lead to no result, the application of various more decisive measures such as threats, the seizure of the obligor's property (or of persons, territory, and so forth in the domain of international and other inter-group relationships such as those obtaining between primordial tribes), or acts taking physical effect upon the person of the obligor to compel him to submit and to carry out what is required.

(c) Actual effectuation of a right where its content is such as to make this possible (as in the case of the right to hunt or to pasture animals in a neighbor's forest) without asking his consent, or notwithstanding his dissent or even his physical opposition: that is to say, the application (in the latter case) of measures of physical violence.

(d) If the obligee has not at his personal disposal the means to attain the realization of his right he may turn to others — to fellow members of his social group (to his tribe in the epoch of tribal life, or to his friends and allies in the international domain), or to organs of higher authority (tribal or family authority, in relations between members of the household and children), to the authority of a master, or to the authority of the state — and make a complaint and request aid against the obligor, or present a demand therefore (in case of consciousness of a right to coöperation on their part).

(e) To the extent that these others, being in accord with the obligee as to his right, render aid, this further manifests the same tendency of the legal mentality to furnish to the obligee that which is due to him, irrespective of the good will and judgment of the obligor. In the lower stages of culture, taking the law into one's own hands — that is to say, appropriate actions of the obligee in person or in conjunction with friends, kinsmen, and so forth — plays an important part in the effectuation of rights, despite the unwillingness of the obligor to fulfill them. In the higher stages of culture and with state organization and authority developed, the effectuation of a right through self-help gradually ceases, and we have the corresponding actions of organs of state authority instead. Moreover, in place of the primitive lack of regulation as to permissible action by the obligee and his allies, a more or less developed legal standardization comes in, defining what persons are bound — and in what order — with regard to the obligee to coöperate to achieve the realization of his right, what actions they have a right to undertake with reference to the obligor, and so forth. This standardization reflects, in the very content of the law, the tendency of the legal mentality with which we are concerned.

Moreover, it is permissible even in cultural states to effectuate a right by force (of the obligee himself, or of persons who happen to be associated with him) to the extent of resisting an attempt to violate a right (*vim vi repellere licet*) and in certain other cases; and there are, also, various spheres of life — in the field of relationships between children, in the less cultural strata of society, and so forth — where the aspiration to effectuate a right by violence is often manifested in fact in the direct form of unregulated self-help.

In those spheres of legal life where there is no higher authority and no corresponding force above the parties — as where legal claims between states, or relationships between the members of a newly formed colony, which has not yet a definite organization and authority, are involved — there are in general no means of effectuating a right (despite the unwillingness of the obligor to perform) other than that the appropriate measures be taken by the obligee in person or in conjunction with his friends.

Notwithstanding the diversity and the change of the forms recorded in history, the essence of the relevant phenomena and their causal connection with the attributive nature of legal impulsions is everywhere identical: whether we are concerned with the unregulated and violent (or covert or other) acquisition of that which is his due by the obligee and those who chance to help him, or with the juridically regulated actions of definite organs of state authority, it is specifically the attributive character of the legal mentality that psychologically explains the movement of individual and social forces in every case.

Because the nature of morality is purely imperative, freedom in the choice of conduct by the obligor is recognized in that sphere, where physical constraint and verbal incitation (in the form of a declaration of the corresponding demands or claims) are alike unnatural and inappropriate. In the field of law, on the other hand, the need and desire, corresponding to the attributive nature of the law, to achieve the furnishing of that which is owed to the obligee (regardless of the obligor's attitude) are manifested in various forms, not only when the time of performance is impending and the obligor is unwilling to perform, but at earlier stages also: thus various measures, agreed upon when legal obligations are being established, to assure that what is owed to the obligee will be furnished (pledge, guaranty and so forth) are particularly characteristic of law and altogether alien to morality.

(2) *The repressive tendencies of the law and the peaceful character of morality.*

In accordance with the general laws of the ethical impulsions actions of B with reference to A which seem to A to be a causing of good — the bringing about of a plus — have a tendency to evoke in the mind of A caritative, benevolent, and grateful impulsions. On the other hand, those actions of B with reference to A which seem to A to be a causing of harm or injury — the bringing about of a minus: aggressive actions and encroachments — have a tendency to arouse impulsions of the opposite character: those of hatred, malice, and vengeance. These experiences tend to be extended as well to persons surrounding A to the extent that they psychically make common cause with him.

In law, because of the attributive nature of the law, fulfillment on the part of the obligor (even though it be the furnishing of something extremely valuable) is not experienced as the causing of a plus (of good, of benefaction) with regard to the obligee, but only as his not being deprived of that which is attributed to him with higher authority: his obtaining, for his part, of "his own" (*suum tribuere — suum accipere*); while nonfulfillment by the obligor is conceived of as the obligee's being deprived of that which is owed him: as the causing of a minus (a loss: *laesio*), as an encroachment, an aggressive action.

In morality a different psychic situation obtains in both cases (of fulfillment and nonfulfillment). Since the nature of this branch of ethics is purely imperative, the furnishing of something by the obligor (though in fulfillment of a moral duty) is not experienced as the furnishing of that which is due — not as the obtaining by the other of what was "his" — but as a plus: a benefaction; while nonfulfillment is not experienced as the causing of an injury (or of a minus), nor is it conceived of as aggressive action.

In conformity with this, and with the general laws of ethical impulsions, the reactions to fulfillment and to nonfulfillment of a duty by the obligor also possess a different character in law and morality.

In morality there is a tendency — where material advantages or other services are furnished by others — to experience caritative impulsions (and a tendency for the corresponding dispositions to be manifested: love, gratitude, sympathy, and so forth), together with the corresponding discharges (impulsive actions): expressions of gratitude, or other benevolent actions in respect to those who have done good; while in cases where the moral duty is not fulfilled there is no basis for the malicious or vengeful reactions aroused by consciousness that a loss has been suffered and that aggressive acts on the part of others are being passively tolerated.

In the law, on the other hand, there is no ground for the tendency toward caritative and grateful reactions to be operative in cases of fulfillment, while a tendency to malicious or vengeful reaction operates in cases of nonfulfillment.

According to the seriousness of the evil conceived and other circumstances, these stimuli vary in intensity from a condition of weak vexation to powerful anger and "fury," a "thirst for blood," and the like, and are manifested in external conduct in various forms: verbal protests and expressions of "dissatisfaction," anger, impatience (with corresponding facial expression, intonation, and gesticulation), or other repressive actions up to and including murder — blood vengeance. These are supplemented by resort to others (friends, allies, neighbors, kinsmen, and so forth) for help in the matter of vengeance, and the corresponding conduct of the others in making common cause with the person who has suffered, as well by recourse to representatives of a general, superior authority (to parents in relationships between children, to the head of the house or the patriarch in relationships between members of the household or of the *gens*, or to representatives of state authority in the political sphere, and so forth) with a complaint against the wrongdoer and a demand that he be punished.

The repressive tendency of the law — like its tendency to impel the obligor to perform and in the direction of coerced realization in general — influences the very content of law and is reflected there in the regulation of vengeance and of punishments. As the state authority and organization develop, the treatment of wrongdoers in summary fashion (alone or in the company of others) is gradually limited and done away with, and a system of state punishments takes its place. Still outside regulation by state law are the less harsh manifestations of the emotions of hatred and of the vengeful tendencies when there has been a breach of law: verbal protests and expressions of impatience, exclusions from society, and the informal legal repressions customary as between children. The harsher forms of vengeance — lynch law, and taking the law into one's own hands — are forbidden by the law of cultural states; but not infrequently these prohibitions turn out to be impotent in fact (as in cases of lynch law and summary dealing with horse thieves, and the like). In the international field, the principles of lynch law and the taking of law into one's own hands — up to and including blood vengeance — prevail even now in various forms.

SECTION 14. *The Unifying Tendency of the Law*

It is clear, from the psychological definition of the nature of law and morality herein established, that moral and legal norms and obligations represent nothing actually and objectively outside the minds of the individuals asserting or denying their existence, and apart from those individuals. They are merely reflections or projections of the psychic states of those individuals. Obligations or norms which exist or "undoubtedly" exist in the opinion of some can be nonexistent (or have another content) in the opinion of others. There can be no objective verification, as by examining the person to whom an obligation is ascribed: it is solely and specifically a matter of the opinions of these individuals — and not of material things objectively existent — and these opinions can differ.

In morality, there are frequently discrepant opinions of this sort. They are not harmful or dangerous. In consequence of its purely imperative nature, the moral mentality is *a peaceful mentality* — disposed neither to require by violence that which is not turned over voluntarily, nor to exact bloody retribution for a breach of that duty — and neither dangerous conflicts nor destructive consequences follow if those to whom others ascribe moral obligations hold different opinions in relation thereto. This is not the situation where the legal mentality is concerned. By reason of its attributive nature, it is characterized by a tendency to get by force that which is due, and to act in a repressive fashion where there is a breach. If some ascribe legal obligations to others and corresponding rights to themselves, and those others do not acknowledge the existence of such obligations-rights (either in general or to the extent asserted by the other side), this represents a psychological ground favorable for dangerous dissentions and conflicts, bitterness, violence, and bloodshed.

A psychic source of destruction, malice, and vengeance — a dangerous explosive material — is latent in the attributive character of the legal mentality where the opinions and convictions held by individuals or by masses clash; unquestionably many millions have suffered death, and countless human groups have been destroyed and exterminated, because of the non-coincidence of opinions regarding the existence and compass of mutual obligations and rights.

Associated with this on the ground of, and explained by, sociocultural adaptation is the tendency of law to development and adaptation in the direction of bringing the legal opinions of the parties into unity, identity, and coincidence, and in general toward the attainment of decisions as to obligations-rights which possess the utmost possible degree of uniformity and identity of content for both sides, and — so far as may be — exclude or eliminate discord. This tendency (which is alien to morality) may be called briefly the unifying tendency. It is manifested in law in various forms and directions, so that — side by side with the general development and adaptation of law just indicated — it is possible to establish a whole line of corresponding special tendencies. The most important of these — for the general characterization of law as compared with morality, and for explaining the phenomena of legal life — may be indicated as follows.

(1) *The tendency for a single pattern of norms to develop.*

In order that the opinions of the parties may be caused to coincide with reference to concrete obligations-rights, or that a common solution (which neither side could impugn) of doubts and discords that have arisen may be found, the first requisite is the working out and acknowledgment of uniform general rules — general norms of a single pattern — from which concrete rights and obligations should be deduced, and in accordance with which discords which arise should be decided.

Positive law is a suitable means to this end. It is a special characteristic of positive law that opinions as to that which is due to some from others are not here individual — independent and autonomous opinions: they are heteronomous opinions, defined by various objective facts (normative facts) such as that our fathers and grandfathers so acted, that such is the established order, that others act thus (customary law), that it is so ordered from above (statute law), and so forth. On this basis a pattern of norms is obtained (uniform for masses of people), defining mutual rights and obligations and deciding the doubts and discords which arise. It is thus characteristic of law that it tends broadly to work out and to develop a unifying pattern, and to give that pattern decisive significance so that dissensions as to obligations and rights may be eliminated and solved. In general, modern jurisprudence neither knows nor acknowledges any law other than positive (customary and statute) law. Morality, on the other hand, is defined and portrayed as if it were always intuitive (as the word is used herein), and the distinction between morality and law is alleged to be that morality rests on "inner conviction," whereas the law is established *ab extra* and represents "external norms" which are independent of individual convictions.

This is not so. (a) In the first place, even positive law is not external. It represents inward, imperative-attributive experiences whose intellectual synthesis includes ideas of normative facts: of corresponding divine or human commands, of corresponding behavior of our ancestors, and so forth. It is this complex — and not existence somewhere in the outside world — that is the special characteristic of law. (b) In the second place, it must be recognized that — side by side with positive law — still another law exists as well: intuitive law which, as we have demonstrated, consists of imperative-attributive experiences involving no reference to extraneous authorities. (c) In the third place, morality is not merely intuitive. It may also be positive. There is customary morality authenticated by customs, by the mores of ancestors, and so forth. There is legislative morality, referable to divine or human commands (such as the commands of parents). If the phenomena of intuitive law and positive morality — and of the corresponding classification — are unknown and unrecognized there can be neither a scientific (adequate) theory of law nor a scientific theory of morality. The only acknowledgment having a scientific basis is that in law (for the causes already explained) the positive element is particularly developed, whereas in morality the positive element is weakly developed and does not possess the significance that it has in law.

It must also be noted that the species and varieties of positive law are far more numerous than modern jurisprudence assumes: the legal consciousness is charcterized by a propensity to positivize so powerful and so constant that it may be said to take advantage of all possible occasions, cases, and facts to bring about the fixation of defined and positive patterns.

In the absence of a proper, uniform, and definite law — customary or statute law — the legal consciousness strives to find or to create other objective criteria and patterns to define obligations and rights, and so not infrequently raises collections of juridic dicta (assembled by private persons) to the rank of authoritative sources for the solution of legal questions. *Russkaya Pravda*, the Saxon Mirror, and other "mirrors" of German law, the Talmud, the written codes for dueling, and so forth, are merely private collections of this sort which have acquired a significance analogous to that of legislative codes. If in a particular environment — at the card table, for instance, or in a university council or faculty, or in parliament or the like — some legal question (for which there was theretofore no ready pattern for its solution) is solved in a particular way on the basis of intuitive law or otherwise (if, for example, there has been a new deal because a ten-spot was exposed during the deal), there is, upon the recurrence of like circumstances, a positive law pattern already in operation, and the legal mentality claims that the same course should be followed, citing the precedent, and arguing that on the first occasion the matter was treated thus and that the new case should "therefore" be decided in the same way.

(2) *The tendency of legal concepts toward precision and definiteness of content and compass.*

While the unification of norms — of general legal opinions and convictions — with the aid of the development of uniform patterns is as important as it is indispensable for bringing the actual and specific obligations and rights deduced from general norms (the corresponding opinions of the parties) into unity and congruence, it is not *per se* enough. Accord cannot be attained without precision and definiteness as to the content and the compass of the general rules and of the individual ideas and concepts which are integral parts thereof: (a) ideas of the objects of obligations and of rights, of their nature, dimension, and so forth; and (b) ideas of the circumstances conditioning the obligations and rights (relevant facts). If the expressions and the relevant ideas are obscure or ambiguous, or if their meaning, scope, and so forth are elastic, conflicts would be inevitable in view of the attributive character of the legal mentality. Assume that a statute of the following tenor were promulgated: "Persons who have faithfully and truly served for a long time have a right to receive from those served remuneration in the form of an adequate lump sum paid down or a corresponding pension." The ideas "long time," "faithfully and truly," and so forth are indefinite in scope and elastic. Persons representing the attributive side would be disposed to interpret and apply the rule in the direction of asserting the presence of a right (for example, in cases of a service not particularly long — or even extremely brief — and in cases of service of poor quality) and in the direction of expanding the scope of their claims. Persons representing the imperative side would manifest the opposite inclinations. This would occur also where there was no bad faith. Such a statute would, in consequence, be a social ulcer of extreme malignancy, and the relations of various categories of servants and employers would be poisoned by mutual enmity, quarrels, conflicts, and so forth. The less definite and more elastic the sense of the imperative-attributive rule, the more numerous and harmful are the conflicts which *ceteris paribus* it can occasion.

This proposition has no relevancy to morality, whose nature is purely imperative and therefore peaceful: not only are rigidity and precise definiteness unnecessary here — they would positively obstruct the successful effectuation of morality's social-educative function. From the point of view of moral perfection, therefore, it is desirable that moral principles admit — in conformity with the powers of the individual — of elasticity, of movement ever higher and higher in the matter of their realization, and of the stimulation and attraction of others through example, and afford basis neither for self-satisfaction (on the ground that what is required has been precisely fulfilled and improvement may be halted) nor for despair and a general refusal to perform (where ethical forces are weak). Morality should be an ideal light which enables even the weak to move within modest limits in the right direction, and compelling even the strong to go on ever higher and higher. It should not formulate exact precepts as to something being obligatory and precisely what (no more and no less) is required, but furnish directives admitting of the most diverse degrees of realization, from the most modest to the most lofty.

The contrasting tendencies of the development of law and morality, and the characteristic attributes of their content, are in conformity with what has been herein set out: the tendency in law toward exact definiteness of content and rigidity as to the scope of ideas and concepts, and the tendency in morality toward flexibility and elasticity in these respects.

Law is thus characterized by a desire for an exact definition in respect of the *objects* of obligations-rights: mathematically exact in the matter of quantities. Various positive laws — including those of ancient Rome — contemplate that obligees may demand more — albeit a minimal more, or an hour earlier, and the like — than is owing to them (*plus petitio*), in which event serious and disadvantageous consequences follow (such as loss of the entire right). In precisely the same way the obligor is forbidden — and under penalty of disadvantageous consequences, such as doubling the extent of the duty — to deny improperly the right of another even as to a minimal part of its content. These phenomena are at once special means operating to forestall discords and conflicts between the parties at law, and graphic and characteristic illustrations in support of our thesis as to the definiteness of the elements which constitute the content of law (particularly of the definitions of objects). Such penalties as those just referred to presuppose that the dimension of duties-rights can be precisely defined in accordance with the law which is operative.

In precisely the same way, the law evinces a tendency to predetermine exactly the circumstances, facts, *indicia,* and so forth with whose presence that of obligations-rights is associated; with these relevant facts are connected the casuistic character of law and its anticipation of all possible categories of factual combinations.

Morality, on the other hand, is for the most part limited to pointing out the general trends of conduct recommended (be ye gentle and merciful, help the needy, and the like) and nothing more — leaving a large margin of freedom for a diversity of individual views in actual cases as to whether there are obligations and (if so) as to the measure of their fulfillment. To render help to all the needy would be unthinkable, even for the most wealthy; the principle of morality comprises only a general directive, within whose limits the conditions of help, its character, its extent, and so forth are dependent upon individual views and remain wholly undefined.

Certain moral commandments, however, have a seeming similarity to legal commandments in that they manifestly predetermine exactly — sometimes even with mathematical precision — conditions precedent to the existence and the object of an obligation. Such are the particular New Testament commandments as to not resisting evil: of offering the left cheek when struck on the right, of handing over the cloak also if the shirt is taken away, and of going two miles if compelled to go one. The sense of such expressions, however, is not that they should be understood and fulfilled literally (which would be appropriate in the field of law): they have only the sense of picturesque language employed to indicate a general direction of conduct.

Associated with the indefiniteness and elasticity of the content of morality are the concepts of virtues and of perfection characteristic of morality ("be ye perfect as your Heavenly Father is perfect"), of holiness, of the moral ideal of character and conduct, and the like. Virtue signifies a plane or degree of fulfillment of the principles of morality loftier than the average, and perfection, sanctity, an ideal: it designates the highest possible degree. In the domain of law there is fulfillment *vel non* (a breach of the obligation), but no room for degrees of fulfillment; still less can fulfillment be broadened and extended *ad infinitum* in view of the definiteness of the conditions and of the objects of obligations.

(3) *The law strives to have relevant facts susceptible of proof.*

In order to forestall discords and conflicts as between persons representing the imperative and the attributive sides in law, it is extremely important to avoid linking obligations and rights with facts, whose presence cannot be objectively verified and established: to raise facts incapable of proof to the rank of relevant facts would lead to doubt and controversy as regards the corresponding rights and obligations. Accordingly, the law tends to avoid this and to ignore facts of this sort by simply excluding them from attention or by substituting others which can be established incontrovertibly. Thus the fact that a specific person (A) is conceived by his mother (M) and begotten by her husband (H) — a fact not amenable to verification and yet of vital importance in many fields of law (including the law of inheritance and the law of domestic relations) — is ignored by the law and there are instead special rules defining legitimacy by birth.

In addition to various physical facts, there are many psychic facts not susceptible of verification and the tendency of the law not to raise psychic phenomena to the rank of relevant facts is manifested in various fields. In order, however, that the essence of the matter and the causal connection of phenomena be correctly understood, it must be borne in mind that the point is not the distinction between inward and outward worlds, but whether or not facts can be verified. Conception is a physical (a physiological) fact, but it is not amenable to verification: the law does not elevate it into the class of relevant fact, but replaces it by substitutes. Powerful emotional excitation — such as furious anger because of an insult, is a psychic fact, but it can be established (as, for example, through witnesses of a quarrel and a killing "in passionate irritation") and is raised by the criminal law into a relevant fact which mitigates punishment. Another tendency of the law is that legally relevant facts shall be to the greatest possible degree objectively trustworthy and incontestable. The important part played in the law by written documents, notarial attestations, evidential proofs, and so forth is likewise associated with, and explained by, the attributive nature of the law.

The foregoing tendencies and phenomena are completely foreign to morality in consequence of its purely imperative nature.

The lower the culture of a given people, the more urgent is the necessity that the content of law be adapted to precise predetermination of the conditions of obligations-rights and an exact definition of their objects and their extent, and such that the existence *vel non* of facts raised to the class of relevant facts can be objectively demonstrated: the less cultured the folk, the sharper and more bloody are the corresponding conflicts, and the greater is egoistical obduracy, mendacity, and so forth.

(4) *The unification of actual and specific legal relationships: the role of the court.*

In the vast majority of actual cases, the foregoing tendencies of legal development and adaptation result in a unification of the legal opinions of the opposing sides: the obligations or rights which one party ascribes to the other coincide with what he ascribes to himself, and *vice versa.* Not every possible occasion for legal discord between the parties can be obviated by working out a uniform pattern of general legal principles calculated to reduce to one common denominator the legal opinions of the parties and to define precisely the conditions and the scope of rights and obligations. However excellently a law be adapted, in the respects indicated, to bring about a coincidence of the legal opinions of the parties, it may fail in this regard because of doubts and discords as to relevant facts, as to bringing them under this or that general principle of law, and the like.

In addition to, and independently of, the development of a single positive pattern of norms and the proper adaptation of their content to the attributive and adversary nature of the legal mentality, the concrete rights and obligations (the corresponding opinions) must, as such, be brought into unison in order to forestall or to eliminate harmful and dangerous conflicts associated with the imperative-attributive nature of the law. A means of accomplishing such unison is for the contesting parties to request a disinterested third party to analyze and decide their dispute as to that to which they are bound — that is to say, to examine the circumstances of the matter (the relevant facts) and state his opinion as to the claim that one side may assert against the other (or as to the mutual claims that each may assert). This opinion (which must be equally binding upon both sides) takes the place of the individual and diverse legal opinions of the respective parties as the legal opinion of a third person (or group of persons) which binds both sides by a single decision. The working out of such a legal opinion we will term the trial and the opinion of the third party a court decision. This is, incidentally, a particular instance of the positivization of law —

the working out of positive law of a particular species. The parties ascribe to themselves definite obligations and rights, citing the decision of the court as an authoritative-normative fact.

From the point of view of the psychological theory of law, not only do the examination of the case and the entry of the decision by state courts — special official institutions — come within the established concept of a court, but the same is true as well of innumerable other psychologically analogous phenomena similarly connected causally with the imperative-attributive nature of law: the examination and determination (on the part of the father, the mother, the nurse and so forth) of disputes of children (which are legal disputes in our sense) as to the one to whom playthings belong, how sweets shall be divided, how their childish agreements shall be carried out, and the like; the court of comrades as between children or adults considering offenses and sentencing an offender to make an apology or the like; the trial and determination (by the chief of the gang) of disputes of robbers with regard to the person to whom the booty (or a certain part of it) belongs, and so forth.

Consciousness of the need to resort to third persons for a decision and to submit to such decisions as positive-normative facts constitutes an extremely widespread manifestation of the legal mentality in the most diverse fields, and is a psychologically natural supplement of the imperative-attributive nature of that mentality, exemplifying the general legal tendency in the direction of unification.

Assuredly it is no novel proposition for legal science to find that the phenomena of law and the court are linked together: the corresponding ideas are firmly associated in the minds of the public and of jurists so that the word and the idea "court" evoke the idea "law" and so forth. The nature of the causal connection between the phenomenon "court" and the specific nature of law remains, however, unascertained in European jurisprudence and cannot be scientifically explained in the absence of a proper concept of law. In general, a scientific and adequate theory of the court — which is a phenomenon by no means characteristic solely of the sphere of phenomena which jurists refer to law — can be attained only on the basis of law that is conceived of and studied as imperative-attributive experience.

SECTION 15. *The Social Functions of Law.* (1) *The Distributive Function*

Associated with a differentiation of the specific nature of law and morality is a differentiation of the functions fulfilled by these two branches of ethics in social life. Their difference as regards the motivation of conduct has already been demonstrated. Law, in conformity with its imperative-attributive nature, is characterized by bilateral motivational action: side by side with passive ethical motivation (the consciousness of a duty) there is active ethical motivation (the consciousness of being empowered or endowed) and the result is individual and mass conduct correspondingly coördinated. Moreover, the passive law motivation — in consequence of the attributive force of the relevant impulsions, by reason of the consciousness that what appears as an object of our duty is owed to the other side — exerts a more decisive and steady influence on conduct than does purely imperative motivation: it becomes a general rule which is observed with great regularity. Furthermore the legal assets include not only the stimulating-sanctioning motivation in aid of the effectuation of law, but also (a) the tendency to strive for what is due independently of the judgment and will of the obligors (to demand, to importune, and to compel obligors to submit, employing various means including violence), and (b) the tendency toward vengeful and repressive reactions in general with regard to those violating the law. This exerts additional motivational pressure upon obligors toward undeviating observance of the demands of law. In general, these two tendencies influencing the conduct of both sides toward the constant effectuation of the demands of law, give to the social coördination of conduct already indicated a particularly firm and stable character, which is further promoted by the unifying tendency of the law — and especially by the broad development of a positive pattern of norms (uniform for members of the community), of controlling importance where there are doubts and discords, and by the precisely predeterminate character of the conditions precedent to obligations-rights and establishment of the exact content and scope of these obligations and rights.

The foregoing tendencies of legal mentality and of the development of that mentality operate to produce *a stable and coördinated system of social conduct evoked by law — a firm and precisely defined order* — with which individuals and masses can and should conform, and upon which there can be reliance and calculation as regards economic and other plans and enterprises and in the organization of life in general. In the minds of the public and of jurists, the ideas "law" and "order" are constantly associated, and it is extremely common to use the expression "law and order" in place of the word "law." What has been set out above indicates the cause of this association and explains the peculiar capacities and functions of legal ethics in general — as compared with purely imperative ethics — in the matter of organizing and standardizing social life.

Morality creates no coördination of conduct: not only is its motivation unilateral but it is relatively unstable and unreliable as well. Moreover, its character and content, in so far as it does operate, are such that individual opinions differ greatly, as to the character, direction, and degrees of performance. It does not — and by its nature it cannot — create a definite "order" or a system of social conduct precisely predetermined and coördinated, or a firm basis for foreseeing and adapting conduct and constructing economic and other plans and considerations. It makes social conduct better and more gentle, evoking in individuals conduct and an improvement of character which are sometimes highly ideal and outstanding and animate and stimulate others to do likewise. However it cannot, by reason of its purely imperative nature and other typical attributes associated therewith, provide what social life commonly and imperatively requires: that conduct be firmly standardized (and social-educative discipline steady and unremitting).

The precise and definite standardization and coördination of social conduct created by law are manifested in the social functions which characterize law as distinguished from morality. Two of these are of the utmost importance for social life: the distributive function and the organization function.

The function of endowing separate individuals and groups with social benefits (which depend on the conduct of members of society with reference to each other) corresponds to the attributive function of the legal mentality. This is conspicuous in the domain of national (and international) economy, in the division of the fertile soil and other means and instruments of production and objects of consumption (economic benefits in general) as between individuals and groups.

The fundamental type and chief basis of this distribution — and, at the same time, the fundamental basis of economic and social life in general — is the institution of property: individual property (on which the so-called private economy or "capitalist" order of society rests), or collective property (on which the primordial — or other — collectivist social order is based).

What is property? How can the corresponding social distribution be explained? By what forces are the instruments of production and other economic benefits distributed and made secure in behalf of individuals or groups? Wherein does this making secure consist? The phenomenon of property is so familiar as ordinarily to raise no problems of any kind. That estates and various other objects are made secure for definite individuals as by some invisible bonds is naively thought to present no enigma whatever. It neither arouses curiosity nor calls for causal explanation.

This is the attitude of modern jurisprudence as well, although it must have a special concern with the law of property — with a definition of property and so forth. Here, as in other fields of jurisprudence, the naive-projection point of view is dominant, and this, in general, neither knows, or even takes a cursory glance at, the relevant real phenomena or chains of causation. Attempts to define the nature of property from this (projection) point of view have never been successful, and this, like other most important and fundamental problems of jurisprudence, is still a matter of dispute.

Many jurists, particularly those whose studies do not extend beyond civil law, fail to penetrate into the more general problems of the science of law and consider property as an immediate ("invisible") bond between the individual and the thing, and the power of the individual over the thing — complete and exclusive dominion thereover — as the essence of this bond. The manner in which the law is able to create "immediate bonds between persons and things," and the nature of these supposed "bonds," remain unascertained. As to the dominion of an individual over a thing (in which the essence of the law of property is ordinarily said to consist), it must be noted that even where the "thing" is not in the power of the owner but vice versa (as where the owner of a menagerie is in the paws of his bear or his tiger), the law of property is in no wise either concerned therewith or violated thereby.

Consciousness that the prevailing theory is unsatisfactory has recently led to attempts at other definitions of the essence of property. Some jurists suppose that property consists in prohibitions (of the "legal order," the state, or the like), and specifically in prohibitions addressed to all persons (except the owner) against encroachment upon a particular thing. This theory, unlike that set out in the preceding paragraph, holds that property is a relationship to other persons (and not to a thing) — a relationship existing between the owner and all other persons — so that property is not power over the thing but power over all other persons. But this theory, too, is unsatisfactory. One objection is its strange logical sequel that if anyone makes or buys a pin or other object in a store, all other persons alive on earth come to be in a peculiar relationship as regards the purchaser: prohibitions arise with reference to them, and the like. Some jurists assume that the prohibitions arise only with reference to persons conceiving a design to encroach upon the *res* of another, and not with reference to all. But what of the case where there is no one who desires to encroach? Then it would seem that there is no property at all because there are no prohibitions.

Even if these difficulties are left on one side, however, and it is believed that prohibitions do arise, in respect of all or some persons, the theory still fails to attain its purpose. It is utterly incomprehensible how prohibitions (addressed to all persons except one) against encroachment upon a thing can be the source of a right of disposition, a right of enjoyment, and so forth deemed to be vested in that person. If we forbid all persons to enter into an enclosure, or into a part of the forest, where there are deer or bison, these animals do not thereby become the owners of that particular parcel of the forest, and this is so *a fortiori* as to the attempt to interpret property in terms of prohibitions addressed to certain people.

The starting point of a scientific theory of property must be that property is not a phenomenon of the external and objective world. Property is neither a bond between a person and a thing nor the sum total of the prohibitions issued by anyone in respect of anyone. It is a psychic, impulsive-intellectual phenomenon. It exists solely in the mind of one who attributes to himself or to another a right of property. He who ascribes to *another* a right of property considers himself (and others) bound to tolerate any relationship toward the thing (any influence brought to bear upon it, any use or abuse, of it, *uti et abuti*) on the part of that other, and on his part to refrain from every sort of action with regard to the thing (without the permission of that other: the owner). Consciousness of these obligations is experienced in an imperative-attributive manner: the use and the freedom from interference by others is experienced as something which is due and owing to the owner. One who ascribes *to himself* a right of property in a given estate or other object considers others bound to tolerate any economic dealing therewith that he fancies and to refrain from interference (bound not to "step in"). He experiences these psychic acts with attributive force: any dealing with the property which he pleases — and he alone, free from the interference of others — is due and owing to him, and others are bound to submit thereto.

The impulsive force of the corresponding imperative-attributive experiences creates a pressure upon the conduct of those who ascribe to themselves and to others rights of property, and results in individual and mass conduct, which would not and could not exist in social life if they were inoperative. Specifically — as concerns owners — the consciousness of one's right (to exclusive dealing) authoritatively sanctions a corresponding relationship to the thing and to those near it, creating that motivation and that conduct specifically in evidence in actual social life as the behavior typical of owners.

In the persons who ascribe to others a right of property, the imperative-attributive consciousness of their duty to refrain from encroachments upon things of another, and to tolerate any dealing therewith — consciousness that a different conduct would be an encroachment upon the right of another, depriving him of that which is authoritatively attributed, and is due and owing, to him — creates that motivation, and evokes that conduct, specifically in evidence in actual social life as "perfectly obvious" and prevalent throughout the community: a general social relationship toward things belonging to others and toward their owners (nonobservance being merely sporadic and fairly rare, on the part of subjects with some exceptional idiosyncrasy: ethically undeveloped or degenerate, thieves, robbers, and the like). This bilateral, coördinated motivation and the corresponding conduct result in a social process whereby estates, instruments of production, and so forth seem to be made secure, as it were, in behalf of others by certain "invisible bonds."

The idea that a special bond exists between the person and the thing — and the corresponding theories, which reflect naive and fanciful speculations — is due not alone to the association of ideas (which are created on the basis of the phenomena just pointed out) but also to other psychic processes directly evoked by the attributive experiences. The attributive nature of legal impulsions leads to the projection upon various objects of the character of being owned, attributed, and belonging, to certain subjects, and because of these impulsions there is a projection of duties (resting on some and belonging to others), of rights (belonging to them), and (upon duties and rights) of the character of belonging. What is required of the obligor appears as authoritatively attributed — as belonging — to another. If it is a matter of paying a certain sum, or of furnishing other objects, the projection of the quality of belonging is (on the basis of attributive impulsions) then extended to this sum or to these objects also. Obligees receive "their own." In the discharge of mutual debts, they retain what is "theirs" — that is to say, that which is due to them from the other side. The tendency to project the character of different objects as belonging naturally operates with special force, and particular continuity and persistence, in those fields where the rights (secured in favor or some) are not limited in operation to another definite person (relatively secured rights) but are unlimited in operation, extending to all other persons whatsoever (absolutely secured rights). This explains why the character of a thing as belonging to the subject of the right is stubbornly and constantly ascribed, and why the term "property" (proprietas, Eigenthum) is used likewise. The character of a thing as "belonging" to its "owner" is an impulsive projection of phantasm, precisely like the "appetizingness," "attractiveness," "repulsiveness," "prettiness," "ugliness," and so on ascribed under the influence of impulsions to objects and phenomena of the external world. Ignorance of the nature of the corresponding phenomena, and fidelity to the naive-projection point of view, lead to the confident belief that there is some bond — even though it be "invisible" — between the individual and the thing.

The foregoing demonstrates that property is to be found, not as a real phenomenon anywhere in space in the shape of bonds (between people and things, or between people), but in the minds of the owners and of the others who ascribe rights of property to someone. In order that naive and fantastic speculation may be replaced by authentic scientific study and cognition of the real phenomena, these must be studied psychologically with the aid of the corresponding methods: self-observation, and the joint method of inward and outward observation in the form of simple or experimental observation. Experiments with children in order to study their mentality in relation to property, the time and degree of development, the intensity of the relevant legal impulsions, and so forth constitute one of the important and interesting tasks of the future psychological study of the law, which is far from being exhausted in the foregoing general and brief observations.

Such study does not exclude the possibility (and the usefulness, for the technical ends of practical jurisprudence) of defining property from the projection point of view, provided that study were not from a naive-projection point of view, but a conscious and critical investigation of property as the obligations of some made secure in behalf of others. The subject of the obligations is "each" person, whoever he may be: "each and every one" — that is to say, that which the corresponding pronouns designate, that which is conceived by those who apply the corresponding expressions — and in no sense the billions of people on earth or the like. In grammatical analysis of the sentence: "every man knows best for himself what he likes" — or in the logical analysis of the corresponding judgment — it would certainly be naive to suppose that the subject is here the enormous mass of people scattered over the entire planet, but no less are the ideas of jurists as to incalculable numbers of subjects of obligations and addressees of prohibitions in the law of property (and of other rights — absolute rights — wherein the subject of the obligation is each person whoever he may be) due to a basic misunderstanding of principle. As to the obligation itself — the right of property itself — we are here concerned with a complex obligation: a complex right — a combination — made up of the two elements now to be examined.

(a) The first constituent element of property is the legal obligation (of "each and every one") to suffer or to tolerate actions by the owner of whatsoever type with regard to the thing (that is to say, the legal powers of the owner to act upon the thing in any way that his fancy may suggest). *The object of the obligation* is *the tolerance of action of whatsoever type* upon the thing which the owner cares to take; *the object of the right* of the owner is *any action upon the thing* (any dealing with it on his part and so forth) — with the necessary caveat regarding actions (if any) which may constitute special exceptions under the law of a given time or place. In order to make it clear that the owner's right is not a right to actions especially defined and enumerated but to actions of every sort (whose very diversity makes it impossible to enumerate them) — aside from those actions within this caveat — the right of the owner may be termed a "general" right of action upon a thing, and the obligation of the opposing side a "general" obligation to tolerate the actions of the owner upon the thing ("general" not meaning absolutely general but contemplating the possibility of particular exceptions).

(b) The second constituent element of property is the "general" obligation resting upon every person, and made secure in behalf of the owner, against encroachment upon the property of another: the "general" right of the owner to freedom from encroachments. Here the object of the obligation is abstention from taking any action whatsoever upon the property of another (aside from special exceptions, if any, as we have indicated by the expression a "general" obligation of abstention from actions), while the object of the right is freedom from outside actions of every sort (aside from those particularly exempted).

What has been said with regard to property is applicable *mutatis mutandis* to other legal phenomena, including *jura in re aliena*, such as the servitude of watering or pasturing cattle on the land of another. They represent duties (made secure in behalf of the obligees) resting upon each and every person — including the owner of the servient property — to tolerate the corresponding actions on the part of the obligee: such as pasturing his cattle, and conversely to refrain from such use or other action as would lessen the enjoyment granted to the obligee. As distinguished from the general right of property (in the foregoing sense of a duty of tolerance and abstention) the right here involved concerns special obligations of tolerance and abstention: of tolerating specifically defined conduct on the part of the obligee. The same is true as to various monopoly rights consisting in the duties of others (made secure in behalf of subjects of the legal asset) to refrain from competing with the obligee in respect of certain actions such as the manufacture or sale of specified products. The real phenomena corresponding to these obligations-rights consist in corresponding impulsive-intellectual processes of an attributive character in the minds of the persons ascribing such obligations and rights to themselves or to others, which leads to the corresponding coördinated conduct. The monopolies themselves, however, the servitudes, and so forth, and their character of belonging to definite persons, are impulsive phantasmata — projections — and in no sense real bonds, either between individuals or between individuals and things.

Side by side with the distribution of economic goods, the imperative-attributive mentality causes citizens to be endowed with various ideal benefits (personal inviolability and honor) and civil freedoms (freedom of speech, freedom of the press, freedom of conscience, freedom of assembly and association, and so forth).

Morality, on the contrary, by reason of its very nature as purely imperative ethics, endows no one with anything: it neither makes benefits of any sort secure from anyone nor creates any character of belonging. It merely imposes obligations, whose fulfillment is recognized as depending upon the good will and the discretion of the obligor. It is a precious element of the human mentality but insofar as it is necessary for social life, and valuable in the life of the individual, to be socially endowed with the different benefits of community life (material benefits, various inviolabilities and freedoms and so forth), this is a function to be carried out by the law and by the law alone.

SECTION 16. *The Social Functions of Law.* (2) *The Organization Function*

Included in the objects with which the imperative-attributive mind endows various subjects is "authority": the endowing of individuals with authority is at the basis of every sort of social organization including the state organization. The nature of social authority and especially of state authority is debated in modern political science. The prevailing opinion construes *state authority as the single will of the state* (*regarded as a personality of a special character*) *possessing coercive and irresist-*

ible power. Some identify state authority with the will of individual rulers who have coercive force at their disposal. Others simply identify state authority with force. Insofar as they invoke the existence of a single will these doctrines are of a naive-projection (partly naïve-fantastic) character and in so far as they are concerned with force and constraint they are naive-realistic. The real phenomena they neither explain nor touch.

Like social authority in general, state authority is neither will nor force. Nor is it, in general, anything real. It is an impulsive projection: an impulsive phantasm. It signifies a particular species of rights ascribed to certain persons. Starting our analysis, for convenience, from what we know to be the projection point of view, we can say that the legal relationships we are examining consist of the obligations of some (the subjects) to fulfill certain commands — or, in general, all sorts of commands — of others (those who are endowed with power) and to tolerate certain actions — or in general all kinds of actions — on the part of the latter. Obligations possessing this content are made secure in behalf of others as their rights (claims to obedience, and legal powers to perform the corresponding actions such as the infliction of corporal punishments, rebukes and the like with regard to the subjects). To define the nature of state authority requires that various classes and varieties of these legal relationships be distinguished. First and foremost we must differentiate general authorities and special authorities.

(1) General authorities are legal relationships consisting of (a) general legal obligations of obedience (to obey commands of every sort issued by the other party — whatever their content — or to obey commands of every sort with specified exceptions); and (b) general obligations to tolerate actions (to tolerate actions of every kind — including corporal punishments which involve maiming or death — by the dominant person, or to tolerate actions of every kind with specified exceptions — such as capital punishment). General authorities are, therefore, either unlimited or limited by particular exceptions.

(2) Special authorities correspond to special obligations of some and rights of others in that they are limited to a definite field of conduct. Thus the authority of the president of a learned society, legislative assembly, meeting, and the like is a special authority since it extends only to such actions and arrangements as relate to the observance of the proper order of considering the appropriate questions (and not, for example, such as relate to the private domestic life of members of the assembly). The authorities of university, school, ecclesiastical or military superiors with regard to subordinates are also special authorities.

Authorities must be further divided into two categories: (1) ancillary or social authorities, and (2) dominant authorities.

(1) *Ancillary or social authorities are those with which are associated legal obligations to be concerned for the welfare of subjects or for the general welfare of a certain social group* (a family, *gens*, tribe and the like): these are to be effectuated within the bounds of such obligation and as a means of carrying it into effect.

(2) *Dominant authorities are those which are to be enjoyed freely on the part of the dominus or master for his own individual purposes and interests, material or otherwise*; with these are ordinarily united the obligations of the subjects to serve by rendering to the master services of every sort (a general obligation of service) or of a definite class (a special obligation of service).

As to authorities of the first class, the subject of the authority plays a subservient or ancillary part with reference to the subjects or to the social group wherein he is endowed with authority in order that he may be solicitous for the general cause. As to authorities of the second class, the opposite is true: the subject of the authority is the end or purpose, while the subordinates are the means and play a subservient or ancillary part. Authorities of the latter class include such as the authority of a master as to a slave, of a squire as to serfs, of a master as to domestic servants, and of an employer as to his hired laborers and salesmen.

Contemporary jurisprudence holds that the essence of slavery is that slaves are things like animals and not subjects of legal relationships. This is a mistaken view. Slaves are, specifically, subjects of a general duty of tolerance and obedience (and of certain other obligations as well: service, fidelity, and loyalty) with regard to their master; and the master is the subject of dominant authority and can employ the corresponding right for any personal ends whatsoever: for his economic interests, or to amuse himself or his guests. In the lower stages of culture the right of authority of the master is unlimited and includes even the right of life and death, but subsequently limitations appear and the right to impose the punishment of death comes to an end.

Dominant authority like that of a master as to a servant or of a storekeeper as to his clerks is not a general but a special authority.

Ancillary authorities include the authority of a guardian over his ward, of a nurse, or governess, of the director of an educational institution or foundling hospital and the like as to persons entrusted to their care. The right of authority of a guardian or educator exists in order that he may take care of the wards or persons being educated and has the corresponding content, so that employment of the right to command or to manage the person and property of the ward for the personal gain of the guardian or educator is not permitted by the law.

Family authority — that of a father, mother or husband — possesses an ancillary character with regard to a social group and its general welfare. The nature of family authority is unknown to modern jurisprudence: the father's authority (*patria potestas*) is currently defined as his authority over children born in wedlock and others put upon an equality therewith (adopted person, and so forth), and the definition of the husband's authority is analogous. Such definitions, however, neither clarify nor set out with exactitude anything of the substance of the matter. If jurisprudence had had at its disposal a precisely defined general concept of authority as a specific category of rights, its definitions would then have indicated at least the nearest class (the *genus proximum*) to which the concept to be explained and defined is related, and would then have suffered only from the defect (an extremely essential defect, however, from the point of view of logic) that they would not indicate the distinguishing attribute of the species (the *differentia specifica*). There is, however, no such concept in modern jurisprudence, and the words "authority" and "domination" possess in modern juridic literature a character scientifically unsettled and fluid as to scope and content alike.

The real phenomena at the foundation of the authorities belonging to various persons — that is to say, the authorities which are ascribed to them by the legal mentality — consist in impulsive-intellectual experiences of the legal type: (a) in the imperative-attributive consciousness of some that there is due to them from others (from slaves, servants, children, juniors in the *gens*, subjects, and so forth) obedience, the tolerance of directions in an imperative tone and of other influences, reprimands and other punishments, and so forth; and (b) in the imperative consciousness of others that they are bound to obey their masters, parents, or chief, and to endure — to suffer without repining — imperative directions and other influences issuing from them as actions possessing a higher sanction: as something granted to the masters, parents, and so forth with loftier authority.

These impulsions evoke corresponding coördinated (individual and mass) conduct: some command, direct common affairs, punish offenders, and so forth; others tolerate this without repining, carry out the directions of the former without demur, and so forth. Where subordinates are unwilling to submit, the tendency (characteristic of law) to compel the recalcitrant to submit, to punish for nonsubmission, and so forth operates in the minds of those who ascribe to themselves authority (the right to obedience and so forth) and in the minds of others who psychologically make common cause with them. Insofar as there are other persons subject to the authority — other members of the household, slaves, servants, and so forth — the powers of these are at the disposal of the potentate, the patriarch, the householder, the prince, and the like independently — or in place — of his own in order to overcome the recalcitrance of the refractory and unsubmissive subordinate. The more there are who ascribe to the given person — even though he be a decrepit and impotent old man — the right to obedience from them and so fulfill his orders, the greater is the collective force at the disposal of the dominant person the holder of authority and the more powerful are his commands.

Certain considerations must be borne in mind if the nature of social organizations and of the corresponding individual and mass conduct, and in particular the nature of the state, are to be made clear. In families, and *a fortiori* in tribal groups made up of numerous families under the power of a chief, and still more in state organizations, there is ordinarily not one power alone but several — there may be a great many powers and subjects endowed with powers: rights to impose commands and so forth as regards subordinates are ascribed to two, three, or more persons. In the family the obligation of obedience is ascribed to children as regards: (1) a nurse, governess, or the like; (2) the mother; and (3) the father; or even to others such as an older brother, or an aunt or a grandmother living in the family. In tribal groups there are, besides such domestic authorities, tribal authorities, the authority of a chief and so forth. In the military sphere the right to exert authority over soldiers belongs to a whole series — sometimes a very long series — of persons: various officers of the lower ranks, the colonel, the general, the commander-in-chief, the monarch, and so forth.

Endowing more than one subject with the right to exert authority over identical subordinates would, in accordance with the attributive and adversary nature of the law, lead to more or less sharp (and possibly sanguinary) conflicts if the various persons possessing that authority could issue different (perhaps diametrically opposed) commands with a like claim to require the execution thereof. Characteristically, the legal consciousness tends so to adapt the relevant convictions and the actual experiences (the consciousness of a duty of subordination and of a right to obedience) that in individual cases — in particular where the orders of various superiors are contradictory — the actual duty of obedience is acknowledged with regard to one, and not to two or more, of those who issue the commands. In precisely the same manner, the legal consciousness of those who issue the commands ordinarily eliminates the idea that substantially diverse commands of others be obeyed at the same time. Thereby conflicts are prevented.

In particular, the power of some subjects of power (in the family, the tribe or the state) normally has the character of a preferential right to command: that is to say, the corresponding legal convictions and opinions are of such content that the rights of some to command are conditioned upon there being no different orders of others, and if the various commands are in conflict only the orders of the latter are binding. Accordingly we may establish two categories of authorities: (1) those having precedence or priority, and (2) those which are subsequent or yielding. The authority of parents as regards children is thus precedent as compared with other domestic authorities over children. The authority of the husband over the wife, where such authority is inherent in the law, is precedent as compared with that of parents.

It is characteristic of many fields, where authorities over the same subordinates are distributed between various subjects, that to some of these is ascribed not only higher authority as regards others but also authority over these other subjects of authority as well as the claim that the subjects of authority subordinate to them be properly concerned about the welfare of the subordinates entrusted to their care or that the matter entrusted to them be carried on properly. Such is the relationship of the authorities possessed by nurse and parents over children, by owner and foreman over workmen, by monarch and minister, and by further authorities subordinate to the latter, by the monarch, by the commander-in-chief of the army, by his immediate subordinates to him and by theirs to them, and so forth. This relationship of authorities may be called hierarchical, and the authorities hierarchically subordinate (or lower) are to be distinguished from those hierarchically dominant (or higher). That general social authority above which there is none in the hierarchy — so that the subject of this authority is bound to be concerned about the general welfare only as regards subordinates or definite social groups — but not as regards any subject of higher authority — may be termed the *supreme social authority.*

Human societies united by one supreme social authority may be called independent social groups. These social groups are united and made cohesive not only by the corresponding imperative-attributive consciousness but also by consciousness of the duty of mutual solidarity and loyalty to the group. Thus, for any one of its members (even for the monarch or other subject of supreme authority) to join its enemies for action against the interests of the group is regarded as a most serious offense (treason). Moreover, as regards any outsider the duty is ascribed to him that he tolerate the effectuation of supreme authority and wholly refrain from interfering in the internal affairs of the group and from encroaching thereon or on the separate members thereof.

On the basis of imperative-attributive convictions and the corresponding coördinated conduct, mankind is divided into separate agglomerates: single bodies, as it were, isolated and tightly cohesive. The hierarchic distribution of authorities, headed by the subjects of supreme authority issuing general directives and having a system of hierarchically subordinate authorities executing them, evokes the idea of a complex mechanism with a single motive power, or of a complex organism "with a single will" and a system of "organs" carrying out that will. What we actually have is a special complex consisting of impulsive-intellectual experiences and individual and mass conduct which is evoked and sustained by imperative-attributive impulsions.

For a scientific study of the phenomena of social organization (a study which knows the real facts and the causal relationships) and, in particular, for the creation of a political science which shall be truly scientific, it is not enough to reason from associations of ideas: the relevant impulsive-intellectual processes and their causal attributes must be examined by means of the empirical method of observation (self-observation and the joint method of inward and outward observation, simple and experimental).

When one is concerned with independent social groups made cohesive and organized by imperative-attributive convictions of the content aforesaid, the rules for forming adequate scientific theories (and for building a political science which shall be truly scientific) require that two sub-classes or varieties be carefully distinguished. (a) Certain independent social groups do, or did formerly, consist of people united by the bonds of kinship (as well as by the foregoing legal convictions): by the corresponding legal relationships (consciousness of mutual obligations and rights) of a property nature (by obligations and rights of sustenance, inheritance, and so forth) and of a personal nature. This is so as to family groups in the narrow sense (groups of persons — relatively very few in number — united by legal relationships of marriage and by parental authority) and as to tribal groups (which do or did consist of sundry related families under the authority of a chief or patriarch — or councils of elders) insofar as these do or did (prior to the development of state organizations) have the character of independent groups not subject to any other authority whatsoever. (b) Other independent social groups are unions of persons not related by blood, to which the legal relationships of kinship are not ascribed: these groups we call states.

The psychological background of these two groups, and their social structure, differ so substantially that it is both possible and appropriate to construct special and adequate theories concerning them as a complement to the general theory of social organizations.

The prevaling view holds that possession of a definite territory is an essential element of a state. Tradition distinguishes three elements in the state: territory, population, and authority. It must, therefore, be emphasized with particular force that neither a definite territory nor a settled population is of any significance whatsoever from the point of view of the psychological theory that the state organization consists of impulsive-intellectual phenomena of the kind indicated above plus the corresponding coördinated behavior. Even nomad social groups, or groups formerly settled but later shifting to other territories under the power and leadership of their princes are to be included in the class "state" if the other attributes, indicated above, are present.

Supreme power in the state belongs (that is to say, is projected: is ascribed by the national legal mentality) to various beings. In theocratic states it belongs to the gods: here government is in fact carried on by priests or other deputies of the particular deity as hierarchically subordinate subjects of authority. In secular states it belongs to definite persons (such as monarchs) or to collective institutions (like supreme councils or to parliaments).

Besides the supreme authority in states there is a host of authorities hierarchically subordinate thereto, related *inter se* partly as further hierarchical subordinates and partly as possessing precedence without hierarchical subordination (compare the relationship of judicial and administrative authorities, and of courts having different jurisdiction).

The view prevaling in modern political science is that authority in the state is always one and single and always belongs to the state as a specific person. The monarch, the ministers, and so forth are held to be only "organs" of a single authority (of a single mighty "will" possessed by the state); their will has no authority as to citizens or as to each other. The norms of law which regulate the relationships between various "organs" of a single power are regarded as objective norms of law which endow no one with any rights of any sort. These propositions are flatly contradictory of the doctrine set out *supra* as to supreme authority belonging to the deity, the monarch, and so forth, and a host of other authorities (the right to command and so forth) belonging to diverse other persons, with mutual rights of authority and obligations of subordination as between the subjects of supreme and of subordinate authorities.

That such fundamental and striking discord could exist is explained by the error of modern political science and jurisprudence in general as to the sphere wherein the real phenomena corresponding to the theories they have constructed are found and their nature, and as to the scientific methods whereby real and factual knowledge of them may be attained, and the result is fantastic elaboration of things which do not exist and ignorance as to what actually does exist, instead of a study of the facts of the relevant sphere of mental phenomena.

If the relevant real phenomena were studied — if there were introspective analysis of the relevant imperative-attributive experiences and projections of corresponding rights — such theories would be unthinkable as denying innumerable rights of authority possessed by a host of persons in the state.

Study of the real imperative-attributive mentality which sets the state machine in motion — which evokes and directs the corresponding coördinated behavior (the oral and written imperatives issued by some and fulfilled by others, and so forth) — readily demonstrates incontrovertibly that the national legal mentality endows with rights of authority (which are not uniform in content) a host of persons in the state — not only monarchs, ministers, governors, and the like, but even district, city, or village policemen — and that these persons in exactly the same manner ascribe to themselves the corresponding rights, act under the influence of the corresponding consciousness of their rights, and are impatient if others are unwilling to submit to orders corresponding to their rights. Furthermore these same persons ascribe to themselves a duty of obedience as regards their superiors (those having corresponding rights as such superiors and standing higher on the hierarchial stairway) — for example, policemen with regard to district superintendents, bailiffs, chiefs of police, governors, and so forth — and act in conformity with this consciousness of the rights of others to issue orders to them.

To this the student of political science, firmly believing in his familiar fomulae as immutable truths, might object that, while such is the actual working of the popular mentality, this is so because it is naive and uneducated, unfamiliar with the science of constitutional law and ignorant of the fact that corresponding rights belong only to the state as a special subject with a single will. The answer, however, is that the naïveté lies in supposing that law and rights exist somewhere independently of the people's minds, and can be scientifically analyzed without studying them or knowing their intellectual and emotional content, the corresponding projection processes, the motivational action of the corresponding impulsions, and so forth.

SECTION 17. *The Relationship of State and Law. The Concept of Official Law*

State authority is social-ancillary authority — not a "will," which can do what it likes and rests on force, as modern political scientists mistakenly suppose. It is a general right, ascribed to certain persons by these persons and others, to command and otherwise to act upon subjects in order to carry out a duty to care for the general welfare.

The most important service by state authority (subjects of the corresponding obligations and rights) to the general welfare is service to the law: it is ancillary authority, above all and preëminently, with regard to rights of citizens and to the law in general. Being a phenomenon of the legal imperative-attributive mentality, the state organization develops ordinarily in conformity with the need for stable and secure effectuation of the attributive function of the system of legal norms which endow individuals and groups with certain aggregates of personal and material benefits.

Characteristic of the legal mentality, because of its attributive nature, is the tendency to obtain satisfaction for the party opposed to the obligor (using force for this purpose if necessary) and to deal retribution when the law has been violated. Hence the further necessity for a higher authority which would have at its disposal force adequate to furnish satisfaction to the subjects of rights and, eventually, to punish the lawbreaker. Such force is created and put at the service of the law by the development of the legal mentality of the social-ancillary authority. The motivational action of the legal mentality of those subordinate thereto makes it possible for the subjects of this authority to dispose of the corresponding collective force; they have the right — and are obligated in accordance with the duty of social serving — to avail of this force to defend the law against injustice. Members of the state community (citizens) are entitled as of right to have those in authority employ the authority given them by law to defend their rights against injustice. The collective force dedicated to service is thus on the side of the law and against the lawbreaker, and this very greatly strengthens the guaranty that the attributive function of law will be correctly and unswervingly effectuated: this executive function of state authority with reference to law comprises both the right and the duty to punish lawbreakers.

The attributive nature of the law makes it essential that there be courts, and that legal matters be impartially examined and the corresponding rights and obligations authoritatively established. To this demand of the legal mentality state authority ministers, meeting it in a form particularly well developed and suitable. It provides citizens — as it is bound to do — not only with force for the defense of their rights but also with "justice according to law" which is regulated and standardized by law: the impartial investigation and authoritative decision of the relevant problems. This does not require voluntary assent to the judicial examination by both sides: it is enough if this is demanded by one side. Here the application of constraint (for fulfillment) or of repression (like the punishment of a lawbreaker) is subsequent to an examination of the facts of the matter in court by the subject of general supreme authority (prince or king, or specific persons or institutions endowed with corresponding special rights and obligations).

This in turn further promotes the correct and unswerving effectuation of the attributive function of law. With the obligation to furnish to citizens justice according to law is combined the obligation of state authority to defend them from the arbitrary application to them of constraint and repression by others without regard to the form therefore established, from persons who — having been injured — would take the law into their own hands, and so forth. Citizens have a right not to be subjected to violence from other citizens, and to have constraint and other repressions applied to them only by persons duly representing state authority and in cases defined by law, and usually only after the matter has been judicially investigated.

This is extremely important and valuable from the point of view of social peace and order, and of the guaranty to each citizen of a sphere of personal inviolability, freedom and other rights granted to him by law. Its beneficial consequences are enjoyed not only by peaceful citizens who have committed no violation of the law, but also by criminals: the latter are punished only as provided by law for action of the type specified and pursuant to a court order issued after an impartial investigation of the matter. Beyond this measure of punishment they suffer no violence, while their other rights — unaffected by the punishment which the law provides — are protected by authority. On the other hand, it is oustide the bounds of moderation and propriety for one who has suffered and his friends — or for the mob — to deal with the criminal.

Finally, the organization of authority contributes also to greater satisfaction of the need to develop uniform and precisely defined legal patterns and to effectuate the unifying tendency which is connected, as explained *supra*, with the attributive nature of law. The satisfaction of this need and, in general, the improvement of law is subserved by the legislative function of state authority, which creates positive legal standards (for areas and problems for which such did not exist formerly), and defines what positive law should be applied in what fields.

The foregoing ancillary or service functions and obligations of state authority with reference to law do not and can not extend to all the spheres where the legal mentality of citizens exists and acts. To set in motion the mechanism of courts and the executive authority entails a more or less serious expenditure of social energy and is inapplicable to petty legal questions without serious social significance or not requiring official intervention. In certain areas where the legal mentality acts — in intimate life, the various mutual rights and obligations based on love, and the like — official interference by the representatives of authority and crude measures of constraint are inappropriate and inadmissible. Again, while scientific, artistic, and other oral and printed criticism — and in general the appraisal of the merits, character, and conduct of others — is regulated by the legal mentality, which indicates what is here due and to whom, conduct which puts no biting affront upon another's honor and does not constitute defamation or the like, is free, and official regulation or other official interference is inadmissible.

As the state authority and organization develops, a progressive differentiation of law within the state takes place, whereby it is divided into two categories: (1) that which is to be applied and sustained by representatives of the state authority in accordance with their duty to serve society; and (2) that which does not possess this significance in the state. Law of the former class we will term *official law*, and that of the latter class *unofficial law*.

It is manifest from the foregoing that official law is not only privileged law in the state but is at the same time better adapted to satisfy the demands of the attributive nature of law. In this sense it is law of a higher sort than unofficial law.

The foregoing division of law into two categories, and the development of official law with its superior advantages, do not exist in the area of the legal relations between states ("international law") which defines the mutual rights and obligations as between states that are independent social organizations. But there is no superior authority above the states. There is no common legislative power which can issue laws binding on them, classify the corresponding law according to importance and its cultural character, and so forth and define what law should be of decisive significance in what cases. Nor is there a common executive authority, which could provide the law with superior force against injustice and prevent the assumption by states of a right to resort to violence, to take the law into their own hands, to reach decisions by the spilling of blood in wars, and so forth. International law consequently lacks the valuable advantages of official law pointed out *supra*: it is law of a lower character than official law.

SECTION 18. *The Nature and Social Function of Jurisprudence*

Emanating from the attributive nature of law is the social necessity for the establishment of legal norms uniformly patterned for all persons and independent of the diversity of the subjective legal views of individuals. The content of these norms must be defined with the utmost possible precision. The norms must themselves subserve the goal of unifying legal relationships. To aid in the realization of these aims, a special class of persons — learned jurists — devote their activities: their scientific and practical activity is called jurisprudence.

Jurisprudence is a very old science whose existence and development characteristically accompany legal life even in the stages of cultural development which preceded the appearance and development of scientific (theoretical) knowledge and investigation. When modern scholars think of the origin of jurisprudence and the time of its appearance, they have particularly in mind the jurisprudence of ancient Rome. In reality, however, jurisprudence existed and flournished at a far earlier time — specifically in the nations of the ancient East (Assyria and Egypt) and among the ancient Hebrews on the basis of a law which possessed a religious and ritualistic character.

At the present time it occupies a peculiar and exceptional position among European sciences as a strikingly hypertrophied branch of knowledge in comparison with the evolution of science in general, and of the science of morality in particular. Special departments in universities are devoted to the advancement of legal knowledge whereas they commonly have no professorships for the science of morality. This anomaly should, in the interest of sicence, be set right. As a historical phenomenon, however, the difference in the position occupied by the sciences of law and morality respectively, and in general the earlier broad development of a special science and a learned profession in the field of law, is a characteristic phenomenon requiring scientific explanation from the point of view of the specific nature of law.

Even more striking — and more imperatively calling for explanation — are the particular character, methods, and direction of the intellectual labor of jurisprudence, although the learned jurists themselves — their attention dulled by a habit of thinking — usually find nothing that is remarkable or that demands explanation.

The causal explanation of these phenomena, and in general of jurisprudence — its nature, its social function, its content and methods of work, and the specific distinctions making it different in these and other respects from the science of morality and so forth — must be sought in the specific, imperative-attributive nature of law and the social need for, and tendency to, unification therewith associated: the necessity for full development of well-established patterns of legal propositions, uniform for all and independent of the diversity of individual opinions, with the utmost precision as to the content and scope of the ideas and concepts. With this necessity the development of definite legal customs, and the positivization of law in general, correspond, as we have seen. Official law is the higher, more complete and perfect form of satisfying the same need and other social needs which are associated with the attributive nature of law.

However, positive law, as it existed prior to the development of the authority and organization of the state (and now exists only in the international field) cannot, even in conjunction with official law (in the amplified form of legislation), satisfy the demand that legal relationships be unified in such full form that all possible legal questions be anticipated and predetermined with due precision and definiteness, and that ideas and concepts entering into the structure of legal propositions have a compass so precisely defined as to exclude doubts of every sort regarding the limits of their application in the various and infinitely diverse cases and combinations of actual life. Always and inevitably a host of problems not immediately anticipated, and capable of stimulating quarrels, remains. Statutes always contain numerous words borrowed from everyday speech and corresponding to ideas of a content not precisely established: obscurities, contradictions, and other shortcomings which may excite quarrels, conflicts, arbitrary action, the necessity for the weak and dependent to yield to the divergent opinions of those on whom they depend, and other social evils incidental to the inadequate unification of legal relationships, are inevitable. Jurisprudence is, therefore, an intellectual activity and technique directed at the development of positive — and especially of official — law in the direction of unification. Its essence and meaning, as such special activity and technique, are so to fashion legal opinions concerning positive law that a system of propositions would emerge which would (in a form more complete and perfect than law itself) satisfy the need to bring legal relationships into unity and to make them objectively definite and incontestable.

This is manifest from the content of the intellectual work and the achievements of jurisprudence. Activity in this field is ordinarily held to include (1) criticism, (2) interpretation, and (3) the scientific arrangement of law (eliciting the general principles of law from concrete material, and reducing these principles to a single system).

(1) Criticism in legal science ordinarily means the establishment of the authentic text of legislative norms. From the viewpoint of the psychological theory of law, which distinguishes in principle between norms of law, on the one hand, and legislative expressions and other normative facts on the other, criticism is directed at establishing — incontrovertibly and beyond doubt — the existence and composition of the normative facts of positive law as objective data and patterns for eliciting positive, heteronomous decisions of legal problems.

The unification of normative facts is one of the main objectives of criticism. The development of the positive law is itself calculated to bring about the utmost unification of normative facts. Legislation in particular, and especially recent legislation, seeks to anticipate the various possibilities of doubt as to what normative facts should possess decisive significance in what cases, and to establish rules of decision in this regard. The function of jurisprudence is to fill in the relevant gaps and to find solutions for problems left unresolved in the statutes — in general, to amplify and perfect what the corresponding unifying tendency of positive-official law has produced.

(2) A further stage of work in jurisprudence is interpretation, whose aim is usually defined as the explanation of the meaning of legal norms. Certain considerations must be borne in mind in order to maintain an attitude at once consciously scientific as regards interpretation and critical with reference to what juridic literature ordinarily has to say about it.

(a) Modern jurisprudence fails to discriminate between norms of law on the one hand and legislative expressions (normative facts) on the other, and so purports to be interpreting norms of law whereas it is actually normative facts (including legislative expressions) that are the objects of interpretation.

(b) From one normative fact, whether taken by itself or along with others, a multitude of different legal norms can be deduced. Thus, from the legislative statement that one who has committed larceny is subjected to such and such punishment, the following deductions may be made: (1) that all persons are bound, with regard to owners, to refrain from corresponding encroachments: that owners have a right to corresponding abstention on the part of others; (2) that one who has committed larceny is bound to tolerate the corresponding punishment: that the subject of punitive authority has the right to punish; (3) that a judge is obligated to the state to condemn the thief to the corresponding punishment; (4) that the public prosecutor is obligated to charge the person who has committed larceny and to obtain his punishment; and (5) that the police are bound to conduct investigations, make arrests, and so forth.

(c) What jurists call interpretation therefore embraces not only interpretation, in the sense of the elucidation of the thought expressed in a legislative enactment, but also innumerable other intellectual maneuvers designed to produce special juridic judgments or (from the projection point of view) norms to subserve the need that norms and legal relationships be unified: that a single system of juridic concepts be worked out, as complete as possible, and with corresponding concepts whose content and scope are precisely fixed. Such at least is the general tendency of the traditional works and of the methods (or habits) historically employed in producing them.

(3) The activity, or stage of activity, of jurisprudence usually called the scientific study of law in the narrow sense, consists in bringing the content of law into a scientific system. Here two species are to be distinguished.

(a) Generalization: the creation (on the basis of the special concepts and propositions of law) of more abstract and general concepts and propositions, and bringing these into systematic order.

(b) Deduction from these of additional propositions and the fashioning thereby of decisions for various problems neither directly contemplated by statutes nor predetermined in general by normative facts.

Each of these processes alike — the logical movement upwards (the creation of higher and more general concepts and propositions) and the logical movement downwards (the deduction of particular and special propositions and conclusions) — means unification, directed at the scientific and authoritative predetermination of possible doubts and disputes, and the elimination of that which is arbitrary.

(4) If for any problem these operations fail to furnish an objective decision, based on a positive pattern, statutes, or other normative facts, the final means of unification is the application of analogy, so-called. Analogy — "interpretation by analogy," although it is not interpretation — is the decision of legal problems (not anticipated by statutes

or other normative facts, and impossible of solution by the general legal principles accumulated by jurisprudence) through the application of statutes or general principles which contemplate cases most nearly resembling in nature those to be decided (*similia*). Analogy is one of the most characteristic indicia of what jurisprudence means, and of the unifying tendency of law in general. It signifies an eagerness to find an objective decision, independent of the diversity of individual opinions.

The foregoing represents, in general, the fundamental propositions of the theory not only of jurisprudence (the fashioning of law by learned jurists as such) but also of the practical application of positive law to individual cases which actually arise: "practice," so-called, and in particular, practice in the courts and before administrative tribunals, and the practice of international law. While the chief concern of the former is not with the concrete rights and obligations of specific parties, but with general categories thereof (the making and preparation of decisions for indefinite and innumerable concrete questions in the future), practice deals with concrete cases and specific parties, and is occupied with the examination of more general questions only to the extent that this is essential for the solution of individual problems. To the extent that science has already decided the corresponding more general problems, the task of practice is lighter and more simple: merely to bring an actual case within the corresponding general proposition so as to infer deductively the concrete decision which is sought.

To suppose, however, that the social significance of jurisprudence is nothing more than that it facilitates and shortens the work of practice would be a grave error. There is something else immeasurably more important and valuable. In the field of concrete legal problems as to property rights and obligations as between private persons, or as between private persons and the treasury, and the like, or various other rights and obligations between adversary parties — as between the administration or representatives of authority, on the one hand, and individual citizens and the like, on the other — more or less important financial, political, and other interests are sometimes affected. Conflicts, more or less serious (war, in the international field), threaten where doubts and discord obtain. To the extent that the position of the parties is unequal — as in the relations of weak states with powerful, or of citizens and others subject with authorities, or of workmen, servants, and others with employers, masters, and so forth — one of the parties must, in case of disagreement, yield. The result is a social evil, since the interests of the weak are suppressed in favor of the strong; while insofar as the matter gets into court or comes up to be decided by the authorities, the corresponding interests may exert pressure and influence on the decisions, where different views are possible. In such cases works in the field of jurisprudence may forestall and eliminate these social evils. The system of legal propositions worked out by jurisprudence through its authoritatively scientific, impartially objective work (which has no regard for individuals or their financial, political or other interests and desires) reduces to a minimum the scope for various individual opinions and conflicts, tendentious interpretations, and arbitrary actions which trample on the interests of the weak. This is the justification and the lofty mission of dogmatic jurisprudence.

In the field of moral (purely imperative) ethics, social life needs no such labors as are accomplished by jurisprudence in the province of law: morality can in general get along without unification, and without a pattern precisely and uniformly established. Accordingly, the science of morality emerges relatively late — chiefly under the influence of the awakening of philosophic thought — and possesses a character completely different from that of jurisprudence. It even manifests tendencies which are to some extent directly opposed to those of jurisprudence. For example, in place of the tendency in legal science toward the precise establishment of the scope of the ideas, the opposite tendency — of attributing to terms an indefinitely (sometimes infinitely) elastic meaning — operates among moralists: even such terms as murder, adultery, larceny, and the like, which in ordinary language signify relatively definite classes of phenomena (and in the workshop of jurisprudence have a meaning defined with absolute precision and more narrowly) appear infinitely elastic in the moralists: one who feeds his servants badly, or does not provide healthy quarters for them, or is — in general — not concerned about their health is a murderer, as is even one who leads others into temptation or brings up children badly (spiritual murder) and so forth. Thoughts or looks are enough to constitute adultery. One who by any means whatsoever makes a profit at the expense of his neighbor is a robber. In place of marking off the spheres where norms apply, in order to avoid their collision, moralists so stretch the meaning of particular norms that the fields of action of various norms are confused and — to a significant degree coincide — with each other.

Jurisprudence resembles mathematics in that the scope of its concepts is fixed precisely. Its thinking follows the strict methods of deductive logic and its propositions can be proven conclusively, whereas moral science has the most inexact and beclouded character to be found among sciences, and presents the sharpest contrast to mathematics and jurisprudence.

SECTION 19. *The Nature of Law in the Juridic Sense*

The class, and the class concept, of law which we have formed are directed at the cognition and explanation of real phenomena, and not at the definition of what jurists have been accustomed to call law. This same class concept, however, in connection with further theories logically and causally bound up with it and with the further subdivisions of the class into (1) intuitive and positive law, and (2) official and unofficial law, *enables us to determine what law is as the term is used by jurists*: "law in the juridic sense." This problem jurists have tried and are still trying — without success — to solve when they seek a definition of their concept of law.[1]

To solve this question, and to explain at the same time the special characteristics of juridic terminology, we must keep different fields of law distinct. (1) *International Relations*. Here the unifying legal pattern is the corresponding positive law (founded chiefly on international legal customs and compacts). Conformably with its general social function, jurisprudence fashions this (positive) law in the direction of extending and perfecting the unification; but only the system of legal propositions founded on relevant normative facts is acknowledged by jurisprudence as a binding system of international law ("international law" simply): any individual opinions differing in content from the positive propositions and, in general, not based on the relevant normative facts, the science of international law ignores or rejects as devoid of juridic significance and unrelated to law (that is to say, to the legal pattern worked out by its science). If and insofar as any state were unwilling to acknowledge and to observe a rule established by international law, opposing thereto its own differing legal (intuitive-law) conviction, jurists would say that the views of this participant in international relationships, and its refusal to acknowledge that rule, are contradictory to international law and have no juridic significance. (2) *Intra-state Law*. It has already been demonstrated that positive law in our sense is here divided into two classes: (a) positive law *simpliciter*, and (b) official law, which is of decisive significance where there are conflicts, and in general possesses various advantages over other law (particularly as it represents a higher degree of the unifying systematization of law and of objective definiteness). Here jurisprudence, in conformity with its nature and social function, acts to unify official law. Only the system of law fashioned by jurisprudence is acknowledged as law by

[1] Cf. Section 1.

jurists, or by legislators, judges, or other representatives of state power: they reject the idea that obligation and legal significance attach either to the intuitive-law views (in our sense) held by citizens or to positive-law propositions (in our sense) such as those resting on customs which prevail in particular social spheres but are unrelated to a single, official pattern. Thus the rights in the field of sports — including the right of a winning partner to obtain what he has won, the right of the honored guest to first place at the table when younger company is present, the mutual rights of ladies and their escorts based on the customs of the dance, the obligation (legal in our sense) of a young child to give the quantity of nuts promised by him to another child of the same age in return for the plaything which he has received, and the like — are acknowledged neither by state judges nor by the learned jurists as rights and obligations. As to the examples cited, judges, attorneys, and jurists would agree that "contracts of minors have no legal significance, and give rise to no rights or obligations"; the assignment of places at the table, the rules of play, dance, and the like, are not touched by the law at all; this is a province not of law but of nonobligatory social customs, *mores*, social decorum, and the like. Law in the sense of jurists' terminology is accordingly *official positive law within the state, and positive international law without qualification.*

Starting, as does modern legal science, from the concept of norms we may say that *legal norms* in the sense of jurists' terminology *are positive imperative-attributive norms — in the international field without qualification, and in intra-state life insofar as they have an official character.*

Clarification of the nature of law in the juridic sense is important and valuable for jurisprudence for the legal practice within a state and in international law. This obviates the strange abnormality that modern jurisprudence and practice are ignorant of the nature of that with which they are concerned, the boundaries of their field of study and activity (and its relationship to contiguous fields), and the *indicia* denoting whether or not anything ought to be referred to that field, and are consequently unable consciously and reliably to solve the corresponding problems arising in concrete cases. The traditions and habits of calling certain phenomena law, and other phenomena not law are far from always being reliable guides, especially as regards problems of international or state law where firm habits of nomenclature have not yet been formed, as, for example, in the field of newly arising phenomena and problems of law.

The absence of higher concepts entails upon the disciplines under consideration the disastrous consequence that all their other concepts (absolutely and relatively subordinate concepts) comprise an unknown and unreliable quantity. The concepts which we have established herein enable jurisprudence to overcome this defect and the further vices therewith associated. Moreover, the science and practice of international law on the one hand, and the science and practice of intra-state law on the other, can select as their superior and central classes and class concepts two different sub-classes and two different subordinate concepts of the general theory of law which is being set out. Specifically, inasmuch as international law is a science of the corresponding branch of positive law without qualification, and the jurisprudence of internal law is the science of official (and not simply of positive) law, so for the former the superior concept and basis for the scientific formation of all further concepts is the class concept of positive law (in our sense), and for the latter is the concept of official positive law.

SECTION 20. *Law in the Juridic Sense and the Scientific Theory of Law*

The foregoing propositions as to the nature of law in the juridic sense have special reference to dogmatic jurisprudence and the corresponding practice. As a practical discipline which studies and determines the sort of conduct obligatory in accordance with the international positive law existing at a given time and with the official law of a given state, dogmatic jurisprudence must be scrupulously differentiated from theoretical science: the theory of law which studies the general nature and the specific attributes and tendencies which are common to law of every kind wherever and whenever it can be observed — a science of law as a particular class of psychic phenomena without reference to the actual and specific content, place, or time.

It would be unscientific to choose law *in the juridic sense* as their object of study, for the building of *this science* as modern scholars do (although they have no definition of that regarding which they construct their theories), even if the nature of this law were clarified: or, rather, if the nature of law in the juridic sense were clarified, this would make it specifically clear that the relevant group of phenomena is unsuitable for the construction of any scientific theory whatsoever.

It has been demonstrated [1] that to build a scientific theory, and to gain a proper knowledge of phenomena and to set out an appropriate causal explanation of them, requires the formulation of classes as to

[1] Cf. Section 4.

which adequate theories may be established: that is to say, propositions in which what is asserted (with the basis thereof) is true with reference to an entire class and not to some part thereof only (in which case the theory "jumps"), as well as special with regard to the given class (and not of any more general class: in which event the theory "limps").

Not only is law in the juridic sense — those phenomena (positive international law plus official, positive intra-state law) to which jurists usually apply the word law — a class unsuitable for the formation of adequate theories, it does not in general even constitute a class (that is to say, something at once homogeneous within itself and distinct from everything else). It is a heterogeneous and eclectic group of phenomena — the sum of various elements of a broader class (law in the sense of imperative-attributive experiences in general). It has been shown that in their professional terminology specialists are prone to unify under a general term heterogeneous groups of phenomena not uniquely alike in their nature because, in the field of their special practice, these phenomena tend to provoke conduct which is identical. This use of words according to professional practice leads to a concept of law corresponding to that held by professional jurists. It is no more possible to build scientific theory as to a corresponding eclectic group than to fashion one as to "greens," "vegetables," "game," and the like as a cook uses those words. Actually, everything that characterizes all the elements making up law in the juridic sense inevitably characterizes as well much that is homogeneous with what is in that group but is not found there. Positive law without qualification is included in the group insofar as it is a matter of international relations, and outside its boundaries insofar as other classes and fields of relationships are concerned. In these other areas, jurists no longer deign to give the name "law" to that which does not enjoy official acknowledgment and protection, although they call it law in the international field. Consequently every theoretical proposition which is true (and does not suffer from the vice of "jumping") with reference to all law in the juridic sense must inevitably suffer from the vice of "limping," since it refers not to a proper and adequate class, but only to a part of it (like the proposition that old people need nourishment).

Common, therefore, to both elements of "law in the juridic sense" (international positive law and official law) is the imperative-attributive nature of each and that which is logically or causally connected therewith. Also common to both constituent parts of "juridic law" is the character of being positive (the citation of objective normative facts and that which is connected therewith). But the corresponding propositions, referred specially to law in the juridic sense, would be "limping" theories: misdirected expressions which cover only a part of that to which they should be referred. Actually they do not represent anything which is specific for law in the juridic sense, but are truths as to far broader groups of phenomena (as to all law — or all positive law — in our sense).

The foregoing exposition of the theory of law as imperative-attributive experiences has demonstrated that it is the attributive nature of law which specifically and uniquely characterizes this branch of human ethics and that the corresponding class concept is a valuable basis for the cognition and explanation of phenomena, the ascertainment of their causal relations, and in general the formation of scientific and adequate theories. All the relevant propositions, however — past, present, and to come — would be unscientific and misshapen ("limping") theories if they were referred specifically to law in the juridic sense. Their character would be less grotesque if they were referred to all positive law in our sense, but this, too, would leave them substantially worse off inasmuch as they have a far broader application — and correspondingly greater scientific value — since they are in reality related not only to positive law but to intuitive law as well: and even if they were specially related to positive law — a far broader field of phenomena than law in the juridic sense — they would still be malformed ("limping") theories.

The specific attributes, which are foreign to what is found beyond the boundaries of the eclectic "law in the juridic sense," are the special properties of official law, and the corresponding propositions would therefore be free from the fault of "limping," but — being referred to law in the juridic sense — would inevitably suffer from the other scientific fault of "jumping" since official acknowledgment by authorities and what is connected therewith characterizes only a part of law in the juridic sense: it does not characterize international law.

Modern legal theorists, then, neither know nor suspect the true nature of the group of phenomena which they have been accustomed to call law, and refer everything else to what is not law (*mores,* morality, religion, and so forth). Striving to construct a theory of law in the juridic sense, they find themselves in the tragic position that in avoiding the Scylla of having their propositions "limp" they must inevitably come to grief on Charybdis: the opposite fault of having their propositions "jump" and vice versa. It can be asserted *a priori* — and without any particular examination of that which jurists have hitherto succeeded in finding and establishing as to law in their sense — that all they have done is of no avail: at best (that is, even if they are not completely false) their theories (and all possible theories of the same kind) must and will suffer from one of two scientific faults. Either they "limp" or they "jump."

Contemporary jurisprudence is in fact chiefly and preëminently official-law jurisprudence, worked out and nurtured on the basis of studying and applying official law: even when it is not shaded out and altogether lost from view, international law plays no great part in the occupations and ideas of most jurists. Their current ideas and opinions as to law, norms of law, obligations, rights, and so forth accordingly correspond to the nature of official law. Ideas of standardization by the state and by the authorities, of organized defense on the part of the judicial and executive powers, and of organized constraint, and so forth, are firmly associated with the idea of law. The typical and predominant fault of their opinions and ideas is therefore that of "jumping": all the corresponding propositions collapse if we take into account the different nature of international law and the absence there of the foregoing attributes which are mistakenly ascribed to law in general.

In building a scientific theory of law, the first and fundamental task is to form the corresponding concept: law. Jurists "seeking a definition for their concept of law" hold fast to their terminology in the province of legal theory, and understand the corresponding problem as the search for general and differentiating attributes of all that is law (that is to say, of that which they are accustomed to call law). There are and can be no such attributes. Consequently it is perfectly natural that the definition of the concept of law in modern jurisprudence represents an object which is still being sought notwithstanding the vast amount of labor and wit spent thereon.

What has been said as to the Scylla and Charybdis of "limping" and "jumping" refers to all conceivable attempts to define law in the juridic sense — that is say, to search out general and distinguishing attributes for the objects of the relevant eclectic group: (1) Definitions which would help to distinguish law from that which is not law in the sense of jurists in the field of internal state life — that is to say, definitions which would correspond with official law as distinguished from positive law — must inevitably suffer from the fault of "jumping" since they do not correspond with the nature of international law, where there is neither higher authority nor the characteristics of official law imposed by authority. (2) Definitions which would correspond with the nature of international law — which would be definitions of positive law without qualification — must inevitably suffer from the fault of "limping"; the corresponding attributes are characteristic as well of much which is not related to law in the juridic sense, and leave it impossible to distinguish law from what is not law in the juridic sense in the internal legal life in the state.

CHAPTER IV

THE LEGAL NORMS

SECTION 21. *The Elements of Law*

Knowledge of the nature of complex objects or phenomena presupposes knowledge of their content: of their constituent elements. Accordingly, when defining the nature of ethical phenomena, as a general class embracing law and morality, we pointed out the general elements of these phenomena: (1) ethical impulsions; (2) ideas (a) of objects of obligations, (b) of subjects of obligations, (c) of relevant facts, and (d) of normative facts. Then, when forming concepts of morality and law by dividing ethical phenomena into two varieties, we pointed out the elements of experiences of each of the two species, and the specific differences of the impulsive and intellectual content of law and morality. It was demonstrated (1) that the fundamental distinction between morality and law lies in the difference of the corresponding impulsions which have a purely imperative character in morality and an imperative-attributive character in law; and (2) that a difference of intellectual content corresponds to this distinction; where the legal mentality is concerned, the intellectual content is more complex and possesses a dual character: equally with ideas of subjects of obligations, there are ideas of subjects of rights, and equally with ideas of objects of obligations there are ideas of objects of rights.

At the present time there is no theory — either in legal or in moral science — concerning the elements of ethical phenomena in general, and of moral and legal phenomena in particular. No such theory could emerge, if only because of the complete lack of knowledge of the existence of impulsions as a special class of psychic phenomena, their attributes, and the methods whereby they might be discovered and comprehended.

There is, however, in legal science something to a certain degree corresponding with and parallel to the doctrine concerning the elements of law: the doctrine of "law in the objective sense" (norms of law and their elements, hypotheses and dispositions) and of "law in the subjective sense" (legal relationships and their elements: obligations and rights, and the subjects and objects thereof).

The chief difference is that whereas the doctrine as to the elements of legal phenomena which has been advanced above touches the real elements of legal phenomena, the prevailing doctrine starts from a projection point of view and so conceives the elements to be found dispersed in space in a world external as regards persons experiencing legal phenomena, and not where they actually are (that is in the consciousness of the person experiencing the legal phenomena and the corresponding projections).

There is as yet no developed theory whatsoever as to elements of morality, so that in this regard moral science lags behind jurisprudence. This is associated with the fact that, in accordance with the imperative-attributive nature of law and the unifying tendency bound up therewith, jurisprudence leans toward clear and exact differentiations and delimitations, and so toward breaking up complex entities into clearly distinguished and defined elements. This tendency is alien to moralists and, since unrestrained elasticity of ideas is appropriate in morality, misty and indefinitely expansive ideas and judgments are customary and typical.

SECTION 22. *The Nature and Functions of Legal Norms*

Law in the objective sense (objective law) is ordinarily defined as the totality or aggregate of norms of law. The aggregates of norms of law which regulate a certain special kind of relationships are called legal institutions — such as that of marriage, of property, of paternal authority, and the like. The totality of the institutions relating to a broad field of relationships, or embracing all the (official) law of a given nation or (positive) international law, is called a system of the corresponding law — such as the system of civil law, the system of criminal law, the system of Russian law, or the system of international law.

The concept and expression "norm" is found in various sciences — and not only in that of law and that of morality — in the sense of rules of conduct in general, such as technical rules, rules of hygiene and the like, rules of opportunism, and rules of expediency. It is ordinarily assumed that all rules of conduct are rules of expediency, and definitions of norms as rules of conduct are accordingly amplified sometimes by pointing out that they are conditioned by this or that purpose or have in view a definite goal.

Norms or "imperatives" in the field of law (and "social" norms in general, to which norms of morality and *mores,* as well as norms of law, are ordinarily held referable) mean, according to the prevailing view, those rules of conduct which are "expressions of the will of some with respect to others," or simply "commands." These norms or commands are divided into positive (orders or commands — in the narrow sense — to accomplish something, and demands of positive acts) and negative (prohibitions, demands of abstention from certain actions). Whether or not all law in the objective sense can be reduced to commands and prohibitions is a matter of controversy in legal science, some asserting that there are other classes of legal norms on the same plane as commands and prohibitions (or, if norms are to include only commands and prohibitions, other classes of legal propositions): negative, definitive (or explicative), and permissive norms.

The existing doctrine of legal norms rests on substantial misconceptions. This is due primarily to a failure to distinguish between norms on the one hand and the normative facts of positive law on the other. Precisely because normative facts are confused with norms, the very concept of normative facts does not exist in modern legal science. In statutory positive law various commands, prohibitions, and other expressions of the species indicated above do in fact exist, but these are not norms of law: they are only normative facts, whereby the corresponding legal opinions of persons and the relevant projections (including norms) are defined and to which which are referred.

Jurists could readily be convinced that these facts, on the one hand, and norms, on the other, differ in principle and are completely heterogeneous, even though they know neither of intuitive law (where in general there are neither commands emanating from authorities nor normative facts of any kind) nor of various other species of positive law (where it is not commands and so forth, but facts of a wholly different sort, that constitute normative facts). They need only to turn their attention to the point that commands, prohibitions, and so forth are actions — human behavior — of a particular type: actions of monarchs, of members of the legislature, and so forth. These phenomena pass swiftly and disappear, ceasing to exist the moment the corresponding words are spoken (in the field of oral legislation, oral commands of absolute monarchs, oral enactments of the national assembly, and the like) or the corresponding document signed. On the other hand norms, which are studied by these very jurists despite their failure to distinguish between the concept of norms and the concept of commands, appear as existing continuously or over a prolonged period. The legislative commands of deceased legislators are thus bygone events which have passed into the annals of history, yet jurists speak of the corresponding norms as if they actually continued to exist. It is true that when legislation is in written form, the relevant actions may still be traced in the shape of the corresponding document, but jurists are not so naive as to take these documents — that is to say, the leaves of paper with spots of ink, or these spots of ink on the paper — for norms of law: the documents and the characters merely evidence (in the form of symbolic signs) bygone actions of monarchs or other legislators.

We have already pointed out that on the basis of one legislative pronouncement (taken separately or in connection with others) in legal life — and in particular in jurisprudence — a multitude of legal judgments may be expressed, and the existence of a host of legal norms of the most diverse content may be asserted. Thus, from the legislative pronouncement defining punishment for a certain crime (mistakenly taken to be a norm commanding the court to punish the criminal accordingly) sundry binding norms and obligations are deduced, for criminals as well as for the administration, the police, examining magistrates, state attorneys, and so forth. Conversely, from two or more legislative pronouncements in their entirety, the legal consciousness sometimes deduces a single norm: thus a whole line of legislative pronouncements contains a description of the form of a contract and enumerates other facts which must be present in order for a certain person to acquire a certain right with regard to another (relevant facts). The result is one norm for the conduct of the corresponding persons provided all the requisites indicated in a number of paragraphs of the legislative code are satisfied. If a statute notes that such and such earlier or other paragraphs thereof extend also to other cases or other categories of persons and so forth (or the contrary), this is a normative fact: a basis for denying the existence of a host of norms which would be asserted on the basis of other paragraphs if it were not mentioned that they did not so extend (as a basis for reducing the number of norms) or conversely for producing a host of new norms.

Normative facts in the field of statute law play the part not only of facts which create positive norms (evoke the corresponding legal judgments and projections in the human mind) but also of facts which eradicate norms from the minds of the persons concerned (nullify the corresponding legal experiences and projections). The legislative declaration as to the abrogation of slavery, serfdom, imprisonment for debt, torture, corporal punishment, the death penalty, and so forth are normative facts: legislative acts of vast and mighty importance as facts which eradicate from the law a host of legal convictions, opinions and the corresponding projections (norms) which were formerly present.

The current doctrine concerning norms fails to distinguish between legislative enactments and norms, and represents abrogative or negative norms as not independent, not important, and the like. Here are at least two serious misconceptions. Actually, imperative and negative "norms" — and in particular abrogative statutes — are alike normative facts and not norms at all. As normative facts, however, negative — and in particular abrogative — legislative pronouncements are acts possessing independent significance (sometimes of the utmost importance), productive of radical revolutions in the law (revolutions in the national mind as to matters of principle) and putting an end to whole systems of legal convictions which defined the earlier social order.

Normative facts that do not create but abrogate "norms" (eliminating earlier legal convictions, opinions, and the corresponding projections from law) may be termed "norm-abrogating" or "negative" normative facts, as distinguished from those operating on the legal mind in the opposite direction ("norm-creating" or "positive" normative facts). Having done their work and purified the legal mentality from the corresponding legal convictions, many norm-abrogating facts lose all legal significance thereupon (reference may be made to the right of blood vengeance and torture, and a squire's rights in peasants), so that when the laws in force are collected there is no reason to mention them (as is the case with regard to a host of statutes such as those relative to the law of serfdom, the burning of heretics and witches, and the like). Most of the norm-creating statutes are at the same time norm-abrogating as well: when they create new norms they thereby eliminate earlier norms regulating the same fields of conduct.

In addition to norm-creating and norm-abrogating facts, we might distinguish, as a further category, norm-modifying facts: those which change the law; yet since the change is to add or create, to eliminate, or to unite, all normative facts may be reduced to two categories: positive and negative, as the simplest elements. All the phenomena, now mistakenly held to be different species of norms — imperative, prohibitive, negative, abrogative, explicative, and so forth — come down to these two categories of normative facts. But it must be borne in mind that imperative, prohibitive, explicative pronouncements do not in fact exist either in the intuitive law, or in other species of positive law where the normative facts are completely different: with various sorts of these we shall become acquainted in detail in the doctrine as to positive law and its various kinds. Even modern jurisprudence uniformly admits the existence of customary law although it comprises no commands or orders, no definitions of concepts, and no declarations of abrogation. Here the actions of others — the conduct of our forebears: "our fathers acted so," and the like — rather than imperative, explicative, abrogative, and similar pronouncements of anyone, act as normative facts.

The nature and the specific attributes of norms of law — as well as of moral norms, aesthetic norms, and so forth — can in general be known and correctly defined only on the basis of familiarity with the relevant impulsions and their properties, and in particular with their capacity to produce phantasmata of a particular class: impulsive projections. Like all other norms, legal norms are impulsive phantasmata. In conformity with the peculiar authoritative-mystic character of ethical impulsions and their likeness (as regards the nature of their inner pressure) to the impulsions evoked in us by commands and prohibitions, the idea — based on corresponding experiences — emerges that certain higher "commands" and "prohibitions" are present and exert pressure over people and over other beings (including deities). In reality we have only specified impulsive-intellectual processes. Pursuing the corresponding naive-projection point of view, philosophers, moralists, and jurists call norms commands and prohibitions, and seek or devise — and fantastically construct — realities in accordance with these confused ideas. Jurists have succeeded in finding in statute law what they deem a suitable reality of imperative-attributive experiences, related to the orders of monarchs and the like. In customary law there is no such reality, but its absence was rendered innocuous by the formulation of a supposedly existent "general will": the confusion of will in the psychological sense with commands provided the needed imperatives jurists were seeking (the naive-construction theory).

The prevailing doctrine of law as commands and prohibitions — and nothing else — contradicts the specific nature of the legal mentality. Rights (of which the representatives of this doctrine talk at every step in jurisprudence) thus represent a *deus ex machina*: something inexplicable from their point of view which should not have existed at all. The puzzle is, how can commands addressed to some create rights in behalf of others? But this objection as to the theory of commands — of expressions of the will of the stronger to the weaker, and the like — is only relatively significant: not rights only but obligations as well refuse to fit into the framework of this theory. In order to save his life the traveler who has fallen into the hands of a band of robbers can fulfill the commands of the more powerful and hand over his purse, but probably even the robbers would not assert the presence of an obligation as such.

Neither law nor morality has anything in common with commands and prohibitions as such.

SECTION 23. *The Elements and the Species of Legal Norms*

Legal norms have been divided into unconditional (categorical) and conditional (hypothetical), depending on their being unconditional commands to do or not to do something (not to commit murder), or only conditional commands to do something in case certain possible circumstances occur (to punish a criminal in case of murder). Two elements are distinguished in conditional norms: the hypothetical part (or condition), indicating the conditions, and the dispositive part, containing the command itself (the disposition). The hypothesis may take the form of a subordinate clause starting with "if," but the same meaning can be arrived at in various other ways. For example, "he who does so and so," or "he who has done so and so," or "for doing such and such a deed" (the hypotheses: if a person does such and such a deed), "the guilty person is subjected to such and such punishment" (the disposition); the hirer (meaning if one hires) is bound, and so forth.

Categorical norms contain the dispositive element only. Recently it has come to be widely held that all legal norms are conditional commands of a hypothetical nature, while the existence of categorical norms is in general denied.

If the doctrine of hypotheses and dispositions of norms is to be formulated correctly, and the problem as to the existence *vel non* of categorical norms solved, the corresponding theory must be put on the basis of scientific psychology, and in particular ideas of commands addressed to others for the attainment of certain ends replaced by a study of ethical experiences and their projections. The solution is then easy and free from doubt: categorical legal and moral norms do exist and are in fact experienced with very great frequency.

Self-observation and the joint method of internal and external observation corroborate this at every step. Very frequently the experiences and norms of intuitive law have a categorical character. In our behavior with regard to neighbors we are guided by innumerable intuitive law (and moral) convictions, which unconditionally — and not merely when and if special circumstances are present — reject certain encroachments and prescribe other conduct. Many norms of positive law also possess a character undoubtedly categorical. In support of the proposition that all legal norms are of a conditional character it is pointed out that even the prohibition of murder is only conditional: the law admits of punishment by death, of killing in war, and the like. This, however, is a misunderstanding. In the minds of persons normally brought up and not engaged in the profession of executioners or the like, the norm as to murder is of a categorical character. That the positive law admits of death sentences, killing in war, and the like means simply that exceptions to the general principle exist, and not that the norm which forbids killing is of a hypothetical character. There are, however, many norms which not only are experienced as a rule in categorical form (like that concerning murder), but also correspond to general principles of law which in the civilized world have the character of absolute principles not subject to exceptions of any kind. This is the case as to the norms which do not admit of torture, racking, aggravated death sentences (such as crucifixion, pouring molten metal down the throat, quartering, and breaking on the wheel), rape, forgery, enslaving and trading in human beings, and so forth. Whatever the "interests" or "purposes" in view, these and similar encroachments upon the personality and rights of another are rejected by cultural law. It is far from true, therefore, that hypotheses are characteristic of all legal experiences and norms.

In accordance with the imperative-attributive nature of legal experiences, dispositions of legal norms are not "commands" but imperative-attributive propositions. The existing doctrine concerned with the analysis and the elements of legal norms should therefore be amplified by distinguishing two elements in the dispositions of these norms: (1) imperative and (2) attributive. It is clear from what has already been set out that the corresponding nature of the dispositions of legal judgments and norms is reflected in dual, imperative-attributive phraseology which indicates (by two corresponding propositions or otherwise) both the obligations of one side and the rights of the other: these could, however, be shortened into one of the abbreviated forms — the abbreviated-attributive, the abbreviated-imperative and the doubly-abbreviated. In the imperative and the attributive elements of the legal dispositions further elements must be kept distinct.

(1) Subject definitions: ideas (a) of subjects of the asset attributed — subjects of a right — and (b) of subjects of the liability resting on the other side — subjects of the obligation. Since from the projection point of view, norms appear as higher dispositions or arrangements with reference to those whom they endow with assets and burden with liabilities, so from the conscious-projection point of view the corresponding beings can be designated as the active and passive addressees of norms.

In the sense of the psychological theory of law the addressees of norms are those pairs of beings between whom imperative-attributive standardization occurs: those from whom something is required and those to whom it is attributed. Clearly, from what has gone before, the beings that can be passive and active addressees of juridic norms are not only officials, but also simple mortals, as well as all other possible kinds of beings: deities, the dead, animals, and so forth. This will be corroborated in the exposition which follows. Addressees of norms may be either definite individuals — concrete subjects (I, you, John, Peter, George I, the city of St. Petersburg, or Russia in international relations) — or classes — subjects defined by class — such as children, parents, landlords, lodgers, or states in general (in international law).

Accordingly, norms may be divided into: (a) individual or concrete norms, and (b) general or abstract norms. To assert that all norms are "abstract imperatives" is willfully to contradict the facts. Through self-observation one may become familiar with norms (with the projection of norms) with reference to "I," "you," "comrade A," and others. Even in the field of statutory law, we are concerned with individual norms at each step: in tax legislation the addressee of the attributive is the "treasury" of the given state; the rights of monarchs to a certain maintenance (on the basis of the so-called Civil List) or of other specifically named individuals to a certain pension, to a special reward for services, and so forth, are not infrequently established by special acts of the legislature, and the corresponding positive norms have an individual character.

It is not uncommon in the history of positive law for general norms of a certain content to be preceded by the appearance of corresponding individual norms. Thus, in most contemporary states, corporations are created on the basis of a general statute so that a special statute for each individual company is not required, whereas in earlier periods when this form of business unit was developing, it was sanctioned by special statutes. In precisely the same way, the right of authors to exclusive enjoyment of the publication of their works (the so-called right of literary property) was originally granted to individual authors by separate statutes. The corresponding norms were individual norms.

The norms of international law, based on compacts or conventions between individual states, are likewise individual norms.

Passive or active addressees of general, abstract norms may be either definite categories of persons, or "all": "each whoever he may be." Thus the norm which endows one with a right of property has, as the *passive* addressee, "each," or "all others," or "outsiders of every sort" (that is to say, that which is conceived as designated by this expression). The norm which requires abstention from torture, racking, rape, and the like has as its active addressee — the addressee of the attributive element — "every person whoever he may be," or "everyone," having (according to this norm) a right not to be subjected to such evil actions.

Conversely, the norm defining that children are bound to obey their parents — that parents have a right to obedience from their children — or the norm that the debtor must pay interest, forfeit, and the like in certain circumstances and that the creditor has a right to receive such-and-such interest, forfeit, and the like, have as their addressees only a definite category of persons: children-parents, debtors-creditors.

General norms may therefore be divided according to their addressees into: (a) those addressed to each and every one (absolute norms), and (b) those addressed to definite categories of subjects (relative norms). Absolute norms may then be divided into: (a) imperatively or passively absolute norms, wherein the addressee of the imperative element is each person whoever he may be; (b) attributively or actively absolute norms, wherein the addressee of the attributive element is each whoever he may be; and (c) bilaterally absolute norms (absolute in the narrow sense), wherein the addressees of the imperative element (the obligors) and the addressees of the attributive element (the obligees) are "all" or "each": thus norms requiring abstention from the evil actions above are bilaterally absolute norms.

(2) Object definitions: ideas of the conduct — of the "furnishings" in the general sense — required from addressees of the imperative elements, and of the "receivings" in the general sense authoritatively attributed to addressees of the attributive elements of the norm dispositions.

It has already been pointed out that all objects of the imperative element — all the species of conduct required of obligors — may be reduced to the following as their simplest elements: (1) positive actions (*facere*), (2) abstentions (*non facere*), (3) and tolerances (*pati*); while all objects of the attributive element — all the "receivings" in the general sense — may be reduced to the corresponding: (1) positive receivings in the narrow sense (*accipere*), (2) non-tolerances of certain actions or freedom therefrom: "inviolability" or "safe-guardings" (*non pati*), and (3) actions tolerated on the part of obligors, positive freedoms, freedoms of action (*facere*).

Accordingly three classes of norms are to be distinguished in accordance with object definitions: (1) positive-attributive norms or norms that grant (objects: *facere-accipere*), (2) negative-attributive norms, or norms that safeguard (objects: *non facere-non pati*), and (3) empowering norms, or norms that authorize (objects: *pati-facere*).

An indistinct consciousness of the difference between these three types of norms is probably at the basis of the differentiation by ancient Roman jurists of the three functions of statutes: *jubere, vetare, permittere*; it is reflected in the opinions of those modern jurists who — notwithstanding the prevailing theory of imperatives — still assert the existence of so-called permissive norms. The latter term, and the contrasting of permissive norms with imperative norms, is inadequate: norms which we call "empowering" or "authorizing" are likewise imperative (as are others) but the special characteristic of their imperative element is that they impose an obligation to tolerate certain actions of the obligee.

In its doctrine concerning the elements of norms contemporary jurisprudence, which knows and admits only positive law, leaves out of sight a further element (of positive law in general, and of positive norms in particular) to which special attention should be paid: ideas of the corresponding normative facts. This may be termed "the positive basis" or "the positive referral." In positive norms of law we may thus distinguish three parts: (1) positive basis or positive referral, (2) hypothesis, and (3) disposition. For example, on the basis of the statutes of such and such a year (the positive basis), in such and such circumstances (the hypothesis), such and such conduct is due (the disposition).

As already set out, positive legal judgments and the corresponding norms are not infrequently inferred not from any one fact but from aggregates of normative facts, and the positive referral of one positive norm not infrequently consists in pointing out several normative facts. Thus, on the basis of articles 5, 15, and 20 of the Criminal Code in connection with paragraph 50 of the Rules of a Criminal Procedure (a complex positive reference), in such and such cases (the hypothesis), the order should be so and so (the disposition). Positive "bases" or positive "referrals" may, therefore, be either simple or complex.

The normative facts mentioned in a complex positive "basis" or "referral" may be related to a single category of normative facts (for example, to a category of statutes or customs) or to various categories thereof (for example, one to statutes and others to customs: "on the basis of such and such custom of commercial intercourse in connection with such and such a paragraph of the Commercial Code and such and such rule of Commercial Procedure . . ."). Complex positive "referrals" may therefore be divided into homogeneous and mixed.

The presence or absence of a positive "basis" determines the classification of norms as intuitive or as positive. Positive norms must further be divided into species and varieties: statutory, customary, resting on precedent, contractual, and so forth, having regard to the particular categories of facts mentioned in the positive "referrals."

From what has been pointed out with regard to complex "bases" or "referrals," it is clear that positive norms may be not only statutory, customary, and so forth but also complex: statute-customary, customary-contractual, and so forth.

Failing to distinguish between norms and normative facts, contemporary jurisprudence knows neither of the existence of such complex norms, nor in general of positive bases or referrals as a special element of positive norms. That which from the point of view of the psychological theory of law appears as one of the parts of positive norms or as a normative fact represents — from the point of view of modern legal science — the norms themselves.

Bringing together what has been set out as to the elements of legal norms, we may establish the following scheme of their content: (a) positive "bases" or "referrals," (b) hypotheses (in hypothetical norms), and (c) dispositions, whose elements are imperative and attributive. The imperative element indicates (i) the addressees of the imperative (the obligors), and (ii) the objects of the imperative (the objects of obligations — objects of the relevant conduct: *facere, non facere, pati*). The attributive element indicates (i) the addressees (the obligees), and (ii) the objects — that which is to be received (*accipere, non pati, facere*).

This is a complete scheme and guide for legal analysis (the mental resolution of the complex into simple elements) and synthesis (the mental formation of the complex out of simple elements), and for the proper interpretation and exposition of the sense of legal norms, as well as a basis for the classification of norms.

This scheme is transferable to the science of morality with some simplification, and specifically with the removal therefrom of the attributive element of the disposition. Aided by this scheme, representatives of the science of morality could essentially promote their science and replace their misty and confused ideas and judgments concerning moral norms with clear and exact knowledge and analysis.

CHAPTER V

LEGAL RELATIONSHIPS

SECTION 24. *General Characterization of Modern Theories of Legal Relationships, Obligations, and Rights*

Ethical experiences (moral and legal) are accompanied by the projection of peculiar and seemingly real conditions of subordination and obligation upon various beings. These impulsive phantasmata are to be explained by the peculiar character of the ethical impulsions already analyzed. In accordance with the specific distinction between moral and legal phenomena, the relevant impulsive phantasmata have a distinct character in law on the one hand and in morality on the other. In morality obligation or duty appears as a state of being unilaterally bound, while in law it appears as a state of being bilaterally bound: the obligations or the duties resting upon some are made secure in behalf of others and represent duties belonging to them as their rights.

In languages which are less developed, these projections, although they appear to be bilateral bonds, have a single name which corresponds to the modern expressions duty — obligation. In more developed languages, especially in the sources of Roman law which have played a decisive part in the evolution of contemporary legal science, three different names for these projections are found, depending on the point of view from which they were regarded. To designate the bilateral bonds (insofar as they are not being examined especially from the point of view of either obligor or obligee but from a neutral point of view) Roman law employs the expressions *juris nexus, juris vinculum,* signifying a bilateral bond between the parties: legal relationships. Insofar as they are examined from the point of view of the active belonging of the duty — from the point of view of the party opposed to the obligor — we have the expressions: *jus* and *jura* (rights, competencies, legal claims). Modern jurisprudence follows the corresponding terminology and assumes that three different objects exist because of the presence of the three different names (obligations, rights, legal relationships). It knows nothing of the impulsions and the phantasmata they evoke. It has no suspicion of the impulsive-projection nature of obligations, legal relationships, and rights. Accordingly, it takes for granted the existence of three different realities, and proceeds to examine legal relationships, rights, and obligations and to fashion three separate doctrines.

The doctrine concerning legal relationships has in modern science a dual and fluctuating character. On the one hand rights and obligations are distinguished as elements of legal relationships, and to various combinations of rights and obligations (considered as distinct phenomena), such as the rights of the creditor and obligations of the debtor, jurists are always giving the name legal relationships. On the other hand, legal relationships are identified with life relationships (such as marriage) regulated by law.

From the scientific point of view, this doctrine is vulnerable even on the ground of the data which jurists know and acknowledge in other parts of their works (to say nothing of criticism from the viewpoint of the psychological theory of law).

(1) This doctrine is based on the premise that legal standardization — "the establishment of rights and obligations" — necessarily presupposes that there are particular life relationships between the persons connected with each other by rights and obligations: in other words legal standardizations — rights and obligations — are imposed like a stamp on an actual substratum — life relationships — already existent between specified persons. This assumption is mistaken. The establishment of rights and obligations between persons by no means necessarily postulates that there are any life relationships whatever between them. The very nature of the so-called absolute rights — wherein the obligor is each and every person — such as our right to life, the right of corporeal inviolability, the right of honor, rights of an author, and so forth, refutes the premise from which the prevailing theory of legal relationships starts, and it is strange that this could have escaped the notice of jurists familiar with these legal relationships. Moreover, there are also legal relationships wherein the obligees appear as each and every one.

And even in the field of relative legal relationships — those between two only, or between some definite persons — closer examination shows the error of the assumption that life relationships must necessarily exist between them. Various legal relationships in the field of inheritance by will (mutual rights and duties as between co-heirs, as between heirs and legatees, and so forth) presuppose nothing like the presence of any life relationships between these persons, but only that a valid will was drawn up by a third person and that he is dead, or that other events contemplated by positive law have occurred; but in general these occurrences have nothing in common with any life relationships between the persons named in the will and not infrequently ignorant of each other's existence. Thus in his will T (testator) imposes on the person designated as his heir (A) the duty of paying 1,000 rubles to B. A and B stand in no "life" relationships with each other. They have never personally met. In the domain of interests they have never encountered each other. A does not even know that there is any B somewhere beyond the ocean, nor does B suspect the existence of A. Yet A, having accepted the inheritance after T's death, comes thereby into a special legal relationship toward B even though the former may not yet have known of T's direction to pay the 1,000 rubles: he becomes a debtor of B, and B becomes his creditor. Between them a legal relationship has arisen but there is a complete absence of any life relationship between them. In such a case no jurist would inquire whether there were or are any life relationships between A and B: where there is a valid will of T, every jurist would acknowledge that a binding obligation has arisen — a binding legal relationship between heir and legatee. The same is true as to all the other relative legal relationships where the disposition of a third person or other neutral event, and not any life contact between them, is a condition precedent to their coming into being as between definite persons (to the corresponding projections, and the ascription of the mutual obligations — rights to those persons).

Legal history contains many examples of marital rights and obligations arising as between two persons of different sexes who were in no life relationships of any kind with each other before, when, or after these mutual rights and obligations arose. Modern marriage, it is true, presupposes mutual acquaintance, the assent of those being married, and the like, but there was a time in the history of marriage law when marriages were concluded without their consent, and even without their knowledge, as when they were joined by means of a contract between the heads of the families: sometimes only after marital rights and obligations had come into being, did husband and wife know that they were married, become acquainted with each other, and enter (or not) into life relationships.

(2) Besides the concept and the doctrine of legal relationships as life relationships regulated by objective law, an important part is played in legal science by the concept and the doctrine of legal facts, which is incidentally one of the happiest and least vulnerable of the general concepts of jurisprudence. The generally accepted view is that legal facts are those conditioning (or evoking) the application of legal norms, or the emergence, change, and termination of legal relationships (or of rights and obligations). If this definition is compared with the foregoing

definition of legal relationships, it cannot but be noted that these furnish no criterion for distinguishing legal facts from legal relationships. This is a serious scientific defect in the traditional system of fundamental legal concepts. It has escaped the attention of science hitherto only because the traditional definitions of legal relationships seem terminologically dissimilar to those of legal facts.

In the first place, the expression "life relationship" manifestly signifies a somewhat protracted state, whereas the word "fact" clearly expresses an instantaneous event which is not of a protracted character. Here, apparently, is an essential distinction between "life relationships regulated by law" (legal relationships) and facts which condition the application of legal norms (the emergence of rights and obligations: legal facts). No such distinction, however, exists in reality, and insofar as the idea of such distinction is evoked by the usual formulae, it is a false idea.

Prolonged conditions, sometimes extending over a very long period, may undoubtedly be related to legal facts: in the law of ancient Rome the essential legal fact in marriage (*usus*) was uninterrupted cohabitation in marriage for the period of a year, and therewith was associated the emergence of the corresponding marriage rights and obligations, *manus mariti,* and so forth. Possession of a thing for ten years, or leaving a debtor undisturbed for the same period, is an extremely important legal fact in certain civil codes, since it leads to changes of legal relationships: the acquisition of a right of property *in rem,* and the suspension of the debtor's duty. Immemorial prescription (*vetustas*) — for 100 years in certain civic laws — shows still more graphically the incorrectness of the idea that the concepts "legal fact" and "life relationship" are to be theoretically distinguished from the point of view of protracted existence.

Moreover, the customary definitions of legal facts and legal relationships evoke — or may evoke — the idea that a legal fact, as distinguished from *the life relationship* of a person to a person (or of a person to a thing), is inevitably a collateral *event* distinct from the life connection: the *relationship* between persons or between a person and a thing. In reality, no such distinction exists, and insofar as the idea of such a distinction is evoked by the usual formulae, it is a false idea.

The foregoing examples of legal facts show that they may consist specifically in particular relationships either of a person to another person (cohabitation in marriage for the period of a year, or exacting an assessment or taxes from a certain settlement from time immemorial, or leaving a delinquent debtor undisturbed for a long period and the like), or of a person to a thing (possession of a thing for the period of limitation).

Is it possible, however, to discern in the prevailing theory a criterion whereby to distinguish between legal relationships and legal facts in that legal relationships are defined as "regulating" life relationships, while legal facts are "conditions relevant to the application of legal norms" (conditions precedent to the rise of rights and obligations, which "produce" legal relationships)?

Again the answer must be that, insofar as the idea of a difference in essence is evoked by these expressions it is a false idea. Perhaps the expression "the law regulates life relationships" can evoke the idea that it is possible for law to affect "life relationships" directly: that law is some powerful and ubiquitous subject which in the street, in homes and the like establishes certain regulations, separates persons who are scuffling, apprehends and punishes criminals, and the like. Actually, the relationship of objective law to life phenomena — to life facts and life relationships — consists simply and solely in what jurists call the establishment of rights and obligations. This constitutes "the regulation of life relationships." Accordingly, the expression "life relationship regulated by law" can designate nothing other than a life phenomenon "with which objective law connects rights and obligations." It signifies precisely what is meant by the concept of a legal fact as a fact which "conditions" the rise of rights and obligations or the application of legal norms, "produces rights and obligations on the basis of objective law," and the like. Thus we can at will call *usus* (cohabitation in marriage for a year) or the possession of a thing for the period prescribed by the statute of limitations "a life relationship regulated by law," "a fact with which the law associates legal consequences," or "a fact producing rights and obligations."

Manifestly, then, the prevailing theory is guilty of having confused concepts and sought (unsuccessfully) to limit the concept of legal relationship, on the one hand, and of legal fact on the other.

(3) Since the prevailing theory proceeds on the basis that this attempted distinction is perfect, further logically malformed products of thought develop. The essence of legal facts is held to be that they condition the emergence and existence of legal relationships. They "produce" or "evoke" legal relationships, and the like. The legal fact is the logical *prius* for the legal relationship: it should appear and be present in order that the legal relationship may arise. Since, however, the current definitions identify legal relationships and legal facts, this is logical nonsense: the appearance of A presupposes the presence of A; A must exist before

it emerges; for the production of A it is necessary that A, which also produces A, exist. For example, under the law of ancient Rome *usus* is undoubtedly a life relationship regulated by law: a legal relationship from the prevailing point of view; but *usus* is likewise and incontrovertibly a legal fact — in other words *usus* must emerge and be present prior to *usus,* as a condition precedent to its own emergence.

The foregoing considerations suffice to demonstrate the complete indefensibility of the prevailing theory of legal relationships. But to regard a legal relationship as a combination of obligations and rights is no less indefensible: this, too, is a naive-realistic view, since modern theories of obligations and rights have already been demonstrated to be of a naive-realistic character and to possess other fundamental faults.

Similar is the state of the doctrine of obligations. Jurists, moralists, and philosophers constantly talk about obligations, but so cautiously skirt the problem of what an obligation is that their works do not afford even an approximate idea of how the authors understand the nature of what they are talking about. The only thing that is clear is that they start from the naive-projection point of view, and regard the obligation as something real, to be found at the place to which the projection of the obligations is directed. How they understand the nature of these supposed realities does not appear.

The gist of the observations of philosophers and moralists is that an obligation presupposes the presence of an imperative — a higher command — addressed to the will of a reasoning being, or the presence of "two wills," one of which requires something while the other has been or is being subordinated to the former. Moreover some (chiefly moralists) identify obligation with a corresponding command; others treat it as identical with pressure or "constraint" emanating from a superior will or superior command; others, again, identify it with the condition of unfreedom — of boundness, "of being bound by the norm" — as regards the person to whom the command is addressed; still others treat it as identical with the very will which is bound by the command; and finally there are those who identify obligation with the very actions prescribed by the imperatives (in philosophy and ethics there is a fairly widespread confusion of obligations with their objects: actions).

The observations of jurists as to the nature of obligations are of the same general content, with the further presupposition of greater force on the part of the commanding will — authority to compel subordination, and so forth — or, coupled with this, the further threat of causing certain evil in case of non-fulfillment. Accordingly, "constraint" with which obligations are sometimes identified in the observations of jurists is given the character of physical or psychic constraint emanating from the threat. Sometimes the nature of obligations (including moral obligations) is seen in psychic constraint (the reaction of social opinion and the disadvantages connected therewith) and it is held that for legal obligations physical or mechanical constraint as well is essential. When obligations are identified with the condition of the person under the influence of the constraint — and not with constraint itself — legal obligations are not infrequently characterized as the "necessity" of certain conduct because physical constraint is present or the application of a threat is to be avoided. There are also jurists who identify obligations with the will of him to whom commands are addressed. Finally, some identify obligations with the corresponding actions or behavior.

To criticize the foregoing doctrines as to the nature of obligations seriatim would require more space than their importance merits. Insofar as they are connected with the theory of norms as commands, what has been already said with reference to that theory applies to them. Aside from this, they are all unaware of the projection nature of obligations and evidence an uncritical belief that something real can be found in the beings to whom obligations are ascribed. Finding nothing real which corresponds to the ascribed obligations, they all seek salvation in accepting other realities (which have nothing in common with obligations) as what they are looking for: they are naive-realistic theories which confuse obligations (impulsive projections) with phenomena which are completely heterogeneous. This fundamental misunderstanding, and a symptom thereof, is naturally followed by failure on the part of philosophers, moralists, and jurists to distinguish between obligations and things which are altogether different *inter se*: (1) commands, (2) psychic or physical constraint, (3) the condition of one under the influence of commands, threats, and the like, (4) the will of these subjects, and (5) their actions.

Whereas the problem of the nature of obligations is ordinarily passed over in silence, that of the nature of rights (legal claims, legal competences) is examined in the science of law with the greatest animation, and this and the nature of law in the objective sense are considered the most interesting, important, and difficult problems of that science. There is an extensive literature on the subject which is extremely keen and profound in some respects. Nevertheless the matter remains controversial and the problem unsolved. Earlier attempts to define the essential nature of rights have ordinarily been reduced to two: the theory of will, and the theory of interests.

Will and interest, however, are phenomena equally alien to the essence of a legal right. This is readily demonstrable from the data and the concepts of modern jurisprudence itself, and without reference to the propositions of the psychological theory of law.

(a) Do rights — such as a property right, or rights of children as to their parents or of a husband as to his wife and vice versa — cease to exist because the "interest" of the obligee therein has ceased, or because the "will" to make use of a corresponding right no longer exists, or even because an interest directed at terminating these rights (or perhaps a wish — even an intense will — to terminate their existence) appears? Any jurist would at once answer in the negative. There are rights whose subject cannot dispose of them: he cannot even terminate them however much he may wish and be interested to do so. There are other rights from which only exceptional circumstances can liberate him — thus he may be freed from marital rights only if specific grounds for divorce are present, otherwise no interest in terminating these rights — no efforts or exertions of any kind — will avail. Even where the subject interested in terminating his right can freely dispose of it, such termination ordinarily requires the accomplishment of various actions, and sometimes the observance of complex and onerous formalities (such as the preparation of a formal writing, or recording). Briefly, there can be no doubt from the legal point of view that our rights can — and not infrequently do — continue despite our will and our interests, or at all events with no interest on our part or direction of our will corresponding to the content of the right.

(b) Is an interest in becoming an obligee, or the will to acquire the particular legal rights, an essential condition precedent to the acquisition of a right? Not at all. There are innumerable cases which, by their nature, embody and demonstrate the possibility of acquiring a right not only without, but even in spite of, the corresponding will and interest, as where rights come into being in our behalf by the operation of the forces of nature (which consults neither our will nor our interest). The owner of the soil acquires a property right to its various products even if their appearance was alike contrary to his interest and to his wishes — including plants injurious to beneficial plants or to animals, or dangerous to persons, such as poisonous mushrooms and berries, parasites, weeds, and darnel. He has a right of property in branches broken by the hurricane, or fallen and rotting, as well as in brushwood, although he were not only not interested in their presence but even wished that they would disappear as soon as possible. By the same laws which acknowledge a right of property in game found on one's land, the owner of the soil acquires a right to property in hares and other wild animals which have run into his forest or garden, although these may be objects of property which he is extremely unwilling to have. Increment to land occurring in consequence of the action of volcanic or ocean forces (the appearance of an island, the increase of land by reason of alluvion and the like) becomes an object of the property of the owner of the parcel although such acquisition of a right of property may be extremely undesirable for him (for example, because of tax considerations). There are also entire categories of cases where rights are acquired by one in consequence of events happening to the legal personality of others, independently not only of the wishes and interests of the former but also of the will and the wish of the latter. Thus rights of inheritance, and rights to security, to a pension, to insurance, and so forth are acquired by reason of the death of another. Particularly illuminating and interesting, as militating against the will theory and the theory of interests, are those laws which (like the ancient Roman law) recognize the institution of compulsory inheritance (*sui et necessarii heredes*), by virtue whereof the totality of the rights and obligations (debts) of the deceased is fastened upon persons contrary to their will and their interests, so that the acquisition of the inheritance may mean to them ruin which they cannot avoid since the right of inheritance cannot be renounced. There are other laws, too (not embodying such strict provisions, but allowing an inheritance to be renounced), under which the complex of rights of inheritance — and therewith of the obligations — not only may be but sometimes is acquired against one's will and wish by reason of inadvertence (because certain formalities were not observed, and so forth). Moreover, rights are not infrequently acquired by us because of arrangements made by others with no inquiry as to our will or our interests. We have seen that according to certain laws — especially of an earlier period — the rights of husband or wife were fastened upon persons unwilling to acquire them and altogether without interest therein, so that the acquisition thereof was more than once accompanied by weeping and sobbing, or even by suicide. In the example of a legacy cited above, of a testamentary disposition in behalf of a person beyond the seas — the legatee acquires the right independently of his will and wish: if an American, who knew no Russian and did not wish to learn Greek, were bequeathed a manual of the Greek language written in Russian — or a pair of old slippers — he would nonetheless acquire a right to the legacy, not only where interest in this right was altogether absent but even though he did not know of its existence. Certainly even such rights as are ordinarily acquired by a corresponding "expression of will" of him who is acquiring them are often gained independently of knowledge and will by our representative. Ordinarily we voluntarily confer authority to represent us in legal matters, but compulsory representation may be fastened upon us: a conservator may be designated for a spendthrift, contrary to the will of the latter, and acquires for him rights without consulting him as to whether or not he wishes, or is interested, to acquire them.

Proofs of the possibility and presence of rights resting on neither will nor interest — or contrary to the will and interest of the obligee — could be extended ad libitum, but the foregoing completely justify the proposition that both theories — both the theory of will and the theory of interests — see the essence of rights in that which not only does not constitute their essence but does not even always accompany them (and the theories therefore "jump"). Not only, then, do rights exist which are undesired by the obligee and possess no interest for him (and so are devoid of "will" and "interest" alike) but a particular will, "acknowledged" by others or by "the general will," or "an interest protected by objective law" may exist without any legal right whatever being present. Thus, according to an official law which recognizes slavery, a slave is, in general, a being without rights. If, on the contrary, one takes his stand on the theory of will, or on that of the interests safeguarded by objective law, it appears that slaves have a great many rights. The interest of the slave that he be not killed or poisoned, or have his hands or feet broken, that he be not robbed on the way, that there be no arbitrary obstacles to his riding or going along the street, his interest or his wish that the tradesman who has sold him eatables on the way in return for money actually deliver the goods purchased — assuredly all these enjoy "the defense of objective law." Robbery, larceny, and the like are forbidden by law, and are prosecuted if the robber attacks the slave. Objective law furnishes dominance to the will of the slave to go unimpeded into a neighboring city, and safeguards his interest in preserving the provisions he has taken for the road or in obtaining those he has bought on the way, yet it would be heresy, under the will theory as under the interest theory, for a jurist to come to the conclusion that we were concerned with the rights of a slave, notwithstanding the theoretical view of the essence of a right. The explanation would be that here our concern was partly with the rights of the master and partly with those of the state: the state has a claim that there should not be robbery within its territory (that all refrain from such conduct) while the master has a claim that his slave be not beaten or corporeally injured, precisely as he may demand that no one torture or kill his horse or dog.

In a degree highly significant, the interests or the will of children are preserved and defended because various rights belong to their parents and, conversely, various interests of the parents are guaranteed by norms of law from which rights — not for them but for their children — flow. The objective law safeguards many interests of city dwellers or of members of a rural society by rights belonging to the city or to the village, and so forth.

The theory of will and the theory of interests are thus refuted. However, even aside from the problem of the nature of rights and their definition, it is asserted as incontrovertible (a) that all rights are established in the interests of those to whom they are given — for the sake of, or to safeguard, the interests of specified persons — and (b) that the sense and the significance of rights is the furnishing of advantages — the satisfaction of the needs and interests of those to whom they belong. These propositions are entirely distinct from the definition of the concept of rights. Each of them is alike indefensible. We have already dealt with rights of ancillary and social authority. These rights illustrate clearly and graphically the ineptitude of the positions taken by Ihering and his school as to the "purpose" or "end" of rights. These — such as a guardian's authority in respect to those under guardianship, rights of instructors or educators, or of directors of educational institutions with regard to subordinates and so forth — by no means "exist in the interests" of the guardians and other subjects of rights of this sort, but in the interests of the obligors. In precisely the same way, various rights attributed to agents, managers, salesmen, and others in public or private enterprises and institutions, as a means of carrying out their functions of service, do not exist in the interests of those to whom they are attributed. Clearly the current views of the relationship of rights to interests are "jumping" doctrines at least.

Even as to these rights (ordinary rights of property, money claims, and the like) it is extremely naive and superficial to suppose that it is for the sake of the interests of any subjects that the corresponding imperative-attributive convictions develop. Like morality, law is produced by subconsciously adequate social adaptation to the welfare and the prosperity of societies and the spiritual and cultural education of mankind. The social significance of these or other rights — such as rights of property, of contract, and of inheritance — requires regard, not to the pockets of any owners, creditors, or heirs, but to the national economy and the national culture, and study of the function of the individual legal institutions involved in the mighty and complex processes involved.

The foregoing are by no means all the attempts that have been made to define the nature of rights in the subjective sense. Rights are not infrequently so defined as to indicate constraint or defense on the part of the state, and the like, as an important attribute. Inasmuch as these definitions merely undertake to say that, in case of non-satisfaction, the obligee has a *right* to demand the application of coercive measures upon him who fails to perform — that protection be furnished to him, and so forth — this only worsens the relevant formulae by referring to "X," which still remains to be defined.

All opinion of this type as to the essence of a right is based on ignorance of the impulsive-projection nature of rights. It rests on the assumption that there is something real in the subjects to which rights are ascribed. It has the character of a naive-projection theory. To the extent that rights are not distinguished, in these theories, from something real and actually present — from the corresponding wishes, interests, factually favorable positions, and so forth — the theories are of a naive-realistic character. Insofar as they refer to nothing real these doctrines are of a naive-constructive character. Modern literature as to rights also contains naive-nihilistic doctrines denying various rights because the relevant reality is not found and cannot be stated: in constitutional law, various political scientists deny different categories of rights, and declare that the corresponding norms are merely objective and do not produce rights for the reason that there are no corresponding individual interests in those to whom these rights are ascribed.

SECTION 25. *The Nature of Legal Relationships*

The ineptitude of the existing teaching as to legal obligations, legal relationships and rights corroborates the foregoing doctrine of the projection nature of obligations, legal relationships and rights.

If the usual faith of the public and of science that moral and legal obligations exist as something real and present in subjects of the obligations, in the form of something psychic or otherwise — some special factual condition, position, relationship, or the like — were justified, it cannot be supposed that the age-long work, thought, and investigation of a multitude of scholars toward discovering the nature of the corresponding something would have been wholly barren of result — least of all as to the nature of rights, in view of the particularly zealous and energetic work of philosophers and jurists in this field.

Our thesis that moral and legal obligations and rights are impulsive projections, and that the corresponding real phenomena actually exist in the mind of the person experiencing the corresponding processes and projections is not only affirmatively supported by the psychological theory set out above but is negatively confirmed in the history and present condition of the teaching of philosophers, moralists, and jurists which starts from an allegedly realistic point of view.

The doctrine of legal obligations — rights — relationships set out *supra,* explaining them as the duties of some secured in behalf of others in the sense of projections whose basis is imperative-attributive impulsions, introduces into the theory of law and into jurisprudence in general an essential simplification: three distinct theoretical doctrines of (1) legal relationships, (2) legal obligations, and (3) rights, and the corresponding threefold series of problems and definitions are replaced by a single doctrine and the work of thought and memory is shortened by two-thirds. Moreover, that single concept — defining at one stroke the nature of legal relationships, obligations, and rights — comprises as well an indication of the *differentia specifica* of legal and moral obligations, and sets out a scientific classification of obligations (together with a causal, psychological explanation of the special characteristics which distinguish them).

It must not be forgotten that classification is adapted to problems of the adequate and scientific cognition and explanation of phenomena, and not to the particular nomenclature used by professionals. The concept of legal obligations — rights — relationships which is established herein embraces immeasurably more than jurists include in these terms: intuitive legal relationships as well as positive relationships which are without official significance in the framework of the state. There is no difficulty in ascertaining the nature of legal relationships, rights, and obligations in the juridic sense on the basis of our concept of legal relationships, in association with the two divisions of law: (1) intuitive law and positive law, and (2) official law and unofficial law. This is a miscellaneous group, comprising: (1) positive legal relationships — obligations — rights in the international field, ascertained on the basis of the relevant normative facts (with citations thereof), and (2) official positive relationships — obligations — rights in legal life within a state. For the science of international law on the one hand and that of intrastate law on the other, there are two distinct concepts of legal relationships — rights — obligations.

With the general doctrine concerning legal relationships, the system of modern jurisprudence associates a doctrine as to their elements and their rise and termination.

The elements of legal relationships usually differentiated are (1) rights, and (2) obligations (both being taken as distinct realities, as we have seen), (3) subjects of rights and obligations, and (4) objects of rights.

This division reflects the logical inconsistency of the prevailing doctrine. It is self-contradictory in identifying general legal relationships with life relationships (regulated by objective law or the like). Starting from this concept (of legal relationships as life relationships) it should logically discover in legal relationships, not rights and obligations, but innumerable and extremely diverse "life" elements, such as the relationships of neighbors, disputes, quarrels, trade connections, life relationships between teachers and pupils, and between master and servant, and the like. The fact is, however, that after serving their purpose in defining the nature of legal relationships as apparently possessed of an appropriate reality (corresponding to the general naive-realistic tendencies of jurisprudence) life relationships disappear, and legal relationships turn into a combination of rights and obligations with their subjects and objects of rights as further elements. Moreover, diverse realities are found in the external world, apparently suited to serve as backgrounds for obligations and rights and their elements. Again most systematic treatises particularly accommodate their doctrines as to subjects and objects, as well as those relative to the rise and the termination of legal relationships, not to legal relationships as such, but to rights. Legal relationship, having been first defined as a bilateral phenomenon, is thereafter treated as unilateral. Obligations and obligor disappear. The nature of obligations in general is passed over in silence. A paragraph devoted to legal relationships is immediately followed by doctrines as to rights, subjects of rights and objects of rights, and the rise and termination of legal relationships or the manner of acquiring and losing rights.

In the modern doctrine concerning legal relationships the attributive side — that of the obligee — comes unilaterally into prominence, while the side of the obligation is more or less shaded out and ignored. The entire theory therefore has a one-sided character. Even where doctrines of subjects and objects are adapted to legal relationships, the doctrine of subjects is in fact characterized by concern, not for subjects of obligations and rights, but chiefly (if not entirely) for subjects of rights, and the doctrine of objects for objects of rights. The concept of objects of obligations, and the corresponding doctrine, simply do not exist and the distinction proposed above between objects of obligations and objects of rights is an innovation. Conversely, the modern theory of law in the objective sense (legal norms) suffers from the opposite defect: the attributive function of law is ignored, while norms of law are reduced to commands and prohibitions.

Since doctrines concerned with law in the objective sense and in the subjective sense (legal relationships — rights — obligations) have this character of being unilateral in opposite directions, the entire modern doctrine concerned with law is incongruous and self-contradictory: its content as to law in the objective sense is such that only the imperative side could be discussed further (obligations, obligors, and so forth) yet the converse appears: in subsequent development not only do rights appear — like a deus ex machina — but the chief or exclusive concern of the texts is with them, while the imperative side is shaded and disappears.

This shortcoming must be corrected, both parts of the system must be brought into accord and made congruous by taking into account and developing the attributive side equally with the imperative in the former field, and the imperative equally with the attributive in the latter.

Aside from this, the usual analysis of legal relationships — the resolution of legal relationships into elements — is incomplete as is the modern analysis of norms (which merely distinguishes in them two elements: the hypothesis and the disposition). In addition to subjects and objects in legal relationships other elements, now lost from view as we shall see, can and should be discovered and identified.

The analysis of obligations in moral philosophy and ethics is still less developed — or, more accurately, does not exist at all: what is essential here is not correction but the creation for the first time of a doctrine concerning the elements of obligations.

SECTION 26. *Subjects of Legal Relationships and of Moral Obligations*

Legal science defines subjects of a given legal relationship as those participating in that relationship as obligors or obligees, and subjects of a right as persons capable of taking part in legal relationships as obligors or obligees (regardless of whether or not they are at a given time subjects of any obligations or rights). Capacity to participate in legal relationships as obligor or obligee is called legal capacity, and this jurists ordinarily define — in conformity with the general unilateral direction of their doctrine concerning rights — as the capacity to have rights. This should be corrected: a distinction must be drawn between active legal capacity (the capacity for rights) and passive legal capacity (the capacity for legal obligations).

The initial premise of the modern doctrine as to subjects is the proposition that the law regulates only relationships between human beings, as it is created for the sake of persons. Hence only persons are subjects of rights. That this "truth" was not always known and obvious is sometimes mentioned: rights were ascribed formerly as well to various other beings (deities, spirits of the departed, animals, and even inanimate objects) but this is concededly the result of ignorance, backwardness, and superstition to be corrected by the modern "enlightened" theory of subjects of rights.

Modern jurisprudence sees man's legal capacity as beginning at the moment of birth and ending at the moment of death. It belongs to all persons, but (according to traditional theory) this is so only as to modern law which does not recognize slavery — in the period of slavery, only people who were free possessed legal capacity. Slaves had no legal capacity. They were things or objects, and not subjects or persons in the legal sense. It has already been shown that this proposition is erroneous: the essence of slavery — of the power of the master — was that the slave was the subject of a general obligation of obedience, tolerance and so forth with reference to the master. While admittedly slaves are more or less completely without active legal capacity — the capacity to possess rights — according to the official law of states recognizing that institution, the unofficial law, and intuitive law, and even the positive law (customary law, for example) ascribe to slaves various rights in domestic and business life.

Legal capacity may be complete, or it may be limited and not extend to certain rights. Depending on the class, sex, or religion of a person, and on whether or not he is a citizen of a given state and the like, greater or lesser limitations on legal capacity are possible: one may be incompetent to hold certain offices, to acquire right of property in land, and the like. More or less important limitations of legal capacity are likewise imposed by the courts as punishment for crime.

From legal capacity we must distinguish the capacity for legal acts, the predication of legal significance to one's acts (to his contracts, for example). Children and lunatics have legal capacity, but not capacity for legal action, according to official law.

These propositions and concepts are generally admitted. The doctrine concerning persons as subjects is one of the very few general theories of jurisprudence which is not a combination of "disputed questions," and in which obviously all is well. However, modern science encounters serious difficulties as regards the doctrine of persons by reason of the fact that official law ascribes various rights and obligations — like the right of property, the right to require payment of debts, and so forth — not only to individuals but also to institutions, societies, and the like, to states, the treasury, counties, cities, churches, monasteries, universities, learned and other societies, business corporations, hospitals, almshouses, libraries, and so forth. Thus a right of property in a given parcel of earth is said to belong to the treasury, to the city, to a monastery, or to an agricultural association. With cities, with the treasury, and with corporation contracts are concluded through representatives — contracts for loans of money, leases, and the like — according to which these "subjects" assume various obligations, acquire rights, are called "creditors" and "debtors," and appear as plaintiffs and defendants if the contracts are broken. The rights and obligations of such persons are sharply differentiated from those of even the component individuals. What is due to the corporation is not due to its individual members, nor what is owed by a corporation owed by its individual members. Things wherein the corporation has a right of property do not belong to its members and vice versa.

Such subjects are called juristic persons, as distinguished from the individuals who, as subjects of rights, are called physical (or natural) persons.

Juristic persons are traditionally divided into (1) corporations (*universitates personarum* — the *collegia personalia* of medieval jurists) usually defined as a union of persons which is capable of legal rights, or whose substratum is its members, including various societies, companies, and the like, and (2) institutions (*universitates bonorum*, the *collegia realia* of medieval jurists), ordinarily defined as property complexes or independent properties, devoted to a defined and useful end, or juristic persons whose substratum is a complex of property (almshouses, houses of industry, institutional foundations in whose behalf an independent capacity of legal rights is acknowledged, and the like). Transitory or mixed forms, too (*collegia mixta*), are usually recognized. Whether or not the so-called juristic persons are actually persons (subjects), whether or not such subjects exist in reality, and (if so) who or what specifically has the capacity for rights — or is a subject of rights — and what is the actual nature of these subjects, has given rise to extended dispute in science and produced an enormous literature. A multitude of different theories has been proposed as solutions, and they are sometimes extremely intricate and difficult to understand and to communicate. To criticize them in detail, with all — or even the most important — of the objections thereto, would require much more space and is unnecessary. Remaining on the ground of the traditional ideas and doctrines concerning law we may state that the presence of what is assumed by the various existing theories in that regard is not at all essential to the existence of a juristic person: under existing official law it is enough that certain formalities be complied with and certain documents prepared and confirmed by certain authority for its existence to commence. This demonstrates at once and without further criticism the complete ineptitude of the whole long line of existing theories of juristic persons. Specifically, it is not a condition precedent to the emergence of a juristic person either that there be any present individuals to whom an advantage is furnished or whose interests are satisfied in consequence of the existence of the given institution, or that there be any present property. The existence of a social organism is not a condition precedent to the emergence of a juristic person. No organism is born when a will is drawn up or the minister affixes his signature — no "being" will appear except on paper — but in the meantime a juristic personality emerges and can acquire independent rights from the moment the document is signed by the proper person.

Patently modern legal science is in a tragic situation from which there is no escape: on the one hand, rights and obligations without subjects are inconceivable; on the other hand, the search for appropriate subjects for a multitude of rights and obligations is all in vain, notwithstanding the enormous expenditure of labor and the acumen of countless outstanding jurists. This suggests that the search is being conducted in the wrong direction, as founded on error regarding the sphere where the object of the search exists and can be discovered.

All appears to be in order, with no disputes or doubts emerging, in respect of the first part of the doctrine of contemporary jurisprudence regarding subjects. This is so, however, only because various circumstances which contradict and refute it are left out of account. The very doctrine that physical persons are living individuals, possessing capacity for rights from the moment of birth to the moment of death, is contrary to the fact that death does not necessarily terminate legal capacity since even the dead can have rights and duties. So, after the traditional observations to the effect that the existence of the physical person begins at the moment of birth and ends at the moment of death, treatises on the civil law proceed to set out the doctrine of *commorientes* (persons dying in a common disaster) and of absence without being heard from. The former is to the effect that if a number of persons perish in a shipwreck, battle, or similar disaster, and it is not known which of them died first (although the decision of this question may determine rights and obligations), they are deemed (by Roman law and in many modern statutes) to have died at one and the same moment, so that none of them inherits from any other; but if they were related by ascending and descending kinship (father and son, grandfather and grandson), it is assumed that the adult descendant survived the ascendant and the minor predeceased him. As to the other doctrine, where a person is absent without being heard from, there are rules of the official law defining the period during which he is recognized as living (with rights of property in his farm ascribed to him and his existence as contract creditor and debtor and so forth conceded), and thereafter he is deemed dead, so that his rights and obligations pass to his heirs.

These propositions seem at first glance to be in accord with the ordinary concept of a physical person and the proposition that death terminates personality. If the law in these cases ordains the continuance of personality in the juristic sense (the independent capacity for rights) this is specifically upon the basis of an assumption as to life. However, to assume that he is alive does not turn the dead man into a living man: the sense of the law does not consist in making assertions (correct or otherwise) as to what has been or what is, but in molding conduct, rights, and obligations. "Life is assumed" asserts nothing: it directs that obligations be performed in the name of the absent (whether he be living or dead, and irrespective of what anyone thinks in that regard). Debts are to be paid out of his property. His rights are to be effectuated (debts due him are to be paid in his name to the person in charge of his affairs). The assumption of "life" merely prolongs the separate existence and effectuation of legal capacity and the possession of rights, and protracts the existence of personality regardless of the possible death of the person long before. If this is so, the doctrines of absence without being heard from and of death in a common disaster manifestly refute that of physical persons as actually "living" and of personality and legal capacity ceasing at the moment of death.

Some modern laws (to say nothing of unofficial law, or of the official laws of earlier periods of culture) continue the existence of the personality and the legal capacity of the dead until the acquisition of the inheritance by the heir. At all events the situation in the interim between death and the acquisition of inheritance by the heirs (the appearance of new subjects of the corresponding rights and obligations) causes jurisprudence no little discomfort and difficulty: who is here the subject of rights and obligations? As to this there is an extensive literature, but to find a satisfactory solution of the problem (satisfactory to modern jurisprudence) has proved impossible. This has caused many scholars — including those who hold juristic persons to be real subjects, social organisms and the like — to concede that here rights are present without a subject (sometimes consoling themselves with the observation that this situation is only temporary).

The other proposition, that capacity to acquire rights begins at the instant of birth, is equally indefensible. This is obvious from legal propositions as to children still unborn: side by side with the traditional denial of legal capacity and legal personality down to the moment of birth, there is the traditional assertion that various rights (including rights of inheritance) are preserved for the child still unborn, and that a special guardian or curator or the like may be designated to safeguard those rights (that is to say, to bring suit as representing the child). Sometimes it is actually said, simply and clearly, that the unborn child "has certain private and public rights." As it is developed, the doctrine as to when legal capacity begins contradicts what it stated at the outset, whether the incongruity is masked under obscure expressions about preserving rights, or is frank and open.

If modern jurisprudence were not confined to propositions of Roman and contemporary laws as to subjects, but broadened the horizon and material of its study by turning to the laws of other stages of culture, it would be manifest that not even conception is a condition precedent to the acknowledgment of human beings as subjects of rights and obligations: laws to be found on certain levels of culture (and particularly when tribal life had developed and was strong) contemplate the making of contracts, the acquisition of rights (including rights of property), and the assumption of obligations, not only in behalf and in the name of the living, but also in behalf and in the name of all their descendants: "of all their seed forever," and so forth.

However that may be, the existing doctrine of physical persons combines propositions which are mutually contradictory and destructive. Aside from the difficulties, riddles, and incongruities in which this doctrine abounds, symptoms of inadequacy are conspicuous in other fields and problems of jurisprudence which traditionally are unrelated to the theory of subjects. Thus, in the law of property and as to other so-called absolute rights, the errors of the customary doctrine regarding subjects give rise to an appalling multiplicity of subjects: the purchase of a pin or a pencil occasions a revolution among all persons and nations on earth, since "all" are bound with reference to the owner of the pin: to all, the jurists fancy, prohibitions go out; all are bound to conceive of the corresponding will; all fall into a "life relationship" toward the pin; and so forth. There are, of course, various efforts to exterminate these subjects whose extraordinary numbers give off so unpleasant an impression, but these are as arbitrary and unsuccessful as are the attempts to find or to create subjects where only one subject is required.

In order to build successfully a doctrine of subjects, and to solve such difficult problems as that of the nature of juristic persons or the *hereditas jacens* in particular, we must start from the simple proposition that legal phenomena and their elements are phenomena of the mental, and not of the material, world. These phenomena must be sought out and studied, not by scouring the external world, but by examining the minds of those who experience specified psychic processes: who ascribe to themselves or to others rights, obligations, and so forth. Here, in the minds of individuals and only in that sphere, is where legal phenomena are present. The entire doctrine of modern jurisprudence as to subjects rests on the false assumption that search for the relevant objects must proceed elsewhere than in the sphere where they are found.

Earlier in this work the example was cited of a logician or grammarian who — in order to define the logical subjects of three judgments or sentences: "The servant is in the ante-room," "Zeus is the King of the Olympian Gods," and "The treasury possesses vast property" — set out for the ante-room after the servant (a naive-realistic solution) to find the subject of the first sentence, declared that he did not believe the subject of the second sentence existed (a naive-nihilistic solution), and built up fantastic theories as to the existence of some super-organic being with reference to the subject of the third judgment (naive-constructive solution). This is precisely the picture of the doctrine as to subjects to be found in modern legal science.

When they ascribe to the "treasury," and to other so-called "juristic" and "physical persons," rights and obligations — when they experience the corresponding legal judgments: "The treasury has such and such rights," and so forth — jurists actually have the relevant subjects "extremely close at hand," so to speak, in their own minds, where it is very easy to become acquainted with their nature. In the legal experience: "The treasury has a right," the subject of the right ascribed is the logical subject of this judgment — that which is conceived of and to which is referred the logical predicate: "has a right"; the content or object of the idea to which the word "treasury" corresponds. Undoubtedly this is the real, logical, and juristic subject. It is found there in the very judgment: "The treasury has a right." The same applies to the logical and juristic subjects in the experiences: "Zeus has a right to obedience from gods and men"; "the deceased has a right that his memory be not insulted"; "St. George has a right of property in such and such a parcel of land," and so forth. Jurists, however, do not comprehend that, when they are studying law and occupying themselves with legal analysis, they must move in the sphere of mental life and address themselves to the minds of the individuals experiencing the legal phenomena and ascribing rights, obligations, and so forth. Failing to realize this, they search in an entirely inappropriate sphere: in the external world or somewhere in space. The natural and inevitable result is the strange incongruities observed in the foregoing examples of naive-logical or grammatical analysis, and searches for predicates carried on in the ante-room or the clouds of Olympus.

The doctrines of modern legal science regarding subjects are naive-realistic to the extent that all persons living on earth are treated as subjects of obligations (in the law of property and of other absolute rights) and juristic persons are dealt with as realities actually existent. They are of a naive-nihilistic character insofar as — failing to find in the external world anything real which seems appropriate — they concede the impossibility of finding, and refuse to believe that there exist, innumerable subjects of rights (which undoubtedly do exist or have previously existed). Thus modern legal science denies the existence (actual and potential) of all those categories of subjects not coming under the heading of "living people," "physical persons," "human organizations," or "juristic persons," which (particularly in earlier stages of culture, including the Middle Ages) played an important part in the legal mentality and in official law: incorporeal spirits, the dead, deities, saints, devils and similar beings, animals, inanimate objects, and so forth. Misinterpreting medieval documents in the name of saints and the like (so that for these subjects monasteries, churches, and the like are substituted), refusing to believe that deities, souls of the deceased, devils, stones, and the like could be subjects (notwithstanding the corresponding historical evidence), and adopting the attitude that these phenomena are naive misapprehensions reveal a fundamental misconception of the very nature of law. With a naive-nihilistic attitude toward these categories of subjects, are associated other misunderstandings in modern science, partly of an extremely general and essential character: first, the doctrine that law touches only human conduct and regulates only relationships between persons.

Knowing and taking into account the categories of legal subjects denied by the naive-nihilistic approach provides excellent material for verifying the correctness, and disclosing the mistakenness, of the existing doctrine of law and its elements. In our criticism of the theories of law in general, and then of doctrines of norms, legal relationships, obligations, rights and subjects of a right, we used only data known to and acknowledged by contemporary jurisprudence.

To know and to heed the indubitable fact of legal history that Jehovah was a subject of various legal obligations and rights by ancient Hebrew law is enough, *per se*, to demolish all the extremely "realistic" and "practical" theories as to law in general and its separate elements. How naive, in the result, is Ihering's general characterization of law as a policy of force — or, in general, the theory of physical or psychic constraint — as contrasted with the legal obligations of Jehovah with reference to Israel and all its seed! In precisely the same way, the view (of Ihering and his followers) that norms in general are addressed to weaker persons by a "will" possessing force — and, in general, the prevailing doctrine that norms are commands and prohibitions — is patently incongruous as applied to Jehovah *qua* the addressee of various norms. The same is true as to doctrines to the effect that obligations are conditions of unfreedom in view of commands and threats when they are compared with the legal obligations ascribed by Israel to Jehovah, and so forth.

On the other hand, such subjects as stones, chariots, and animals subjected to criminal courts and to punishment under medieval and other law are no less instructive for various other general theories of law— for theories of a general will, of general persuasion, of general acknowledgment — in view of the fact that these theories have to ascribe to stones and so forth participation in the general will, in the general conviction or in the general acknowledgment. But these subjects are stumbling blocks for other theories, too, including that of physical or psychological constraint, theories of freedom, theories of the protection or delimitation of interests and the like, as well as for existing theories of norms as directions addressed by one will to another, and of obligations and rights.

But subjects of medieval and other primitive laws such as devils, goblins, spirits of slain animals and the like are particularly instructive for the theory of law and of morality. They not only destroy the entire structure of modern jurisprudence, but at the same time demonstrate the general road upon which this science must enter as a science concerned with special phenomena of the human mind. Moreover they point clearly and suggestively to the correct solution of various special problems of legal theory. Thus the very obligations of devils pursuant to a contract for the sale of a soul and the like communicate to the thinker who is toiling over the problem as to the nature of these obligations — their projection nature; at all events they attest the fact that the real phenomenon is not where it seems to be present but is solely in the mind of him who ascribes the obligations. If the devils themselves, or the spirits of slain bears, elephants, and so forth exist in the mind of the superstitious man, and not somewhere in space, it is clear that the obligations of such subjects as well are not found outside the mind of the person experiencing the relevant psychic processes, and so as to rights, norms of law as to the fulfillment of contracts and so forth.

The doctrine as to subjects is of an essentially different character and content when regarded from the point of view of the psychological theory of law developed herein.

(1) As in other fields of legal science, the sphere where the relevant phenomena are found and studied is transferred from the external world to the mind of the person experiencing legal processes and ascribing obligations and rights to various beings: the proper method of studying subjects is therefore self-observation and the joint method of inward and outward observation.

(2) The relevant investigations and doctrines seek to achieve familiarity with the facts of legal consciousness and to state without arbitrary misinterpretation what is present therein as subject ideas and in what shape. As the subject of a right, the "treasury" must not be interpreted to mean that the subject is the state: this would be an arbitrary interpretation contrary to reality. Self-observation and the joint method readily demonstrate that when we ascribe to the treasury rights with regard to ourselves or to others, we are concerned with an idea entirely different from the idea to which the word "state" corresponds. The idea of "state" ordinarily comprises the idea of territory and nation. There is nothing of this in the idea of "treasury," which is akin to the idea of a cash box and the like. The nature of other so-called juristic persons: monasteries, churches, and so forth is misinterpreted in another sense if they are understood as combinations of persons, social organisms, and the like. In reality, the content of the relevant ideas is different: thus the notion of buildings and so forth enters into the idea of "monastery," especially if it is a matter of a particular monastery known to the individual.

In various fields of law, the application of the scientific-psychological method of study (in this case the joint method of inward and outward observation and the study of written sources) reveals varied and heterogeneous beings as subjects (various subject ideas). Thus the subject of rights and obligations, after the death of a person and before the acquisition of the inheritance by the heirs, may be the dead testator according to one law and the *hereditas jacens* according to another. This should be so stated, without misinterpretation and without fanciful speculation. The attitude of the contemporary legal consciousness as to the legal nature of an estate between death and the receipt of the inheritance often consists, however, in ascribing corresponding rights and obligations neither to the deceased nor to the *hereditas jacens* as such, but to a subject less definite by nature and approximately corresponding to the pronoun "someone." A confused consciousness that a certain right — for example, a right of property in something that has been found — belongs to "someone" is a phenomenon which is extremely common and of great significance in legal life.

The nature of what in the external world corresponds to subject ideas is not among the problems to be investigated scientifically by legal theory. It would be as inconsistent to describe the nature of "social organisms" in a doctrine of persons (even if the existence of superorganic beings were revealed) as it would be out of place to discuss the anatomy and physiology of man in a doctrine concerned with "physical persons."

(3) Like general theoretical investigations and theories of law in general, investigations concerning subjects should extend as well into the field of intuitive law and of all positive law also (whether or not it is officially acknowledged) in order that various scientific faults — particularly that of "limping" — may be avoided. What is now formulated as a general doctrine concerning subjects is accepted as such only by reason of a misunderstanding. In reality it is an inadequate interpretation of contemporary official law. A study of unofficial law through the introspective and joint method shows that such subjects as animals, the dead, saints, and so forth have by no means passed into the field of history. They play a part even in modern legal life. The same investigations — psychological analysis which is not limited to the narrow framework of official law — can greatly broaden the horizon, and vastly increase the material for a doctrine concerning juristic persons. In unofficial law there are innumerable and diverse juristic persons. If we do not know the proprietor of a shop or the like with which we are concerned, our legal mind ordinarily conceives of the establishment as a juristic person, although by official law the subject is the proprietor. The presiding officer of an assembly, the council of elders, and the "student body" of a university, are all juristic persons of unofficial law and so forth.

(4) As to who or what can be the subject of legal relationships, obligations, and rights, the psychological theory holds that subject ideas can correspond to all possible ideas of a personal or individual character: insofar as legal impulsions and other ideas — object ideas and so forth — are associated with them the objects of these ideas are the subjects of rights. These can be objects not actually alive but assumed to be animate (such as stones, plants, and so forth), animals and their spirits, persons (including their embryos and their spirits after death), human societies and institutions, and various deities and other incor-

poreal spirits. Everything depends upon the level of culture, religious creed, and individual peculiarities of the given man, his age and so forth (in child law there are such subjects of a right as dolls which are not found in the legal mind of adults, and vice versa).

It must be especially emphasized that *not only are individuals who actually exist subjects of obligations and rights, but so are classes and species thereof,* although classes neither exist in the external world nor designate real combinations of objects now present: they are purely ideal quantities (embracing as well future and other imagined objects, once they possess specified attributes). Thus in the legal relationship: "Parents have a right to punish children, children are bound to endure punishment by their parents," the subjects of the right and of the obligation are not individuals but classes: the class of parents and the class of children.

Legal relationships, rights, and obligations must accordingly be divided into individual (concrete) and class (general). However, "abstract legal relationships," in the sense of general concepts of legal relationships or general ideas of legal relationships of a certain type, must not be confused with general (class) relationships in the sense indicated *supra.* Whereas it follows from the essence of the prevailing doctrine as to law that "legal relationships" between those who are not individuals — between classes or species of beings — are utterly unthinkable, such relationships are in fact not only thinkable but experienced by us at every step, as self-observation shows — further demonstrating the ineptitude of the prevailing ideas and theories of law.

Among the countless classes which act in the legal mind as subjects of rights and obligations, special significance must be attached to that designated by the pronouns "all," "each," "everyone whoever he may be," and the like. Reference has already been made to absolute rights known to modern jurisprudence but incapable of being explained thereby. These include the right of property, the right of life, the right of bodily inviolability, the right of honor, and so forth. They are simply rights the subject of whose obligation is the class: "every," or "each." As there are absolute rights, so it must be conceded that there are absolute obligations, wherein the subject of the right is the class "every," or "each and every." Such is my obligation to refrain from encroachment upon life or honor, whosesoever the life or honor may be.

In the science of morality there are no particular doubts or difficulties as to subjects of obligations. There is no doctrine or controversy such as those of jurists with reference to juristic persons — but not because the science of morality is in advance of jurisprudence in this respect as having successfully examined the actual position of affairs and so forth. On the contrary here, too, as in many other fields, it has lagged behind, and is a science feebly developed as compared with jurisprudence: it still has not come to the point of knowing that the problem exists or of noting the existing facts and questions therewith connected. It is clear from the reasoning of philosophers and moralists as to morality and moral obligations that they start, as from something self-evident, from the postulate that morality may be, and is, "addressed" only to a "reasoning and free" will and that the obligor must necessarily be a person possessing such a will. This assumption is not at all in conformity with the nature of morality and is contradicted by phenomena of actual moral life. If, instead of deliberating from the point of view of what seems reasonable, philosophers and moralists occupied themselves with the psychological study of the facts of moral life, they would readily see that the subjects of moral obligations include states, communes, cities, counties, universities, corporations, and the like. To such subjects are ascribed moral obligations to be concerned for the poor, to administer education, and to have an honorable and benevolent attitude toward those who serve, work, and so forth. In other words, if moral science possessed even such knowledge regarding subjects of obligations as does jurisprudence, the problem of moral persons would have come up. The same problem should exist also in the field of aesthetics, for the rules of elegant conduct extend likewise to the conduct of states and so forth. But the science of aesthetics is backward, not only in that it has no doctrine of aesthetic subjects, but it lacks even a doctrine of aesthetic norms and normative experiences and still concerns itself exclusively with the interpretation of enjoyments from the perception of beauty.

The fact that states and other so-called juristic persons are subjects of moral obligations and aesthetic decencies as well as of legal obligations — a fact which may readily be verified, and profitably studied, through self-observation and the joint method — is instructive not only for the science of ethics and aesthetics but for legal science as well. Attention thereto also broadens the horizon of the legal theory of subjects, and discloses the superficiality and ineptitude of various doctrines adapted especially to law. In the light of morality and aesthetics, the very term "juristic persons" appears unfortunate and expressive of mistaken ideas.

Furthermore, subjects of moral obligations (and of aesthetic demands) may be and are even animals, the spirits of the dead, deities, and so forth, and comprise both individuals and classes (including "each").

In general the foregoing with regard to subjects of a right is true as well of moral subjects (subjects of moral obligations) and of aesthetic subjects: the essential difference is that in law there are pairs of subjects whereas in morality and in aesthetics there is only one.

SECTION 27. *The Objects of Moral and Legal Obligations and Rights*

In the prevailing view, objects of rights are objects of the dominance, or of the realization of interests, which are furnished or guaranteed by subjective rights.

It is customary to distinguish various objects, depending on the various types of rights. Things are recognized as objects of the right of property and of limited *jura in re aliena.* The prevailing doctrine of objects, developed on the basis of the science of Roman law, contains little more than the doctrine of things and various kinds of things: movables and immovables, simple and complex, and so forth. By the prevailing view, objects of rights created by contracts and other obligations are the actions of the debtor, positive and negative (abstentions). Objects of family rights — of rights of marital and parental authority in particular — are the personalities of subordinate parties. The object of a right of inheritance is the property remaining after the death of another. It is also widely held that the very personality of the obligee is the object where rights of life, body inviolability, honor, and similar so-called rights of personality are concerned.

Opposed to the traditional and prevailing theory — the pluralistic theory — of various species of objects of rights are monistic theories of objects, by which something single and homogeneous is considered an object of rights. Some of these hold that only things are such objects, and others that actions (including abstentions) are such objects, while still others recognize persons as such objects (because the law grants them dominance over other persons) or the "will" of another (opposed to the obligee), or the forces of nature and human forces. The part played by monistic theories in literature is not, however, important: they have only single supporters, and even in the works of these they are for the most part decorative and introductory observations after which the authors pass to the common point of view of the plurality of objects of various rights and assemble more or less extensive and motley collections thereof.

The chief shortcoming of the prevailing doctrine as to objects — as indeed of other doctrines of contemporary jurisprudence — is that it searches for objects elsewhere than in the proper sphere. In the science of morality there exists no doctrine corresponding to that of jurisprudence concerning objects.

The building of a proper theory of objects is extremely important for both legal and moral sciences in order that obligations, rights, norms, and so forth may be correctly understood. Such a theory and correct classification of objects must start from the methodological principles already indicated, studying that which is in the mind of the person experiencing the moral and legal processes and achieving the corresponding projections, employing self-observation and so forth, and keeping clear of arbitrary interpretations and conclusions from preconceived theories about interests and the like. Thereafter a general scheme of objects of obligations — a single scheme for the legal and the moral sciences alike — can be constructed, and on this basis a supplementary doctrine of objects of rights worked out in accordance with the attributive nature of the law.

Ethical impulsions are abstract impulsions not endowed with specific responses (being distinguished therein from special impulsions: hunger, fear, anger, and the like) but operating in favor of the conduct whose idea is experienced in connection with the given ethical impulsion. Accordingly the essential intellectual element of ethical experiences is the action idea: idea of the conduct in favor of (or against) which the given ethical impulsions operate. An experience of obligation without the idea of conduct to which the given subject is bound is unthinkable: to be bound to nothing means not to be bound at all. The corresponding necessary intellectual complement of the predicate "obligation" — in other words, the conduct conceived of as due — we term the object of the obligation. Effectuation of the relevant idea — the real performance of the relevant action — is the fulfillment of obligation. In accordance with the abstract nature of moral and legal impulsions, the objects of obligations may be all possible classes of conduct, including any conceivable actions, external and internal — even the purely internal in the field of law and the purely external in the field of morality — and comprising (in both fields) not only actions which we conceive of as reasonable, advantageous for others or for society, and increasing the amount of happiness and the like (as sundry philosophers, moralists and jurists mistakenly suppose), but unreasoning and harmful actions as well.

It has already been shown that all possible classes of conduct can be reduced to three categories: positive actions, abstentions, and tolerances. This threefold division of actions was known even to the Roman jurists long ago, who distinguished *facere*, *non-facere*, and *pati* as three possible classes of obligatory conduct. Recently a twofold division has prevailed, distinguishing positive actions and negative actions (or abstentions), on the ground that norms prescribing tolerance of something do in essence signify that to offer resistance is forbidden, and so tolerances are ordinarily not mentioned at all as a special category of obligatory conduct.

The reduction of tolerances to abstentions from opposition results from the application of an unscientific method: the facts are arbitrarily misinterpreted from the point of view of the practical consideration (that one equals the other in practical result) whereas the psychological method studies what is in reality found in one's own or in another's mind.

It is indisputable that obligations to tolerate anything and obligations of abstention (including obligations to refrain from opposition) are distinct phenomena from the psychological point of view. The content of their object ideas is completely different. There are, incidentally, cases of the consciousness of a duty of tolerance in a field wherein ordinarily there is not even a thought of opposition or of abstention therefrom, and from which the corresponding association of ideas is excluded: such are cases of the consciousness of a duty to tolerate patiently and without repining — to endure submissively — diseases, ruin, the death of those near to us, and other misfortunes sent down by an omnipotent God. Here the idea of opposition and of abstention therefrom — as in general in the field of relations to the Almighty — does not ordinarily arise at all: it is already forestalled and eliminated by the idea of omnipotence. Moreover, it is ordinarily a matter of enduring, not actions or events which are impending (so that the idea of averting or hindering them is admissible), but events which have already taken place. The obligation to endure with submission the death of one who is near, or other unhappiness sent down by God, excludes the thought of opposing or hindering: not merely because the other party is omnipotent, but because the event has already occurred. As to the time prior to the event — for instance, before the onset of the death of one who was dear — consciousness of a duty to endure misfortunes sent down by God does not exclude resort to the physician and the like, although this means an attempt not to permit the onset of the threatening event.

In accordance with the division of conduct into actions, abstentions, and tolerances, three classes of moral and legal obligations are to be distinguished: "action" obligations, "abstention" obligations, and "tolerance" obligations.

The object of moral and legal obligations may, moreover, be such conduct (conceived of as due) as consists in more or less complicated combinations, sequences, and systems, of various separate actions, abstentions, and tolerances. The obligation to bring up children, to govern a country and the like represent obligations directed at complex systems of diverse actions, abstentions and tolerances unified by the general ideas and terms: "to bring up children" and "to govern the country." Accordingly (1) simple or elemental objects, separately conceived of as due, positive and negative actions and tolerances and simple obligations, are to be distinguished from (2) complex objects and complex obligations.

The fulfillment of various legal and moral obligations — the actualization of the corresponding objects — ordinarily presupposes accomplishment by the obligor of various other positive or negative actions, or tolerances on his part, or both, as the means or the necessary conditions for realizing the required effect. Thus fulfillment of the legal obligation to pay another a sum of money owing to him, or of the moral obligation to render financial assistance to another, presupposes acquisition by the obligor of the corresponding amount, abstention by him from spending it on his own needs or pleasures, tolerance by him of the corresponding deprivations, and the like. Fulfillment of the obligation of a railroad switchman by the time the train passes presupposes his refraining from sleep and intoxication, his presence at the place where his obligation is to be performed, his endurance of bad weather and cold, and so forth. Originating in the consciousness of a given condition of duty, ideas of actions, abstentions, or tolerances — essential for the performance of that duty — appear (through the association of ideas or by inference) and to them ethical impulsions are extended, so that they in turn become objects of obligations. Such objects — as well as the corresponding obligations and norms, and in general the corresponding moral and legal experiences — may be termed "auxiliary" or "subsequent," to distinguish them from those which are primary or basic.

Auxiliary objects may accompany all possible primary objects — and, in particular, not only positive actions but abstentions and tolerances as well — and may in turn consist in various species of conduct — in particular, in positive actions, abstentions, and tolerances — irrespective of the nature of the primary objects. The foregoing examples show that objects auxiliary to positive actions as primary objects may be positive actions and also abstentions and tolerances. The same is true as to objects auxiliary to abstentions and tolerances. Thus where there is a duty to tolerate paternal punishment, confinement in prison, the carrying out of a death sentence, and the like, the auxiliary objects may be various positive actions (appearing before one's father, admitting that one had done the criminal act, returning to one's own country, appearing before the police or prosecuting officer, and so forth), various abstentions (from concealment, falsehood, escape, or opposition), and various tolerances (of arrest, of preliminary confinement, of examinations, of speeches by the prosecutor, and so forth).

Auxiliary objects are chiefly referable to the stage preceding the realization of the primary objects. Thus abstention from opposition — as an object auxiliary to the duty of tolerance — is related ordinarily to a time preceding the time of tolerance: to the time of an actual attempt by another (who is not sufficiently powerful to exclude the idea of opposition) to cause us a certain evil, or the like. Non-opposition as an object auxiliary to the duty to tolerate confinement in prison, carrying out of a death sentence, and the like appears precedent to the primary, obligatory effect. Auxiliary objects may, however, be related to the time when the chief object is being realized (for example, refraining from escape while one is serving a prison sentence) or to a subsequent time. Thus, the object auxiliary to the duty to give something to another may be abstention from taking it away later. One bound by contract to surrender to the authority of another as captive, hostage, and the like, who — having accomplished this "formality" — immediately runs away, cannot be said properly to have fulfilled the duty, because he has violated the corresponding auxiliary duty and so forth. Thus among auxiliary objects and the corresponding obligations and norms, a distinction may be drawn between precedent, concurrent and subsequent. The Hebrews often violated their obligation of tolerance with regard to the actions of Jehovah, in that they repined during or after these actions: it was chiefly in this manner that their obligations were violated.

The concepts suggested, and distinction between primary and auxiliary objects, obligations, and norms, as well as the study of the corresponding phenomena of the moral and legal psyche, are valuable for the moral and legal sciences in various respects.

To interpret correctly the sources of positive morality (the Christian morality, for example) and of positive law and to build the corresponding doctrines on correct principles requires constant attention to the fact that the corresponding association of ideas frequently causes auxiliary objects and obligations (in place of, or on an equality with primary objects and obligations) to be mentioned in written or oral communications of moral and legal ideas.

In the moral system of Christ, as correctly understood, obligations of tolerance are of the highest importance but — like other obligations — they are often depicted and explained in the New Testament by pointing out various auxiliary objects, and since those who interpret them do not have at their command a proper theory of morality and its elements, the result is misunderstanding which may be extremely serious and can substantially distort the meaning of the moral philosophy of the New Testament. Thus the derivation of a moral system of apathy — of abstention from struggling with evil and from counteracting it — is drawn from the Sermon on the Mount, with its allusion to not opposing evil and offering the other cheek (Matthew 5:39). The Sermon contains two propositions which manifestly have in view two species of obligations: the first is concerned with the negative obligation to abstain from opposition; and the second with the positive obligation to offer the other cheek. But it is manifest, if the logical connection of these propositions, and what has been said as to primary and auxiliary objects and obligations — particularly as to auxiliary objects in the field of obligations of tolerance — are taken into account, that the Sermon is here expressing a single moral idea and illustrating a single moral obligation, which is not an obligation of abstention and not an obligation to positive actions, but an obligation of tolerance (willingly to tolerate evil caused to us: an insult, for instance). To illustrate this obligation — and, in general, the corresponding moral idea — two auxiliary objects and obligations are pointed out, and it is manifest, when the logical connection of the foregoing language from the Sermon with that which immediately precedes it (the former commandment of blood vengeance, on the principle of talio, an eye for an eye, a tooth for a tooth and so forth) is taken into account, that there is still a third class of auxiliary objects and obligations which are consecutive with reference to tolerance: specifically, abstentions from vengeance. Only upon such an interpretation is the contrast understandable and logically justified: "But I say unto you" and so forth. The same is true of the later propositions as to the shirt and the cloak and so on, which are obviously not further independent obligations to positive actions, but additional explanations of the obligation of tolerance as the primary obligation. To consider the injunction as to non-opposition separately and to regard the corresponding obligation of abstention as an independent general obligation leads to a completely different moral doctrine: the apathetic and inert attitude towards evil which has been proclaimed by some because of their faulty understanding of the Sermon on the Mount. The other interpretation does not exclude the struggle for the good and against the evil which Christ and His disciples carried on in its most sublime form. It is in and by means of this struggle that the lofty obligations of tolerance may be realized: tolerance of misfortunes, persecutions, and insults, and the willing endurance without malicious and egoistic reactions, demonstrated in the great example of the Teacher Himself.

Similar expression and illustration of moral obligations by pointing out auxiliary obligations are very common in the New Testament and other written sources of moral philosophy, and not infrequent even in legal sources — including modern statutes and codes — in spite of the prevailing tendency of the law toward exact formulation (a tendency which is foreign to morality).

Besides ideas of the bodily movements and other actions, as such, the structure of the object ideas (in our sense) also includes — in the fields of morality and law — ideas which define more precisely what is necessary for proper fulfillment of the obligation — modal or complementary object ideas and their modal or object complements. They comprise (1) ideas of the time when the action must be accomplished (such as aid without delay, or payment on such and such a date), (2) ideas of place (to bring an object to such and such a place), (3) ideas of attributes of obligatory action (of the means or order of accomplishment, of quality or quantity and so forth: for example, with due caution, willingly, zealously, gradually, as necessary, and so forth), (4) ideas of things or other benefits which should be furnished to obligees, from action upon which obligors should refrain or whose use by another should be tolerated, and (5) ideas of the addressees of obligatory actions — of persons or other beings for whose benefit certain conduct, abstention, or tolerance is required — for example, those for whom something should be furnished, from encroachment upon whom abstention is required, or whose actions must be tolerated.

In law, the addresses of action are ordinarily obligees (subjects of rights): in other words, the ideas of addressees of obligations coincide with or are absorbed by ideas of subjects of a right and so are not separately experienced. Hence the addressees and obligees are sometimes identified in theory. This, however, is to confuse concepts which should be kept strictly distinct. From the psychological point of view, ideas of addressees of obligatory (moral or legal) action, on the one hand, and ideas of subjects of a legal claim, on the other, play essentially different parts and occupy different positions in the structure of ethical experiences. By no means do the terms "addressees" and "subjects" of a right always coincide in legal experiences: if a father hires a nurse for his child, or makes a contract with the owner of an apartment or boardinghouse in the city for furnishing lodging and food to his children, the corresponding legal experiences comprise both the idea of children as the addressees of obligatory actions (feeding and other concerns) and the idea of the other contracting party (the father) as the subject of the claim. To states are ascribed mutual claims and obligations whose addressees are individual subjects. In religious law various claims belong to deities in respect of men: that their relations with their neighbors be of a certain pattern, that they accomplish certain actions in their behalf, that they abstain from encroachments on their life, honor, and property, and so forth. Obligors may themselves be addressees in law: thus where the action of subservient and social authorities is concerned — the authority of a guardian or parent, or of the state — the subjects of the relevant authorities have a right to fulfillment of these commands by those under them although they issue the commands not for their own sake but for the sake of the very persons who are under their authority. Sometimes this is specifically indicated: as where passengers are forbidden to go upon the platform of a moving train lest their lives be endangered.

In contemporary moral science ideas of addressees play an extremely important part notwithstanding the complete lack of the corresponding scientific concepts and doctrines, as is the situation with respect to the other elements of moral experiences. The relevant ideas are at the foundation of the commonly accepted classification of moral obligations (and virtues) and of the scientific system which is itself built upon a classification of obligations (or virtues). Modern moral philosophy distinguishes two classes of moral obligations: (1) obligations with regard to onself (individual obligations, "individual" virtues); and (2) obligations with reference to neighbors and others ("social" obligations, social virtues). Earlier the prevailing doctrine had divided obligations into three classes and set out the system under three headings: (1) obligations with regard to God; (2) obligations with regard to oneself; and (3) obligations with regard to one's neighbors; and this threefold division still prevails in Christian ethics, in the corresponding learned treatises and in catechisms.

Neither of these classifications and systems, resting manifestly on a differentiation of moral issues depending upon addressees, can withstand the test of criticism: each must be rejected for the following reasons. (1) First of all it must be conceded that the proposition at the foundation of the classification and system now under criticism — that all moral obligations presuppose a certain addressee: that they are all obligations with reference to someone — is unsound. There are, on the contrary, a multitude of obligations (and of moral experiences in general) wherein there are no addressees of any sort. This is so as to the majority of obligations traditionally classified under the heading of obligations with reference to oneself (so-called individual obligations), such as the obligations (and virtues) of moderation, self-possession, courage, wisdom, modesty, and so forth. If the proper method of study (self-observation and so forth) is employed, the conclusion readily follows that the relevant obligations are experienced ordinarily with no ideas of any addressees whatsoever. We are bound to be modest, moderate, and so forth; but this is so *per se*, and not for the sake of — or in relation to — anyone: there is ordinarily no idea whatever of oneself, or of anyone else, as addressee, although sometimes this idea is present (in which case the relevant obligations are obligations with addressees). But the same is true also as to many obligations traditionally qualified as obligations with reference to others: self-observation readily demonstrates that the obligations traditionally set out as obligations with reference to others under the heading "truthfulness" are likewise in reality obligations which are ordinarily without addressees: "one should speak the truth," "one should not lie" and the like *per se*, and not for the sake of another. It sometimes happens, however, that the obligation not to lie is experienced as an obligation with reference to others — the person experiencing it has the idea of another to whom a particular lie might cause harm, and considers himself bound to abstain therefrom in reference to and for the sake of that other. But in such cases abstention from the lie is ordinarily not an independent object of the obligation of truthfulness as such, but only a consecutive auxiliary object to the obligation not to cause harm to another. The same is true as to a multitude of other obligations for which moralists arbitrarily devise addressees in order to bring them under the traditional heading of a system and classification. In general, the traditional classification of obligations, the system of exposition and the corresponding interpretations and misinterpretations of various obligations and virtues on the part of modern moral science may be said to be an essential distortion and destruction of genuine morality.

(2) Again, if we leave on one side the misunderstanding just pointed out, and pause especially on moral experiences and obligations wherein there actually is an idea of some personal addressee of the relevant actions, the assumption on which the traditional classification of obligations and the corresponding doctrines is based is erroneous. Many moral experiences and obligations which do have individual addressees of the relevant actions are directed at causing those addressees not good but evil: death, insult, and so forth. The relevant addressees, and the corresponding obligations and ethical experiences in general, may be termed odious, to distinguish them from addressees of good, and of the corresponding obligations and ethical experiences in general, which may be called caritative. To prove that such odious obligations, norms, and so forth (incompatible with the traditional theories of moralists) can and

do exist we have not far to go: the propositions as to suffering evil, seen above in the New Testament, are set out in the Sermon on the Mount, as contrasted with the earlier commandments prescribing vengeance; further propositions thereto as to loving one's enemies are opposed to the earlier commandments enjoining hatred (Matthew 5:38, 43).

Obligations to hate enemies in the international, inter-tribal, and inter-individual sense — to injure them in every possible way, to persecute them and exterminate them without mercy — constitute the basis, or at any rate an extremely important element, of morality in all nations at a certain stage of development. It is from the point of view of those principles, and the obligations and virtues therewith connected (bravery, craft, implacability, and even cruelty in general), that the ethical appraisal of persons is made in these stages of development. The opposite types of conduct and character traits — such as gentleness and forbearance towards enemies, readiness to compromise with them, lack of militancy, pugnacity, bravery — are considered to be evil. Even in the Bible which is the chronicle of a comparatively lofty culture, compromises with enemies, sparing their lives, and so forth are considered grievous transgressions (see the story of Saul). Even Plato, admittedly the greatest philosopher-idealist of the most cultured nation of antiquity, ascribed to the citizen-warriors of his ideal Utopian state the virtues which distinguish vicious dogs. "Barbarians" — that is, all persons except the tiny tribe of Greeks — seemed to him natural enemies who must be neither indulged nor spared. Lack of militancy and bravery entails banishment from his ideal state: the greatest rewards and honors, in life and after death, are won by bravery against enemies. Education is organized accordingly: children are inured to pictures of mass killings, battles and so forth. Even now among so-called civilized nations — to say nothing of barbarians and savages in the narrow sense, and notwithstanding the outward confession of Christian teaching — manifestations of similar moral principles with regard to persons of another nationality, religion, and so forth are by no means alien. The purification of factual morality from elements of revenge is still the task of the future. The lower the culture, the less in general is the significance of caritative obligations (and the narrower is the circle of their addressees) and the greater is the significance of odious obligations and the sharper and harsher is their content (and the broader is the circle of their addressees).

The current doctrinal identification of morality with altruism — with conduct directed at the general happiness and the like — illustrates and emphasizes the fact that the nature of morality is essentially unknown and that the practical views and reasoning of particular individuals are substituted for the objective-psychological study of phenomena. In conformity with what has already been set out herein, the traditional classification of obligations from the point of view of addressees must be abandoned, and replaced by division into: (1) obligations without addressees (neutral or objective obligations), and (2) obligations having addressees and subdivided into (a) odious, and (b) caritative obligations. Only with reference to the second species of the second class of obligations could the prevailing classification be correct — and that only if it comprised a correct classification of caritative addressees. This, however, cannot be conceded. The division of caritative obligations into obligations with reference to oneself (or so-called individual obligations) and obligations with reference to others (or so-called social obligations) is a "limping" classification which embraces only some out of many species of caritative obligations. Somewhat better — though likewise far from satisfactory — would be the old threefold classification which did not forget God as the addressee of moral obligations.

A multitude of other categories of addressees exists over and above the addressees of moral obligations known to current moral science and taken by it into consideration: there are all the categories of assumed beings already pointed out in the doctrine concerning the subjects of moral and legal obligations and rights, as well as all imagined beings in general including the spirits of the deceased, animals, beings whom jurists call juristic persons, and so forth. Examples and proof may readily be found in abundance through self-observation and the joint method, and need not be cited here.

What has been set out *supra* as to the division of moral obligations — and in general of moral experiences — from the point of view of the idea of addressees is applicable as well, *mutatis mutandis*, to legal obligations and experiences in general. Here, too, neutral or objective obligations (obligations without addressees), caritative obligations and otiose obligations are to be distinguished. Here, too, addressees may include not only persons but animals, the spirits of the dead, deities, juristic persons, and so forth. The traditional view of the jurists — particularly of the criminalists — is that the law safeguards only human interests, and that its prohibitions as to the cruel treatment of animals, the violation of graves, blasphemy and the like are not for the sake of animals, the dead, or God, but for the sake of people: so that unpleasant feelings may not be aroused among them. This is an arbitrary and methodologically inadmissible misinterpretation of facts dictated by the practical views of particular individuals.

The foregoing exposition contains a scheme of objects of obligations and their elements which is common to moral and legal experiences, and capable of serving as a guide for the analysis, interpretation, and other study of moral phenomena, as well as of legal phenomena insofar as it is a matter of the imperative side of the latter.

In the field of law this scheme of object ideas needs amplification in accordance with the law's attributive nature. It has already been pointed out that, in accordance with the attributive nature of legal impulsions, legal experiences comprise ideas of the positive effects — the "receipts," in the general sense: the plus — due to the obligees as well as (or instead of) ideas of actions required from the obligor (ideas of objects of obligations). The furnishing to the obligees of these "receipts" (the realization of the objects of the right) plays a decisive part in the law, whereas fulfillment on the part of obligors of the actions to which they are bound (the realization of the objects of the obligation) is merely a means of attaining this effect, so that if the corresponding "receipts" are furnished to the obligee by whatever means (though it be without the fulfillment of the relevant action on the part of the obligor) the legal mentality is satisfied thereby as the appropriate accomplishment of what was required. In precisely the same way it has been shown that positive "receipts" — receipts in the narrow sense as objects of the relevant rights: *facere-accipere* — correspond to positive actions (actions in the narrow sense as objects of obligations); non-tolerances of the relevant actions — "inviolabilities" or "safeguardings" (*non facere — non pati*) — correspond as objects of rights to negative actions — abstentions; the relevant actions tolerated by the obligors, or freedom to act (*pati-facere*) correspond as objects of rights to tolerances. There may, therefore, be said to be three species of rights and of legal obligations, norms, and so forth: positive-attributive, negative-attributive and empowering; or legal claims in the narrow sense, legal safeguardings and legal empowerings. In other respects what has already been set out as to ideas of the objects of obligations in general is applicable *mutatis mutandis* to ideas of objects of rights.

Here, too, primary and auxiliary or consecutive objects, and primary and auxiliary rights, can and must be distinguished. Thus the power to undertake various actions which are the means or the preliminary stages of punishment (such as the arrest of the criminal or other means of achieving power over him) and various negative claims (to abstention by the person subject to punishment from what would impede the realization of the right of punishment and so forth) correspond, as auxiliary rights, to the right of punishment as the primary right. If property should come into the possession of another — if, for example, it was found in his shed — the claim of the owner to have the thing handed over or to be admitted in order to take it, to have the closed place opened, and so forth, corresponds to the primary right of the owner: capacity to use his property and, in general, to do with it whatever he pleases.

Moreover, even where ideas of the objects of obligations are concerned, we must distinguish — exactly as in the case of ideas of objects of rights — modal or supplementary ideas: (1) of the time of the relevant receiving, (2) of the place, (3) of attributes, quality, order, and so forth, (4) of material or object ideas, and (5) of ideas of addressees: for example, the father has a right that such-and-such a thing (the object idea) be furnished to his son (the addressee) at a certain time (time) at a certain place (place). The relevant ideas: time, place, and so forth are modalities or amplification of objects of rights.

Combinations of objects of obligations and of corresponding objects of rights are objects of legal relationships. Our proposed threefold scheme of objects of obligations and objects of corresponding rights: *facere-accipere*, ***non facere-non pati***, and ***pati-facere*** (with their modalities) is a scheme of three species of objects of legal relationships.

In combination with the concept and the scheme of modalities, this scheme comprises a general theoretical enumeration and classification of the relevant elements of legal phenomena, and a guide to their correct and clear interpretation and analysis — as well as to the synthesis — of legal phenomena, rights, obligations, norms of law and legal phenomena in general. It does not, however, signify that a given legal experience completely expresses the objects of legal relationships in the shape of paired ideas in accordance with the twofold scheme *facere-accipere*, and so forth, which occurs only in certain legal experiences and expressions. Ordinarily object ideas and the corresponding verbal expressions have a shorter and more succinct character.

As to the forms of expression of legal experiences in general, it has been shown that, in addition to the complete and adequate form, three abbreviations exist: the abbreviated-attributive (which points out only the subjects and objects of the right), the abbreviated imperative (which points out only subjects and objects of the obligation), and the doubly abbreviated or neutral (which points out impersonally what is appropriate: compensation for damages, for example). Accordingly, in the field of object ideas we may distinguish four forms of experience and expression: the full or the adequate, and three abbreviations.

Besides these there are various other abbreviations. There are complex rights, consisting of legal empowerings and legal claims, portrayed in abbreviated form through pointing out the actions to which the obligee has a right, as if it were a matter of empowering only: thus a great many rights consist of two elements, (a) the legal power to make certain declarations so that others are bound to tolerate these actions (such as addressing another in an imperative tone, or propounding a question in parliament) and (b) a claim that what is expressed be taken in this or that sense (of fulfillment, of consideration, or of an answer, if it is a matter of questions, or in the sense of considering and satisfying or refusing if it is a matter of requests, applications, and so forth). Such is the characteristic composition of a vast number of legal relationships in political life. A typical form in which complex legal relationships are expressed is to point out that one has the right to make certain declarations or to issue such-and-such directions and the like (the monarch or the president has the right to declare war, to make such-and-such dispositions, to convene and to dismiss legislative houses, to command the army, to pardon criminals, and so forth; so as to rights of suffrage, to cast a decisive or a deliberative vote in the legislature, to administer, to file a petition or a complaint, of litigants to make certain declarations, and so forth). Here there is a combination of two abbreviations: (a) the abbreviated-attributive form and (b) an indication only of the corresponding legal power without pointing out the legal claim.

A broad category of legal relationships — including the right of property — consists of a combination of the legal power to do something (such as to use property or in general to do with it as one will, and the obligation of others to tolerate the relevant actions) with the negative claim that others refrain from the corresponding actions (from using the property and so forth). Here the typical form of expression consists in pointing out the abbreviated-attributive form of the legal power, with the addition sometimes of a hint at the negative claim in the form of ascribing to the use and the like the term "exclusive."

In pecuniary obligations — as is perfectly natural — national languages work out special abbreviated and simplified expressions for object symbols: thus instead of pointing out that A is bound to *pay* B so much, and B has a right to *receive* so much, it is stated simply that "A owes B so much," or "B has a right to so much, to interest," and the like. And in various other positive legal claims directed at the acquisition of a certain object, pointing out this object (one of the modalities of the complete object idea) not infrequently takes the place of a complete indication of the object of the right (A has a right to an order, a pension, alimony, a flat in a government-owned house, and the like).

As is true in the field of objects of obligations, auxiliary or consecutive objects (and rights) are not infrequently mentioned in legal expressions instead of principal objects (and rights), while positive and negative legal claims are not infrequently expressed in the inexact and mutilated form that the right to demand or to forbid something is ascribed to the obligee.

In these cases of abbreviated or inexact expression of the objects, the task of interpretation is to define and to express them in complete and proper form according to the scheme set out above.

SECTION 28. *Legal Facts and Morally Relevant Facts*

Associated with the doctrine of legal relationships — or, ordinarily, with that of rights — is a doctrine as to legal facts intimating that rights or legal relationships do not remain immutable: they arise, change, and come to an end in consequence of facts to which objective law appropriates the capacity to evoke them, or which by objective law condition them. These are called legally relevant facts, or legal facts, and the changes evoked by them in the field of legal relationships are termed their legal consequences. Legal facts are divided into two species: legal actions, and legal facts in the narrow sense or legal events.

The usual definition of legal actions as those manifestations of will which evoke legal consequences, or as legal facts evoked consciously by the will of man, rests on the psychological misunderstanding of assuming that there is always a will at the basis of psychologically determined bodily movements or inward actions. It is clear from what has been set out in Chapter I that actions are ordinarily evoked immediately by impulsions, and only in certain cases is there a will as an intermediate psychic link. Legal events include all other facts which entail legal consequences (death, birth, lapse of time, and the like).

Legal actions are divided into: (1) positive (actions in the narrow sense of the word) and negative (abstentions, omissions), while the third category (tolerances) slips out of sight; (2) actions of the parties participating in the legal relationship and actions of the authorities (such as court decisions or administrative orders); and (3) permitted and unpermitted actions.

Unpermitted, forbidden actions are actions or omissions contrary to the demands ("commands") of law and therefore evoking certain legal consequences disadvantageous to the lawbreaker — such as the obligation to make compensation for damage caused or to suffer punishment.

Their common identification with violations of law is incorrect since many such violations — for instance, violations of *leges imperfectae* or norms without sanctions — entail no legal consequences whatever.

Legal transactions are specially studied as a particularly important category of permitted actions. They are usually defined as expressions of will directed at establishing, terminating, or changing rights.

Transactions are divided into unilateral and bilateral (contracts). Unilateral are those which represent expressions of will by one side: expressions of one will, such as a will or the acceptance of an inheritance. Bilateral (contracts) are those which represent a concurrent expression of will of both (or of several) sides presupposing the unity or coincidence of wills, such as a contract of hire, purchase, or loan.

Legal transactions — chiefly contracts — are very important in the law and much has been written about them. However, this literature refers chiefly, if not entirely, to only one field of law: civil law, and does not touch public law (constitutional or international law). Consequently the term "legal transaction" commonly designates the relevant civil law acts whereas acts substantially similar have a place and play an important part in other fields of law as well. Leaving this out of view, jurists borrow the corresponding ideas, terms, and propositions from existing literature which is not adequate to the task and content of general legal theory. This should be corrected; and in particular, besides the concept and term "transaction" as a special concept and term of civil law, a more general concept and general term should be introduced, embracing corresponding acts of all fields of law. A suitable term for this is "legal act." From the point of view of this terminology, transactions form one species of legal acts: viz, legal acts of the civil law.

Moreover, this literature is essentially deficient in that it is not based on such familiarity with the nature of the legal (imperative-attributive) mentality as is essential in this field, but makes use, instead, of unsuitable substitutes which do not correspond to the nature of contracts and of legal acts in general — ideas "of will," "unity of wills," "expression of will," and so forth.

The very appearance of contracts and other transactions (legal acts in general), creating bonds with regard to another — securing a duty in behalf of others — or involving the management or disposal of duties of others already existing and secured in behalf of a given individual as his property, can be explained by the attributive nature of the law and represents its peculiar characteristic. In morality there neither are nor can be obligations established by contract or disposed of by any transactions whatsoever.

Contracts and unilateral legal acts are not expressions of will or of the coincidence of wills, and so forth, as assumed by the traditional theory; they are expressions of specific experiences of the legal imperative-attributive type.

In different cases, acts of the legal mentality are expressed symbolically. First of all, the nature of contracts which create obligations and rights as between the parties (in their minds, and in general in the legal mind) is expressed by symbolic actions already described.[1] One side extends its hand or some other object to the other, and the other side grasps it — thereby symbolizing the assurance of the duty of one in behalf of the other: the establishment of an obligation with reference to another — of a right for the other. What occurs and is symbolized here is something wholly different from an experience of will, or of the coincidence or unity of wills. Will is a purely active psychic process, combined with the idea of certain future action of the subject of the will, and directed at future realization of a specified action idea. Here, however, actual binding of one side with reference to the other takes place, and is symbolized, in the minds of the parties, as an actual and final securing of the obligation of one in behalf of the other. The corresponding acts of the legal minds are accompanied by corresponding projections and their symbolic expression: on the side of the obligor is consciousness of the legal binding of one's self (attributive with reference to the other side), while on the side of the obligee there is consciousness of the legal acquisition of assurance of the duty in his behalf. In view of a theory that in these cases wills coincide or are made one, it must be emphasized that the relevant acts of the legal minds have a distinct content, corresponding to the distinct position of the imperative and attributive sides, as is portrayed by the accomplishment of correspondingly different symbolic actions. Oral or written declarations of the parties when the contract is made carry the same meaning as do these symbolic actions: that is to say, that one side is bound, assuming an obligation in the present, while the other side is granted the right to do thus and so, to require thus and so, and the like. Insofar as a future time is sometimes applicable — it is said in behalf of the obligor that he will do so and so, or will not do so and so — these declarations mean, not that he is expressing a will to accomplish the corresponding actions in the future, but that he is in the present taking upon himself the corresponding obligation. Moreover, before a contract is concluded, or at the time of concluding it or thereafter, there may be a genuine expression

[1] Cf. Section 7.

of will — of a "firm will" and the like — actually and exactly to carry out the corresponding obligation (to accomplish the corresponding action, and so forth), but this is neither required for the contract nor referable thereto. Sometimes when a contract is concluded an intention is assumed — or even openly expressed — not to carry it out in case of difficulties, or simply of unwillingness (this may sometimes be more advantageous for the other side than performance because of the right to compensation and the like). But this in no way lessens the legal force of the contract. On the other side, an expression of the will to do something in the future in favor of the interlocutor does not, as such, signify the assumption of the obligation to do this and has no legal significance. Of course, the conclusion of the contract may itself be produced by a preceding decision of will — of a will to conclude a certain contract, to take upon oneself a certain obligation, and so forth; but, as is true of other actions, it may likewise be — and often is — not a will action but an impulsive action (although this is likewise unessential and irrelevant as regards the contract). It is no less true that the expression of a will to conclude a contract — to take upon oneself an obligation, to accomplish the corresponding actions in the future — by no means signifies that one assumes an obligation in the present, and has no obligatory significance.

Since, in conformity with the attributive nature of law, the obligations or duties of some appear as belonging to others, the latter (if there are no special obstacles in the way) can dispose of them as of their own property; hence in law, as distinguished from morality, there can be various contracts (and unilateral acts) consisting in the management and disposition of existing duties-rights, with or without the participation of the obligor. These contracts may be termed right-dispositive, in the narrow sense, as distinguished from the contracts which are right-creative.

The creditor — the obligee — thus can, if there is no fundamental obstacle thereto, remit the debt and thereby free the obligor. The nature of the contract of release is expressed in the corresponding symbolic actions, consisting in the return of the debt, document, or other object symbolically representing it by the owner to the obligor, or in other conduct showing the end of the holding thereof by the obligee. While consciousness that a legal obligation has been created — that the debt has been secured — exists and is expressed in right-creating contracts, consciousness of legal emancipation — of terminating the boundness — and of ending the situation of a debt actually belonging to the obligee is manifested in right-dispositive contracts. As in the field of right-creating contracts, what occurs here is not an expression of will as to the future, but a present disposition of the debt.

Contracts whereby the parties produce changes in the legal relationship existing between them — diminution of the debt (partial liberation), increasing the debt (the addition of a new burden), the substitution of one object of debt for another (liberation from the former and replacement thereof by another), and so forth — have partly the character of right-establishing contracts and partly that of emancipating contracts.

Moreover, the creditor may, as owner (and insofar as there is no specific fundamental obstacle), transfer it to a third person. The symbolic expression is the transfer to the third person of the document or other object embodying the debt. Such contracts may be called transmissive. Dealing in obligations of another occurs on the stock exchange. Paper money is the symbolic embodiment of obligations of the treasury to pay the corresponding sum in gold — or, in general, in valuable money — so that the movement of these funds from hand to hand signifies a transfer of the possession of the debt of the treasury from some persons to others.

Like the transfer of other absolute rights, such as that of an author, the alienation to another of property belonging to one — the transfer of a right of property — comprises likewise a transfer of duties of others secured in our behalf: specifically a transfer of the corresponding duties "of each and every person" with relation to us. Moreover the person alienating a right of property or other absolute right to another person is under precisely the same obligation with reference to the latter as is each third person: thus, he is bound thereafter not to encroach upon the property transferred, to tolerate the use thereof by the person acquiring it, and so forth.

The right of property comprises the right to every possible species of enjoyment thereof — and in general a host of different special and private rights (that is to say, the various corresponding private legal powers and legal claims are ascribed to the owner in the corresponding cases) — and the same is true of various other rights. Corresponding to this is the phenomenon of handing over to third persons special legal powers and legal claims on the part of those who possess broader rights. The owner may grant others special rights of enjoyment; the subject of general authority (the subject of a general duty of obedience on the part of a subordinate) may endow others with special rights of authority with reference to the subordinate, and so forth.

The different classes of transmissive contracts — as may readily be shown by self-observation and the joint method — are expressive, not of a will, but of acts of legal consciousness which correspond to the character of the legal changes produced as of something actual and accomplished by the subject.

The same is true as to unilateral legal transactions, and in general to unilateral right-dispositive acts. In different fields of the law, the participation of both sides is not required for the establishment of a legal relationship, the securing of the duty of one in behalf of others, the liberation of another by renouncing one's right, and other cases of disposing of obligations-rights: it is enough that there is the relevant dispositive act of one side, such as a declaration renouncing such and such a right, and so forth. A contract is essential as to many dispositions of rights (particularly as between private parties in private law) whereas in relations between representatives of state authority and subordinates a unilateral disposition by the representatives of the former is sufficient. The imposition upon citizens of taxes and various other obligations in favor of the treasury, the state, or the commune, liberation from the payment of taxes or other obligations, the supplementary assessment of arrears, the exercise of the pardoning power (that is to say, liberation from the duty of enduring punishment), and so forth are effected through unilateral orders of authorized representatives of the state authority.

In addition to the particular corrections already indicated, the prevailing doctrine as to the emergence, change, and termination of legal relationships and as to legal facts requires reform of a more general character and in point of principle. It ascribes the significance of legal facts to the corresponding objective events: to the phenomena of nature, to the actions of persons, to contracts and so forth, as such. From the viewpoint of scientific psychology, however, these facts can play no such part, since the legal relationships themselves — the rights and the obligations — are impulsive phantasmata or projections. They do not exist objectively. The most that can be said is that the relevant facts evoke corresponding impulsive phantasmata or projections and appear as the cause or condition of the ascribing by persons of obligations and rights to themselves or to others. But even this effect cannot be evoked by the events of the external world as such: it can be and is evoked, not by those facts as such, but by the idea that the relevant events have taken place. This must be the understanding and the definition of the underlying causal connection as well. If the general idea of causing loss to another contrary to law is connected in the given subject's mind with the idea of compensating him for the loss and of the corresponding imperative-attributive impulsion, then by the general law of associations the emergence in the mind of this subject of the concrete idea that damage has been actually caused to A by B evokes the corresponding imperative-attributive impulsion: the idea of compensation by B for the damage. This occurs — in accordance with the general laws of the human mind, and the special laws of the legal mind — even if the fact of causing loss is only a supposed fact which does not in reality exist. If, on the other hand, the damage has actually been done but neither the subject, nor indeed anyone at all, knew about it, no experience ascribing to A a right to compensation for losses emerges. The same is inevitably so as to all other legal facts, including contracts. Thus in sacral law, the significance of contracts with deities — fundamental contracts defining for hundreds and thousands of years the relationships of tribes or nations to their deities, the order of their political and other life and so forth, and of private contracts of individuals with deities about certain services in return for certain offerings and so forth — by no means depend on whether or not the relevant deities did actually take part in the contracts and so forth. What is important and of decisive significance in legal life is not the fact that such contracts were actually made, but the belief in the fact that they were so made — as where, in reliance on divination, it is believed that the deity actually entered into the contract and has a right to the fulfillment thereof, or that so many hundreds or thousands of years ago the deity carried on personal conversations and concluded a contract with representatives of the nation, and so forth. It would be naive for a historian or a jurist to deny the existence and development of a law for the sole reason he did not himself believe that deities take part in the conclusion of contracts and other legal transactions. In precisely the same way, the prevailing doctrine as to legal facts and their significance in legal life must be held to be erroneous in principle insofar as it considers real events of the external world as relevant facts and ascribes to these facts a significance in legal life which does not and cannot exist.

Here, as in other fields of legal science, contemporary scientific thought is not operating in the proper sphere, and must be translated into another — the minds of those experiencing legal phenomena — if actual knowledge of phenomena is to be attained and their causal connection explained. Our concern is with one of the intellectual elements of legal experience. The very concept of legal facts must therefore be modified and replaced by another, in the sense that legal facts must be understood not as external and objective but as mental events: the content or objects of the relevant ideas.

In legal relationships and the analysis thereof legal facts in the above sense appear in dual form and play a twofold part.

(1) They may appear as possible in the future, and act as conditions precedent to the emergence of the corresponding legal relationships, rights, and obligations. Sometimes the legal consciousness assumes that the very "existence" or "emergence" of a duty, right, and so forth depends upon the relevant event. Sometimes, however, it assumes that while the duty (the right) is present even now, it is as a conditional duty (or right). If A was bound to provide B with a room in his hotel in case of the arrival of the Emperor, the existence of the duty-right is conceived of (prior to the fulfillment of this condition) as conditional. This, by the way, is a proof of the projection character — of the absence of objective existence — of legal relationships, obligations, and rights: real objects and phenomena cannot be conditional: they either are or are not, there.

(2) They may appear really to have taken — or to be taking — place. Here they serve as psychological starting points for ascribing obligations and rights and may, in this character, be called the factual bases of legal relationships, obligations, and rights. The causing of loss conceived of as real appears as the factual basis of the claim to compensation for the loss sustained.

In positive law the projection of obligations and rights may have one further foundation: normative facts (a legislative directive, a legal custom and so forth) which may be called the "positive basis" of the relevant positive obligations, rights, and legal relationships. Thus on the basis of such and such a statute (the positive basis) A is bound in relation to B to do so and so in view of B's having performed such and such an act (the factual basis).

Intuitive legal relationships, rights, and obligations are legal relationships existing independently of any normative facts or positive bases whatsoever.

Although the concept and the doctrine of normative facts and positive bases of legal relationships, obligations, rights in the sense herein established are alike foreign to the contemporary doctrine of legal relationships and rights, the corresponding phenomenon of the legal mind is reflected in contemporary jurisprudence in the form that "objective law and order," "the norms of objective law," "statute," and so forth act therein — equally with legal facts — as factors creating rights. Clearly, this is a misunderstanding: the actual relationship between statutes and other normative facts, on the one hand, and legal relationships, rights, and obligations, on the other, is this: ideas of normative facts evoke corresponding legal experiences with their projections, with the ascribing of rights, and so forth.

Moreover, the prevailing view starts from the assumption that the presence of both a statutory or customary basis and the corresponding legal fact is a condition precedent to the "emergence" of every sort of right: rights are produced by the interaction of these two factors and a right cannot exist if either is absent. Insofar as statutes are concerned, the assumption that this combination of conditions is essential is bound up with the exclusive concern of modern jurisprudence with positive law but the assumption is itself unsound even from the point of view of the law with which modern jurisprudence does deal. To the existence of such rights as that not to be subjected to torture, and the like no special factual foundation — no particular legal fact "producing" such a right — is a condition. The existence, on a par with conditional or hypothetical legal norms, of unconditional norms (even in official-positive law) has already been demonstrated [2] and sufficiently proves the existence (the ascribing) of rights which do not presuppose the presence of any legal fact whatsoever.

In contemporary moral science there is no doctrine corresponding to that of jurisprudence concerning legal facts. In defining the nature of morality it was pointed out that ideas of factual circumstances which correspond to ideas of legal facts in the field of the law enter into the structure of moral experiences. Concepts and terms of morally relevant or moral facts, and of ideas thereof, were formed accordingly. Here it need only be added that the relationship of the relevant ideas to the consciousness of duty and the projection of moral obligations is of the same character as the relationship of ideas of legal facts to legal consciousness and the projection of legal obligations and rights. In general, what has already been set out as to legal facts is applicable to moral facts (with certain changes, flowing out of the purely imperative nature of morality). In the field of positive morality — on a par with morally relevant facts — there are morally normative facts as the factual foundations of moral duty (such as statements of the New Testament).

SECTION 29. *A Final Survey of the Elements of Legal and Moral Phenomena*

Modern jurisprudence devotes no little attention to questions regarding the possibility of some elements of legal phenomena existing without others and to the precedence of some elements over others. The views

[2] Cf. Section 23.

underlying the controversies on these points rest on misunderstandings as to the nature of law and its elements (and the proper method of studying the latter) and are eliminated automatically when these defects are eliminated. Norms of law, obligations, and rights are not independent and separate phenomena capable of existing one without the other, or preceding one another in history, or having in general an independent existence. They are simultaneous reflections or projections of the real legal experiences — of the impulsive-intellectual processes which contemporary legal science neither knows nor studies, although this is the only knowledge that could furnish scientific understanding of law in general and of its elements. In the same way doctrines of legal relationships without obligations and rights, of legal obligations without rights, and so forth — like the controversy as to their preceding each other — are all manifest misunderstandings from the point of view of the psychological theory of law. The inability in different cases to find legal norms or to discover the obligations corresponding to the rights — and the failure of the search for subjects for certain rights and obligations — are bound up with the absence of psychological understanding of the relevant phenomena and the lack of a psychological method of investigating them.

Instead of these and similar doctrines the psychological theory of law must investigate problems of another sort. First of all, the doctrine concerning the elements of legal phenomena must be transformed. In place of one doctrine of the norms of law and another of legal relationships (now mistakenly taken to be real elements of legal phenomena), the doctrine of the impulsive and intellectual elements of legal experiences must be developed, dealing with subject ideas, object ideas, and their elements; with ideas of the relevant actions (of furnishings and receipts and their modalities: time, space, addressees, and so forth); and with ideas of legally relevant facts and normative facts. A doctrine concerning norms of law and legal relationships should constitute a special division of the general theory of law strongly emphasizing their character as legal phantasmata or projections. The real elements of legal experiences must be analyzed seriatim, and it must be explained how, in accordance with their imperative-attributive nature, legal impulsions are reflected *qua* projections in the assumed existence, on the one hand, of authoritative commands binding some and endowing others and, on the other hand, of the corresponding states of being bound or endowed (empowered), the duty of one side being secured in behalf of the other as its assets (legal relationships). The part played by subject ideas in projections is that their content appears: in norms as ideas of addressees of legal imperatives and rights, and in legal relationships as ideas of obligors (subjects of obligations) and of persons endowed (subjects of rights). In precisely the same way object ideas are reflected qua projections in that the corresponding furnishings and receipts with their modalities appear in norms as objects of higher commands and endowings, and in legal relationships as objects of obligations and rights. Norms and legal relationships and their respective elements completely correspond *inter se* and are completely parallel. The two parallel lines must be understood as the (projection) reflection of a third line: a line of real elements — of real legal experiences, of corresponding impulsions and ideas.

Meantime it is clear from the foregoing exposition that contemporary legal science — which neither knows nor studies real legal phenomena and their impulsive-intellectual structure but accepts as real the projection phantasmata and their elements — at the same time so construes these phantasmata (norms and legal relationships and their elements) as to reveal no such parallelism or correspondence as between the nature and elements of norms on the one hand and those of legal relationships on the other. The corresponding doctrines: (1) concerning norms and their elements, and (2) concerning legal relationships and their elements, seem to speak of things that are different and dissimilar. This lack of harmony is due chiefly to a misconception of norms as commands, an undeveloped doctrine as to elements of norms, and the lack of a proper doctrine as to the objects of obligations and rights. If these and other defects were eliminated, the doctrines concerning "objective law" (norms) and its elements and "subjective law" (legal relationships) and its elements would seem sufficiently to correspond *inter se,* and to be so closely parallel in content, that if this present formulation (though with its inaccurate content) were kept, the result would be, in substance, a repetition of the same thing.

The content of the realistic psychological doctrine as to the elements of legal phenomena should be broadened and enriched by the creation and full elaboration of theories of these elements in the sense of studying the laws of nature and tendencies acting in the corresponding fields of phenomena and explaining and illuminating the latter. Thus the doctrine concerned with object ideas should not be limited to the establishment of the major categories of ideas: three species of furnishings-receivings, and modal ideas of time, place, and so forth. It should further comprise doctrines which start from the specific attributive nature of law and the general characteristic attributes and tendencies of law associated therewith and establish the characteristics peculiar to object ideas, the distinctions between them and corresponding ideas in the field of morality, the corresponding tendencies of historical development, and so forth. Thus, in addition to the special characteristic of legal object ideas immediately connected with the attributive nature of law, a series of other characteristic peculiarities and tendencies could be established. The circumstance that in law what is required from one is unfailingly required to be furnished to another — should, so to speak, reach the other — whereas in the field of morality what is required from the subject is required as such, and not as secured in behalf of another and due to be furnished to him, must be associated with a special adaptive tendency as to the choice of objects of obligations other than the one operative in morality. In law, in other words, that which is unsuited — or less suited — for furnishing to others or which cannot reach the other side is excluded. This tendency is connected with the fact that the chief concern of the law is with external actions as objects of obligations. This is a particularly important and interesting theme for scientific investigation.

Then the general unifying tendency of law, associated with its imperative-attributive and adversary nature, must be manifested in the endeavor to achieve precise definiteness in the formation and choice of object ideas.

Hence it is easy to foresee *a priori,* and to disclose, an abundant development of supplementary modal ideas in the law more exactly defining and particularizing that which is required from the obligor and the relatively poor development and minor significance of these ideas in morality. In various categories of modal ideas — ideas of time, ideas of things — this tendency of the law must be manifested in correspondingly different forms which should be specially studied; the relevant investigations and their results — such as an explanation from this point of view of the particular rules of law as to defining time, as to the day from which and how periods are computed, and the like — would shed valuable light in these areas and contribute to a conscious attitude toward the law. Since the serious danger, lurking in every sort of indefiniteness in the lower stages of culture, becomes less and less as civilization advances, it can be established by deduction, and verified in fact, that the tendency to require precision weakens *pari passu.* This is manifested in different forms in the various compartments of law and requires corresponding investigations of a special historical-theoretical character, and so forth.

In the field of ideas of relevant facts there are — in addition to the foregoing special characteristics of law (immediately associated with its imperative-attributive nature) such as the existence of contracts and other legal transactions — other characteristics bound up with the attributive nature of law. These tendencies are manifested in different forms, requiring special study, in the various categories of ideas of relevant facts — including contracts and crimes — and they in turn operate with a different degree of intensity and in different form in the various stages of culture, so that here too investigation of the corresponding historical tendencies is required. Thus the particular manifestation of the unifying tendency of law — the tendency to choose legal facts readily susceptible of proof and verification, and to furnish them with special accessories for greater provability and incontestability — is manifested in the field of contracts and other legal acts more sharply in lower than in higher stages of development. In the lower stages of culture the aim of the law is to make contracts dependent on a multitude of witnesses and other formalities, so that they may be proven beyond doubt or dispute: in the contracts themselves and their content, only the words spoken and the signs made are acknowledged as relevant, while the actual intent — the true thought and so forth — of the contracting parties fades into the background and is ignored as being more difficult to prove. With the progress of culture, the content of contract law in both particulars gradually changes, and more and more reliance is put, so to speak, upon the honesty and the peaceful disposition of men. Analogous theoretical and historical-theoretical propositions may be established in the field of violations of law as legally relevant facts.

With regard to ideas of normative facts, there is — in addition to the foregoing special characteristics of law, associated with its attributive nature — a like tendency in the direction of the exact definiteness and provability of the corresponding facts: a tendency (foreign to morality) strictly to limit the spheres wherein the different categories of these facts are of decisive significance.

What has already been set out as to the formulation of a theory concerning the elements of law appropriate from the point of view of theoretical science is applicable *mutatis mutandis* to the theory of moral experiences as well. Here, too, we must start not from the projections (norms and obligations) but from the real elements of moral experiences: imperative impulsions and ideas (subject and object ideas, ideas of moral facts and normative facts) and — not content with establishing the corresponding concepts and categories — develop corresponding theories, investigate the corresponding tendencies of historical development, and so forth.

The correct formulation and successful development of doctrines concerned with the elements of moral and legal phenomena in these directions presuppose that these doctrines will be referred to proper and adequate classes of phenomena: there must be a corresponding classification of ethical phenomena and correspondingly formed classes and class concepts of law and morality. On the other hand, the doctrine as to the elements of legal and moral phenomena attests the correctness and the fruitfulness of the classification herein developed.

The existing doctrine concerned with the elements of law is distinguished — over and above other shortcomings — by what, from the point of view of scientific theory, is a fundamental error: the individual propositions are not related to the proper class but are directed to the wrong address. The adequate class is by no means that selected by contemporary jurisprudence (that is, law in the juridic sense), but law in the sense of an imperative-attributive branch of human ethics: an immeasurably broader class. The characteristics of law, reflected in the historically developed doctrines, are typical of the entire range of imperative-attributive ethics and not alone of that part comprised in the eclectic group "law" as the word is used by jurists. Even in the field of positive law which does not have official significance — as well as in that of intuitive law — claims correspond to obligations, there are two subjects and so forth. Whether contracts are unifications of wills (as assumed by the prevailing doctrine) or are psychologically different (as it was our purpose to show), the relevant phenomena do at all events characterize the entire field of imperative-attributive ethics, and not merely that which jurists call law. Contracts are concluded and carried out in more or less good faith, even in bands of robbers regarding a division of the booty, and so forth. Whether or not a thing should be considered the object of a right of property does not relate merely to the property specifically recognized by the official positive law, but also to the property of the positive law not officially acknowledged and equally to the property of the intuitive law — such as a right of property in playthings as between children, or a right of property ascribed by an honorable vendor, who has received payment and transferred possession (and by others) to the purchaser although by reason of the nonobservance of certain formalities the seller is still admittedly the owner according to official law, and so forth. Thus all the corresponding theoretical propositions and problems of modern jurisprudence, insofar as related by the latter specially to law in the juridic sense are phenomena suffering from the vice of "limping," and misshapen and monstrous from the point of view of theoretical science. Only deep-rooted tradition and custom can explain the failure of contemporary jurists either to note or even to suspect this "limping," although in most fields it is conspicuously manifest.

Certain doctrines concerned with other elements of law avoid the vice of "limping" since they are especially adapted (though unsuccessfully) to intra-state, official law, but because of the very nature of law in the juridic sense, they inevitably "jump": rights in international law cannot possibly be explained as interests defended by legal proceedings.

It has already been demonstrated that the doctrine as to elements of law does not correspond even to law in the juridic sense. A corresponding analysis in the field of morality no less sustains the correctness of the established class and concept of morality and of the resulting classification of ethical phenomena in general. The further development, over and above this, of theoretical and historical-theoretical investigations of the tendencies manifested in law and morality should attest the value and the fertility of this classification as a tool for acquiring more scientific knowledge.

CHAPTER VI

SPECIES OF LAW

SECTION 30. *Intuitive Law and Positive Law*

In order to gain complete familiarity with a genus of phenomena it is important to become thoroughly orientated with regard to its species and sub-classes. The division of law into species most significant from the theoretical point of view is that already proposed on the basis of the concept of law as imperative-attributive experience: (1) intuitive and positive law, and (2) official and unofficial law.

The division of law into intuitive and positive is most intimately associated with the broad generic concept of law herein established, embracing incomparably more than does law as jurists use the term, and comprising imperative-attributive experiences which are altogether independent of the idea of any authoritatively normative facts (such as statutes, customs, and so forth). This division and the corresponding species concepts are inevitably alien to modern jurisprudence which, being dependent upon juridic terminology and the correspondingly narrow sense of the term "law," and not suspecting the possibility of another scientifically free classification of phenomena, could not — even if it were familiar with the phenomena herein termed intuitive law — acknowledge that they were law.

Even for the formation of the concept "positive law" as a scientific concept with a scientific content and a scientific meaning, in particular, modern jurisprudence lacks alike the scientific and the logical basis, for this would presuppose the existence of a more general concept of law and the division of that genus into two species: positive and non-positive.

Nevertheless, the *expression* "positive law" is not foreign to modern jurisprudence: it is applied time and again in various literary contexts as if the corresponding class and species concepts existed. This is due to special historical causes: before the doctrine of the so-called historical school of jurisprudence appeared and was widely accepted at the beginning of the nineteenth-century, philosophers and jurists of antiquity, the Middle Ages, and modern times believed that a law other than that originating in legislation or in custom (and differing in content in various nations and historically variable) existed on the same level, external and changeless for all nations and times, and rational and just in its nature. Ancient philosophers and jurists supposed this law to have been established by Nature Herself (personified by some philosophical theories and endowed with divine reason) and it was called the law of nature or natural law (*jus naturale*) — a term which was still employed although philosophers and jurists of later periods ascribed its establishment to God (in the Middle Ages) or to various metaphysical beings and forces (Reason, Objective Will, and the like), or deduced it from human nature, from the nature of things and relationships, and the like. The historically variable and imperfect law, established by the people, acquired the name positive law (*jus positivum*). The doctrine of natural law developed particularly and flourished in the seventeenth and eighteenth centuries, *pari passu* with positive-dogmatic jurisprudence. At this time a special science, dedicated to working out the principles of natural law under the name "philosophy of law," or "natural law," was developed — chiefly by philosophers and in connection with philosophy. Great treatises were written and even special codes of natural law were compiled. At the beginning of the nineteenth century this doctrine was dealt a decisive blow by the historical school, chiefly under the leadership of Savigny and Puchta. This school not only denied that natural law — external and changeless, and suitable for all times and races — existed, but also that the origin of positive law was arbitrary and fortuitous, holding that the latter (like language, *mores*, and so forth) is produced by and manifests the national spirit and that its development is gradual and unnoted, and altogether independent of the arbitrary will of anyone. The doctrine of the historical school quickly attained general acknowledgment, and took the place of that of the school of natural law, so that thereafter faith in the existence of other than positive law was deemed an error to be relegated to the archives of history. Until the end of the nineteenth century the task of legal science was recognized as the study and treatment of positive law exclusively.

Although the new "historical" jurisprudence thus refuses to acknowledge a law other than what was formerly considered merely one of the species of law, the expression "positive law" is applied even now by the force of the historical tradition. In this context, however, the word "positive" is a superfluous addition to the word "law." It signifies the contrast not of one species of law to another, but of a new doctrine to an earlier doctrine which acknowledged the existence of natural law. Accordingly, as regards the word "positive" in its application to law, explanations are not infrequently added to the effect that it designates law actually and uniquely existing, or law possessing a real existence and obligatory, historically emerging and changing law, and the like.

However in the literature of the last decade of the nineteenth and beginning of the twentieth century there is again an acknowledgment of natural law which had apparently been finally and decisively eliminated from the sphere of scientific thought. Even a renaissance of natural law is discussed. The author of this treatise has sought, by a series of special investigations and the general considerations founded thereon, to stimulate and to establish the idea that it is possible and necessary, on the basis of the psychological study of law and its motivational and cultural-educative action, to create a special science of legal policy and, in particular, a science of civil policy in the civil law dedicated to the working out of the principles of desirable rational law and legislation.[1] Moreover, it was pointed out that to a certain degree the earlier doctrine of natural law fulfilled the function of a legal policy, indicating the paths of progress and ways the law could be made better, and that in this sense the renaissance of natural law may be seen in the emergence of civil policy. The reasoning in support of the "renaissance of natural law" in this sense, fortified by the results of special investigations in legal policy to illustrate the new method and the fertility of its application, manifestly undermined the formerly axiomatic faith that the task of legal science was only to study and to work out "positive" law. Gradually the idea of legal policy, which had been greeted at first with skepticism as a return to the errors of natural law, began to gain adherents in the sphere of jurisprudence, and the term "natural law" to be applied to the corresponding propositions of the rational, desirable, and "correct" law to be created — with the manifest result that once again two species of law (positive law and natural law) are acknowledged to exist. It is impossible, however, to agree with such a concept of natural law or to believe that it should be set off against positive law. Ideas as to a desirable, rational law — worked out by science or by anyone at all — and the corresponding legislative-political proposals and demands are not law: they are merely projects of legal enactments. The objects of such ideas — rules of law conceived of as rational, reasonable, and so forth — cannot be erected into a particular species of law under the name of natural law, for this contravenes the principles of classification. It violates the rules for forming class concepts. The latter embrace — and should embrace — not the sum total of the corresponding objects and phenomena existent in reality, but all objects or phenomena (including those possible in the

[1] Cf. 17 Boston University Law Review 793 *et seqq.*

future) which are thought of as desirable and the like, once they possess — or are thought to possess — the corresponding class attributes. Hence a concept of law, correctly formed and understood, should embrace as well law which is possible in the future, desirable law, and so forth. To divide law into two species or sub-classes according to the criterion that it exists, or that it does not exist but is merely possible or desirable and the like, is as incongruous as to classify dogs by dividing them into two breeds: existing dogs and future or ideal dogs. Moreover, it is not only propositions about law which is possible in the future, and is conceived as desirable, that may be and are rational and correct: this is so as well regarding countless propositions about existing law, and from this point of view it would be logically absurd to reëstablish the division of law into positive (existing) law and natural (correct or appropriate) law.

Of an essentially different character is the division of law into the two species — positive and intuitive — on the basis of whether or not the corresponding imperative-attributive experiences comprise a reference to normative facts. This is not to contrast desired or ideal law, or the like, to existing law. The content of intuitive law can be — and even is — extremely irrational and barbarous, more laggard and less reasoning, than existing positive law, and the division of the class of psychic phenomena already established under the name of law into two species according to their psychological structure is in complete conformity with the general principles of classifying phenomena.

The formation of the intuitive law concept is concerned with phenomena each of which is capable of being stated, observed, and studied with the aid of effective scientific methods (the introspective method and the joint method of inward and outward observation), and there can therefore be no scientific question or controversy as to the existence of an underlying reality, such as those regarding the existence of natural law. The only possible questions are (1) as to whether there is a scientific reason to form a general class of phenomena and class concept under the name of law embracing also these phenomena (which undoubtedly exist), and (2) as to the differentiation, within the boundaries of this broad class, of two species or sub-classes in accordance with the criterion indicated (or would what we call intuitive law be more correctly referred to morality, and the concept of law limited to the corresponding positive experiences). These questions are actually serious and vitally important, not only for the science of law, but also for that of morality. The answer thereto, and proof of the scientific necessity of the proposed classification are to be found in the preceding exposition in its entirety, which has demonstrated that all the important propositions as to law and its elements (excepting special propositions concerning positive law and normative facts) relate as well to intuitive law and would be of a mutilated and "limping" character if related only to positive law in our sense.

SECTION 31. *Intuitive Law*

As already indicated, the general propositions herein established as to law are applicable to intuitive law; this is so as to the doctrine regarding the nature of law as imperative-attributive experiences and its distinction from morality as purely imperative experiences; the doctrine as to further special characteristics and tendencies connected with that nature, as concerns the motivational and educative action of the corresponding experiences; the doctrine of the elements of law: of the relevant impulsions and ideas — object ideas and subject ideas — and of revelant facts; the doctrine of the corresponding projections: of norms, legal relationships, obligations, and rights. The task of a special doctrine concerned with intuitive law is to examine further what specially characterizes intuitive law as compared with positive law. With the fundamental difference (*differentia specifica*) set out *supra*, as differentiating intuitive law from positive law, which is found in the intellectual content and consists in the absence (from the content of intuitive law) of ideas of normative facts — various further characteristics, peculiar to intuitive law as compared with positive, are associated.

(1) Whereas — because its content is definable by perceptions of external facts (which can likewise be known to and authoritative for many persons) — positive law can furnish a corresponding uniform pattern of rules for larger or smaller masses of people (notwithstanding the differentiation of their character, upbringing and so forth), the character of intuitive law varies with each individual. Its content is defined by each person's individual conditions and life circumstances: by his character, upbringing, education, social position, professional occupations, personal acquaintanceships and relationships, and so forth. Of course, the fact that certain conditions and factors of the development of the intuitive law mentality of a number of individuals (of children in the same family, for example) — or of larger or smaller masses thereof — are common, can and does result in their intuitive law being more or less congruous. Thus we can talk about the intuitive law of a given family, of a given circle, or of a society (such as modern cultural society), or of the intuitive law of a given class of society (such as work-
the more sacred"). In the customary law mentality of the latter (sec-

men, factory employees, peasants, or squires) and of a child, wife or husband, and so on, in a sense of pointing out a certain common content of the relevant intuitive law. Certain problems of intuitive law find a similar solution in the intuitive law of large circles or of broad categories of people, while others find a solution less general. Investigation of the corresponding uniformities (and distinctions) is an interesting problem of the psychological study of law. In principle, however, intuitive law remains individual — individually diverse — in content: it is not stereotyped law, and there may be said to be as many intuitive laws as there are individuals. (To avoid misunderstanding as to the expression "individual," it may be noted that law of every sort — even positive law — is individual in the psychological sense, as every sort of psychological experience is a phenomenon of the individual mind: we are here concerned with the content of the relevant individual experiences.)

(2) Being diverse and individual in content, intuitive law is at the same time distinguished from positive law by the fact that its directions freely conform with the specific, individual circumstances of the given case — of the given life situation — and are not constrained, as they are in the field of positive law, by a preordained pattern of corresponding precepts, settled customs, and the like, with preëstablished decisions for general categories of cases — decisions which ignore a multitude of the individual peculiarities of each actual specific case which they cannot foresee and with which they cannot conform.

(3) Intuitive law is further distinguished from positive law by free variability and adaptability. Positive law, precisely because of its positive character (the fixation of its content by normative facts — facts of the past — sometimes of the extremely remote past) is subjected to delay in development and is backward with regard to the present spiritual and economic life. This is so in a particularly high degree as regards customary law, which cites the traditions and habits of our forebears, and in the period of its flourishing seems "sacred in proportion to its age"; but even legislation cannot avoid lagging to some extent behind life which is constantly and uninterruptedly developing. On the other hand the development of statute law may be inept in the opposite direction — the premature enactment of positive law — for whose beneficent action the national mind is inadequately prepared and the necessary economic conditions are absent — or be determined by individual folly or thoughtlessness or by individual or group motives and considerations of gain or malice. Intuitive law develops in a different fashion: these phenomena (which are due to the content of positive law being dependent upon normative facts) are foreign to intuitive law. The latter develops

gradually and symmetrically, neither subject to fixation and fossilization nor dependent upon the arbitrary caprice of anyone.

It by no means follows, however, that intuitive law is necessarily better in content or that it is more perfect or ideal. On the contrary, it is possible — and often happens — that its content is of poorer quality than that of the corresponding positive law. In the first place, as has been pointed out, the intuitive law of individuals differs and is unique in content, depending upon the conditions of individual development. These may be such that the resultant intuitive law is unsatisfactory — or even extremely bad. Its development may be of a pathological character under the influence of unsuccessful legal education in the family.[1] Moreover, intuitive law worked out by mutual psychic communion in different circles (larger or smaller) of persons whose common interests are opposed to those of others tends to develop towards the unilateral preference of the former interests to the prejudice of the others. Ordinarily the content of legislation is in this regard better than that of the many intuitive laws of groups and classes in the nation. Furthermore, since the nation includes strata which are backward in culture (particularly in ethical culture) as compared with that part of society which guides and directs legislation, this takes on in various spheres a more enlightened and cultural character than the intuitive law of such elements. Whereas by the law of a given time or particular state, citizens are deemed equal as regards rights of honor, rights to be free from bodily punishment and so forth, there is the greatest inequality under the intuitive law of various spheres as to the individual rights of different members of the community. Thus, according to the intuitive law prevailing in the sphere of domestic service, the position of the master as regards honor and dignity is often completely different from that of the servant, while that of the butler is altogether different from that of various persons of lower service. The statute may establish a progressive marriage law, but the intuitive law of certain strata of society ascribe to the husband the right to beat or to torture his wife while denying the wife the right to complain against him. Still greater differences between the intuitive and the positive elements of ethics may be found in the field of morality: one need only compare the content of positive Christian or Buddhist morality with the former and present intuitive morality of Christians or Buddhists.

(4) Associated with the intellectual content of intuitive law (which is more meager and simple than that of positive law) and the absence of ideas of normative facts in its structure is the great scope and broader

[1] Cf. Section 9.

applicability of the propositions of intuitive law. The binding force of the rules of conduct in positive law is conceived of as dependent and based upon authoritative-normative facts, and therefore as referring only to the time subsequent to the emergence of the relevant fact. The existence and operation of this binding force are therefore limited (a) to the time subsequent to the publication of the corresponding authoritative command and prior to its abrogation, (b) to the place for which the relevant fact is of authoritative importance (the territory of a state or city, or even a house), and (c) to persons to whom the particular authoritative-normative fact is related and for whom it has significance. These limitations — associated with ideas of normative facts — and their decisive significance in the field of positive legal consciousness, are altogether foreign to intuitive legal consciousness which is of infinite scope and unlimited applicability.

With this are also associated differences between positive law projections and intuitive law projections. From the naive projection point of view positive norms appear as higher laws existing and holding sway over a given territory and during the course of a certain time and so forth, whereas intuitive law norms seem to be higher laws existing and dominant everywhere, always, and with reference to all persons insofar as the subject ideas or the ideas of relevant facts entering into the structure of these experiences introduce no particular limitations. In positive law obligations and rights appear as temporary, local, and so forth, but in intuitive law they seem to be universal and to exist always and everywhere.

Furthermore, since the relevant impulsions are bound up with ideas of certain conduct as such, or with certain relevant facts as such (irrespective of anyone's commands, local and temporary customs, and so forth), intuitive norms appear true and valid *per se*, as distinguished from positive norms whose significance is conditional. In the legal mentality, therefore, intuitive law norms have higher standing or rank. They are significant as a loftier criterion for the appraisal of positive norms and disapproval of these if their content does not correspond with that of intuitive norms. With this is associated the capacity of intuitive law to attain a higher emotional uplift, amounting sometimes to sublime enthusiasm or fanaticism. In general the emotional vivacity — the intensity — of legal impulsions in the field of intuitive law is manifestly greater, *ceteris paribus*, than in the field of positive law, and if this is so, the motivational action of consciousness of a duty — of another's right (passive-law motivation), and of active consciousness of a right (active-law motivation), and likewise the corresponding auxiliary action must then be, in general, stronger in intuitive law than in positive law. Of course, another relationship may obtain in actual cases; the greater authority, the greater vivacity, and the more powerful pressure to conduct, may be on the side of positive law, as is the case regarding customary law in the minds of those who cherish a lofty respect for the traditions and customs of their forebears. Moreover, in positive law (chiefly official positive law) various collateral motives of a nonethical character frequently operate — considerations of cautious calculation, fear of punishment, and the like — to reinforce or to replace the specific legal motivation in the more or less complete attainment of the corresponding conduct.

Study of one's own and another's conduct with the aid of the introspective and joint method, to the extent that this conduct is defined by legal motivation, leads readily to the conclusion that intuitive law does in fact play an extremely great and essential part as a factor of individual conduct and of social phenomena. Many areas and elements of our relations to our neighbors — especially to those near us in family or domestic life — in the field of love, and in relations of friendship, acquaintanceship, and comradeship — are foreign to regulation by positive law, and insofar as they are defined by the legal mind — by consciousness of that which is owing to others from us and from others to us — intuitive law operates here exclusively. And in those numerous fields of life where the relevant problems of conduct are foreseen and decided by positive law (such as renting a lodging, hiring a servant, or buying things in shops), people are in fact ordinarily guided not by what is enjoined in this regard by the civil or criminal laws (which are ordinarily unknown to the vast majority), but by their intuitive law and the directions of their own intuitive law conscience. In other words, it is not positive law but intuitive law that is the actual basis of the corresponding "legal order" and the power which actuates the corresponding part of social life. Only in exceptional pathological cases of conflicts, infractions, and the like does the matter go so far as to involve the application of positive law. It is in certain fields, chiefly in those of official relationships involving courts and administrative agencies, that positive law plays an exclusive or a decisive part.

Availing ourselves of self-observation and the joint psychological method to study the relationship of the intuitive law to various questions of conduct, we can state that certain questions solved in this or that sense by positive law find no response in the intuitive law, and that the observation or the idea of this or that factual conduct in the relevant province (in accord, or not in accord, with relevant precepts of a statute) awakens in our minds no intuitive law reaction of censure, of rejection, or of encouragement. There is for example, a certain order in making up the state budget in accordance with law, a definite arrangement for preserving an inheritance, or the teaching of such and such objects in certain schools: if, with reference to the corresponding questions, we try to bring our intuitive law conscience into action our efforts will fail completely. We shall get no such answer — in other words, the corresponding intuitive law experiences simply will not appear at all in our mind. Here are interesting questions, which are important from the point of view of the character and significance of intuitive law and the understanding of legal life in general: To what provinces of conduct does intuitive law standardization extend? What provinces of conduct does intuitive law (as distinguished from positive law) leave untouched? This is the problem of the sphere of action of intuitive law and of its relation to that of positive law.

Psychological observation sustains the following thesis: intuitive law standardization extends to those relationships in which a certain good or evil is to be caused to others or certain benefits or evils distributed as between subjects. It is typical of the human mind to tend in the direction of working out, and giving definite intuitive law decisions to, questions conceived of as questions of causing good or evil to others, or of the receipt of certain benefits or the experiencing of certain evils by others. To problems and relationships of another sort, however, the intuitive-law conscience does not react: formalities (which may be rational or necessary) and the technical methods and arrangements of actions (which may be appropriate or necessary from the point of view of expediency, policy or pedagogy, but are matters of indifference from the viewpoint of distributing good or evil in the general sense). The intuitive law consciousness is therefore apathetic with regard to the arrangement and forms of making up the state budget but not to problems of distributing the corresponding burdens (such as the tax burden in general, or a definite tax as between different classes), apportioning a certain tax or obligation among individuals (such as the householders of the commune), or distributing specified benefits as between different classes of subjects or different provinces or nationalities (such as equal or unequal distribution of resources among the national schools of different nationalities and so forth). As to these intuitive law exists.

Intuitive inheritance law does not touch the procedure for citing heirs and for safeguarding an inheritance, but does ordinarily answer problems as to who is entitled to the inheritance and as to the proper distribution of the inheritance among the co-heirs, so that none be affronted.

The intuitive law of public service does not touch the formal arrangement of designating for service or the conditions of age or other qualification, nor does it define hours of service; but if a less worthy candidate is preferred and appointed to service or promoted, by reason of patronage, or if the burden of service or its rewards are distributed from personal motives to the injury of some and the advantage of others, or if one suffers an unfounded reprimand or other disciplinary punishment (loss of position and the like), the intuitive law consciousness reacts with censure and sometimes with strong legal indignation.

In positive law the situation is different: here the field of actual or possible standardization is broader and its content — and that of the corresponding obligations and claims — more diverse: the content of positive law is defined by normative facts, and these (including customs and legislative enactments) are such that they can touch any areas of conduct whatsoever, irrespective of their relationship to the distribution of good or evil or the consciousness of such a relationship. This is incidentally one of the important advantages of positive law as compared with intuitive law, and one of the reasons why positive law is not less useful and necessary socially than intuitive law. On the basis of intuitive law alone, normal social life could not exist and successfully develop — not merely because there would then be no proper unification of legal relationships and no social peace or stable order, but also because many fields of conduct where legal regulation is essential would altogether lack it since intuitive law cannot provide it.

There are, however, topics of legal standardization which by their nature exclude, if not positive standardization in general, at least positive standardization corresponding to the essence of the matter. Here intuitive law standardization is required if the proper results are to be attained, as where obligations and rights must remain freely susceptible of change and adaptation to actual and specific circumstances. In literary, artistic, and other criticism — in general, in the distribution of praise and blame, which plays an important part in social life — an intuitive law is in operation, suggesting what is due to whom and what one has deserved, whereas any sort of (even unofficial) positive standardization would be out of place. The more material rewards for merit — for outstanding services to the state or to society — cannot be rationally standardized without entrusting to intuitive law the decision of whether or not a given individual deserves reward and, if so, in what measure. The mark due to a person for an examination is a matter of the intuitive law conscience of the examiner: it cannot reasonably be predetermined by positive law. It is extremely important that punishments in various spheres of life (in the family or school, or of crimes) be commensurate with the degree of guilt, and this result can be attained only by means of intuitive (but not of positive) law: here either the positive law does not intervene at all but gives the matter over to be acted upon by intuitive law, or establishes only a certain framework (as in punishments, by stating a minimum and a maximum) within the bounds of which intuitive law operates freely. Under the powerful pressure of the unifying tendency, primitive law established for criminal acts punishments which were positively fixed in advance and bore no relation to the degree of actual guilt. The criminal law of advanced nations fixes only the boundaries, leaving the decision itself to the action of intuitive law. As to rewards there is no positive pattern, even in the lower stages of culture: intuitive law prevails.

Since the pressure of the unifying tendency of the law grows gradually weaker *pari passu* with the ennoblement and socialization of the human mind, we can deductively establish the proposition that — as a tendency in the development of law — the sphere given over by positive law to the operation of intuitive law must constantly increase as time goes on.

From the point of view of the mutual relationship of intuitive law and positive law, then, legal life clearly falls into three fields: (1) that wherein positive law alone exists and operates, (2) that wherein intuitive law alone exists and operates, and (3) that wherein the existence and operation of intuitive and of positive law are parallel. As to the last — which is an extremely important and broad field — various problems emerge as to the mutual relationships between the two competing laws.

First, certain propositions may be settled as to their relationship in respect of content.

(1) Between parallel and coexisting intuitive law and positive law, there is and must inevitably be accord in content as to foundations and general direction. This, and the corresponding *mutual support* and reciprocal reinforcement of intuitive law consciousness and positive law consciousness, constitute the foundation of the actual legal order and the corresponding social order: political, economic, and so forth. The causal necessity of this relationship has its roots, on the one hand, in the fact that the development of both intuitive and positive law is alike defined, in its general and fundamental features, by the action of the same social processes, operating according to identical laws. On the other hand, the inevitable agreement of positive law and intuitive law as to their principal bases is due to the fact that such accord on general and fundamental features is a condition precedent to their concurrent existence and operation: where their divergence goes beyond certain bounds, the posi-

tive law must inevitably break down — and in case of resistance the debacle will be in the form of a social revolution.

(2) Differences as to details are, on the other hand, inevitable in the nature of things: they not only can but do exist between positive and intuitive law. No positive law in any nation either accords or can accord with the parallel intuitive law as to all the parts and elements of its content. The bases of this assertion — which indicate at the same time the character of the different categories of inevitable divergences — are as follows:

(a) Since intuitive law has a content which varies in the different elements of society (in the different classes and individuals) there can be no positive law whose content could coincide with that of the intuitive law of all these elements. Satisfying the intuitive law demands of some, positive law thereby fails to satisfy the intuitive law demands of others; and the more diverse the structure of the population in education, nationality, religion, class interests, and so forth — and, in general, the more the bounds of the intuitive law mentality differ and vary — the more abundant and the greater are the discords and collisions between the positive law and the intuitive law of the different social elements. Variants of this category may be termed class and individual conflicts between positive and intuitive law.

(b) Since intuitive law develops, and consequently changes its content in history constantly and gradually, whereas the development of positive law — by the very nature of the latter — is subject to retardation and to other deviations from such constant and gradual development, positive law must in its various parts lag behind the development of intuitive law. *Ceteris paribus*, conflicts of this sort between intuitive and positive law are more frequent and more acute as the actual incongruities (which are inevitable within certain limits) between the processes of development are greater and more numerous, the mobility and flexibility of the customary or other law less, and the maladjustment of the legislative mechanism to cause statute law to conform with the intuitive law more serious. These may be termed historical or evolutionary conflicts.

(c) Since positive law — in conformity with its nature and its unifying function — does and must diverge from intuitive law in the degree to which it can be adapted to concrete circumstances — and must, in particular, establish sharp boundaries and define its scope and content precisely as regards objects and relevant facts, and ignore facts not susceptible of verification — it follows that (even if the foregoing areas of variation and conflict did not exist) there must inevitably be discords between positive law and intuitive law *decisions of actual, specific cases*. Judgments of official courts pursuant to statutes — even though the statutes are perfectly reasonable and excellent — must within certain limits arouse intuitive law disapproval in the minds of the parties and of the public; and the more positive law develops under the pressure of the unifying tendency — the more the essence of the matter is sacrificed to the precise definiteness and provability of relevant facts and so forth — much the more abundant and sharp, *ceteris paribus*, will be these discords and conflicts (which are inevitable within certain limits) in the area of actual decisions. These are "casuistical" conflicts between positive and intuitive law, arising out of the specific facts of life.

There are, therefore, lower and upper limits of accord (or discord) between intuitive law and positive law with reference to content: their factual relationship oscillates between these boundaries in the various periods of history, in different nations, and so forth. The greater the accord within these limits at a given moment, the better and the more correctly *ceteris paribus* does the law function in general in a given nation, the more uniformly is it observed, and — in particular — the greater are the respect and sympathy for and with the existing positive law and the satisfaction with the existing social order, and the stronger this order is, and vice versa.

Insofar as the contents of intuitive law and of positive law diverge, the problem of solving the possible conflicts in specific cases arises. To the extent that the intuitive law opinions of the parties as to their mutual obligations and rights coincide in content, and both act in conformity with the directives of their intuitive law conscience (whether or not they know that the positive law would give a different solution), the intuitive law prevails; and the same is true when the solution of discords is sought, not in the positive law, but in the intuitive law of third parties — by invoking arbitration according to conscience, and the like. And, *ceteris paribus*, the area wherein intuitive law is of such decisive significance should grow broader in proportion to the growth of culture.

Insofar, however, as the matter is considered and decided in accordance with positive law from the very beginning — or if the discord between the parties causes the positive law to be invoked subsequently — that law then becomes of controlling importance. Yet even here the intuitive law is by no means without actual significance: it exerts pressure upon the interpretation and application of positive law in the direction of securing decisions in accord with (or as little as possible divergent from) the directives of the intuitive law conscience. The practice of the positive law is a resultant whose direction is defined, to a more or less significant degree, by the pressure exerted by the intuitive law of the parties making the decision. Even upon the scientific fashioning of positive law — upon learned jurisprudence — intuitive law exerts the same pressure, defining in a corresponding fashion the trend of the interpretation of sources, the application of analogy, the direction of generalizations, and the derivation of special propositions from general principles. This in turn is reflected in the direction of the practice of positive law in court and otherwise.

This influence of the intuitive law on the evolution and the application of positive law serves in a certain degree to forestall, eliminate, and mitigate conflicts between positive law and intuitive law. A more essential factor operating in the same direction is the psychic pressure exerted by intuitive law on legislation, on the formation of customary law, and in general on the development of positive law, in order to bring the latter into accord with the former. Statutes, the mass legal conduct of people which serves as the normative fact in customary law, and other normative facts to be investigated *infra*, are to a significant degree merely products and manifestations of the intuitive law of individuals and masses. These later acquire an independent significance in the minds of others as determining their positive law experiences. To this extent intuitive law is the creator of positive law. However, it must be observed — in order to avoid misunderstanding — that by no means all the laws, customs, or normative facts of positive law in general are products and manifestations of intuitive law, nor does all positive law derive its origin from intuitive law. It has already been pointed out that intuitive law has its limited sphere of existence and action (*distributio bonorum atque malorum*), and that questions of formalities, technical arrangements, and so forth, are referable to the exclusive cognizance of positive law insofar as they are subjected to legal decision. In this field positive law is not, and cannot be, a product of intuitive law. Even in fields related to the cognizance of intuitive law, however, it is possible in particular cases for normative facts and the corresponding positive law to emerge independently — or even in spite — of intuitive law. Thus, legislative enactments may be based on considerations of interests and the like, which contradict the intuitive law conscience of the legislators themselves — or of the masses — and nevertheless bring to life the corresponding positive law.

The accord between positive law and intuitive law, prevailing when positive law at first emerged and due to the dependence of normative facts upon intuitive law, tends gradually to be replaced by ever-increasing discords on account of the fixation of the content of positive law while intuitive law is developing freely. As these discords are manifested and become intense, however, the psychic pressure of intuitive law becomes manifest and more powerful in the direction of the repeal of the positive law which contradicts it (and its replacement by another law which is in accord as to content), and, in particular, of weakening and destroying, or correspondingly changing, the relevant customary law or of reforming it by legislation. The idea of abrogating a particular statute and replacing it by another, or of revising the relevant code, or of replacing non-statutory law by a legislative enactment arises and spreads under the influence of intuitive law. Demands for reform — becoming constantly more insistent — are presented. Supporting arguments are sought out and accumulated. Aside from this, when statutes are compiled — whatever the occasion — the intuitive law operates to eliminate the propositions of the earlier positive law which are contradictory to intuitive law and to replace them by propositions in accord with itself. As the discords between intuitive law and positive law gradually appear and become intense, there are countless partial and petty — or more or less important — repeals of and changes in positive law. If, notwithstanding the growing pressure of intuitive law, this process of destruction and renovation is held back by the resistance of representatives of interests associated with the existing law, and important and essential problems of law and the social order are involved, there is a further increase of the pressure of intuitive law. Being resisted, this pressure gains ever increasing impulsive force, reaching the point of enthusiasm and fanaticism in more and more individuals and leading them to maniacal hatred of the existing order and its representatives. Finally the pressure evokes an explosion: a revolution. The coming of the revolution is ordinarily accelerated and facilitated by the fact that those who take advantage of the existing legal order, extracting thereform material benefits (as from slavery before the American Civil War, or from feudal privileges before the French Revolution), or sustaining it upon any other inducement or consideration without the ethical sanction of their intuitive law conscience and without faith in the sanctity and justice of their conduct in the matter (or even despite contrary directives of their intuitive law conscience), are inevitably poisoned ethically and decay. An ethical decay of the upper strata of society and of the state mechanism sets in, compromising abuses appear and spread, and there is a notable lack of honorable and outstanding persons acting with faith and enthusiasm.

The current explanation of the phenomenon of social revolutions is that they are evoked by class interests which are not acknowledged, but are trampled under foot, by the existing law. These — if the former equilibrium of forces is upset and superior force is gained by the rising class — are supposed to evoke a violent revolution. The facts of history, however, contradict this explanation: for hundreds or thousands of years slaves, serfs, and various lower classes, occupying a disadvantageous social position under the rule and dominance of a negligible number of masters or overlords, caused no revolutions so long as faith in the sanctity and justice of the existing law prevailed — so long as the existing positive law was in accord with intuitive law — and the explanation is further contrary to fact in that those taking part in the internecine revolutionary struggle are distributed among two opposing camps, not in accordance with the theory of interests, but according to other sociopsychic laws, with age, intelligence, temperament, and so forth playing an important part as well. The result is that in both camps masses of persons are struggling who, according to the theory of interests, should have been in the opposing camp. Furthermore, from the psychological point of view, the foundation of the theory of interests is not study, knowledge, and understanding of the human mind and the motivation of conduct: the "interests" mentality is not *per se* one which can compel a multitude of persons to sacrifice their well-being, their careers, and their lives. Seeking, as it does, to reduce everything to egoism and material calculation, the theory of interests must at the same time haul in a *deus ex machina* in the form of a (hypothetical) opposing psychic element which is alike unexplained and unknown. The nature of the conduct here to be clarified by psychology is such that explanations should be sought in the phenomena and laws of the ethical mind: the moral or legal mentality should be the object of study. However, the moral mentality is a peaceful mentality, neither inclined nor able to realize its demands by force: such propensities and tendencies belong only to legal mentality.

There was constant talk of the rights of the man and the citizen during the French Revolution and of the right of every man to freedom and to the fruits of his labor during the Civil War in the United States. The issue was joined, and the struggle carried on, in support of these rights, and against the opposing order of things which had come to be hated.

With reference, however, to the action of intuitive law in favor of specific changes in the positive law, and the influence of intuitive law on the interpretation, scientific evolution, and application of that law, it must be noted that the action of intuitive law remains for the most part latent and unobserved. Not only is there no corresponding verbal or written expression, but the actors themselves neither know nor understand what compels them to act in the direction they do when, for example, they are defending a certain interpretation of existing law or a certain reform thereof, because of the pressure exerted by the intuitive law. This law operates as an invisible factor, behind the scenes so to speak, while various other arguments and considerations appear on the stage and sundry theories, political and social, are advocated. Although they are superficial — sometimes extremely so — and of a unilateral and arbitrary character, the argumentation, doctrines, and theories (once their direction corresponds with the demands of the intuitive law which is being conceived and implanted) seem extremely cogent and convincing, and spread and become popular. Sometimes they win the faith and veneration commonly to be found in the province of religion. The root of their power is not in their intellectual content but in the impulsive intuitive law subsoil.

Besides the influence of intuitive law upon the development of positive law, there is as well the reverse process: the positive law influences the development of intuitive law. The intuitive law of the individual develops in childhood, in the family, and in school, and in later life, to an important degree, under the influence not only of the intuitive law views of those around him and of prompting on the part of parents and others but also under the operation of suggestions originating in the positive law (legal customs and statutes, and in general the existing positive law social order), particularly if that positive law is held in respect in that social milieu and not subject to doubt and criticism. The derivation of positive law from intuitive law proceeds in the manner already indicated: intuitive law evokes actions whic htake on the significance of normative facts, and these later operate independently of the intuitive law which evoked them. Analogous processes, whereby the intuitive law is derived from the positive law, consist in legal experiences suggested by the normative facts of positive law (and originally dependent on ideas of these facts) which thereafter — and especially if they are repeated frequently and acquire impulsive vitality — take on an independent character, and appear *qua* intuitive law independently of the corresponding normative facts and ideas thereof. This occurs through the formation of stable dispositive associations of the corresponding object ideas and imperative-attributive impulsions. By the action of these processes, the intuitive law mentality of those who are specially and constantly concerned with positive law — such as learned specialists, judges, attorneys, and so forth — is subjected incidentally to a specific regeneration and develops unilaterally in that the positive law which these specialists constantly study, expound as professors, or apply —

which, in other words, they experience frequently so that it leaves corresponding dispositive traces — becomes to a significant degree their intuitive law, crowding out and destroying various elements of their former intuitive law. Then, their intuitive law consciousness acquires to a considerable degree a complexion other than that of the intuitive law consciousness of non-specialists and this is sometimes a source of mutual misunderstanding and controversy. Positive law acts in the same way — but in a weaker and less conspicuous degree — upon the intuitive law consciousness of other members of the community.

Aside from its immediate value, a rational and efficacious positive law is a valuable school of intuitive, imperative-attributive ethics for the nation (sometimes even of purely imperative ethics: morality and law are reciprocally interactive as already pointed out). Irrational and malignant positive law, on the contrary — such as admits and encourages malicious conduct and treatment and persecution as regards a part of the population according to religion, race, nationality, or the like — poisons and destroys the intuitive law (and moral) consciousness. So long as it possesses adequate authority and is respected, a positive law which is itself backward in content somewhat retards the development of intuitive law as well. Advanced positive law — in particular, statutory or other positive law which outstrips the development of the intuitive law of certain elements of society (such as the less cultured strata of the population) — accelerates the development of their intuitive law.

To what degree the positive law can modify intuitive law in conformity with its own content depends to a considerable extent upon the qualities of that content — on how far it corresponds to the demands of social life, the tendencies of its development and so forth. Accordingly, the influence of backward positive law in retarding the development of intuitive law is less than that of advanced and progressive positive law in accelerating that development. The regenerative action of positive law of the latter class upon intuitive law is sometimes extremely swift and radical, and produces fundamental revolutions in the nation in intuitive law mentality. Undoubtedly the abolition of serfdom in Russia under Alexander II — a tremendous legal reform, realized under the action of the intuitive law of cultured and advanced personalities headed by the monarch — was far in advance of the development of the intuitive law of the great majority of the population. The intuitive law of this part of the population — of the majority of the squires and most of the peasants — was, at the time when the Emancipation Manifesto was promulgated, the law of master and slave. The squires ascribed to themselves corresponding rights with regard to serfs, while the latter ascribed to themselves corresponding obligations with regard to their masters and corresponding rights to the latter — in general, not merely on the basis that such was the mandate of positive law but also (and independently thereof) in conscience and according to their intuitive law views. Many did not even conceive that any other law — a law of freedom — was either possible or admissible. The legislative reform produced in this regard a revolution which was extremely swift and radical. Some peasants — chiefly those who were aged — preserved for decades, and to the end of their lives, the earlier intuitive mentality of the law of serfdom and were unwilling to know and to acknowledge the reform, declaring to their former masters that they considered it their sacred duty to serve faithfully and truly for the future also. But the vast majority — especially the young — were liberated very swiftly indeed from their former servile, intuitive law consciousness and imbued with the opposite intuitive law convictions, and the converse reform would have been absolutely unthinkable a year, or even less, after the publication of the manifesto because of the corresponding intuitive law revolution in the national mind. Similar revolutions in the intuitive law mentality of the nation — great and more or less swift revolutions — have occurred in the history of other nations as well under the influence of far-reaching and progressive reforms of like content in the positive law — as, for example, under the influence of the legislative grant and effectuation of political rights. The reception by Western European nations of the more cultural Roman law as positive law (the Roman law being advanced as compared with their national laws) was accompanied by the corresponding processes of changing as well the intuitive law consciousness, and was itself facilitated and accelerated by this action upon intuitive law: in particular, the most cultured elements of the society of that time — having become familiar with the content of Roman law — enthusiastically accepted a number of its elements as legal truths. These accordingly came to be their intuitive law; previous intuitive law opinions seemed barbarous to them, and due to their earlier ignorance of the true law and the absence of true legal clarification.

SECTION 32. *Justice*

People discern in justice the loftiest guiding light. In faith that justice exists, they find peace and solace in the calamities and sufferings of life. But what is justice? Where and in what form does it exist? Wherein do its principles consist? What is the fundamental basis of justice?

For a very long time the nature and the principle of justice have attracted the attention and the interest of thinking people. These problems were conspicuous in the philosophy of antiquity, of the Middle Ages, and of modern times. Moralists relate them specially to their field, and their treatises unfailingly contain a chapter devoted to a doctrine concerning justice: justice is conceded to be one of the most important of the moral virtues, and attempts are made to explain its essence and to establish a single principle of justice. At the same time, legal science is conscious that justice is closely related to the law, and specialists in the general theory of law usually seek, in their turn, to define the nature of justice and its distinction from — and relation to — the law. These are also considered in certain special legal sciences: civil law (especially Roman law, in view of the great part played by justice or *aequitas* in the sources of the Roman law) and criminal law.

Despite the thought devoted to these problems over the ages in the foregoing sciences the nature of justice still continues to be unsolved and controverted.

It is very widely held that justice consists in equality: a relationship of equality as regards others. Some see justice as essentially a combination of the principle of equality with various other principles: the principle of benevolence, the principle of freedom, and so forth. Justice appears not infrequently in moral philosophy as sympathy and nothing more and is defined as a special form of sympathy, or as a special form of applying sympathy (applying it equally, and the like), or as a combination of sympathy with other elements, such as wisdom. Some hold that justice must correspond with truth. Expediency is often considered an essential element of justice or justice is identified with expediency.

The doctrine herein developed concerning law in general and intuitive law in particular comprises all the premises needed to solve the problem of the nature of justice: actually, *justice is nothing but intuitive law in our sense.*

As a real phenomenon justice is a psychic phenomenon, knowledge of which can be acquired through self-observation and the joint method. Employing these we ascertain without difficulty that we are not here concerned with experiences of sympathy (caritative emotions) in regard to anyone, or with judgments as to social expediency, or with any opportunist judgments or calculations whatsoever. We have to do with normative experiences of principle: ethical experiences in the sense of the concept hereinbefore formed. Ethical impulsions are here dominant. The corresponding conduct is conceived of as due regardless of any purpose or calculation whatsoever (and not as convenient for some specific end). The idea or the awareness of another's behavior which seems to us manifestly and sharply unjust as to any third person evokes corresponding ethical censure or indignation. Recollection of such conduct of our own causes gnawings of conscience. Moreover, when we observe and analyze experiences of justice from the viewpoint of the division of ethical experiences into two classes — purely imperative (moral) and imperative-attributive (legal) — we have no difficulty in arriving at the conclusion that these experiences are related to the second class: imperative-attributive impulsions are present and operative, and the corresponding consciousness is consciousness of what is due from some and owing to others, and not of a unilateral and purely imperative duty. In the light of the theory herein developed it is equally incorrect to refer justice to morality (as the moralists do) and to contrast it to the law (as jurists do). These misconceptions should be corrected by transposing justice from the class of morality into that of law. Finally, if the division of law into two classes (positive and intuitive) and the corresponding concepts are employed, and the experiences of justice from this point of view are studied, it is not difficult to state that we are here concerned not with phenomena of positive law but with those of intuitive law, not with judgments as to what is supposed to be done according to statutes and the like but what is due to another and so forth in "conscience," according to our independent convictions without reference to any external authorities. Statutes and legal customs are themselves criticized from the point of view of justice as a higher gauge and criterion: some are approved as in accord with the demands of justice, while others are censured — or even indignantly rejected — as unjust and at variance with those demands since they deprive a person of what is due to him.

It has been shown *supra* that the sphere of action of intuitive law is the distribution of benefits and ills — as distinguished from the positive law, which also decides matters not related to this sphere — matters of formalities, technical arrangements, and the like. The distribution of benefits and ills is likewise the especial concern of justice, and the sphere of its action: it has no jurisdiction over problems of formalities. In a word, suitable study demonstrates that the experiences of justice are intuitive ethical experiences of an imperative-attributive type: intuitive law in our terminology.

As is usually the case in ethical experiences, the trite and ingenuous view relies on the illusion evoked by impulsive projections and regards those in the field of justice as real, taking the term "justice" to signify the corresponding norms, or the totality thereof, apparently existing and immutable, which define with higher authority what is due to whom from whom. This is shown by such expressions as "justice demands or enjoins," "the principles of justice," "in justice," "according to the lofty principles of justice, there is due," and so forth. This is to say that, from the projection point of view, justice means intuitive law norms. And as there is a projection of norms in the experiences of justice, so there is a projection of the corresponding obligations ("an obligation of justice," "according to justice he is bound, obligated") secured in behalf of others: of legal relationships of rights ("in justice he has a right to so and so, he may claim"). In this (projection) view a distinction may be drawn between justice in the objective sense (intuitive law norms) and justice in the subjective sense (the corresponding legal relationships, obligations, competences, and legal claims).

A further product of the projection action of the impulsions which enter into the structure of experiences of justice is that a special nature is ascribed to the corresponding conduct (conduct in accord with our intuitive law). To conduct which contradicts or is discordant with the intuitive law demands of the person judging is ascribed — there is projected upon it — the opposite quality of unjust ("unjust conduct"). Furthermore, the projection of the qualities "just" or "unjust" is directed even upon persons or other beings (such as divine beings) who appear to act in accordance with or contrary to the demands of justice: that is to say, of intuitive law (a "just man," "God is just," and so forth). Moreover, in intuitive law norms the word "justice" signifies also the corresponding attribute of conduct or quality of character — a laudable quality: "virtue," the inclination and desire always to act in accordance with the demands of justice in the former sense (that is to say, in accordance with the norms of intuitive law). The contrary attribute of conduct and character — the vice which consists in the tendency to infringe the demands of justice in the former sense — is called "injustice."

As terms to signify laudable qualities of conduct and character (merits and virtues), and the opposite and blameworthy qualities of conduct and character, the expressions "just" and "unjust" are naturally applied chiefly where the relevant subjects (of the conduct or of the character) appear to act by free choice and not under the pressure of necessity, coercion, authoritative commands of others, or the like (which exclude praiseworthiness and the presence of merit: the virtuousness of the corresponding conduct). The expressions justice, injustice, and so forth are accordingly applied chiefly when the concern is with the conduct or the character of those who are standing higher and are dominant as regards those who are standing lower and are subordinate or dependent, and not vice versa. Justice is thus ascribed to deities as the higher distributors of benefits in relation to persons (but not conversely: not to beings who are dependent upon deities and impotent with regard to them, being unable either to endow them with benefits or to deprive them of anything). It is ascribed to legislators with regard to those subject to the legislation, to monarchs in relation to subjects, to masters in relation to slaves or servants, to authorities in reference to subordinates, to judges in reference to those before them, to parents in relation to children, to critics in relation to those who are criticized, to examiners in relation to examinees and so forth, but not vice versa. It is obvious, however, that those standing above others in one regard may, with respect to such others, be in the converse position in other areas of conduct, and we then speak of the just or unjust relationship of the latter to the former. Thus in respect of an examination and the giving of marks to the examinees according to their merits, as they are due in conscience, we are concerned with the justice of the examiner and not of the examinees; but if, after the examination, the examinees considered the conduct of the examiner — rendering him his due by acknowledging his virtue or justice, or refusing such acknowledgment — there would be here the converse relationship, those who were previously at the bar becoming the judges, so that the epithets just or unjust are applicable to their judgments.

Inasmuch as justice is law — is related to the class "law" — the corresponding real phenomena are legal imperative-attributive experiences, the corresponding norms are legal imperative-attributive norms, and so forth. So all that has been set out herein as to law in general, as to legal impulsions, and as to various categories of ideas entering into the structure of legal experiences, as to legal projections, norms, and legal relationships, obligations, rights, and their elements, as to the characteristics peculiar to law as compared with morality, and so forth, is relevant as well to justice. The structure of experiences of justice — as distinguished from purely imperative experiences (moral experiences, in the sense of the classification established) — comprises attributive (and not purely imperative) impulsions: bilateral subject and object ideas, ideas of those from whom and of those to whom something is owed, ideas of what the obligors are required to furnish and of what the other party is entitled to receive. Because of the attributive nature of the relevant impulsions, consciousness of justice exerts a more powerful pressure upon conduct than does purely imperative moral consciousness.

Furthermore, inasmuch as justice is intuitive law, everything hereinbefore set out — especially as to intuitive law and its relation to positive law — is relevant to justice. Since it does not depend upon normative facts, statutes, and so forth, justice is distinguished by variability in respect of content, possessing a distinct content in different classes of persons and individuals, and being more capable of adaptation to concrete circumstances than positive law. Its development is gradual and unnoted, without the complications typical of the development of positive law. From the naive-projection point of view, the norms of justice appear (because they are independent of local laws, customs and so forth) as external and immutable, and of universal significance. Discords and conflicts — class and individual, evolutionary and so forth between justice and the corresponding positive law — are inevitable. Various elements of positive law and concrete decisions must therefore inevitably appear unjust from the viewpoint of the various classes of a given society and of particular individuals. The consciousness of justice exerts pressure upon the interpretation, application, and scientific working out of the positive law, and likewise appears (operating peacefully or by revolution) as a factor in the creation, abrogation, and change of positive law.

SECTION 33. *Early Natural Law*

The foregoing doctrine as to law in general and intuitive law in particular comprises premises for deciding what natural law is in the sense of theories of earlier legal philosophy and whether or not it actually exists.

The psychological method of study applied to the content of the treatises expounding the norms of natural law shows that their various propositions are nothing but reflections and expressions of intuitive law processes in the minds of the authors, who are setting out the content of their intuitive law convictions and of the corresponding projections. The prevailing form of outward expression is unilateral-attributive: the concern is not so much with natural law obligations as with rights — rights of man, citizen, husband, father, and so forth which are inherent and established by nature herself. Moreover, the authors start from the naive projection point of view, and are influenced by the corresponding fallacy as to the sphere of existence and the nature of that with which they are concerned — accepting as real, not the relevant psychic processes, but their projections supposedly existing in a world which is external as regards their minds. In conformity with the specific character of intuitive law projections — which is associated with the absence (in the intellectual structure of intuitive law experiences) of ideas of normative facts — the authors of treatises on natural law ascribe to natural laws norms eternity, immutability, ubiquity, significance independent of place, and so forth, and talk of the universal and innate rights of man which are independent of any grant by any state. The character of loftier mystic authoritativeness possessed by imperative-attributive impulsions explains the tendency of natural law doctrines to ascribe the corresponding commands and grants to higher beings: Nature, the Deity, and so forth. Finally, what was ascertained *supra* as to the nature of justice explains the fact that the quality of true justice, of correspondence with the principles of higher justice, and the like is ascribed to these norms, obligations, and rights.

The doctrines of natural law contain, however, various additional elements. These include (a) various considerations of expediency — especially considerations of legislative policy as to the unsatisfactory character of existing statutes and institutions from the point of view of the ends and problems which the authors considered they should satisfy (such as the expediency of this or that punishment from the point of view of successful eradication of crime or the correction of criminals, or the unsuitability of torture as a means for disclosing the truth in criminal proceedings, and the like); and (b) normative judgments of a nonlegal type, in particular moral or aesthetic judgments.

Likewise various propositions which, from the viewpoint of our classification should have been referred to the positive law, are found in different natural law doctrines under the name "natural law" — sundry legal propositions cited in medieval philosophy from the New Testament or the Old Testament, and other propositions referring — as to normative facts — to the general opinion among legal philosophers or the opinion of their predecessors who had acquired special authority. The operation of the unifying tendency of law is to be noted in the history of natural law doctrines.

Notwithstanding the naive projection point of view as to law and ignorance of its true nature, and despite the confusion of heterogeneous matters under the name natural law and various other scientific shortcomings, natural law doctrines were intuitive law statements advanced and enthusiastically advocated by forward thinkers, who took part in the working out of propositions of legal policy, and served the useful function of contributing to the progress of law and legislation (and in this sense served as a substitute for the science of legal policy which does not even now exist). The revolution in jurisprudence which occurred in the first half of the nineteenth century — consisting in a denial of the existence of any except positive law and of any activity except the historical and dogmatic study thereof — represents in both directions a retrograde movement: these were two serious errors, to be corrected by the development of the psychological theory of law which embraces both intuitive and positive law, and by the creation of a science of legal policy on the basis of the corresponding psychological data.

SECTION 34. *The So-Called Sources of Law*

By positive law as real phenomena, in accordance with what has already been set out, we mean imperative-attributive experiences comprising ideas of normative facts as the bases of obligation. This concept is of a far greater compass than the sphere to which the expressions "law" or "positive law" are applied in contemporary jurisprudence. It embraces much which is ordinarily referred to various classes contrasted to law (*mores*, religion, and so forth) as well as much which, in the contemporary classification of phenomena in general, finds no place and is lost from sight.

Positive law, in the foregoing broad sense, possesses all the attributes of law in general together with specific attributes which differentiate it from intuitive law. It contains many species and varieties. These species and varieties may be distinguished on the basis of the classes of normative facts to which there is reference in the given positive law experiences. There is already a doctrine as to the species of positive law in the science of law, borrowed from the ancient Roman jurists, but concealed under the peculiar term of so-called "sources of law."

What are the sources of law? There is universal agreement upon the negative proposition, that sources of law in the technical sense must be differentiated from sources of the cognition of law — from historical documents, including the works of private writers, and other data from which we may gain knowledge as to any law that has existed or does exist. But there are many views as to a positive definition of the essence of the sources of law: "the forms of creating law," "the bases for the emergence of law," "the factors constituting the basis of law in the objective sense," "the criteria of the obligatory force of legal norms," or "the different forms of expressing law."

The entire doctrine is indefensible as against scientific criticism and is even curiously abnormal from the viewpoint of elementary logic. If zoologists were to call dogs, cats, and so forth "the sources of animals," and had then started to quarrel about the meaning of the relationships of "sources of animals" and as to whether or not the sources are forms of creating animals or of proving their existence, or are indices of their animal nature and so forth, it would have been absolutely parallel to the thinking of modern jurists responsible for the theory of sources of law.

Cats, dogs, and so forth are not sources of animals. They are not forms of the creation of animals and so forth. Nor are they in general something which is distinct from animals and mysteriously related to the latter in a manner defying definition. They simply are animals. They themselves are animals: species and varieties thereof. In precisely the same way, the so-called "sources of law" (customary law, statute law, and so forth) are nothing but law itself: species of positive law — varieties of law. It is indeed odd to give them the name "sources of law" and to meditate upon their relationship to law. The name of the present doctrine ("sources of law") must be discarded and replaced by the expression "doctrine of positive law and the species and varieties thereof."

A further — and still more substantial — fault is the failure to distinguish between (a) positive law and its separate species and (b) the facts ideas whereof (as of normative facts) enter into the intellectual structure of the relevant positive law. From what has gone before it is clear that three separate things must be distinguished in positive law: (1) normative facts: the corresponding acts of persons, enactments of legislators, and so forth; (2) imperative-attributive experiences associated with ideas of these facts — the positive law itself as a real phenomenon; and (3) the corresponding norms: impulsive phantasmata produced by these experiences. The traditional doctrine, however, neither knows nor distinguishes these three different categories as such: the principal category — real, positive law itself, customary law, statute law, and so forth — it leaves out of view and does not study. It takes impulsive phantasmata (norms) for real positive law and confuses these norms with the commands of the legislators or other corresponding facts.

The proper building of a doctrine concerning the species and varieties of positive law requires us to keep in view that not only are legislative commands and other facts, whose ideas enter into the content of positive law experiences, not identical with positive law itself: they are not even so connected therewith causally that there is necessarily any parallelism between them in fact.

In the first place, what is significant in positive law, as the bases of obligations and determinants of conduct, is not the corresponding objective events (commands of legislators and so forth) but the ideas of them as present or past events. Accordingly, if the idea of a corresponding fact as a real event is present — such as the command of some monarch or deity, or a custom of ancestors and so forth — it is then immaterial, as regards the existence and operation of the corresponding positive law (statutory or customary) whether or not this fact actually occurred: not only may the supposed commands have no place in reality but their supposed authors may themselves exist only in legend or myth and the ancestors may have known nothing whatever of the custom ascribed to them or have acted in a completely different manner. In certain stages of culture, prior to — and for a certain time after — the appearance and development of writing, the positive law was to a significant degree defined by various legendary and mythical normative facts, not only in religious or sacral law but also in secular law. And, conversely, if the relevant fact had place in reality (if a certain statute, for example, had been promulgated and not abrogated) but there was neither the corresponding knowledge nor a corresponding idea (as, for example, if the statute were forgotten) — then the corresponding positive law neither does nor can exist and operate. In certain stages of culture, before — and even after — the development of writing and prior to the invention and spread of printing, it is not without significance as a destructive factor in the development of positive law that legislative orders and other normative facts have been forgotten. Likewise, where oral tradition and memory are operative, the content of ideas concerning normative facts changes with the passage of time, as regards the content of legislative or administrative directives, or the sense and character of customs of ancestors, and the content of positive law changes accordingly although the past facts cannot themselves change. Normative facts, or the "sources of positive law," in the theory of positive law and its species must therefore mean, not the external objective events as such, but the content of the corresponding ideas: assumed facts without reference to their actual existence.

But legislative commands present in imagination, customs of ancestors, and other facts related to the category of those which can in general play an authoritative-normative part, have by no means the significance that a definite positive law invariably corresponded thereto. This depends — as must be borne constantly in mind when the positive law and its separate species are under study — on the psychic condition of the relevant individuals or masses: on their psychic propensities, their habits and dispositions, their convictions (including their intuitive law convictions and their moral or religious beliefs), and so forth. Perceptions and ideas of the corresponding facts (for example, of facts published in the proper form of statutes, or of the customs of ancestors), which sometimes awaken in their minds a positive law reaction which evokes the corresponding positive law, may at other times fail — or even seem in general powerless — to arouse the corresponding positive law experiences. Thus only at a certain stage of culture do legislative orders of those representing state authority gain the capacity to evoke the corresponding positive law experiences in individuals and masses: the capacity of the human mind for legal reactions to legislative orders is a product of culture, and in the lower degrees of culture there is no such product. If a command is provided with threats in case of nonfulfillment, the result may be fear and subordination by reason of fear, but this has nothing in common with law: there are no ethical imperative-attributive experiences with the corresponding motivation of conduct — they do not arise — and therefore there is no true law. Moreover, the existing capacity and propensity for statute law experiences is originally very weak, so that various particularly favorable conditions must be present — such as reinforcement of the statute by intuitive law which is in accord with its content or akin in direction, or the special personal popularity of the tribal leader who proclaims the statute, or the like — if the statute is to have a chance of evoking the corresponding positive law. Only gradually does the mental capacity and propensity for statute law sufficiently develop and become strong to make it possible for legislation to govern mass conduct with relative dependability and success. But even after the capacity and disposition of the masses for the reception of statute law have been strengthened to the point of relative stability, it is only within certain limits and due observance of certain precautions that the legislator can assume to act as master of the situation and issue statutory directives, if the statute is not to fail as not evoking the corresponding content of the legal mentality or becoming sufficiently strong to operate successfully. So in the lower stages of culture (though not so low that there is in general no capacity for the reception of statute law) the authority of customs is extremely strong, and a legislator who should be so bold as to encroach upon these customs — to establish anything directly and sharply contradictory thereto — would merely compromise himself. At a certain stage of the development of the positive law mentality, a phenomenon strange at first sight, but perfectly understandable from the psychological point of view, is noted: statute law smuggled in under the guise of customary law. In order to give force to the statute and to attain legislative success, a statute is deceptively explained as ordaining nothing new and merely formalizing a now forgotten custom of our ancestors, and the like. Moreover, if certain religious convictions — or religion in general — shall have gained strength, statutes must conform therewith, otherwise the result is a fiasco. Always and everywhere the legislator must reckon with intuitive law, so that the statute be not wrecked by reason of a collision therewith. A statute clearly and seriously contradicting the duty of social-ancillary authority — the duty to utilize the legislative authority for furthering the general welfare and not for advancing personal interests — or manifestly immoral, or incoherent and absurd, would likewise appear impotent to call the corresponding positive law to life. Besides the general cultural process whereby the general capacity for a statute law mentality gradually develops, history affords examples of the proper psychological reaction developing and growing strong only gradually as to various particular species of legislation, or as to statutes issuing from a particular legislator: thus in the development of a legal superstructure above small social organizations which were formerly sovereign, the new supra-group legislation is extremely feeble at first. It may successfully concern itself only with certain questions and may easily come to nought. Only gradually does it acquire strength, significance, and a relatively broad scope of action. The same occurs after revolutions, or the overthrow of a dynasty, or a change from a monarchy to a republic or vice versa. Again, a statute which has come into operation may, for various psychic causes (and without being forgotten) lose its normative authority. Not infrequently statutes cease to evoke the corresponding law without being in any sense abrogated, in consequence of the latent and gradually overriding operation of the intuitive law. There are innumerable historical examples of cruel punitive statutes ceasing to function because of the influence of a more gentle and humane intuitive law, which had changed. Statutes fixing certain rates of compensation when the value of a given monetary unit was high cease to operate if the value of that unit gradually but substantially declines. Aside from intuitive law, statutes not infrequently lose their normative force because of undermining causes: because they begin to appear immoral and obviously incongruous from the point of view of expediency where conditions have changed, or because they are at variance with new religious views, or (after religious zeal has subsided) because they seem to have originated in superfluous religious fanaticism or to have been motivated by police suspicion or by a desire to interfere in what statutes should not touch.

What has been set out as to statutes refers, *mutatis mutandis*, to all categories of normative facts (and was therefore set out here rather than in the sections concerned with statutes). They all have the same relative and conditional significance — sometimes arousing to life the corresponding positive law (and sometimes not), depending on psychological factors and conditions. There neither are nor can be categories of facts which would, so to speak, unfailingly operate normatively in the province of the legal mentality by their own nature and independently of other conditions. In the theory of positive law and its species, normative facts must therefore signify, not facts of a definite category with definite objective attributes (such as statutes published in proper form, customs of a certain species as such, court practice as such, and so forth), but only facts which actually do operate normatively, arousing the corresponding positive law experiences. Thus, although they are published in accordance with all the corresponding rules and possess all the attributes required or advanced by contemporary science for their legal validity, statutes are not *per se* positive law — or even normative facts — from the point of view of the psychological theory of law: they can be and are — ordinarily or sometimes — normative facts, and sometimes they are not.

What categories of facts can act as normative facts? and what corresponding species of positive law are present, conformably with those facts? The view that law is an aggregate of norms, and that norms are commands (expressions of will — of the will of the community, of the general will, and so forth) holds that the relevant will can be expressed either (a) by means of words (declaring the will of the community — or of the will of the legislative organ of the community accepted as its will or the general will — in statutes or statute law), or (b) indirectly and *sub silentio* by "expressive" actions (*facta concludentia*): that is to say, by general conduct postulating the presence of the corresponding will, where the social will is manifested in customary law. There are thus two sources of law: statute law and customary law. However, this doctrine — and in general the doctrine of norms as commands — is not ordinarily developed logically in that, as to sources of law, it is frequently acknowledged that still a third source of law (court practice) exists, while customary law theories are ordinarily worked out independently of the theory that norms are commands, and are not brought into logical correspondence therewith.

From the point of view of the psychological theory of law as imperative-attributive experiences, the circle of facts that can act as normative facts in the positive law is far broader, and there are far more species of positive law, than the prevailing doctrine acknowledges and assumes. All kinds of facts besides legislative commands (in the sense of the prevailing opinion), legal customs and court practice can serve as normative facts insofar as the individual or mass legal mind is able and inclined to elicit therefrom certain general rules of conduct or specific directions therefor, and thus give imperative-attributive force to those facts. Moreover, it must be remembered that, in accordance with the general unifying tendency characteristic of law, the legal mind strives to employ all possible occasions and materials for the attainment of a positively fixed pattern incontrovertibly predetermining mutual rights and obligations.

The following exposition investigates and corrects the prevailing doctrines as to statute law, common law, and court practice under the guidance of the general principles hereinbefore set out, and then ascertains the existence and nature of other species of positive law which are either unknown to contemporary jurisprudence or are not acknowledged by it as "sources of law."

SECTION 35. *Statute Law*

According to the prevailing definition statutes or legislative legal norms are norms established by the state, or commands expressing the will of the state (or of organs of the state authority), and it is either assumed or specifically pointed out that these commands should be put together and issued in the form established by the law of the given state. Some authorities are against the inclusion of form in the definition of statute, on the ground that if the relevant form is not observed there is no act of the state — no expression of the will of the state — but only a personal act, manifesting the private will of the person issuing the command.

From the point of view of the scientific theory of law, the principal shortcomings of the prevailing doctrine as to statute law are these.

(1) Identification of statute law with the relevant normative facts, and the failure to distinguish between norms of statute law on the one hand, and statutes — commands of legislators — on the other. The proper study and building of a theory of statute law requires — in accordance with the general principles set out *supra* — a strict differentiation of (a) statutes and the directives of certain persons, as normative facts; (b) statute law in the real-psychological sense: imperative experiences with reference to these normative facts; and (c) the corresponding projections or phantasmata: the statutory norms, rights, obligations, and so forth.

(2) Restriction of the concept and doctrine of statutes to state statutes, and disregard or exclusion of a multitude of essentially homogeneous phenomena which should be united into one class for the building of an adequate theory: this includes legal imperative-attributive experiences, with reference to corresponding commands of deities, direc-

tives of ecclesiastical assemblies and authorities, directives of forebears, of councils of the elders and the like in the period preceding the emergence of the state, commands of a master, father, mother, and so forth in domestic life, orders of the master of slaves, of the possessor of property, factory, trading establishment and the like, or of directors, managers, or other authorities relative to private enterprises, directives of general assemblies and so forth of stock companies and other private associations, and of societies seeking to effectuate purposes which are not material (such as learned societies, political parties, criminal organizations, and so forth).

Even as an essentially narrow doctrine which is concerned, not with statute law, but only with the normative facts of statute law (and is limited entirely to state statutes), the prevailing doctrine is indefensible.

First of all, the hypothesis underlying the current concept of statutes — that in order that there be a statute the relevant command must have been put together in the form established for legislation (or, in the ordinary expression, in constitutional form) — is entirely inadmissible. A multitude of statutes, conceded to be such by contemporary jurisprudence, do not conform to this hypothesis and must (from the viewpoint of the prevailing concept of statutes) be acknowledged as actions lacking the force of a statute. Thus in order that statutes — issued on the basis of the constitution and in the form prescribed thereby — be acknowledged as such, it is necessary, from the point of view of the prevailing doctrine, that the constitution be in turn a valid statute: *videlicet,* issued in the proper form established for the purpose, and so forth. If the corresponding verification is made, it appears as to many states that the relevant constitution is not — and cannot be acknowledged as — a statute because its origin was contrary to statute. This is so, in particular, as to constitutions of revolutionary origin, and those established by a *coup d'état.* Even some constitutions of peaceful origin have been compiled and promulgated without observance of the established form, for the simple reason that, prior to the publication of the constitution, there was no form of any sort established for the publication of statutes — or even that there was no state at all: the constitution declared the existence of the state in the first place and established for it the form to be observed thereafter for publishing statutes. This has occurred for example where for the first time a state was instituted by means of enactment of an assembly of colonists or their representatives, or where a complex state was founded through the working out of a constitution by representatives of the simple states or of their population.

Thus insofar as constitutions defining the form of publication of further statutes cannot be acknowledged (from the point of view of the prevailing concept of statutes) as actual statutes, all further statutes published on the basis and according to the rules of these likewise fail to satisfy the requirements of the prevailing concept of statutes, and must logically be acknowledged as non-statutes.

If this retrospective verification of the legal origin of statutes that have defined the form of publishing further statutes in various states is extended further — to the more remote stages of legislative history — mass destruction of the statutes will follow. If, on the other hand, attention is turned to the beginning of legislative history — to the first statutes of any sort — then the relevant statutes cannot be statutes from the point of view of the prevailing doctrine, since prior to the beginning of legislation there was not even an established form of publishing statutes. When it includes in the concept of statutes the criterion of publication in the established or constitutional form, the current view presupposes that this form is defined by statutes, and to this extent a *definitio per idem* is latent in the formulae: statutes (x) are precepts issued by organs of the state in accordance with statutes (x) defining the order of issuing statutes (x). But besides statutes the prevailing doctrine of law knows still another "source of law": customary law, and to avoid the incongruous conclusion that the first statutes were necessarily illegal for want of an established form of legislation, it is manifestly possible to turn to customary law and to say that the absence of statutes defining the form of issuing statutes does no harm since there can exist a customary law form of publishing statutes. But the objection here is: how can there be a customary form of legislation, antedating the very principle of legislation?

In addition to the fact that statutes published without observance — or in direct violation — of the established order exist and operate, a no less indubitable fact already mentioned must be taken into account: sometimes orders issued in proper form do not operate since they do not evoke the corresponding consciousness of duty and so forth, and so are altogether without significance for legal life, or they lose the force and significance of statutes with the passage of time and without being abrogated at all.

At all events, the proper formation of a concept of statutes requires that no decisive significance be attributed to publication in the proper order, and that the center of gravity of the concept and doctrine of statutes and statute law be shifted to the province of the legal mentality.

What is essential for the presence of a statute and of statute law is not publication in an established form, but that the corresponding imperative-attributive experiences be present: that the act would appear in the legal mentality as a normative fact.

Furthermore, even in the field of official statute law, the proposition underlying the traditional concept of statutes — that statutes are commands expressing the will of the *state* (or of organs of the *state,* of *state* authority and so forth) — must be rejected as erroneous. From what has already been set out, it is manifest that various statutes — including constitutions — may and do issue from other persons, and not from the state or from organs of state authority. Constitutions of revolutionary origin, issued by a revolutionary constituent assembly, as well as constitutions proclaiming the existence of the given state, do not represent acts of the state or of organs of state authority in the sense of the prevailing opinion. The history of legislation contains not a few examples of orders of usurpers which had acquired, in the course of time or (at least in the minds of a certain part of the population) at one stroke, the force of statutes and so forth. Even the common phenomenon of the operation, in recently annexed territories, of statutes published not by the legislator of the given state but by representatives of the authority of another state (of which the given province was formerly a part) contradicts the current concept of statutes, since this has in view the publication of the relevant injunctions by organs, not of any other state, but only of the given state whose law is being considered. Here, too, it must be said that the center of gravity of the concept and doctrine of statute law and statutes should be shifted to the field of legal psychology: what is essential is not the source from which the statute proceeds (a given state or its organs, or any one else) but the fact that in the given state the corresponding act attains the force of a normative fact as evoking the corresponding imperative-attributive experiences.

The foregoing errors in the prevailing concept of statutes are due to the methodological defect of confusing the theoretical point of view (the point of view of that which is or occurs) with the practical-dogmatic point of view (the point of view of that which should — for the future — be observed as binding by the mandates of official law). Once there is a definite established state order, with a constitution defining by whom and in what form statutes should (thereafter) be published, and directing that if the relevant rules are not complied with enactments should be deemed to be without force, the jurist can set out the corresponding rules, but specifically as rules of what should be — as what should (thereafter) be observed as binding according to the law of the given state. Such propositions, however, should by no means be confused with theoretical concepts and truths: that which is prescribed for the future and is binding is not always observed, and prior to the formation of the injunctions there could be no observance thereof. The prevailing idea of statutes is produced by confusing two essentially distinct points of view; and in general the content of the contemporary doctrine concerning statutes represents not so much an actual doctrine concerning statutes and statute law as a practical-dogmatic exposition of the content of the mandates of contemporary constitutional law. In the same way, ordinary statements concerning the legal force of statutes, the moment when they begin to operate, and their further validity down to the moment they are abrogated, and so forth, are nothing but statements of what is prescribed by contemporary legislation as due, while the corresponding propositions are taken for theoretical verities. From the theoretical point of view, it simply cannot be asserted that directives promulgated and published in proper form begin to operate unfailingly and always from a definite moment of time and always operate until the moment of their abrogation, and so forth. Instead of these and similar theoretically incorrect propositions, study of the psychological conditions of action or inaction, or of the initially weak or uncertain action of newly published statutes and the gradual intensification of their action — of their growing strong in the national mind — as well as an investigation of the conditions and different processes whereby statutes grow weak and cease to operate without any abrogation thereof whatever, and so forth, are relevant to the problems of a future doctrine of statute law as a psychic phenomenon *sui generis*.

There are further reasons to doubt the validity of the view that statutes represent commands. First of all it must be noted that in the legal mind the obligation to observe statutes is by no means limited merely to the persons or categories of persons to whom the legislative orders are addressed, but extends as well to various other categories of persons, including the very persons who issue the commands: thus the monarch — even an absolute monarch — is admittedly bound by the statute he publishes, in precisely the same way as are others, until the statute is abrogated. There are even statutes whose meaning and action consist chiefly — if not exclusively — in creating certain obligations (or in renouncing certain rights) for the monarch who promulgates the statute. To interpret a statute as a command by a single superior will to another is obviously unsuitable.

From the point of view of a theory of law as imperative-attributive experiences this phenomenon presents no difficulties. The source of the authoritative and binding character of law in general, and of various species of positive law in particular, is not found in any external events (particularly not in anyone's commands) but in ethical impulsions, which can be united with various ideas, including ideas of extremely diverse normative facts (and not excluding one's own words or other actions, as will appear in connection with the law of precedent, whereby one who has acted in a certain fashion on one occasion is considered bound to act the same on other occasions of the same class).

Moreover, insofar as it is a matter of statutes as directions to others and of the obligatory character of statutes for those others, these directions can — as we have already seen — issue from persons neither endowed with, nor pretending to, rights of authorities (rights to command and to forbid). In general, various legislative enactments — especially collective enactments (in an assembly, council, parliament, session of a faculty, and so forth) — often comprise absolutely no subjective element of a command or an order: the concern is not with ordering or commanding, but with working out and fixing for themselves and for others certain rules of conduct for future observance. It must further be kept in view — and this is essentially important for understanding the nature of statutes — that, in accordance with the imperative-attributive nature of the legal consciousness, statutes have in general a dual imperative-attributive significance: legislation is not only concerned with the establishment of obligations for some, but also with securing corresponding claims in behalf of others and endowing the latter with rights. Legislative enactments are in general not imperative orders but imperative-attributive orders, and this is reflected in their formulation: in the complete and adequate form of directions with two addressees each, and in the use of three abbreviated forms as equal in significance (including the unilateral-attributive form) addressed to those only who are endowed with rights and indicating the rights attributed to them.

In view of the foregoing, statutes should be characterized not as commands but as directives or orders as to what, for the future, should or should not be acknowledged as an obligation for some and a right for others: or, more briefly, as orders regarding a future right.

A final definition of statutes and statute law requires us to take into consideration that our concern is (1) with unilateral orders as distinguished from contracts (which are accords), and (2) with directives (assumed to be real) of natural or supernatural beings, irrespective of whether or not they actually existed or whether what took place was in reality something else and not a legal directive at all, such as an expression of technical advice, an aesthetic rule, or a moral commandment.

These considerations enable us to define (a) statute law as imperative-attributive experiences containing reference to unilateral legal orders of someone as normative facts, and (b) statutes as unilateral legal orders of someone insofar as they are normative facts (in other words, to the extent that the relevant ideas exert a corresponding influence on anyone's legal mentality, arousing, eliminating, or changing imperative-attributive experiences). The classes and class concepts of statute law and statutes thus established — embracing incomparably more phenomena than do current doctrines of statutes — are susceptible of division into different species, sub-species, and varieties from various points of view. One of the most important divisions is that into official and unofficial statutes, having regard to whether or not they possess official significance in the state. Official significance may be and is possessed not only by statutes promulgated by state authorities, but also by various others such as ecclesiastical enactments (insofar as the relevant act enjoys official acknowledgment on the part of the state), and rules and other directives of various private associations recognized by the state (such as stock corporations, clubs, and learned societies).

It was explained *supra,* with regard to official statutes, that the term includes directives of persons having no rights of authority in a given state or in general. The same is true as to other species of statutes. Even in the midst of communal, ecclesiastical, and other units, directives of usurpers or others not endowed with the right of authority in the given social sphere may acquire statutory force. Ordinarily, however, in regulated and normal legal life, statutes issue from persons or institutions endowed (in the minds of the relevant persons) with authority over others — general or special, social-ancillary or dominant, higher or lower, or supreme. These oral or written directives are issued and acknowledged as binding in the relevant social sphere by virtue of the corresponding right of authority and within the limits of that right. In conformity with the general and broadly inclusive concepts of statutes and statute law established *supra,* rights of every kind to give orders — with the consequence that others are bound to conform therewith as with normative facts (however modest and limited the rights are: for example, of a nurse in relation to children, or of a slave endowed with authority over other slaves) — may be called legislative rights or legislative authorities in the broad sense. In conformity with the division of authorities (proposed *supra*) into species and varieties, corresponding species and varieties of legislation and of statute law may be distinguished. Thus legislation may be divided into: (1) general (which may touch any relationship with the exception of some particularly indicated) and (2) special (which are limited to a definite circle of relationships). The legislative authority of the head of the family, of the head of a tribe, and of one possessing supreme state authority is general legislative authority and the corresponding legislation is general legislation. The legislative authority of the head of the church (such as the Pope), or of a minister of national education and the like, is special legislative authority, and the corresponding legislative orders, directives, circulars, and the like are special legislation. The corresponding directives are, in general, operative and have the force of statutes insofar as they remain within the bounds set for the legislative activity of the corresponding authorities.

Legislation may be further divided into ancillary or dominant. That of the first class (such as the legislative authority of the head of the family or the head of a tribe with regard to its members, or of a monarch in regard to citizens) represents legislative rights coupled with an obligation, to subjects and to the social group, to employ them for the welfare of the social group and its members and to carry them into effect within the limits of this obligation and as a means of its fulfillment. Legislative authorities of the second sort (such as those of a master as to slaves or serfs, or of the head of a private enterprise with reference to those serving therein, or of a monarch with regard to subjugated nationalities or state slaves in the narrow sense — as distinguished from free citizens) are rights which are free and not ancillary with reference to the slaves and so forth, not being connected with an obligation to carry them into effect for the welfare of the subjects, and being capable of being effectuated in order to extract property or other advantages from them.

Where there are many authorities arranged in a hierarchy, there are corresponding gradations of legislative authorities and of legislation. Here it is possible to distinguish those which are lower and subordinate in the hierarchy, those which are higher and dominant therein, and those which are supreme. In the life of the family or the tribe there is a relatively small series of gradations of legislative authorities, hierarchically subordinate each to the other, with supreme legislative authorities at the head, while in extensive and complex state or other organizations (such as the Catholic Church) this series is a long one. Supreme legislative authorities — and in general those which are higher in the hierarchy — extend as well to all subjects of all the lower authorities which are bound, within the sphere of their orders, to obey higher statutes and directives of higher authorities — and in particular to carry out higher injunctions by means of corresponding orders below. In this sense legislative authorities which are lower in the hierarchy may be termed executive with reference to the higher, and all the higher legislative authorities executive with reference to the supreme legislative authority. The latter is not executive authority with reference to any other but represents independent legislative authority and may from this point of view be termed legislative authority in the narrow sense. Higher statutes may abrogate all lower statutes, but not vice versa. Statutes of the lower orders have normative force only insofar as they conform with the injunctions of statutes of the higher orders — or at least do not contradict them.

A characteristic peculiar to legislation and to statute law with reference to other species of normative facts and positive law (particularly customary law) is that here one person or a certain group of persons can at will evoke in the minds of others such legal ideas as seem to him or to the group desirable, and similarly eliminate or abrogate existing law and produce various other changes in the legal minds and life of others. Moreover, legislation can produce such changes suddenly, at a single stroke, and at a time chosen at will. With these distinguishing features various further characteristics of legislation and statute law are associated, in particular its merits and demerits as compared with other classes of normative facts and positive law. Employed with reason, enlightenment, and boldness, legislation is an excellent and a powerful instrument of rationally controlling the development of law — of improving its technical form and adapting it to the satisfaction of the general need of unifying legal relationships. Where, on the other hand, it is not employed with reason, it may become an evil more or less seriously detrimental to the nation in various directions. It is extremely important for the spiritual and material well-being of mankind and its progress — particularly and chiefly in view of the foregoing attributes of legislation — to create and develop for the guidance of the legislator a science of rational law-making: the science of legal policy.

The phenomenon of the combination of normative acts with a hierarchical subordination of lower to the guidance of the higher authorities is particularly typical of statute law as compared with other species of positive law. By virtue of this peculiarity, statute law is an instrument not only for creating law directly but also for governing the various subordinate centers (or entire systems thereof) which may produce law. This in turn results in further characteristics of statute law as compared with other species of positive law. Corresponding to the multiplicity, hierarchical subordination, ramification, and specialization of the law-producing laboratories is the multiplicity of the categories and types of the corresponding legal products, with the content and scope of their action related to each other in definite and typical ways. Higher legislation, such as the constitution, may establish nothing more than general directives which presuppose — and are sometimes even incapable of execution without — the settlement of more special and particular rules by other and subordinate legislation; as the system of statutes moves downward to lower ramifications, the content of these becomes more and more particular and special, the scope of their action narrower in territorial or other relationships, and their social significance more modest and less significant.

SECTION 36. *Customary Law*

Customary law is ordinarily defined as law which is in fact observed although it has not been established by statute: as the constant and uniform observance of a certain rule of conduct. As to the nature of customary law, however, the views of jurists are not in harmony: when indicating the structure of the customary law and the conditions of its presence, they set these out with greater precision than is found in the definition. Some of them cling to the so-called spiritualistic theory, founded by leaders of the historical school (Savigny and Puchta), that all that is needed for the presence of customary law is the existence of a corresponding national legal conviction: the factual observance of the norm has no bearing on the substance of customary law, being merely its inevitable result and concomitant and a means of knowing that it exists. Others hold to the so-called materialistic theory: that the essence and basis of customary law is, on the contrary, comprised in uniform conduct constantly observed — in the factual habit — and that legal conviction is not essential. A third and intermediate opinion asserts that the presence of customary law requires two equally essential elements: (1) the prolonged uniform observance of a certain rule, and (2) the conviction of those so observing it ("the general conviction") that such observance is legally obligatory. Those who associate the concept of customary law with the general theory of law as commands or imperatives find the essence of customary law in its being "the general will" or "the expression of the general will."

These doctrines must all be rejected: they do not correspond to the actual nature of customary law. The phenomenon of prolonged and uniform observance of a certain rule of conduct, with consciousness that it is legally binding, does not mean that a particular species of positive law — customary law — exists: it is also found where customary law is absent and other species of positive law — such as statute law or the law of court practice — are operative. It occurs also where there is intuitive law uniform in content in the minds of many persons and successfully operative. Law of every kind may evoke corresponding uniform conduct with consciousness of its obligatory force, and where there is prolonged action of such a law there will also be prolonged uniform observance.

As a particular species of positive law, customary law is found only if imperative-attributive experiences, with the idea of the corresponding mass conduct of others as a normative fact, occur in the mind of someone: I (or we, or he, or they) have a right to this, or are bound to that, because it was always heretofore so observed, because our forebears acted so, because this is an "ancient custom."

The propensity to legal experiences of this class — the tendency to elevate the former conduct of others (principally our forebears) into "law": into a normative fact for oneself and for others — is typical of a more primitive mentality and of people of the lower grades of culture, where respect for ancestors and their customs is more strongly developed and ancient traditions and customs seem sacred, and nonobservance thereof evil and shameful. It is important, if scientific psychological cognition of the relevant legal phenomena is to be achieved, to turn to the corresponding factual material as to ancient life, or in general to the lower stages of culture, and to study the relevant mentality of tribes still living according to the customs of their ancestors.

In certain areas, however, the normative fact of customary law is not the conduct of ancestors, antiquity, or ancient customs, but the corresponding mass conduct of contemporaries: the fact that "so it is done," "everyone acts so," "this is a generally accepted custom" at a given time. Such customary law occurs even outside the sphere where ancestors and antiquity are held in reverence. The relevant phenomena may be observed in the rules of social etiquette (visits obligatory by custom and other civilities) and the rules of various sports, and sometimes even in business life, entering into the sphere of official law (chiefly commercial law, where various claims unregulated by commercial statutes are made and satisfied on the basis that "this is what is done in trade" and so forth).

Accordingly two classes of customary law can and must be differentiated: (1) the law of ancestral customs, ancient traditions, and antiquity, and (2) the law of contemporary customs, of what is ordinarily observed: of what is "generally accepted." For brevity the former may be termed "ancient" and the latter "modern." In the customary law mentality of the former species, the prestige or authority (the impulsive force) of customary law is, *ceteris paribus*, higher: the older and more ancient the given custom appears the higher its standing ("the older the more sacred"). In the customary law mentality of the latter (second) species, that law is, *ceteris paribus*, the higher the more generally it is accepted and the more consistently the particular legal conduct appears to be observed in the relevant sphere.

In each of the two classes of customary law the normative fact is ordinarily the mass *legal* conduct of others (forebears or contemporaries): that is to say, that the relevant actions, abstentions, or tolerances were accomplished as satisfying rights acknowledged in behalf of others and as the effectuation by the latter of rights ascribed to themselves (and not, for example, the fulfillment of purely moral or aesthetic rules, and the like). There can, however, be another manifestation and extension of customary law opinions: the making of claims based upon a citation of certain mass conduct of ancestors and so forth, although the relevant conduct did not in general — or in most cases — have the character of legal conduct. It must further be kept in mind that in customary law, as in other positive law, what is imagined to have been — and not what in reality was — is of decisive importance as a normative fact. Thus, "ancient" customary law may appear and operate with reference to an alleged custom of forebears although in reality the latter acted otherwise: either there was no such custom whatever, or the relevant custom had the character not of a legal custom but of a purely moral or aesthetic custom or technical rule and the like. The phenomenon of the introduction of a new law under the guise of reëstablishing the action of a custom now forgotten or distorted, but supposedly existing formerly, has been mentioned. In general, in the operation of "the older the more sacred" it is extremely easy and natural for customary law opinions (resting on legendary or generally unreliable ideas as to antiquity, customs of ancestors, and so forth) to appear and spread. For persons who because of youth, inexperience, or otherwise are not themselves personally familiar with ancestral or with contemporary customs (such as those defining the rights and obligations of the principals and seconds in a duel), the communications of others are extremely important (communications of elders, or of specialists or would-be specialists in a particular field, such as dueling). Accordingly customary law opinions emerge and operate, based not on observance of the authentic customs but on second or third hand — and sometimes unreliable — communications regarding them. The history of customary law reveals that processes of this class did — and do — undoubtedly play no small part.

Customary law may therefore be defined as imperative-attributive experiences which refer to the corresponding mass conduct of others as the normative fact. From this definition, as also from all that has been set out *supra* as to law in general and positive law in particular, it is clear that customary law is a phenomenon of the individual mind, and may be studied as such with the aid of self-observation and the joint method of inward and outward observation.

It must be emphasized that the proposed concept of customary law embraces all imperative-attributive experiences with ideas of normative facts of the type indicated — including as well those which have no official significance in the state and are not related by contemporary jurisprudence to law in general but are instead contrasted to law under the name of simple *mores,* conventional rules, and the like. Such for instance are opinions on the rights of guests to a place of honor at the table and other signs of attention insofar as they rest on customs obtaining in society. Accordingly, customary law in the foregoing broad sense may be divided into two classes: official and unofficial. From the proposed general definition of customary law and this division, we obtain at the same time a solution of the further question: what is customary law in the juridic sense employed in practical-dogmatic jurisprudence? This is an eclectic group, comprising official customary law in our sense in the intra-state field and customary law (in our sense) without qualification as that of international law. The traditional doctrine of customary law rests on ignorance of the eclectic content of the group "customary law" in the juridic sense. All the theoretical propositions of this doctrine must inevitably suffer — aside from other defects — from the faults of "jumping" or "limping," or even from both at the same time.

Apart from this, an essential defect in the prevailing doctrine as to customary law is that it neither studies nor knows the authentic and real phenomena of customary law, nor the corresponding phenomena of the individual mind and their content, but takes for customary law that mass phenomenon which can only be — and is sometimes — a normative fact (in the idea of those experiencing specified psychic processes).

Before the time of the historical school it was widely held, as regards the relationship of customary law to a statute, that customary law was not an independent class or "source" of law: the fundamental and only independent species of law was the statute, and jurists deduced the obligatory force of custom from explicit precept, or tacit admission of its operation, by the legislator. Puchta's enormous and epoch-making merit is that he refuted such doctrines and demonstrated that customary law is independent of statute. The view now prevailing is that the relation between customary law and statute is not that the former is subordinate and dependent as regards the latter, but that they are coördinate: each possesses equal force, and exists and operates independently.

Neither doctrine can be accepted. Actually the relation between statutes and customs differs in various stages of development and spheres of life, and any theory asserting a single definite relationship between them would "jump." In certain fields — chiefly in spheres and periods in which ancestral customs in general are honored as something sacred and inviolate — the relationship between customary and statute law is not one of equality and coördination: statute law is subordinate to customary law; legislation must concededly conform with customary law, and legislative enactments contravening the sacred customs of ancestors wholly lack normative force. In other situations — chiefly where statutes possess high authority and there are constitutional and other guarantees of legality, and reverence for routine and antiquity is weak or nonexistent — the relationship between statutory and customary law is the reverse. Here, too, there is no coördination, but the subordination is of customary law to statute law. In contemporary society, the official force of customary law is ordinarily defined by statute law: where (as in the criminal law) the statute assumes the application of statute law alone, custom is inadmissible. Where, on the other hand, a statute admits or enjoins the application of customary law, this is done within the bounds established by the statute and on the basis thereof, with citations of the relevant statutes. In continental law the application of customary law is admitted chiefly in the sphere of commercial law and, in general, of civil law (and even then for the most part within modest limits, as where there is no corresponding legislative solution, or a special statute prescribes that the particular question or group of questions be decided in accordance with customary law). In other fields of law, especially in that of the criminal law, the application of customary law is excluded. To this the factual course of official legal life corresponds in general, although particular inconsistencies are possible.

Besides these two types of relationships between customary and statute law, an intermediate transitory type of relationship must be recognized as possible and existent (a relationship raised to the rank of a general truth by the prevailing opinion): that customary and statute law are equal and coördinate.

From the theoretical problem as to the relationship in fact between customary and statute law, practical problems as to a desirable or proper relationship must be kept distinct, although the literature on this question (as on other questions of general legal doctrine) unfortunately confuses these points of view. While problems of the latter class are related to the dogma and the policy of law, the doctrine that customary and statute law are equal and coördinate is no less mistaken qua theory (as not in accord with reality) than it is inadmissible qua practical principle as a rule to guide the courts. It would undermine the force of statutes and lessen their social and cultural value and significance, conflict with the task of unifying the law (of establishing definite and firm legal order), and contribute to arbitrary action and legal anarchy. If customary law regulates certain fields of conduct otherwise than does statute law — as by admitting corporal punishment of apprentices, the payment of workmen in kind, duels and other reactions to insult forbidden by statute and so forth — the doctrine of the equality of statute and custom should then logically hold that judges are free to choose whether to decide by statute or by a custom, so that the outcome would depend on arbitrary choice, on taste, and so forth. Since it assumes that duality of law is impossible, the prevailing doctrine does not note that this logically follows from its view that statute law and customary law are equal: customary law, rejected by statute, becomes (under this doctrine) "not-law," "simple *mores*" and the like. In other words the prevailing doctrine suffers from internal contradiction when it proclaims that statutory and customary law are equal, and at the same time displays a decisive preference for the former.

Under the influence of doctrines of the historical school, which exalted and glorified customary law as compared with statute law, it was usual to ascribe to customary law various lofty qualities and advantages as compared with statute: it appears as the immediate and the better expression of national views and needs, and is further distinguished by flexibility and adaptability to their change, whereas the statute "jells at the moment of writing" and lags behind the constant change of life: it possesses notable productive force and creative capacity, organizes proper standardization where required, and fills in gaps of the statute which could not anticipate all problems of changing life as they arise. On the other hand, Ihering pointed out that the properties of customary law which constitute its merits are at the same time bound up with its fundamental shortcoming: it is dependent upon morality and *mores* and consequently indefinite and difficult to discern and prove. Whether or not it exists depends on the views of the witnesses and on the judge.

These propositions — the praise of customary law by its supporters and its disparagement by Ihering — are alike remote from the actual nature of customary law and are due to a confusion of customary law with other phenomena. They are nearer the nature of intuitive law, which is in reality distinguished by flexibility and mutability, representing the gradual and constant development and change of legal views while having no definite uniform legal pattern and resultant from the outlook of the individual. Where genuine customary law existed or now exists in developed form, it is a uniform mass legal pattern of conduct, sometimes definite down to the very smallest details and fixed with the very greatest precision, and independent of moral and intuitive law views of any individual. It must, moreover, be conceded that it is characterized, not by elasticity and mobility — by adaptability to new views and needs — but by stagnation and immobility, by conformity with the past (sometimes with conditions of the extremely remote past) rather than with those of the present, and by a tendency to preserve routine and antiquity unchanged. It is the most sluggish and conservative species of law. In a particularly high degree is this so as to its principal species, "ancient" customary law, and its aura of "the older the more sacred." Even "modern" customary law, however, is likewise defined by a routine (sometimes of ancient origin, although that origin is unknown and there is no reference to antiquity). A statute is addressed to the future and ordains what should be the law thereafter, whereas by its very nature customary law looks backward and has a retrospective character, inevitably conforming with that which was, in the more or less remote past.

Many customs are accordingly incomprehensible to the observer. The conditions wherein they were understandably important have long since ceased to exist and passed completely from the memory of man, so that the sense and the significance of the corresponding actions, forms, and ceremonies are unknown to the present generation. Yet such is the peculiar psychological nature of customary law that this does not prevent compliance with them. Moreover, more exact and unswerving observance results where the customary law mentality is strong and flourishes, and respect for customs is dominant. Knowing the meaning of the actions, remote ancestors could deviate in various respects in accordance with circumstances, but their descendants — inheriting the same custom, but no understanding of its meaning — fear to deviate in the slightest degree: ignorant of what is important in the custom and why the corresponding actions are necessary, they ascribe like importance and sanctity to every sort of petty detail.

In consequence of the conservative force of the customary law mentality this law (and, in part, customary morality, customary aesthetics, and so forth, as well) is of high scientific interest and value as the archaeological, prehistoric material for reëstablishing the picture of ancient life as to which no written sources have been preserved. Thus the custom of a gift to bind the bargain as a sign that a contract has finally been concluded, and that of a draft of brotherhood as a sign of a contract of friendship, attest the application of blood to corroborate legal acts in antiquity — the importance and seriousness in antiquity of contracts of friendship — and reflect primitive materialistic views as to the nature of the soul. In various contemporary customs of family law there are survivals from ancient periods and stages of development, when a marriage was concluded by the forcible ravishment of wives in company with kinsmen and friends, when a wife was purchased, when spouses were chosen — and the contract of marriage concluded — not by those who were being married but by their lords, and so forth. These and similar phenomena graphically illustrate how far from the truth are the doctrines as to the customary law being a better form of positive law than statute law.

The forward movement of human culture — including economic life and technology — does not keep pace with the movement of time but is swifter, for reasons which cannot be gone into here.[1] In the lower and primitive stages of development, life is relatively stable, and cultural change proceeds very slowly. In the higher stages of development that change occurs ever more and more swiftly. Changes so great as to require tens of thousands of years in primitive stages occur during the course of a thousand years in subsequent stages, and in a period of one hundred years at a still later stage. With regard to customary law, accordingly, certain propositions follow.

(1) Because of the relative stability of spiritual and economic life in the lower stages of human civilization, the sluggishness and archaic character of customary law, the slow pace of its development, and its relative immobility are not an essential shortcoming from the point of view of that life and culture and its progress. The lower the degree of culture, the less negatively significant is the torpor of customary law. It is recognized that, in the lower stages of culture, the conservatism of customary law may be beneficial to the national life, as promoting the accumulation and hereditary transmission from generation to generation of unconscious but valuable acquisitions of collective experience and forestalling the diversion of the social (unconscious and normative) wisdom acquired through centuries of experience. Where life is relatively changeless, the wisdom evolved by preceding generations remains suitable and valuable as well for those which follow.

(2) The higher the stage of culture, the more does the conservatism of customary law become a negative factor of social life and culture and social progress. The swifter the change of the conditions and needs of life, the less can customary law keep pace with the development — the

[1] The author contemplated the preparation and publication of Essays on the Sociology and History of Political Ideas. (TRANSLATOR'S NOTE.)

more it lags behind life — and the more swiftly does the former normative wisdom cease to be suitable and adaptable and become social folly, distorting and retarding the development of the national spirit and of the national economy.

(3) In accordance with the great worth of customary law and, in general, of ancestral customs (including moral, technical, and other customs) in the lower stages of culture as furnishing fundamental and rational guidance in social and individual life, and in conformity with the weakness and failure of the products of conscious individual thinking, these customs enjoy an extremely high social value in those stages — high prestige and great glory — while every sort of innovation is deprecated as evil and shameful. Accordingly, customary law possesses great motivational and cultural-educative force and value, while legislation is relatively weak and of little worth. The situation inevitably changes as customary rules are laggard and constantly less suited and adaptable to new conditions of life, and the consequences of following them — rather than reason — in economic life more and more frequently deplorable. The prestige and motivational force of customs falls and is destroyed, and respect for statute law increases.

(4) The same historical law or tendency of development may be established as regards the so-called "creative capacity" of customary law: the propensity and capacity of the national mind to work out a system of customary rules adequately developed from the point of view of the necessity for unification. In the lower stages of development, the relatively even tenor and general uniformity of life and of the views of mankind (due to the tendency to respect ancestral customs and faithfully to follow their example) leads to the easy and rich development of customary law patterns. In the higher stages of civilization — with the swift changes and diversity of life, the mobility of the population, the diversification of individual and class views, and the weakening and disappearance of the propensity to follow routine — the development of customary law becomes difficult, if not impossible. At any rate there can be no adequate, swift and fruitful development of customary law patterns in areas where positive law standardization is necessary and absent. Hence for the legislator not to fulfill his obligation to furnish the positive law essential for normal social life and adequately developed and defined by means of statutes would be socially and culturally pernicious.

In a comparison of the qualities of customary and of statute law, certain other considerations must be taken into account. Customary law is an instrument whereby inequality, caste and class privileges, slavery and serfdom, the rightlessness of women, and so forth have been developed and maintained. Where, on the one hand, the law is worked out by the interaction of elements of the population occupying positions of power and able to impose patterns of conduct on others (who are weaker and dependent), the developing habits naturally tend to favor the strong at the expense of the weak. On the other hand, the conservatism of customary law and the *vis inertiae* of tradition coöperate to sustain the corresponding class and other privileges and prejudices, and sometimes so stubbornly retard the socially necessary development of a law more free and equal (and, in particular, so clash with intuitive law, which has a content different in principle) that matters reach the point of social cataclysms and even of the dissolution of the social organism.

SECTION 37. *The Law of Court Practice and Related Species of Positive Law*

The law of court practice. Court practice is ordinarily defined as the general, prolonged, uniform application of a certain norm of law by the courts of a given legal area. Court practice has often been deemed a special "source of law" (a species of positive law) on the same plane as customary law and statutes. Other authorities — while not denying the significance of court practice as a source of law — bring it under customary law and consider it a particular species thereof. Some, on the other hand, deny in general the significance of court practice as a source of law, pointing out that in general the function of the courts is not to create law but to apply existing law.

These doctrines are based on the same misunderstanding as that on which the contemporary doctrines as to customary and statute law rest: the failure to distinguish between law and normative facts. Court practice is not a special independent species of law or a species of customary law. It is not law but a phenomenon of an entirely different order: a series of human actions or a line of behavior. The relevant actions (decisions of judges or courts) may be — and ordinarily are — external manifestations of law. They are evoked by the legal opinions of judges. Moreover they can be, and are, manifestations of different species of law: of statute law (correctly or incorrectly interpreting the statute but applying the relevant law), of customary law or of intuitive law if they decide specific questions according to conscience or justice. They may even be manifestations not of law but of lawlessness — of chronic and systematic violation of law — if, for example, in order to gratify the authorities or for other reasons (where the administration of justice is not normal but dependent on administrative authority and the like), the courts decide otherwise than in accordance with good conscience and refuse to acknowledge rights which, in their minds, they deem well-founded and the like. This occasional phenomenon is lamentable and monstrous, pernicious alike for the state and for society. There are, therefore, cases where court practice not only is not law but does not *per se* even prove the existence and validity of a particularly defined species of positive law.

On the other hand, however, court practice does undoubtedly acquire *sometimes* the significance of a normative fact in the minds of men: that is to say, legal experiences are manifested and legal obligations and rights are ascribed with reference to the fact that such is the court practice — that in this way analogous problems were "always" decided by the courts or by a definite higher court.

Citations of former court practice play a particularly important part in contemporary legal life in England, where there are many and extensive spheres unregulated by official law, where the positive law, referred to a series of corresponding court decisions, obtains. Such phenomena are of less, and sometimes of negligible, importance in the states of continental Europe, but they occur even there. Examples of the expansion of these positive law phenomena could be multiplied *ad libitum* in legal history, and such legal imperative-attributive experiences, with reference to the practice of certain courts as a normative fact, may and should be admitted, therefore, as a particular species of positive law: the law of court practice.

When the problem is thus formulated and solved, there can be no serious scientific dispute as to whether or not the relevant phenomenon exists or as to its being confused with customary law (which is referred to normative facts of an entirely different class: not to decisions of any courts but to the corresponding mass conduct of forebears).

The law of separate praejudicia. In earlier jurisprudence there was the view that if there were existing praejudicia (one or more court decisions — cognate in content — handed down earlier as to questions homogeneous with those to be decided at a given time) the court was bound to follow them and to decide the relevant questions in accordance with their import (*stare decisis*). The view now prevailing in continental Europe rejects this doctrine and emphasizes that praejudicia are not a source of law since the court is not bound, either by its own praejudicia or by those of another court (although it be a higher court), and is not obliged to follow them blindly.

Correct understanding of the essence of positive law and of its differentiation from normative facts leads to a solution of the problem altogether different from the earlier and from the modern doctrine. Precisely the same reasoning is applicable to individual praejudicia as was appropriate with reference to constant and uniform court practice: neither of these constitutes a source of law in the sense of a particular species of positive law. On the other hand, however, even individual praejudicia do undoubtedly — sometimes and in certain conditions (chiefly decisions of higher courts, and formerly decisions of monarchs who personally participated in the administration of justice) — acquire the significance of normative facts in the minds of judges and others. They are cited as bases for ascribing certain obligations and rights, with the result of a corresponding species of imperative-attributive experiences which refer to individual praejudicia as the normative fact. This is a positive law phenomenon, which is even more widespread, and plays a greater part in legal life, than is true of the law of court practice in the narrow sense (law referred to the constant and uniform practice of courts).

The law of court practice and the law of separate praejudicia may be combined under the general term: the law of praejudicia. This law is manifested and flourishes chiefly where there is no proper legislation and, in general, no other positive pattern which is appropriate, adequately complete and developed. It is explained by the tendency of law to strive for unification: where there is no definite positive pattern to solve a given problem or an aggregate of problems, the legal mind employs judicial decisions already handed down as a means of establishing a definite pattern. Ordinarily praejudicia law acts as subsidiary, auxiliary, and complementary positive law, applied where there is no other positive law solution of the relevant problems, but sometimes it develops in consequence of conflicts between positive law and intuitive law and even appears under the pressure of intuitive law where there is a positive law solution (statute or customary) conflicting therewith. Decisions deviating from the existing (but seemingly unjust) positive law pattern, handed down by courts acting according to their intuitive law conscience, are then raised to the degree of independent normative facts, with the result that a corresponding new positive law destroys and supersedes the former positive law pattern. Such was the influence of practice of the court of the *centumviri* upon the development of the Roman law of inheritance. In general, the better the legislation, the less is the ground for the appearance and development of praejudicial law.

The foregoing are propositions of legal theory which state the facts (regardless of what seems desirable or proper from the practical point of view) without predetermining questions of legal dogma or legal policy as to whether or not the binding significance of this law should be acknowledged (and, if so, upon what conditions and to what degree).

Judicial law. From the point of view of the theory of positive law as legal experiences which refer to normative facts, there is — besides the law of court practice and of separate praejudicia — still another species of court positive law referred to court decisions. This is incomparably more widespread and important in legal life than the law of particular praejudicia, to say nothing of the law of court practice in the narrow sense. This is a phenomenon intimately associated with the specific imperative-attributive nature of law and with the corresponding necessity of eliminating conflicts and unifying legal relationships. It extends generally into all spheres of legal (official and unofficial) life: the investigation and decision of legal controversies between the parties by an official court, or by other arbitrators, invited thereto (father, mother, nurse or companions in the case of childish legal disputes), and evokes a corresponding change in the legal minds of the parties and of others. It specifically eliminates, or renders unimportant, the earlier (conflicting) legal views of the parties, whether these were based on intuitive or on positive law, and substitutes for them a third legal view with reference to the fact that a court or a judge (official or otherwise) has so decided. This phenomenon is a special manifestation of the law's unifying tendency and is itself a particular species of positive law: imperative-attributive experiences which refer to the court decision of a specific matter. This species of positive law may be termed judicial law, as compared with the praejudicial law referred to earlier decisions on other homogeneous matters.

Of judicial law it may be said that it is the most powerful and authoritative of all the species of positive law, or, more exactly, of all the species of law in general (not excluding intuitive law). By the widespread principle of official law, *res judicata pro veritate accipitur*: whether or not it is essentially correct or in conformity with statutes, a judgment of the court, which is final and has taken on legal force, is recognized as the plain and unqualified truth, incontestably and immutably significant. For that particular case it overrides the statutes, customs, and so forth, and possesses a significance which is alone decisive and absolute (except, of course, in certain special and extraordinary cases). This is, in general, the customary and normal relationship of human minds to court decisions, even in spheres of child law, the law of savages, and the law of criminal organizations and robber gangs.

In the lower stages of culture, when the sanctity and unshakable authority of court decisions are especially important and necessary, subconsciously adequate social adaptation leads to the result that investigation by the court is so organized and proceeds in such a manner that its judgments are deemed to have divine authority and its decisions to be not human but divine. When there are no clear and incontestable data for or against a party, the case is turned over to the judgment of the gods by getting signs from them through the mediation of priests or by lot, or by duel, and so forth (divine judicial law).

Judicial law is an incomparably more widespread and important phenomenon of legal life than praejudicial law: out of many thousands of court decisions which evoke judicial law, only individual decisions acquire the significance of normative facts of praejudicial law. Nevertheless, the prevailing view is without knowledge of judicial law and does not consider court judgments a "source of law." This is entirely natural, logical, and correct from the point of view of the prevailing understanding of the nature of positive law — and, in particular, of its failure to distinguish between law and normative facts — since it is impossible to see a particular species of positive law in judgments of the court themselves *per se*. A decision pursuant to statute is then a manifestation of statute law, one according to custom is a manifestation of customary law, and one according to justice is a manifestation of intuitive law. A particular species of positive law is present and to be found, not in court decisions, but in the minds of those who experience imperative-attributive opinions in connection with ideas of these decisions as normative facts: in other words, where modern legal science does not seek for law.

All three classes of positive law thus established embrace — in the sense of the theory of law which has been set out herein — not only official law but unofficial law as well; only judicial law, however, has serious and important significance in unofficial legal life. As to the law of separate praejudicia and the law of court practice in the narrow sense, the relevant phenomena are associated chiefly with the existence of permanent court institutions, and the chief scene of their development is therefore the sphere of official law. Even these are, however, encountered also in the field of unofficial law: (a) there are permanent court institutions (such as courts of the comrades, courts of honor, and the like) where there is ground for the development of praejudicial law, and, as international law develops, the practice of permanent international courts, general and special (for special matters such as maritime warfare), will undoubtedly play an important part in the future, and (b) insofar as, in a given social group (such as a tribal group or family group), its members turn more and more frequently to the court of one and the same person (such as the elder in the tribe, or the father of the family), legal opinions — the making of claims and so forth with reference to praejudicia (to the fact that the same question was decided thus in an earlier case or invariably in a line of earlier cases) — are here, too, not without significance.

SECTION 38. *Book Law and Other Secondary Species of Positive Law*

1. *Book law.* Collections of legal statements, compiled even by a private person, sometimes acquire in legal life a normative significance similar to that of legislative acts, with resulting imperative-attributive experiences which refer to that which was so written or so stated in such and such a book (the "Saxon Mirror," the "Talmud," and the like). This species of positive law may be termed "book law."

The "books" originate in various ways. Influenced by the insistent demand for the normalization of social life within the framework of definite legal patterns, the national mind is sometimes oblivious of how a particular collection was put together, or by whom or from what materials, if only it seems suitable as a means of setting up a definite legal pattern.

Innumerable books of this class, of normative significance in the law of different nations, have been written by private individuals (former judges, businessmen, clergymen, and the like). The famous "Saxon Mirror," which functioned at one time as a code in the courts in Saxony and far beyond her borders, and sometimes even outside Germany — was compiled in the first third of the thirteenth century by a former knight (Eike von Repkow). Numerous other "Mirrors" were likewise of private origin, as is true also of legal collections with other headings, including compilations of French so-called customs (*coutumiers*). Sometimes the relevant collections were produced by the joint work of many private persons, and sometimes a long line of persons has written, and rewritten them (the "Talmud," the "Shariat," and various other collections of Mohammedan law; the so-called laws of Manu; various collections of the ecclesiastical law of various Christian churches; and the like). Included in book law is also the law which is referred to collections of the law presently operative, compiled for the guidance of officials participating in government, insofar as they are not concerned with legislation and statutory law in the strict sense. Sometimes official collections put together for one locality — such as the so-called *droit coutumier* in France — acquire in fact normative significance for other localities, provinces or countries; legislative collections and codes (or certain parts thereof) enacted in one country may receive in fact — and without legislative sanction of any kind — such authority that the relevant propositions are raised to the degree of normative facts in other countries: in the course of time the *Lex Romana Visigothorum* (the so-called Breviary of Alaric, compiled from various Roman sources), published by Alaric II, king of the West Goths at the beginning of the sixth century (506) for his Roman subjects, gained widespread acceptance as an authoritative normative juridic collection far beyond the boundaries of its original operation — chiefly in France but to some extent in Germany and England. Subsequently, in the twelfth and following centuries, the operation of this legislative collection, and of other special and official juridic collections of Roman and national law, was superseded in various countries of Western Europe by the triumphal progress of another legislative collection compiled earlier for the Roman Empire: the famous code of Justinian (*Corpus Juris Civilis*). The reception of Roman law by Western European nations through the gradual extension of the normative significance of *Corpus Juris* and the operation of that law in Western European states over a series of centuries, until it was replaced by new civil codes (in certain Germanic countries until 1900, when the new German civil code came into operation), is a splendid example of the phenomenon with which we are concerned, but it does not fit into the framework of the prevailing doctrine of legal sources.

There is no uniformity as to the structure of the private and official collections in which book law originated, the origin and character of their content, or the materials employed by their compilers. They include (a) propositions and excerpts from the positive law contemporary with the compilers and known to them; (b) statutes copied by the compilers, or extracts therefrom, or indications of their meaning as the compilers understood it, and inferences therefrom; (c) customary law propositions with information as to the content of legal customs at the time of the compilers and inferences therefrom; (d) propositions of court practice or extracts from separate decisions; (e) propositions borrowed from other kindred juridic collections; and (f) dicta of sundry authorities, legal scholars, apostles, fathers of the church, and commentaries thereon by the authors of the collections. Propositions of the intuitive law of the authors, decisions of various questions according to justice, and not infrequently propositions of a nonlegal character (moral propositions, propositions of expediency, and the like) are also included which, in the minds of persons for whom the collection acquired in general a normative significance, acted as normative facts.

Some collections are simply a confused medley and miscellany of these heterogeneous elements. In some of them some one particular element predominates, such as propositions of statute law, book law, customary law, and so forth. Ordinarily book law, originating wholly or chiefly in customary law, developed, flourished, and played a principal and decisive part in legal life during the times when customary law as such was being overridden or had ceased for some reason to furnish to the nation the essential defined positive law pattern, while legislation had not as yet developed to such a degree of importance as successfully to replace it.

Modern jurisprudence, especially German jurisprudence, emerged, was nurtured and developed in Western Europe — over a period of many centuries and down to the most recent times — on the basis neither of statute law nor of customary law, but of book law (chiefly Roman law, but to some extent canon law and feudal law), which was therefore the principal foundation of its general doctrines concerning law, including those as to the sources of law, through the interpretation of dicta of Roman jurists and of Roman statutes found in *Corpus Juris*. Nevertheless, the particular species of positive law which we have called book law is not to be found among the "sources of law" set out in modern jurisprudence. The explanation of this striking phenomenon is to be found in the decisive part played in this regard by two facts.

(A) Neither earlier nor modern jurisprudence had at its disposal a clear and correct concept of the nature of positive law and of its differentiation from the normative facts to which it is referred. There was, consequently, no criterion whereby to distinguish between the various species of positive law (according to the content of the references to normative facts) and to examine the nature of the separate species of positive law (of customary law and of the law of court practice, in particular). Had the relevant concepts and propositions been available to jurisprudence, it would inevitably have been obvious that the Roman law of *Corpus Juris* received in Germany and other Western European countries (and the law of the Saxon Mirror and the like) cannot come within any one of the three categories of law known to jurisprudence, or of the "sources of law" (customary law, statute law, and court practice). It would have been immediately plain that the law so "received" is referred to a class of facts entirely other than those to which customary law and the law of court practice is referred: neither to the fact that our forebears acted thus, nor to the fact that court practice is of this character, but to the fact that it is thus written in such and such a book.

Meantime — with no adequate concepts and no method for examination — and in particular with the obscure and inaccurate concepts established for customary law and the law of court practice — it was easy indeed to confuse book law both with customary law and with the law of court practice.

(B) In the history of the relationship of legal science to the Roman law of *Corpus Juris,* an important part was played by the fact that this authoritative book of juristic wisdom — from which the doctrines of modern jurisprudence emerged and developed — speaks only of customary law, statute law, and court practice, and says nothing of the class of positive law which we have called book law. The authority of Roman jurists and of *Corpus Juris* exerted pressure in favor of recognizing these three categories and no others — as the sources — and bringing within them legal phenomena of every sort.

The result was that earlier and contemporary jurists — especially those legal historians who were concerned with such phenomena as the operation of the Saxon Mirror and other special juridic collections compiled chiefly by recording legal customs — brought them (and still bring them), with the greatest ease and no doubts of any sort, under the heading "customary law," although the Saxon Mirror and similar German, French, and other collections contain not only customary law propositions but others as well — particularly propositions of intuitive law, which have attained normative force like those of customary law — and even though their action extended as well to other localities and countries which had different customs. Moreover, the problem was bound to arise as to the nature of *this law* and the category to which it belonged, and the answers were in the sense that it must be customary law, inasmuch as *Corpus Juris* is not statute law for modern states. The Romanists taught that Roman law was "received" in Germany through customary law (through court practice as well, according to some) and therefore is itself customary law.

2. *The law of opinions accepted in science* (*communis doctorum opinio*). Earlier jurists held legal science to be a source of law and ascribed binding significance to opinions commonly accepted therein. Some authorities have combined the corresponding law — the law of science, scientific law — with the law of court practice under the general concept and name of the law of jurists. The view prevailing today is that it is an error to raise science to the degree of a source of law and ascribe to the opinions of legal scholars only authority in the narrow sense depending on their scientific validity.

Each of these doctrines, the former (which elevated the opinions accepted in science to the degree of a particular species of positive law) and the present (which denies the existence of the corresponding particular species of law), is alike indefensible.

The general opinion of science does not, of course, constitute *per se* a particular species of positive law: it can be a manifestation of statute law (if it rests on a statute as a normative fact — whether or not the statute is correctly interpreted), or of book law, of customary law, and so forth. Others — judges, for example — may consider a particular opinion mistaken (as based on incorrect interpretation of a statute or otherwise) and follow an interpretation of the statute differing from that held by representatives of science.

It is, on the other hand, possible — and the history of law shows not a few examples of the phenomenon — that opinions of learned jurists do attain the significance of normative facts: that is to say, imperative-attributive experiences appear and become widespread with reference to the fact of the general acceptance of that opinion in science (that such is the *communis opinio doctorum*). When it was being widely held that courts were bound by *communis opinio doctorum*, and the judges followed this doctrine and decided matters on the basis thereof, lawyers asserted claims in behalf of their clients, referring to the existence of the corresponding *communis opinio*. The present doctrine, failing to distinguish between law and normative facts, denies that such a species of positive law can exist and would prevent the emergence of similar phenomena in modern legal life; but its declaration that the earlier theory was mistaken cannot nullify the actual existence of the earlier facts.

3. *The law of doctrines of individual jurists or groups thereof.* Moreover, it must be recognized that doctrines of individual legal scholars or groups of them (such as schools) — as well as opinions widely accepted at the present time in science — sometimes acquire in legal life the significance of normative facts, so that a corresponding species of positive law (in our sense) is present: that is to say, imperative-attributive experiences, with reference to the teaching of such and such a great jurist, or such and such a school of jurists, as the normative fact. Individual jurists or groups do not ordinarily acquire such authority in their lifetime, but only in the course of time, and sometimes after the lapse of centuries. Whereas the law of science in the narrow sense is referred to that which at a given time appears generally accepted in science, the law of doctrines of individual jurists or groups finds its normative facts in the past and is of a retrospective (and sometimes archaic) character. In certain fields where this law is operative — especially in that of sacral law — there is a tendency corresponding to the principle of customary

law of ancient form: "The older the more sacred." Successive generations of priests and jurists develop and fix the law by citing the opinions of earlier scholars and schools as normative facts, by compiling commentaries thereon, and by deducing new decisions therefrom. In the legal collections which emerge from such material and create book law (as in corresponding collections of Hebrew or Mohammedan law) it is possible to distinguish and identify numerous historical strata.

In secular law, too, such phenomena are observed and sometimes play an important part. Such was the case in the evolution of Roman law through the work of learned jurists interpreting, extending by analogy, and developing (casuistically and otherwise) a positive law material (statutory and otherwise) which was fairly meager (the law of the Twelve Tables, the praetorian edicts, and so forth). Gradually a multitude of relevant opinions by outstanding jurists and groups of them (such as the schools of the Sabinians and Proculians) were transformed into normative facts in the minds of later jurists, judges, and others. They were cited, and commented on and elaborated, as if they were equal to, and on the same plane as, statutes. In the course of time, the original positive bases of law (statutes, edicts, and so forth) were so thrust into the background and bereft of normative significance that they were no longer referred to as normative facts, and their place was taken by works of eminent jurists of an earlier time, wherein the varying decisions of specific problems were difficult of application by the courts. Imperial legislation accordingly intervened to promulgate a number of statutes defining what works of jurists of earlier time must have binding significance for the courts and within what limits.

Analogous phenomena have been repeated in modern times on the basis of the reception of the Roman book law in Italy, Germany, and other Western states. As the opinions of Roman jurists had previously thrust into the background and replaced the normative facts wherein they originated, so in modern Western European Romanist jurisprudence the opinions of different generations and schools of interpreters of *Corpus Juris* (the glossators, commentators, and so forth) came to have normative significance, superseding the aphorisms of Roman jurists and the other elements of *Corpus Juris*.

In the history of modern international law, Hugo Grotius, the great jurist of the seventeenth century, played an important part. His statements were referred to in his time as normative facts from which international obligations and rights were inferrred. Subsequently a similar part was played by the opinions of Vattel. In international law and other fields of law, English and American jurists even now refer to the opinions of learned authorities as normative facts: in England for a long time Littleton's *Tenures* (fifteenth century) was treated in court practice as a normative fact, but in the eighteenth century its normative authority was replaced by that of Blackstone's *Commentaries on the Laws of England* which is still operative.

4. *The law of legal expertise.* One of the functions of legal scholars, corresponding to the need of unifying the law, is the solution of complex and difficult legal questions at the request of private persons or societies, administrative authorities and institutions, and occasionally of the courts. This is the work of legal experts. Ordinarily these expert opinions have only scientific authority, being significant to the degree that the view expressed is adequate and capable of proof, and the particular scholar eminent, and so forth. Not ordinarily possessing the authority of normative facts, they may be raised to that degree in order to define the obligations and rights of the parties, being acknowledged as binding by the court having jurisdiction of the matter which occasioned the request for the expert opinion. Moreover, such expert opinions, possessing normative significance, may issue not only from individual legal scholars but also from other persons or institutions, such as collegia of scholars, faculties of law, priests, and collegia thereof, monarchs, state councils, supreme courts, and so forth (in unofficial legal life, such as that of children, from parents, teachers, venerated acquaintances, and so forth). The corresponding legal phenomena — the experiences of ascribing legal obligations and rights, with reference to some expert opinion as a normative fact concerning a legal question involved in the matter in hand — is a particular species of positive law which may for brevity be called expert law. In the legal life of Rome, the part of legal experts, whose opinions had normative significance, was played by individual authoritative legal scholars and emperors (with the advice of legal scholars), expert opinions of the former type being called *responsa* and those of the latter *rescripta*.

Similar phenomena recurred later in the new European states. In the sixteenth century the expert opinions of faculties of law acquired the significance of normative facts. Courts were enjoined by various statutes to resort to the learned doctors, or to faculties of law, for expert advice (*consilia*) in doubtful cases. In the course of time it became customary not only for faculties to compile expert opinions on legal questions involved in matters pending in court, but also for them to draft decisions which were binding on the courts, so that the function of the latter was nothing more than formally to accept them in their own names. Expert law is akin to judicial law and in certain cases, as where faculties thus prepared decisions for the courts, it may not be entirely clear whether the phenomenon relates to judicial law or to the law of expert opinion.

5. Another species of positive law — pre-expert law — with the opinions of legal experts as normative facts corresponds to prejudicial law. These expert opinions sometimes acquire such authority as to become normative facts for the solution not only of the particular case, but also of others analogous thereto in respect of the legal questions involved. Certain rescripts of Roman emperors, as well as *responsa* of Roman legal scholars and *consilia* of modern doctors of law, faculties of law, and so forth acquired such normative significance. Sometimes legal expert opinions become material for the development of book law; there is then law which is referred to collections of expert opinions (*libri responsorum, consiliorium,* and the like).

6. *The law of statements of religious-ethical authorities.* One of the reasons why the prevailing doctrine of positive law and its species (of "sources of law") is unsatisfactory, and in particular why it is narrow and inadequate, is that it rests on a serious dearth of factual material and an extremely circumscribed horizon of legal life. This doctrine is based on dicta of Roman jurists and emperors in *Corpus Juris* and material taken from contemporary European law, while no account is taken of the law of other nations and of other epochs and stages of development. If the representatives of contemporary jurisprudence had attempted to take into consideration the law of the Mohammedan nations or Hebrew law, and to verify their doctrine of the sources of law in the corresponding material, the utter indefensibility of that doctrine would have been conspicuously manifest, since these laws rested for thousands of years — and rest now — on other sources, and not on these at all. Moreover, even from contemporary European law — and even from those elements thereof of which are studied in schools of law — this doctrine takes into account only a part (the secular branch) and entirely ignores sacral law. This law and its history are alike strikingly incongruous with the traditional doctrine of statutes, customary law, and court practice as the only possible sources of law.

In the field of sacral law or, in general, law closely bound up with religion, statements of various persons who have acquired religious authority — prophets and founders of religion, their closest disciples, apostles, saints, Church Fathers, and so forth — act as normative facts. Thus the bases and the chief normative facts of the development of Mohammedan law were the statements of Mohammed, preserved by oral and written tradition, while the basic and most authoritative normative facts of the development of Christian law — of the canon and ecclesiastical laws of Christian countries — were the sayings of Christ and of the apostles, as well as of others who had attained lofty religious authority (Church Fathers, saints, and so forth). In the Middle Ages — and to some extent even thereafter — authoritative significance was attributed to these sayings even in various fields of the secular law, such as international law, constitutional law, and to some degree even civil law (notwithstanding the high authority of the many other sources of law in this field). They were cited as normative facts from which laws were inferred and on which they were based. As late as the sixteenth century, legal scholars declared such rules as the opinion of some saint to be legal rules (if resting on Holy Writ) and of greater force than *communis opinio doctorum* which was then important as a normative fact.

7. *The law of religious-authoritative models of conduct.* In the same areas and periods of legal development the conduct of persons who have religious authority not infrequently attains the significance of normative facts in the sense that it becomes a model of behavior obligatory in similar cases. A certain rule of conduct is raised to the rank of being legally binding on the basis that God Himself behaved thus in an analogous case, or that a certain prophet, or the patriarchs, or the apostles, so acted. Thus certain norms of the ecclesiastical law of the Orthodox Church are deduced from the fact that the apostles visited churches founded by others, aided each other in the performance of certain tasks, and the like.

This positive law phenomenon is encountered in other fields of law as well as in sacral and ecclesiastical law. In the Middle Ages Old Testament models acted as normative facts in international law. Available data authorize the conclusion that from the seventh to the eleventh century the historical books of the Old Testament constituted the chief source of the ideas of international law relationships. In the decree of Gratian even a simple fact of Biblical or ecclesiastical history sometimes serves as a source of law.

In general, ecclesiastical law and international law are highly instructive for the general doctrine of law and positive law, graphically illustrating the complete indefensibility of the prevailing doctrine. Here the law existing at a given time rests upon facts of the remote past, conceived of as real irrespective of their actual existence, as normative facts, even though frequently those facts had *per se* no relationship at all to law: such as conduct not evoked by legal motives, or statements not of a legal but of a purely moral character (such as the statements of the New Testament), or not of a normative character in general.

8. *Contract law.* In the science of international law, contracts, treaties, conventions, and so forth are acknowledged as a source of law on the same plane as customary law. In other fields, especially in the science of civil law (whose representatives chiefly work out the general theory of law), contracts are not ordinarily considered a source of law but are classified as juridic transactions "creating" only subjective rights but not objective law.

Many legal philosophers of earlier ages regarded contracts differently: they not only acknowledged them as an independent source of positive law but also reduced all positive law, and its obligatory force, to contracts. From the point of view of the theory of positive law as imperative-attributive experiences referred to normative facts, legal experiences with reference to a contract concluded between the parties represent a particular species of positive law: contract law; and all the corresponding psychic phenomena — not only of international law but of all other branches of law as well (including civil law) — must be related to this class of positive law. Moreover this is so regardless of whether or not they enjoy official acknowledgment, such as child law referred to agreements, and the like (official and unofficial contract law).

In the modern doctrine regarding the sources of law, the theory that a subjective right without an object can exist or be "created" by this or that act plays a mischievous part as do other misunderstandings. Even in statute law, many authorities decline to acknowledge that acts (such as legislative acts) are a source of law if they do not declare any general rule, but award a pension, define the state budget for a given year, and the like. This is the basis of the contrast between contracts and juridic transactions in general, on the one hand, and sources of law on the other. This contrast should be eliminated from legal theory, and contracts and other legal transactions should be classified among the normative facts of positive law.

9. *The law of unilateral promises.* Unilateral promises to accomplish something (or to do so in certain cases) are also normative facts in various fields of legal life. Thus the promises of monarchs to safeguard or to grant certain laws to the nation, to safeguard and to observe sacredly the earlier law, the constitution or the like, or to give the nation a constitution assume in the legal mentality the function of normative facts which are referred to thereafter as the basis of corresponding rights. A public promise of reward, by organs of authority or private persons, to one who performs a specified act (captures a criminal, finds and returns lost property and the like) is a normative fact for the corresponding obligations and rights. For the derivation of their rights

with regard to Jehovah the Hebrews referred partly to a contract and partly to unilateral promises of Jehovah. Children refer to unilateral promises of their parents as normative facts for certain rights, such as the right to be taken to walk and so forth. Even in international law, unilateral promises (such as to render assistance in case of attack, or not to encroach upon a certain sphere of influence, or to observe certain rules in time of war and the like) are normative facts; so that to count contracts but not unilateral promises among the sources of international law is either illogical or an oversight on the part of the representatives of the corresponding science.

10. *The law of programs.* Sometimes the legal mind elevates even simple communications of certain persons as to the course of their future actions to the rank of normative facts, ascribing to the authors the obligation to act accordingly as regards those for whom the observance of what is announced is important, who had reason to hope for observance, and the like. Such communications may be called program communications, the corresponding legal phenomena may be called program law, and the corresponding norms, obligations, and rights program norms, obligations, and rights. Thus in the international field the governments of different states — or groups thereof operating conjointly — sometimes publish communications or distribute circular notes, informing other governments as to how they will act or what rules they have decided to observe in some international affair: what, for instance, will be their attitude toward states neutral in war (or toward their citizens or their commercial vessels) or how they will act in a province of another state which they occupy. And in the international law consciousness such programs sometimes acquire the significance of normative facts which may be used by interested persons to sustain claims to corresponding conduct on the part of the declarant states.

In precisely the same way, administrative and party programs sometimes play the part of normative facts in intra-state political life: they are referred to as the basis of corresponding claims, legal impatience appears and is expressed on the score of (more or less harsh) violations of them, protests are made and so forth.

Programs of solemn ceremonies — of public spectacles, assemblies and so forth — announced by private persons or by social or state institutions, such as communications regarding the admission of representatives of the press or others, are sometimes raised to the degree of normative facts for the inference of various claims (to a place as reporter, admission to the hall and so forth).

Information by a professor as to a future examination is raised by the legal mind of the student to the degree of a normative fact, permitting the inference of various legal claims which are negative as regards examination questions and requirements, and positive as regards marks notwithstanding inability to answer certain questions, and so forth.

Program law played a great part in the development of Roman law: *jus honorarium*, and specifically the praetorian law resting on edicts of the magistrates (particularly those of the *praetor urbanus*), came to be especially important as normative facts. These were simply programs of their official actions for the next year of their service, announced by the magistrates for the general information when they entered office. The praetor indicated in his edict that in such and such cases he would (or would not) give judicial protection (*judicum dabo, actionem non dabo*), that he would (or would not) turn over and safeguard the possession of anything or of an inheritance (*possessionem dabo*), that he would compel the tendering of an oath or command, the giving of certain obligations or guaranties or the handing over of personal property (*jurare cogam, promitti jubebo, satisdari jubebo, edi jubebo*), or that he would order restitution (*in integrum restituam*), and the like.

Such program announcements, repeated to a significant degree in a line of later edicts of successive praetors (and other magistrates), were raised to the rank of normative facts for the inference of rights and obligations of all sorts, and were subjected to interpretation and other juridic treatment by legal scholars.

11. *Law referred to acknowledgment by the obligor: admission law.* In many fields of legal life we meet the phenomenon that legal experiences are found — rights and obligations are attributed to others — on the basis that an admission by the party to whom certain obligations are ascribed acts as normative fact. This admission may be either express — by written or oral declaration — or implied *sub silentio* from conduct equivalent thereto. Here the acknowledgment is an independent and special normative fact: after the act of admission, claims patently unfounded become proper and enforceable. The corresponding species of positive law may be called the law of acknowledgment or admission law.

The underlying psychic phenomenon is closely associated with the specific imperative-attributive nature of law and the social need for the unification of legal relationships. It performs the valuable function of forestalling and terminating quarrels and conflicts in social life — or at least of confining them to the points not affected by the admission and eliminating other possible disputes. After a certain legal relationship, or certain elements of complex legal relationships, have been acknowledged, that admission cannot be rescinded or the dispute renewed: in international matters a war may not be protracted or begun on the basis of what has been settled by an admission.

If discord arises between private persons, or between private persons and the treasury, or between states, as to money accounts presented, the possibility of further dissension is cut down insofar as various points in the computation of the corresponding claims are admitted (even though they are doubtful or clearly incorrect, exaggerated, and the like) or eliminated (if the account is admitted in full).

During a civil war growing out of disputes over certain alleged rights, such as rights to the throne, the declaration of one side — for whatever reason — that it acknowledges the rights of the other side (even though the claims thus admitted were those of a usurper or revolutionary, or the like) evokes such a revolution in the legal consciousness as to heal the legal sore, stopping the present bloodshed and cutting down the possibility of future conflict. For other states which have directly or indirectly (as by sending envoys) completed the act of admission usurpers become legal monarchs, revolutionary governments turn into legal governments.

If there is armed struggle over the independence of a certain territory of a state, the declaration of the government of the latter that it acknowledges the rights of a belligerent party in behalf of the rebellious province is a normative fact, on which rests the obligation to observe the rules of war laid down by international law rather than those applicable to revolutionaries. On the other hand, the admission by representatives of a group struggling for independence that it is dependent, and that the other side has the right of governmental authority, evokes the converse change in the legal mind and extends the right of the other side to that territory and population, so that the continuation of warlike acts would be considered rebellion and the leader could properly be shot instead of being within the rules of war relating to prisoners.

The tendency of the legal mind to elevate admissions into normative facts of positive law is reflected in contemporary science in the form of the appearance, from time to time, of doctrines which seek to base the obligatory force of all law upon a supposed acknowledgment by all members of the community. Although it seeks to confirm and to prove the obligatory force of law, this doctrine seriously developed, actually involves a negation of law, raises anarchy and arbitrariness to the rank of a legal principle, and makes law depend upon whether or not it is agreeable to a particular subject to acknowledge his obligations, or that norms of law in general are binding upon him. Actual legal life is, of course, of a different nature. Ordinarily rights and obligations are ascribed, and their acknowledgment and observation *required*, with no regard whatsoever as to acknowledgment *vel non* by the obligor. Not to acknowledge them, to impugn them and the like is *per se* regarded as a breach — sometimes cynical and shameless. This is true in international law in the same degree as in other kinds of law.

12. *The law of precedent.* The necessity that legal relationships be unified by the working out of positive legal patterns leads, under certain conditions, to the creation of such a pattern (if none other exists) by elevating to the rank of normative facts the precedents of earlier actions in analogous cases in that given milieu. Thus if in a certain situation — at the card table, in a university council or faculty, in parliament or the like — a legal problem (for whose solution no ready pattern exists) has in fact been resolved, and similar circumstances later recur, a corresponding positive law conviction is already operative, insisting upon the same conduct with reference to the precedent — asserting what was thus done in the first instance, and claiming that this should "therefore" be followed in the new situation as well.

The corresponding law (official and unofficial) may be called the law of precedent. It must not be confused with prejudicial law, which is law referred to prejudicia (not infrequently called precedents in juridic literature), that is to say, to a different class of normative facts — not to the corresponding earlier behavior in the given milieu, but to former decisions of some court or courts.

Precedent law is encountered and flourishes chiefly in closed circles, in groups of subjects constantly or at least frequently in contact: as in groups of players (precedents play an extremely important part in all games and not merely in card games), in organized societies (clubs, learned societies and the like), in trade and other associations, and in state institutions of the collegiate type (including parliament). The same is true of "societies" of nations — alliances of states — as well as of other subjects standing in certain relationships to each other so that there is basis for the formation between them of precedent law relative to their mutual relationships. Moreover, precedent law is of great significance in constitutional and administrative law, not only in the form of the internal law of institutions (especially of collegiate institutions) but also in that of the law between institutions. Such a law may regulate relations between various ministers, between administrative and judicial institutions, between the administration and organs of self-government, and between the crown, the cabinet of ministers, and parliament. In England the extremely broad rights now belonging to Parliament and to the cabinet of ministers as regards the crown were to an important degree gained through precedents, on the basis of concessions by the crown in specific and actual cases which were thereafter raised to the degree of precedents for the ascription of corresponding rights to parliament and the cabinet. The parliamentary form of government developed in England and other states exists by virtue of precedent law and not of statute law. Again, precedent law is of great significance in the relationships between state institutions and citizens, not only where it is a matter of relationships between a given institution and a particular citizen, but also where it is a matter which concerns citizens other than those whom a precedent concerned. If, for example, a given institution decided anything in the case of one, others in the same position cite the earlier case and claim that the solution should be the same for them.

13. *The law of legal maxims and proverbs.* A particular species of positive law is law referred to legal maxims and proverbs as normative facts. This phenomenon is widespread chiefly in the lower stages of culture — during the period of patriarchal life — together with customary law of ancient form. That juridic maxims sometimes play a part in legal life is familiar in contemporary jurisprudence and especially to legal historians; but because the traditional concept of customary law is obscure and widely extended to any and all species of law, this phenomenon is put under customary law, and legal proverbs are put forward as a means of knowing and proving the existence of customary law.

14. *Universal law.* Claims are sometimes made, and obligations are ascribed, with reference to what is ordinarily done "in the whole world" or "in all the nations" or "in all civilized countries" or "in all constitutional states." In legal life, especially in the minds and conduct of persons who are not familar with statutes, an important part is played by the phenomenon of imperative-attributive experiences and the ascription and performance of obligations and rights with reference, not to normative facts which are definite and clearly conceived of, but to what is usual, what is customary, what is established and the like. Sometimes, however, this phenomenon is found as well in professional-juridic spheres. Sometimes Roman jurists used the formulae *hoc jure utimur* (such is the law among us) or *placuit* (it has been established or acknowledged as law) as positive references.

Investigation of the nature of positive law as imperative-attributive experiences referred to normative facts, differentiation of the latter from positive law itself, and the principles which result therefrom have served *supra* as a means of examining into the nature of generally acknowledged "sources of law" (customary law and statute law), solving controverted questions, and finding and proving the existence of numerous classes of positive law unknown to modern jurisprudence. It may be supposed that this series still does not exhaust all kinds of positive law, and that further investigations — guided by these principles — will lead to new (and possibly abundant and important) discoveries in this field.

The same principles and basic concepts may *mutatis mutandis* be transferred as well into the neighboring science of morality, and serve as directives for the building of a doctrine of positive morality and its species and subspecies. The most important species of positive morality may be indicated briefly.

1. *Statutory morality* corresponds to statutory law. The loftiest moral laws are divine laws (*leges divinae*). An example — instructive for the theory of law also — is the contemporary moral propositions deduced (in catechisms, sermons, and so forth) from the Ten Commandments, which in the ancient Hebrew mentality played the part of paragraphs of a contract between Jehovah and Israel: normative facts of sacral contract law.

2. *Customary morality* corresponds to customary law and falls into two species: that of ancient form (referred to ancient traditions, and highly important in the lower stages of culture), and that of new form, which is not unimportant even in modern cultural nations.

3. With the development of a learned priestly class and of sacral science, and with the appearance of written collections of sacral wisdom (legal and moral), *book morality* develops and spreads: purely imperative ethical experiences with reference to the fact that so it is written in such and such a book (sometimes a sacred book) of individual or collective origin: thus from the Talmud purely moral — as well as legal — propositions are deduced, so that the ethics based on the Talmud represent partly book law and partly book morality.

4. Morality plays a leading part as regards modern humanity insofar as it is referred to sayings of the great teachers of morality as normative facts. This may be called *teacher morality*. The most sublime example is Christian morality, referred to sayings of Christ and His disciples. Important, too, is Buddhist morality, with its many millions of followers, referred to the doctrine of Buddha (a philosopher who taught the insignificance of ordinary human interests and preached sympathy of love for all creatures not excluding the lowest). Originally this positive morality had no religious character and acquired it only in the course of time, when the deification of Buddha was widely accepted.

5. An important part in the structure and development of positive

morality is likewise played by so-called *model* morality: imperative experiences, with reference to the behavior of persons having ethical or religious-ethical authority as normative facts. Thus in Christian and Buddhist positive morality, importance attaches not only to the explicit moral aphorisms but also to traditions as to the conduct of Christ, of the Apostles, of the saints, of Buddha, and so forth in different cases, as models to be imitated.

SECTION 39. *Official and Unofficial Law*

The substance of the division of law into official and unofficial has already been set out in connection with the doctrine of the ancillary or subservient role of the state in the field of law.[1] Certain additional points may be made here.

(1) The structure of official law, with which modern jurisprudence is chiefly concerned, is much richer than is assumed in the sense, not only that it comprises various species and varieties of positive law unknown to modern jurisprudence, but also that official law embraces as well a multitude of intuitive law phenomena: intuitive law (in different fields, in different forms, and under different names — or without any particular name) has binding significance in the state and is applied by judges and other organs of state authority.

First of all it should be noted that the positive pattern, whose function is to anticipate and to eliminate legal discords and doubts with their injurious and dangerous consequences, is completely superfluous and unnecessary in those fields of law where intuitive law convictions are so broad and strong that the relevant rules of community life can give rise to no doubt in the mind of anyone except possibly the psychically abnormal. Such propositions may be termed axioms of intuitive law. Thus controversies as to whether by law children can kill their parents, or parents their children, and in general whether we can kill our neighbors or wound or mutilate them, torture or insult them, or destroy or steal their property and so forth, or whether this is impossible, are psychologically improbable. In exactly the same way doubts and controversies are excluded as to whether people have a right to eat, to sleep, and to perform other physiological functions (wash, dress, talk, and so forth), so that all are bound to tolerate this and no authority can forbid it or punish disobedience.

Of such and similar axioms of intuitive law there is a vast multitude in community life of every kind, and the corresponding intuitive law

[1] Cf. Section 7.

is an essential element and basis of law and order of every type. Positive standardization ordinarily does not touch the corresponding problems. It starts from the foregoing propositions as axioms, and supplements them by solving questions which are without axiomatic solution in intuitive law and are capable of arousing doubts.

Insofar as they concern objects within the cognizance of official law, the axioms of intuitive law are acknowledged also by state courts and other organs of state authority. In general the corresponding intuitive law is a constituent part of official law and a fundamental and essential element thereof.

It has already been pointed out [2] that there are fields of legal life to which the positive law pattern seems unsuitable and it is necessary to keep the law freely adaptable to concrete circumstances, as with reference to the degree of fault in imposing punishment, or of merit in awarding recompense, or of knowledge in giving examination marks and the like. This refers both to unofficial and to official law. Thus in the law of state and communal service, the remuneration of those who serve, as well as disciplinary punishments, are or should be defined by the authorities justly and without partiality or prejudice: that is to say (from our point of view), in accordance with intuitive law. Positive regulation is here reduced chiefly to pointing out the classes of recompense and of penalties to be applied.

In the official criminal law of civilized nations, the positive standardization of punishments ordinarily indicates only the minimum and maximum limits of punishments, and definition of the specific punishments within these limits is left to the conscience of the judges — that is to say, to their intuitive law. Even the decision as to whether or not the prisoner deserves punishment and should be recognized as guilty (of an act which has been proved) depends on the conscience of the judges and the jurors: that is to say, on their intuitive law.

Civil codes — especially the more recent ones — likewise entrust the decision of various questions requiring individualization (conformity with individual circumstances) to the discretion of the judge, enjoin the interpretation and fulfillment of contracts and the decision of other questions, "according to good conscience," and the like. In these cases, too, from the point of view of the theory of law which is being set out, it must be conceded that the concern is with intuitive law and its official acknowledgment (although with no conception of its nature).

In civil disputes (excluding certain categories thereof) the parties may turn to arbitration by private persons chosen by them, with the

[2] Cf. Section 31.

proviso that this court has the same official significance as a state court and its decision is carried into execution by the organs of authority if necessary, and the decision of the matter according to conscience and unconstrained by positive statute is entrusted to these courts of arbitration.

According to the law of various countries (as in England and Russia), state courts must in certain conditions decide cases not according to statute but according to justice (equity in England, conscience in Russia) as *judicia bonae fidei* played an important part in the history of Roman law.

As time goes on, however, such intuitive law courts — under the influence of the unifying tendency of law — ordinarily become positive law courts while still nominally courts of justice or of equity. In other words with the passage of time a positive pattern is formed on the basis of decisions according to intuitive law, and begins to operate in place thereof. Thus, in English courts of equity intuitive law was to a significant degree ousted, in the final analysis, by prejudicial law: by law referred to previous decisions in accordance with justice. In the *bonae fidei judicia* of Roman law intuitive law was gradually replaced by positive law, in consequence of the development of the law of learned jurists through interpretation of what is usual according to justice or good conscience, and the elevation of the suitable opinions of jurists to the rank of normative facts.

In another field of law developed by contemporary jurisprudence, international law, intuitive law is also highly important.

(2) The sphere of official law — of official intervention into the national legal life — varies among the nations and at different stages of culture. Nonexistent in lower stages of development before the state has been formed, and growing *pari passu* with the latter, official law is originally of an extremely meager content, and touches only a few matters of legal life — chiefly that of the person to whom authority and command in the matter of defense from external enemies belong, while even such parts of internal legal life as punishment for crime, the exaction of debts, the compulsory return of objects of property which have been removed, and in general the legal relationships between individual citizens or groups and the safeguarding of those relationships do not ordinarily enter into the sphere of official law and official intervention. Alone or in combination with their kinsmen, friends, and so forth, citizens effectively repress criminal individuals and groups by vengeance, forcible repossession of what has been taken, and so forth.

On this level of development criminal law and civil law are represented by unofficial law: official intervention into internal legal life develops, intensifies, and expands — and the sphere of official law grows — only very gradually. Even in periods of developed state life, however, this sphere does not become immutable: it is subject to many different variations. In some nations it is broader, in others narrower; in some periods of the development of one and the same nation it expands while in others it contracts. In theocratic states — or in theocratic stages of development of a state — official law regulation extends to many sides of life and fields of conduct related to religion, while similar types of conduct remain outside the sphere of official law and state intervention in secular states. In the period of the so-called police regime, official law and intervention extend to spheres of life and conduct which are free therefrom in the period of liberalism, when the tendency is to grant citizens the utmost possible freedom in arranging their affairs and to confine state intervention within the narrowest possible limits. The present social-political tendencies lead once again to an expansion of the sphere of official law and intervention.

The structure of official law — in the sense of those classes and varieties of law (of intuitive law and the various species of positive law) whose combinations constitute official law regulation — varies in different nations and at different stages of development. In the growth of Eastern theocratic states and laws, normative facts and species of positive law other than those important in the legal history of the ancient and modern states of Europe played an important part (divine law, both statute and contract, the law of aphorisms of prophets, founders of religions, and so forth; the law of learned representatives of sacral science; sacral book law; and so forth). In the Roman civil law the classes of law and of normative facts whose action was most important (program praetorian law, the law of expert opinion and of other opinions of learned jurists) were not the same as those which were important in the history of post-Roman Western European civil law (customary law, book law of native origin, book law of Roman origin, and so forth). In the modern official law of advanced nations, statutes play a principal and dominant part as normative facts: directly or indirectly they define the spheres of influence of other species of law (intuitive law and the various classes of positive law). This is partly conscious and designed (as with reference to customary law) and partly unconscious and in ignorance of the existence and nature of many species of law (intuitive law, and the various classes of positive law). Moreover, certain species of positive law which formerly played a more or less (or even very highly) important part in the official law of certain nations became obsolete in legal life. Thus book civil law, particularly Roman law which was still operative in certain parts of Germany down to 1900, was replaced by statute law and applied only to cases arising before the new German code began to operate. The law of the common opinion of science and of the doctrines of individual jurists of eminence had already disappeared (except in England) from the official law life of European states in the first half of the nineteenth century. With the decay of the patriarchal mode of life, the customary law of ancient form — which referred to customs of ancestors — disappeared, and customary law of the new form became less and less significant. As the state and law were emancipated from the church and religion, various species and varieties of ecclesiastical law (the corresponding book law, divine statutory law, and so forth) lost their significance.

Certain matters should, however, be borne in mind. (1) Various Christian churches and other religious societies and their special ecclesiastical law — defining their organization, the rights and obligations of priests as to parishioners and to church authorities, the rights and obligations relative to church property and the management thereof, and so forth — still enjoy official acknowledgment by states in varying degree, and to this extent the corresponding species of positive law (divine and human statutory ecclesiastical law, book law, and so forth) are integrated in the structure of contemporary official law. (2) European states with possessions in Asia, Africa, and so forth acknowledge, in greater or less degree, native laws which are in different stages of development — including sacral laws of Mohammedans, of pagans of different categories, and so forth — and the corresponding species and varieties of positive law (customary law of ancient form, book law, divine statutory law, and so forth) thus become incorporated in the official law of the states concerned. At all events, as has already been intimated *supra*, the three traditional classes of the "sources of law" — statutory law, customary law, and court practice — constitute an extremely incomplete and unsatisfactory division of law, not only from the point of view of the theory and history of law in general, but also from that of the actual content of the contemporary official law of European states.

The sphere of action and the content of unofficial law (including international law) also change in history. Here, too, various species of religious authoritative law, as well as of book law, lost their earlier significance, because of misunderstandings in science itself. At all events, even the structure of the modern international law is such that the traditional classification of "sources of law" or "sources of international law" are far from adequate for gaining knowledge thereof. In contemporary science international law means only that part of international law which is related to the more advanced nations (which is incorrect), and it is arbitrarily assumed that international law arose relatively recently, and (although views on this point differ), some deny that it even existed in the Middle Ages, and attribute decisive significance to the Peace of Westphalia (1648). If the sphere of scientific study (theoretical, historical, and descriptive, if not dogmatic) of international law is properly broadened, there will be a corresponding extension of the list of the "sources" of contemporary international law, with the introduction therein of book law, divine statutory law, and so forth.

CHAPTER VII

PUBLIC AND PRIVATE LAW

SECTION 40. *The Highest Division of Law and Jurisprudence*

In modern jurisprudence the fundamental and highest division of law is that into private and public. It is deemed a basis for the fundamental and supreme division of jurisprudence into (1) the science of private law, and (2) the science of public law.

Neither proposition is defensible. It is manifest from what has already been set out herein that the highest division of juridic sciences must start not from a division of law into private and public, but from a classification of scientific propositions in accordance with their nature as they have been established by the various sciences concerning law. From this point of view, the highest division of law in general, and of juridic sciences in particular, is into theoretical and practical: the propositions of the former being objective statements of what is or was, and of the latter an indication of conduct which is desirable or due.

Theoretical propositions and sciences must be further divided — according to the nature of the theoretical subjects of their theses — into class theories in the narrow sense of the word (the theoretical subject of the theses being the class concept), and individual theories and sciences (the theoretical subject of the theses being the individual object or the individual complex of objects or phenomena, such as earth, Russia, the Russian nation). The latter, according to the character of the content of the theoretical predicates, fall into descriptive (such as geography; the science which describes the earth), and narrative or historical (such as the history of the earth, the history of Russia, and so forth).

Practical propositions and sciences fall into normative (such as moral, legal, aesthetic) and teleological — indicating rational means for the attainment of purposes, such as preserving or reëstablishing health (hygiene or medicine), or of certain educational purposes (pedagogy) or social or public purposes and the like (politics). Accordingly there are five classes of sciences in general: (1) theoretical in the narrow sense; (2) descriptive; (3) historical; (4) teleological or purposive; and (5) normative; and five classes of sciences concerned with law in particular: (1) theoretical in the narrow sense of the word (theories headed by the theory of law in general); (2) descriptive (descriptive jurisprudence); (3) historical (the history of law); (4) political, headed by general legal policy; and (5) normative-dogmatic (jurisprudence in the narrow sense).

Philosophy is a complex discipline: it is the supreme theory (the theory of being in general) plus the supreme teleology (a teleological discipline concerning the supreme purpose: concerning the meaning of existence and of the corresponding supreme principles of conduct). Philosophy of law is a complex discipline: it is the supreme theory of law plus a supreme teleology: the supreme policy of law. As to the further divisions of law, conscious classification (as distinguished from that put together historically) should conform with the nature and task of the relevant sciences. At all events, as to the theory of law — and as to the class sciences of law in general — it is impossible to attribute supreme validity to the division of law into private and public. From the theoretical point of view this division is utterly indefensible in its present shape and rests on a complete misunderstanding. But even in an appropriately changed form, it is not of essential importance for legal theory, being in that regard of far less significance than is the division of law into intuitive and positive. As to dogmatic study, which sets out the content of the norms of the official laws of different states and of international law, the position is different. The division with which we are concerned is based on the content of the regulation and possesses, in this content, a significance incomparably greater than it does in the context of theory.

The view attributing supreme significance to the division of law into public and private is to be explained (1) by the fact that the nature of law in general, and the structure and nature of law (as jurists use the word), are unascertained; and (2) by the lack of a proper classification of sciences in general and of juridic sciences in particular, and the (historically natural and socially expedient) overexpansion of dogmatic study, which fills the jurist's field of vision and compels him to ignore possible and desirable sciences of law of an altogether different character and content.

SECTION 41. *Two Types of the Action of the Legal Mentality upon Human Conduct*

The innumerable attempts to divide law into public and private reflect (without conscious grasp of their import) two types of the action of legal mentality upon human conduct. It has already been demonstrated that law is an essentially *psychic* factor of social life and of the development of culture. Its action as such psychic factor is twofold: (a) motivational and (b) cultural-educative or pedagogic.[1]

The very consciousness of one's legal obligation and one's right are motives of individual and mass conduct by virtue of the action of specific legal impulsions (immediate or specifically-legal motivation). But this by no means exhausts the law's extremely complex and multiform motivation of conduct. Already the psychological and physical reactions which, by virtue of its attributive nature, the law tends to evoke on the part of those ascribing to themselves rights and of those making common cause with them in case the obligor does not perform, have the motivational significance that advance knowledge of the possibility or inevitability of these reactions, and the impulsions evoked thereby, represent a supplementary and auxiliary motivational pressure in favor of fulfilling the duty. But the tendency (associated with the attributive nature of law) to secure or to guarantee to the obligee what is due him causes the law to be so developed and molded that there is a whole system of auxiliary motivational pressures promoting the performance of the duty even on the part of those in whom ethical impulsions in the particular fields are weak or entirely absent. Various advantages in case of performance — or of zealous performance — of the duty (rewards, promotion, a pension, and so forth) are brought into view, as are various disadvantages and detriments in case of nonperformance. The relevant motivational processes emanating from law may be called indirect auxiliary motivation, as distinguished from the fundamental ethical, specifically-legal motivation. Furthermore, the consequences of the psychic action of fundamental and auxiliary motivation — the corresponding individual and mass conduct which results — require people to reckon with the relevant individual behavior and social order (as with the laws of nature) and conform therewith even as to problems and fields of conduct left to the unfettered discretion of the individual, for which there are no definite legal precepts. The law evokes motives in favor of innumerable actions which are not *per se* prescribed by the law itself. The corresponding motivation we call free or independent legal motivation.

The motivational action of law consists not only in its evoking positive impulses in aid of this or that conduct (positive legal motivation) but also in its eliminating or forestalling the appearance of various motives

[1] Cf. Section 11.

in aid of certain conduct: it removes "temptations" and so forth (negative legal motivation).

Various species of legal motivation combine, partly so that they confirm each other and partly so that the motivational processes (emanating from certain elements of the law) are paralyzed by other legal motivational processes.

No less complex and manifold is the educative (pedagogic) action of law. The very acts evoked by the law in countless numbers do not pass out of the picture without leaving a trace in the character of those who perform them. The repetition of certain acts develops corresponding habits — positive habits of doing, and negative habits of abstaining — which in turn influence the development of character, instilling certain traits and weakening others. Moreover, as it performs its complicated psychic symphony on different strings of the human soul — forcing some impulsive propensities to operate and exercising them, while refusing to admit others or stifling their action (as brutal, malicious or in general anti-social) — the law leads inevitably to the development and strengthening of some propensities and to the weakening and destruction of others. Rational law represents a complex and mighty school which aims at socializing the national character and adjusting it to rational coexistence. Unsuccessful law may spread demoralization and poison the national spirit — or at least counteract the healthy psychic process and retard the development and flowering of the valuable elements of individual and mass character. The meaning and the significance of all law and of its separate elements — including public and private law — must be considered and explained from these motivational and educational points of view. For example, the institution of "the protection of possession" is admittedly mysterious and requires special investigation, in view of the fact that law is here manifestly protecting interests of thieves, robbers, and so forth as well as those of persons whose possession is lawful. The explanation is to be sought in the following considerations.

The institution of possession has a dual significance which is important and valuable from the social and cultural points of view. (a) From the motivational point of view, it acts in the direction of impelling all persons (including owners) to refrain from socially harmful conduct as to those who are in fact (though unlawfully) in possession: to abstain from the self-willed and headstrong acquisition of possession, or other encroachment upon the possession, of another whether by force (*vi*), secret wile (*clam*), or treacherous cunning (*precario*, as where possession is obtained by a request for temporary delivery upon a promise to return), and to rely instead upon more cultural means: at least upon legal proceedings (if a corresponding right is present), a proprietary action based on a right *in rem,* and so forth. Where there may be doubt as to the side on which the law is, it would be advantageous for one asserting a right of property to deprive the other of possession (by forcible removal thereof, stealing it by night, or the like) so that the latter in case of legal proceedings would be compelled to prove his right and would eventually fail therein (the position of the plaintiff is less advantageous than that of the defendant). The law of possession, however, eliminates these temptations by making it manifest that such devices are purposeless and futile: the thing must be ingloriously returned to the former possessor (and damages, court expenses, and so forth incurred), and it is better to act directly by means more civilized (negative motivation).

(b) From the point of view of educating the nation, the civilizing action of the institution of possession weakens and eradicates habits and propensities to violence and to secret and treacherous machinations, and strengthens respect for the presonality and the rights of another. The psychic action of the institution of possession accordingly consists in the motivational *forestalling* of a multitude of acts baneful from the economic and other points of view (economic disturbances, violence, eventual killings, lawsuits, and the like) and in its corresponding educative functioning.

The obligations to make compensation for damage caused, and the rights of the injured party thereto are to be explained in like manner. The psychic action of the corresponding right is that it creates in the popular masses motives to refrain from innumerable positive actions which are harmful from the economic and other points of view (such as encroachments upon the personality or property of another) or omissions (such as nonperformance of a contract and failure to perform at maturity), and sustains and corroborates respect and a relationship of discretion toward the personality of another (its rights and interests) and to one's pledged word and promise. While the award and the collection of the amount of the damage are advantageous from the point of view of the financial interests of the obligee, they do not represent any plus of any sort from the point of view of the national economy and welfare: that which is given to one is taken away from the other. Moreover, from the economic point of view in the narrow sense (that of the national economy as distinguished from private economy), something worse than a mere zero (which results from A minus A) follows: the legal procedure and the exacting of damages always means a loss of corresponding energy — and frequently legal harm over and above that, and sometimes the ruin and destruction of an active and useful element of national economy: the corresponding economic unit which is subjected to the operation. Moreover the transfer of values, which is detrimental and harmful from the point of view of the national economy (although advantageous from that of the financial interests of one side), tends to intensify the inequality of the distribution of property — and specifically to shift property from the poor to the rich — since *ceteris paribus* the amount of property damage is greater where large properties and great values are involved. If, for example, a rich man strikes and tears the clothing — or sets fire to the miserable hut — of a poor man, his obligation takes the form of payment of a trifling sum in damages, whereas if the poor man acts in the same way with reference to the garment or the house of the rich man, the amount of damages will be great.

Thus where the theory of the protection of interests discerns a plus and a virtue, there is actually a minus and an evil from the point of view of the national economy as regards both the sum total of national wealth and the distribution thereof. This evil has to be justified; and the justification ought to be that the law of compensation for damage is a lamentable but necessary phenomenon — a necessary evil — or more accurately an evil necessary in a certain relatively low stage of the development of culture when — precisely because of that low level — there is no recourse but to operate by corresponding threats in the effort to achieve socially necessary conduct and to exert influence in the direction of educating a better mentality.

Certain points must be borne in mind in order to understand the function of the civil law. The essential elements of certain varieties of the legal order are (a) the obligation of all members of the social group (the tribal group, the commune, and the like) who are able to work to do so for the common good of that group and to take an active part in the collective production of material benefits necessary for its subsistence and the satisfaction of its other needs, and (b) the right of each member of the group to subsistence and to the satisfaction of other needs out of the general store of what has been produced collectively by the use of instruments of production collectively possessed. These elements of law would be restored if a socialistic regime were established whereas, under the present order of social life, the position of citizens is essentially different in these respects. Every adult citizen has a right, in general terms, to organize his life as he pleases. He may choose the kind of activity he wishes, or he may choose none at all and elect to do nothing. On the other hand, and still in general terms, he has no right, such as that just described, to be furnished with subsistence and to be satisfied as to other needs, so that the enjoyment of this right to do what he wishes (or to do nothing) would mean the utlimate right to die of hunger, cold, and so forth.[2]

The essential substance of the legal order in which we are interested may then be reduced to these propositions.

(1) According to the principles of the law of property (and of certain other laws of like import), the fertile earth and other instruments of production (capital, in the sense of national economy), as well as objects which are used or consumed, are secured for the exclusive use and disposition of a multitude of persons. These are not required to deal carefully with the elements of the national wealth entrusted to them, or to use them to produce what society needs. On the contrary, the right of property allows them to act as they please with the objects of their property (*jus utendi et abutendi*) and, in the absence of legal precepts to the contrary, they may leave uncultivated parcels of the fertile earth which are at their disposal.

(2) According to the principles of the law of inheritance, this free enjoyment and disposition, with no obligation to render an accounting, is granted "to one for his heirs forever" — in other words, the law guarantees to those who do not spend (and to those who increase) their property that what is saved or acquired by them will come to those near and dear to them in accordance with their (testamentary) disposition thereof or (if they die intestate) with the corresponding rules of law which take into account closeness of relationship.

(3) According to the principles of modern family law, the upbringing of children (providing them with sustenance and so forth) is a function of the parents — above all and chiefly a function of "the father of the family" — as distinguished from a regime wherein the necessities of food, clothing, shelter, and so forth (of adults and children alike) are satisfied out of the common collective fund of the social group. In general, the principles of modern family law and of the law of inheritance unite with the special characteristics of the contemporary legal order to produce the result that not only his personal well-being but also that of those who are near to his heart depends upon the economic welfare of the subject, not only during his life but after his death.

[2] A more precise juridic exposition of the statement in the text would require the introduction of certain qualifications and the formulation of certain exceptions, relative to standardization of the position of the insane, paupers, those incapable of work, and the like.

(4) Not being in general bound to utilize productively either the parcels of the fertile earth and the other instruments of production entrusted to them, or their own capacity to labor so as to produce and to furnish to others bread and other means of satisfying needs, and having, at the same time, no claim that others should furnish them with bread and the other means of satisfying their needs, those who possess economic goods and the personal capacity to labor can — on the basis of a right to dispose thereof according to their own judgment — obtain by barter what is necessary for themselves in exchange for what is at their disposal, especially by the exchange of economic goods or labor services for money (sale, contract for services) and for objects of consumption (purchase). They are not bound to be concerned for the interests of the others with whom they enter into relationships of exchange: they may develop and defend their own interests ("trade" and so forth) as they like (with certain exceptions, such as the prohibition of usury). But the guiding principle and essential substance of so-called contract law applies: *pacta sunt servanda* (the corresponding contracts possess binding force). The sanction is provided by the further principle of civil law (examined *supra*) which enjoins the payment of compensation for any material damage proximately ensuing if a contract is not performed or is not properly performed.

After the sense and the significance of these principles have been pondered from the motivational point of view, it is easy to see that the corresponding law — which gives the fertile earth and other instruments of production over into the disposition of countless individual separate owners under no duty to render an accounting, with no injunction that they be utilized or one's capacity to labor applied for the common good, and with owners permitted to do what they will (or to do nothing at all) with the property — is indirectly creating, at the same time, motives (partly egoistic and partly altruistic: the well-being and the fate of the family) in favor of energetic and zealous activity in producing for the general benefit. These motives are the more powerful the greater the development, at a given stage of evolution, of family ties and of human — as distinguished from animal — capacity to be guided not alone by momentary impulsions (with no thought or care for the morrow) but by planned concern also for the future well-being of oneself and of those near to one's heart.

In particular the corresponding law creates powerful psychic pressure in favor of zealous concern that the elements of national wealth entrusted to the uncontrolled disposition of individuals be utilized in the best way for the production of new economic goods (corresponding to the social needs of the nation) so that these may be furnished where they are the most useful and the most needed.

Persons of lower intellectual and ethical development have, of course, no interest in the welfare and progress of the nation or of mankind in general. These are no concern of theirs. They think only of themselves, of their own economy, and of their own family. They neither know nor understand that in working for themselves and their family they are working for the common welfare, and that in preserving and increasing their private property they are preserving and increasing the wealth and the well-being of the nation and of humanity in general. They do not suspect that their activity is evoked and directed toward the common welfare by a law of a special character and content which compels them — as a steam or electric motor activates a multitude of wheels and other elements of a complex mechanism — to move as is necessary from the point of view of tasks which they neither understand nor know, and that if this law were abrogated or essentially changed their actions would be altogether different and the interests and aspirations they follow would entirely disappear or take another direction. However narrow these interests and aspirations are, they must by no means be identified with narrowly egoistic concern as to one's own personal and individual well-being.

Manifestly the law of inheritance plays a vital part in the relevant motivation, in connection with the existing law of domestic relations. These motives are of an egoistic character only in part. Concern for others — for the family — which extends not only during lifetime of the subject of the private economy but thereafter is of substantial importance. If, as some authorities deem desirable, the existing law of inheritance should be abrogated or reduced to practically nothing, so that the property remaining after the death of the subject would not go for the benefit of his children or next of kin but would enure to the treasury — without prejudice to the other fundamental principles of civil law — the relevant motivation would then be basically altered. The change would be so fundamental that, in the result, the national wealth and welfare would collapse instead of being conserved and expanded.

The existing law does not enjoin that subjects of private economic units so organize their lives and economic activity — and in particular that they so manage production and limit consumption — that the portions of the national wealth entrusted to them be conserved and increased even for the time after their death. On the contrary, these subjects are free so to organize their lives — and in particular so to raise the level of their consumption — as to absorb not only all their income but even their capital. They are free to turn their private capital into correspondingly high annuities through appropriate contracts, and in general to act on the principle of *après moi le déluge*: what happens after death is immaterial provided one has lived a life of enjoyment. Such conduct would inevitably lead to the ruin of national wealth and welfare. But the present civil law, while neither prohibiting such conduct nor enjoining its opposite, does — through the corresponding premises and guarantees of a right of inheritance — create indirect motives in favor of conduct more rational and socially advantageous. If this right were abrogated or radically undermined, it would mean the destruction or substantial impairment of this motivation. But if, in addition, we were to abrogate the principles of the modern law of domestic relations — and especially if (in accordance with the ideals of Plato) we should introduce the collective bringing up of children by the state (thus removing concern for children even during one's life), or even the corresponding standardization of relationships of the sexes *with the present right of property preserved*, the result would be the dominance of purely egoistic motivation which is mistakenly supposed by many representatives of theoretical political economy to be decisive in economic life.

The motivation examined *supra* may be termed ego-altruistic motivation and corresponds to the concept of independent or free legal motivation already considered. No law ordains that citizens be thrifty as to the elements of the national capital which have been acquired — and are to be managed and disposed of — by them without any obligation to account therefor, or industrious in producing economic goods which are socially necessary and useful and supplying these where needed. Such conduct is not legally obligatory. It is attained indirectly by the creation of motives in favor of the free and independent choice of action which is socially necessary and advantageous.

The foregoing does not purport to be a complete scientific classification and exposition of the relevant motivational action of civil law. For this at least three further investigations must be undertaken.

(1) A study of the psychological motivation of the complex civil law system: creation and direction of the free and independent legal motivation which is our immediate concern derive not from the foregoing principles of the existing legal order only but also from many other elements of private law, in connection with certain elements of public law: only the complex interaction of the many elements of the system of existing law provides the motivation on which the desirable individual and mass conduct rests and by which it is activated.

(2) A corresponding study of the *motivation itself* which is produced

by this law: its elements, character, and direction. The preceding exposition contained nothing beyond brief hints which were far from adequate to any complete analysis of the matter.

(3) A study of the *action* of the relevant motivation in evoking individual and mass conduct. The indications *supra* as to conserving and increasing the national wealth and well-being — as to producing goods socially necessary and useful and supplying them where needed and so forth — merely characterize in a general way the direction of this conduct. Knowledge of the character and direction of the psychic pressures brought about by the law with which we are now concerned would make possible innumerable inferences as to how this motivation could lead to the production of more goods and their movement to those who need them, as well as to the distribution of national capital and income as between various persons taking part in the complex process.

The first two of these investigations have not yet been worked out by science. It is the task of the future to fill this lacuna. The third was worked out long ago, with brilliant success in some respects, and with conspicuous energy since the time of Adam Smith and the appearance of his investigation into the nature and causes of the wealth of nations: a work which may justly be called a work of genius. To the development of this subject (though without proper consciousness of its nature and foundations) a special science, theoretical political economy, is devoted. It has achieved greater success, and is more flourishing, than any other concerned with social phenomena. Inasmuch as the constant and uniform motivational action of the civil law evokes uniform economic conduct, this science has successfully established a whole line of interesting and important "economic laws" which record uniformities of economic conduct — but nothing more. Since this science is wholly unconscious of its nature as a theory of the motivational action of private law (in connection with certain elements of public law), it neither comprehends nor correctly defines its object: the nature of the class phenomena as to which it establishes its theories. Controversies on this score are endless. Nor does it possess either consciousness or a correct definition of the nature of the premises from which it starts in establishing its theories: as indicated *supra*, instead of studying and defining the ego-altruistic motivation evoked by the civil law, it sets out chiefly a hypothetical egoism — the operation of exclusively egoistic motives in economic life — as the fundamental premise for deductive inferences — a premise which (as is manifest from the foregoing considerations relative to the law of inheritance and the like) is indefensible against criticism as well as erroneous in principle (even regarded as a working hypothesis known to be at variance with reality). Notwithstanding such a serious flaw in the very foundation of the science and the fact that its fundamental concepts and premises are neither examined nor ascertained, the theory flourishes in fact and has already achieved great success for the reason that conditions were peculiarly and exceptionally favorable for its development. These successes, of course, are achieved not through the consistent application of the basic concepts and premises at first proposed, but in spite of them: they are inapplicable in fact and are replaced by adequate ideas and propositions of an entirely different sort. Without any reference to the definitions of economy and so forth proposed by the various authors, representatives of the theory of economic phenomena do in fact unanimously describe the action of private law motivation. Nor does a single economist actually carry out his promise further to deduce all doctrines from the hypothesis of the exclusive action of egoism: had any economist sought to do so he must, as we have shown, have ended with the destruction — not the construction — of the national economy: with hunger, pauperism, and so forth. Instead, everything is described in a form approximately corresponding to the actual tendencies of the motivational action of the civil law. In other words the initial hypothesis is abandoned *sub silentio* in favor of other ideas which are unconsciously employed as starting points: ideas of such motivation and conduct as are in fact predominant — ideas which are specifically characteristic of the average *bonus pater familias* (in the language of the Roman jurists), a respectable and good man concerned, not only for his own ego and his own enjoyments, but also for his family and its future, and not at all typical of a monster or an Epicurean egoist.

Two important and valuable sciences stand in an utterly unique, strange, and abnormal relationship to each other: those of law in general and of civil law in particular, on the one hand, and the theory of economic phenomena on the other. They are studying essentially one and the same thing (from different sides) but they do not know each other, their paths diverge, and they are unconscious of their mutual bond and of the fact that they are studying a common object.

The science of law — in particular the science of civil law — reasons about "the protection of private interests" although not far away is the brilliant light of a fine and graceful science: a theory of the action of the civil law (though a partial and incomplete theory). On the other hand, political economy seeks (and fails) to define the object of its study and the basic factors operative therein, all unconscious of the fact that it is a theory of the action of law which is being studied by another adjacent science: that of civil law. This abnormal state of affairs, which is seriously detrimental to both sides, should be eliminated by introducing the sciences to each other and bringing them into association.

Of course the motivational action by no means exhausts the psychic action of civil law. The more profound and — from the point of view of history and the future of mankind — the more essential psychic action of civil law is that of changing human character: particularly of fostering economic efficiency, eradicating laziness, apathy, carelessness, thoughtlessness, and prodigality with reference to economic benefits, and developing thrift, industriousness, enterprise, and the capacity and inclination for planned concern about the welfare of oneself and of others. These are the attributes of character which, to the degree that they have been developed and strengthened in the masses, not only make the action of the respective legal systems substantially more successful and markedly raise the level of the national well-being, but also make it possible to weaken the powerful motivational pressure created by the present law (the threat of death from hunger), or even to eliminate this motivation and to substitute therefor a more gentle and humane system of motivational and educational influence.

Scientific study of the educative action of civil law — study as deep and all-embracing as possible — is an important task of the future: important, in particular, from the point of view of *savoir pour prévoir* (to know in order to foresee).

On the contrary, the socialistic order would represent a standardization of economic life, and a system of legal motivation and education, essentially different from that characterized above. All members of society would have a right to sustenance, and to be supplied with the means of satisfying other needs, out of the general store, and at the general expense, while those capable of work would be bound to work for the common welfare: to take part in the general process of producing economic goods with the aid of common instruments of production, or to fulfill other functions entrusted to them as leaders or subordinate executives, in accordance with the directions of others. Instead of the independent action of a multitude of separate economic units with no general plan or guidance whatsoever from any central authority, there would be a single general economy with a single complex organization, a single plan, guidance and management, a single guiding and directing center, and a complex and numerous hierarchy of subordinate organs with corresponding legal regulation of the activity of central and supreme organs and of a host of subordinate organs.

This system may be characterized as one of centralized or planned organization, as distinguished from the system examined *supra* which may be called a system of decentralization (the system wherein a multitude of individuals and economies are separate and independent).

As to the legal motivation operative in the centralized regime of production, there would be none of the free or independent legal motivation of an ego-altruistic character mentioned *supra*, in view of the right of all members of society (children and adults) to sustenance and to satisfaction of other needs out of the general stock. Instead, in view of the obligation to work for the general good, the operative system of motivation would combine two classes of the motivational action of law: (1) the motivation which was called *supra* specific-law or immediate legal motivation (various activities for the common good, such as work in the field, sewing, and the like which would proceed according to the duty of social service in accordance with the corresponding legal precepts); and (2) the motivation which was called *supra* auxiliary motivation (the intensity of which depends on the achieved level of social education: law, morality, religion, and so forth). The lower this level — as in case of a premature reform, before a certain relatively high degree of industriousness and of the other elements of economic efficiency has been attained with the aid of the law of property, the law of inheritance, and so forth — the more powerful would be the supplementary psychic pressure requisite for the relevant legal order to function well or even tolerably.[3]

In accordance with the foregoing distinctions as regards content and motivation, the educative action of socialistic law would also differ as being more immediately directed at working out readiness and capacity for interest in social matters and corresponding action and so forth, whereas certain elements of the national character brought out by the prior law (such as the proneness to profits and greed and the tendency to hold family ties and associations higher than the general welfare) would be subjected to a reverse development going even so far as atrophy.

In the present legal order each of the two types of legal motivation of human conduct and education briefly characterized *supra* exists and

[3] Accordingly, the usual combination of the idea of social equality with the ideas and aspirations of socialism is a misunderstanding since it assumes such perfection of character in the national masses that the presence of law suffices, without sanctions of any kind, for the relevant legal order to operate successfully, and presupposes that merely pointing out to each his obligations, distributing work, and so forth will suffice to cause all — or almost all — to manifest the corresponding zeal and industry.

acts upon the other: the decentralized system with independent motivation, and the centralized system which is organized and collectivized.

Certain areas of life are regulated through the establishment of a complex system of higher and lower (subordinate and inferior) authorities, with activity prescribed as to object and direction pursuant to plan and a single directing center, a single budget, and so forth. Their activity, which is directed at satisfying the corresponding social needs, is based on legal motivation which combines specific legal motivation (the motivation of consciousness of the duty of social service: state, city, and the like) and auxiliary motivation (promotion in service if the duty is zealously and successfully performed, and so forth). The requirements of state defense (military and naval affairs), of justice, the various branches of communications (the post, the telegraph, and the railroad), and the sale of beverages, tobacco, and the like (where these matters are transferred to collective management through systems of monopoly) thus come within the sphere of action of a centralized system whose principal nuclei of administration are in the capitals of the respective states. Under their paramount administration and pursuant to directives which they issue (statutes in the narrow sense), various subordinate collective economic units operate (districts, cities, and so forth): these may be illustrated by matters of sanitation, hospitalization, and education, city lighting, water supply, telephones, and tramways.

Other national needs — including the most urgent needs such as bread and food in general, clothing, housing, and so forth — are subserved through decentralization with innumerable independent economic centers acting upon their own judgment with independent motivation.

SECTION 42. *The Law of Social Serving and Individual (Free) Law*

The propositions established *supra* are not definitions of the nature of public and private law in the sense of pointing out the common and the distinguishing indicia of what is ordinarily called or referred to public law on the one hand and private law on the other: for the methodological reasons set out in Chapter I one must not, in the province of theory as such, be occupied with a search of this character.

Aside, however, from their importance to explain the action and the social significance of law (particularly of private law), the nature of the contemporary (and of past or possible) social orders and the relations of law and economics, the propositions developed *supra* comprise the foundation for building a classification of law which is independent of terminological habits and other traditions. Solution of this task requires that consideration be given to the foregoing explanation of the organizational function of law, and especially to the clarification of the nature of state authority and the state. Social organizations give the impression, as it were, of single organisms with a single "will" and a single directing nerve center, and a single system of subordinate organs (operating in accord with the needs and the welfare of the whole) and give rise — through the association of ideas — to corresponding quasi biological doctrines of sociology and political science. These organizations are created by the development of psychic phenomena of the legal (imperative-attributive) class. Most important are the phenomena of the law of social-ancillary authority, within whose framework the concomitant legal obligations (to be concerned about the welfare of subordinates or the common welfare of a certain social group: family, *gens*, tribe, and the like) prevail. Such social-ancillary authorities are essentially distinct from dominant authorities — as, for instance, with regard to slaves, servants, or the like — where there is no such (concomitant) obligation.

Leaving on one side, for the time being, the obligation to be concerned for the welfare of subjects, and making use of what has already been explained *supra* as to object ideas, we may now more precisely define the nature and specific differentiation of the two types of rights of legal opinions and convictions. The objects of the rights of the social-ancillary authorities are commands and other actions *for the welfare of subjects or of the social group*, as distinguished from the rights of the dominant authorities whose objects are commands which influence subjects irrespective of any considerations for their welfare.

The object ideas in the consciousness of social-ancillary authorities comprise ideas of the welfare of subjects or of the social group and specified directives for conduct as well as a limitation of the application upon the subjects of the commands, punishments, and so forth. On the contrary, the object ideas in the consciousness of dominant authorities contain no such ideas, directives, or limitations upon conduct: for example, there is no prohibition against exploiting the subjects for personal gain, for satisfying personal whims, for amusing guests, and the like.

In the minds of those experiencing ideas of the welfare of subjects, of the common welfare, or of serving subjects or the common interest, these are for the most part of a more or less confused and indistinct character, or even latent below the threshold of consciousness. If, however, we turn our attention to them — as by questions addressed to heads of households, guardians, representatives of tribal authority, monarchs, and the like regarding their understanding of their right to issue commands and to manage the fate and the affairs of the subjects — we can readily clarify the content of the corresponding legal convictions and demonstrate the presence therein of the ideas we have indicated. Essentially different in this regard is the content of object ideas disclosed by a study of the legal mentality of dominant authorities. *This differentiation in object ideas* is the criterion for dividing the relevant legal phenomena, opinions, convictions, and projections (norms, rights, and so forth) into (a) those which belong to social-ancillary or public law, and (b) those which belong to free or private law.

Sometimes it is asserted that the special characteristic of public law is authority and subjection, and of private law, equality and independence. This is emphatically a misconception from the point of view not merely of our classification (which is independent of traditions, terminological habits, and so forth) but also of the traditional distribution of the material between the two groups: private law and public law. Jurists refer the rights of masters in respect of slaves (perfectly correctly) to private law. In precisely the same way, no jurist refers the relationship between master and servant or employer and employee to public law. This misunderstanding is the more curious because, by the traditional doctrine, both the *patria potestas* of the head of a Roman household (over children, and their wives and children, and so forth) and the modern domestic and guardianship authorities are (in our opinion incorrectly) referred to private law.

In both private and public law, authority and subordination are found. There are, however, two classes of legal phenomena which are distinct in principle: (1) those comprising the idea of the welfare of subjects or of the social group which is being administered (of serving it) and (2) those which comprise no such ideas. To distinguish two species of law according to goal or purpose, and to suppose that the aim of private law is the defense of private interests, is impossible; yet in private and public law we are concerned with distinct "interests," with the welfare of distinct persons, in the sense of legal psychology. In the former the consciousness of rights has an "egocentric," and in the latter an "altruistic," direction (it is a matter not of one's own welfare as such but of the welfare of others: of serving others). From at least the time of Ulpian down to the present this psychological distinction has produced and sustained the idea of the distinction of goal or purpose in the two kinds of law, but could not itself be explained and scientifically formulated since neither the instruments nor the methods of scientific investigation necessary to that end were available: the indispensable psychological concepts and methods of study. Neither in the science of civil law (where even the authority of the father or the husband is indistinguishable from a property right) nor in modern political science (with its concepts of "will" and "force") could this be done while state authority is indistinguishable not only from state property or authority over slaves but even from the will and force of a robber gang. In neither field was it possible to analyze psychologically the relevant phenomena and to clarify the specific distinction between private law authorities on the one hand and social-ancillary authorities on the other.

In social organizations, and especially in states, there are many authorities falling into special arrangements of preëminence and hierarchy (adapted to the needs of social life and of orderly centralized government in accordance with plan). There are also innumerable subordinate special authorities with a higher single general social-ancillary authority.[1] As regards the special authorities, ideas of serving the general welfare of the social group are complicated by ideas of the special matter entrusted to the particular subject — the special social service imposed upon the individual — such as the command of an army, division, regiment, or company, the management of the matter of national education in general or of a school district or of such and such an educational institution or charge of the economic part therein, or of such and such a group of pupils and so forth.

Here we have countless public rights and subjects of those rights, from monarchs and presidents down to policemen, noncommissioned officers, and the like: but in modern political science these rights and subjects are removed from the list of public rights and subjects of rights of authority since the state is understood as a single personality with a single will and a host of organs thereof, and reality is not studied psychologically by means of observation.

Akin to rights of authority are rights to participate in the management of common affairs by certain declarations which must be taken into account by others (the legal capacity to make declarations plus claims that they be taken into account), such as the right of voting in the matter of forming collective decisions (in national assemblies, parliaments, legislative commissions, courts, administrative departmental institutions), rights of legislative or other initiative election rights relative to national representation or local self-government, in universities, and the like.

Even here the structure of the legal consciousness comprises ideas of the common welfare and consequently directives and limitations as to

[1] Cf. Section 15.

the corresponding conduct. Sometimes people vote in parliaments or city councils and the like upon egoistic considerations, of course, such as personal gain or a career or elect others (or do not elect them) upon considerations of personal friendship, enmity, envy, gain, or similar considerations which have nothing in common with the general welfare, but this is conceived of as an abuse and contrary to the demands of the normal legal conscience.

Both categories of rights may be combined in one more general group of public rights: rights to participate in the management (in the general sense) of affairs of common concern for the welfare of social groups (state, *gens*, and so forth). Combined with the rights of the social-ancillary authorities are obligations to be concerned for the welfare of subjects or for the general welfare of the social group, and, in particular, to effectuate the rights of authority accordingly. In conformity with the hierarchical arrangement of authorities in social groups, these obligations also are arranged hierarchically — graphically expressed in the form of a pyramid — with the obligation of general and supreme concern at the top, and a system of descending social services dependent upon directives from above and having a field of action constantly growing narrower and more special (monarchs, ministers . . . policemen, noncommissioned officers, and the like).

Here we have in turn a multitude of legal relationships and of rights. These rights (legal relationships) are more numerous because several classes of legal relationships, with various subjects of the right, ordinarily correspond to one and the same function or service. Certain considerations must be kept in view in connection with the problem of who are those to whom is ascribed the right to demand that the subject carrying on a certain social service do his duty.

(1) The right may be ascribed to the social group as such — to the state in the field of state service; the corresponding obligations *with reference to the state* are ascribed to the monarch, the ministers, the judges, and so forth, while to the state is ascribed the corresponding right (a legal claim to fulfillment). Instead of the social group, as the alleged subject of the right, all the members of the group sometimes figure as subjects of relevant rights: the Caliph who is not concerned about the appointment of judges violates the rights of "all the faithful" and the like.

(2) In conformity with the hierarchical arrangement of authorities and social services, subordinates are bound properly to fulfill their duty with reference to their superiors and eventually to the long line of authorities right to the top of the pyramid, so that there are whole series of

corresponding legal relationships on the basis of one and the same matter of service. To superiors is ascribed a claim that subordinates carry out their work in accordance with the injunctions of the law and, in particular, in conformity with the directions of superiors who in their turn are under the obligation to require fulfillment, to compel the subordinates thereto, and so forth. Accordingly, in theocratic states where the subject of supreme authority is the Deity, all subordinates who are serving and fail to carry out their duty of service violate the rights of the Deity (Allah, Jehovah, and so forth).

(3) Of course no one member of the social group, family, gens, state, and the like has (in a normal legal mind) a right to demand that the concern of representatives of the relevant social authorities be concentrated specially and exclusively upon him, and the welfare of other members of the group and of the group as such neglected. Even individual members of the group, however, have (in the normal legal mentality) a right to demand that the relevant concern for the welfare of the whole and of all extend in accordance with justice (intuitive law) or positive norms to them (among others) by virtue of the duty of the corresponding authority.

Hence arises a multitude of legal experiences with corresponding subject and object ideas: a host of corresponding legal relationships between separate members of the group and subjects of the social authority (including the social group to the extent that it seems as such a subject of a right of authority and of a duty of concern). In particular, the general and supreme obligation of serving and various subordinate and special obligations of this sort include interposition in behalf of the members of one's own group, the prevention of insults, the furnishing of defense to members of the group within the boundaries of the concern for the general welfare, of course, so that in a specific case there may be no obligation to come to the aid of a member of the group (as where disaster threatens the entire group). To this, and within these bounds, individual members of the group who need protection have a right.

The supreme obligation of social concern is differently effectuated and developed in the various classes of social groups and at the various stages of their development. Whereas in social groups consisting of kindred (family, gens, and the like) it includes also feeding and clothing all members of the group and so forth, in official groups not related by kinship — and in the lower stages of development — it is effectuated exclusively, or almost exclusively, in relations toward other social groups (in the form of defending the group and its individual members against external enemies). As the state order gradually develops, the sphere of serving is broadened to include defense against injury even within the group, and so forth. In the socialistic state, as in social groups related by blood, it would extend even to furnishing food, clothing, and other necessities to individual members. Accordingly, in groups related by blood or in the socialistic state, these rights of individual citizens with regard to the group and to the rulers are extremely broad and substantial.

All these categories of legal experiences (and of norms and legal relationships) comprise in their intellectual structure — and specifically in the structure of object ideas — ideas of social service: of serving the social group — the general welfare — as the chief directive of conduct.

The obligation of serving the social group (the common welfare) is ascribed not only to representatives of social authority and, in general, to those having a right to participate in the management of common affairs, but also to members of the group in general. This includes obligations (of those bodily able) to participate in defending the group against enemies (the liability to military service, blood vengeance, and the like) and in satisfying general needs with their individual toil or by payment in kind or in money, or in other ways. The subjects of the corresponding rights are the social groups as such: "all" other members of the group and the relevant superiors (including the Deity in theocratic states).

We combine all legal experiences — norms, rights, and obligations — comprising the idea of social serving into one class under the name social-ancillary law or the law of centralization. All law other than that which possesses this particular character of subject ideas we refer to the contrasted class of law which does not obligate to social serving: the law of decentralization (private law, and the like: it is not the name which is important).

For clarification and the avoidance of misapprehension certain observations are in order.

(1) In the life of social groups a more or less important part is played by rights (analogous to a property right) with regard to others (including other social groups) who are unrelated to the group that they abstain from encroachment of every sort upon the group or its members and from interference in the affairs of the group, and that they tolerate every kind of dictate or prompting of the group and of its authorities with regard to their members.[2] From the point of view of the proposed classification these legal relationships — particularly the corresponding legal relationships between states, and between independent tribal groups — and the corresponding norms and legal experiences are related

[2] Cf. Section 16.

not to social-ancillary law (the law of centralization) but to the law of the opposite class. If a tribe or a state claims noninterference on the part of another, the concern is here not with the service of one subject to another or with joint service to any higher collective whole, but specifically with noninterference by one subject into the affairs of another — as is true where there is a right *in rem* to things or slaves, or the like. The relevant law does not unite or centralize: it "disunites" and "repels others." Accordingly, in Roman law, or in modern family law, we distinguish two elements which are different in principle: (a) law within the family and the like on the one hand (the law of domestic authority and concern: the right of the *pater familias* to obedience from other members of the family) and (b) external law eliminating interference: law effectuated in Rome by *vindicatio filii* (and in general actions built on the model of actions involving a right of property). The former has the same nature as the law of the state organization, the latter the same as the law of property, international law, and so forth.

(2) In certain fields of the law jurists — with no appropriate general criterion at their disposal for the differentiation of private and public law — take the presence of free will or spontaneity in an accord (the presence of a contract) as an auxiliary *differentia specifica* in order to refer certain phenomena such as joint stock companies to private law. With this it is impossible to agree. Social organizations in our sense may be founded by means of contract, and this is so even of states: sometimes new states are instituted or annexed to existing states by contract. From the point of view of our classification it may be observed that the family is founded by means of a contract — the marriage contract — while the rights of children and of parents may alike be acquired through a contract of adoption. The same is true of other social groups. The reason, however, why joint stock companies, trading partnerships, and the like must be referred to private law is not because they are established by contract, but because there is no trace of social serving in the foregoing sense: there is, on the contrary, the dominance — the legally admissible dominance — of the psychology of individual gain. Jurists who put forward the criterion of contract should refer international contract law not to public law but to private law (and this would be correct): this, however, they do not do.

The established classes of law according to the content of the object ideas may then be divided into sub-classes, species, and varieties. In speaking of social organizations, we had chiefly in view general social organizations: social organizations with general, rather than special, social-ancillary authority and concern. However special social organizations, such as ecclesiastical organizations (and, in particular, the universal organization of the Catholic church with its center in Rome), may be referred to the same class. Accordingly we divide social organizations and their law into two species: general and special. General social organizations and their laws must then be divided into two varieties: (1) those of kinship (family, tribe, and the like), and (2) those not related by blood: official organizations (states).

The law of social decentralization may in turn be divided into two species: (1) the law as between independent social groups, such as modern international or inter-state law, the law obtaining between different *gentes* at the time of independent tribal groups and the like (external or inter-group decentralized law, further divided into sub-species in accordance with the classification of independent social groups), and (2) the law within the social groups (internal or inter-individual law, in the conditional sense that it *chiefly* regulates relations between individuals or members of a tribe or state, but is by no means limited to these relationships). This second species of law may then in turn be divided into sub-species in accordance with the classification of social groups.

Not only, then, do the traditional groups termed "private law" and "public law" fall far short of embracing all the species of law (being adapted only to a definite stage of the development of law) — they so arrange the law that heterogeneous phenomena are combined into one group while homogeneous phenomena are separated from each other. The chief faults of this sort are that inter-state law is referred to public law together with the law of state organization, while the law of family organization (and wardship) is referred to private law. These branches of law should change places.

Nomenclature not being a matter of prime importance, the terms "private" and "public" law may either be transferred to the two classes of law established *supra* as a higher division of law according to the content of the object ideas (social-ancillary or centralized law, and individual — free or decentralized law) or be reserved especially for the law with which contemporary jurisprudence is concerned after necessary regrouping has been duly effected.

The scientific basis and justification of the proposed division of law into social-ancillary law and free law is that it provides a foundation whereon to construct adequate theories for the successful cognition and explanation of phenomena.

Contemporary jurisprudence contains something like embryos of the two theories (of civil law and of public law) in the form of certain general assertions as to these alleged classes. Certain propositions are relevant in this connection.

(a) It has already been shown that the independence of subjects is found in civil law whereas there are authority and subordination in public law. Leaving on one side the phenomenon of slavery and of the private law authority of the master in general, this characterization is admissible but only upon the essential condition precedent that the branches of law just mentioned be first transposed, since this characterization of private law is particularly well suited to international law and not at all appropriate to the law of family organization (an indication of faulty classification). With the faults of "jumping" thus eliminated, it is proper thereafter to extend the relevant characterizations to the two broad classes of law proposed above in order to eliminate the faults of "limping," for the phenomenon of authority is bound up with the nature of social organizations in general and not with the state organization in particular.

(b) In public law rights are connected with corresponding obligations, whereas in private law rights do not, by the general rule, carry any obligation that they be effectuated. It is manifest from what has already been set out that there is a category of public rights embodying no such obligation. The foregoing characterization is therefore admissible if the classification is corrected as indicated *supra*: specifically, the special characteristic now ascribed to civil law is typical of inter-state (and other inter-group) law.

(c) As a general rule, freedom to dispose of one's rights — to assign them to another, to renounce them and the like — is found in the civil law, whereas there is none of this in public law. What has been said *supra* with regard to the first two propositions is here applicable *mutatis mutandis*. These — like the foregoing — distinctions are associated with the nature of the two classes which we have established. Consequently that which is referred to public law by the proposition cited suffers from the fault of "jumping" in that international law is referred to public law.

(d) The freedom of disposition characteristic of the civil law is manifested also in civil proceedings in court; in the freedom of the civil obligee to initiate action or not, to demand that everything due him or (if he wishes) only certain elements thereof, be adjudicated upon, to forgive and to terminate the proceedings, and so forth. Of this there is nothing in the proceedings concerning public rights. Again we can say that the relevant freedom is characteristic specifically of international law insofar as the sides wish to hand over their problem for judicial examination.

(e) The civil law norms are for the most part of a dispositive nature: they are applied only insofar as the interested parties have not established anything different through a corresponding arrangement (thus rules of inheritance according to law apply only if there is no will). The norms of public law are on the contrary of a "coercive" character. Here, too, unfortunate grouping has led to the mistakes pointed out *supra*. Freedom of the subjects is particularly characteristic of international law (and in general of inter-group law) with reference to the international courts, and so forth.

(f) All social-ancillary rights including the absolute monarch's rights of authority, are relative rights: in public law in our sense there are and can be no absolute rights binding on all and sundry, since here it is a matter of organizing and governing a definite social group rather than of authority over all the people in the world or other subjects, states, and so forth. In the law of decentralization, on the contrary, absolute rights are not only possible — they play an important part. The basis of all kinds of decentralized law, and so of civil law also (in the traditional sense) as well as of international law, is a principle which may be formulated as *noli me tangere*: no one dares to touch me or mine or to interfere in my affairs — all are bound to refrain from encroachment, and to tolerate acts of dominion of every kind by me within my sphere.

This principle embraces the vast majority of rights — and they are the most important rights — of international, inter-tribal, inter-individual law, and so forth. A second principle of international, inter-individual law is most important for the residue not embraced by *noli me tangere: pacta servanda sunt*. On the basis of this principle, as well as on the ground of sanctions if rights are violated (the principle of compensation for harm), relative rights, too, are found in international law and so forth. Hence it is apparent that the presence of the subject idea "all and sundry" (or "no one shall" and the like) is practically a suitable and infallible criterion for excluding the relevant law from the sphere of public law and relating it to private law. This is so as to the right of life, honor, bodily inviolability, and so forth — rights which even now some jurists refer to private rights. Criminal law and the corresponding obligation of state authority are, of course, public law.

(g) Social-ancillary law is characterized by the decisive predominance of positive obligations (of positive actions of social serving) and of corresponding norms, rights, and so forth, whereas free law which embodies no obligation of social service (international law and so forth) is characterized by the decisive predominance of the two remaining types of obligations, rights, norms, legal opinions and convictions, having object ideas of "abstentions" and tolerations (*noli me tangere; pacta sunt servanda;* even here positive obligations also are of course possible).

There is, however, something else more important, from the point of view of the theory of law, than the establishment of such comparative characterizations. The proposed division clarifies the content of the law and brings it into plain and intelligible relations — not only the content of the contemporary law of civilized nations but also that of the law of other nations, other epochs, and so forth. The essence and content of the law of social organizations of every possible type and stage of development may be reduced to a few fundamental principles, and this is important for theory, for a doctrinal system, for the history of law, for descriptive jurisprudence, and for legal policy.

The most important consideration is, however, that the proposed definition represents a classification which can serve as a basis for establishing and working out corresponding adequate theories. In particular, the difference between the basic (centralized and decentralized) economic orders, human conduct and its governance in general, and the distinction between the nature of motivation in the one case and in the other provide a foundation for the building of two different adequate theories of legal motivation and legal education. This in turn is of enormous importance from the point of view of the future science of legal policy: there should be — besides a general supreme policy of law — two subordinate systems of policy, of decentralized law and of centralized law. The construction and development of these theories — as well as of theories of the origin and development of each of two laws — lie beyond the scope of this treatise.

CHAPTER VIII

LAW AND SOCIO-PSYCHIC LIFE

SECTION 43. *A Bilateral Causal Bond between Law and Socio-Psychic Life*

Law is, on the one hand, a factor of socio-psychic life since its development evokes certain processes in the minds and conduct of individuals and masses. On the other hand, law is itself a product of certain socio-psychic processes: it is created and changed by them in accordance with laws of causal significance. Accordingly, besides the study of law for itself as a special class of phenomena possessing a special nature, a special content, special characteristic attributes and so forth, legal theory must study this bilateral causal connection. It must study law both as a factor (building a theory of the causal action of law) and as a product (constructing a theory of the origin and development of law).

The first doctrine, as to the causal action of law, does not yet exist at all in contemporary science, nor is there even any consciousness that it is appropriate and necessary to study law from this point of view. Some altogether unsatisfactory rudiments of such a doctrine are to be found, if at all, in various attempts to define the concept of law which comprise direct or indirect indications of the causal action of law as it appears to the authors of these definitions. Thus implicit in definitions of law from the point of view of coercion is an indication that the action of law consists in constraining people to certain conduct. In definitions of law from the point of view of freedom are intimations that the action of law consists in the establishment, safeguarding, and organization of freedom. A similar view, obtaining from the time when Ihering's doctrines became widespread, is that the action and the significance of law consist in the protection of interests.

The construction of a scientific and adequate theory of the action of law presupposes an examination of the nature of law. If the starting point is that law represents commands of a will possessing greater or insuperable force, addressed to a weaker will which is constrained to submit thereto, the idea that the action of law consists in constraint — in defending interests by commands and compulsion and so on — is perfectly natural. But if law is regarded as a psychic process of a special sort — a special variety of ethical experience — such views then collapse of themselves as being incoherent and at variance with the nature of that whose operation is under scrutiny. The theory of causal action of law as psychic processes must be a psychological theory. The chief and basic propositions of that theory have been noted *supra*.[1]

The problem of the origin and development of law stands somewhat better in modern jurisprudence: at least the problem is stated, and a solution is offered by some jurists. The origin of law or of "statutes," in the sense of the norms of community life, is a matter that has interested human thought from antiquity. We have already pointed out [2] that the tendency to ascribe the establishment of law and morality to higher beings of a supernatural order corresponds to the particular character of higher mystic authority possessed by ethical impulsions. Accordingly, the most ancient and widespread doctrine as to the origin of norms of community living is that of their divine origin. It has been replaced by diverse metaphysical and mystical doctrines which substitute for deities sundry other supreme forces and beings: "Nature" conceived of as a higher being, world "Reason," "objective spirit," and the like. Most of the relevant doctrines have in view so-called natural law. As to positive law, various representatives of the legal philosophy of earlier ages (before the doctrines of the so-called historical school appeared and became widespread) ascribed its creation to conscious and designed human activity for the attainment of certain ends: peace, well-being, and so forth. Some authorities identified positive law with statutes, and reduced its origin and development simply to the will and discretion of legislators, monarchs, and so forth, while others ascribed the establishment of the positive law to a contract, whereby — in order to obtain peace, order, and the like — people consented to set up a superior authority and to obey it, and that authority later issued laws and so forth acting in accordance with this contract. But the obligatory force of the contract rested in natural law which required the observance of contracts. Periodically in the history of human thought theories appear which reduce all law — as well as morality, religious beliefs, and so forth — to the insidious invention of persons seeking better to dominate others and to effectuate their own interests. Such doctrines are seemingly expressive of lofty criticism but are essentially naive.

At the beginning of the nineteenth century the so-called historical school came out against doctrines that the positive law was consciously

[1] Cf. Sections 7 and 49.

[2] Cf. Sections 6 and 8.

and arbitrarily created, and asserted that law like language, *mores* and so on is a cultural product which develops regularly, unnoted, gradually and independently of any human will, design, or consciousness whatsoever, and manifests the national spirit. In this national spirit the principles of national law are originally dormant. Gradually they are disclosed in history in the form of corresponding general convictions manifested in the better and immediate form of customary law, and then in the activity of the legislator and of the science of law which appear (or at all events are bound to appear) as organs and representatives of the national spirit and interpreters of the common conviction. This theory, too, must be referred to the category of mystic doctrines: its national spirit represents a lofty but inscrutable concept distinct from the national mind as a totality or aggregate of individual minds, and "general conviction" is something distinct from the convictions of the particular individuals whose thoughts may even not harmonize with the supra-individual "general conviction."

The doctrine of Ihering is supposed to have created a further epoch in the theory of the origin and development of law, and to have defined the modern views of jurisprudence regarding that problem. His fundamental propositions are (1) that the law, like the state, is the effect of conscious and designed human creativeness in the pursuit of definite and practical ends: the development and safeguarding of practical interests; and (2) that — in accordance with the nature of legal norms as commands which originate in a will having at its disposal adequate force to compel obedience — the law emanates from force and authority and represents a policy of force and egoism. The authority of the state is the source of all law. Inasmuch as the law depends on force and therefore on overcoming and crushing opposition if interests clash and struggle ensues, Ihering ascribes to struggle an important part as a factor of legal development. This doctrine corresponds to the "practical" and "realistic" spirit of the time when it appeared. It was considered a great discovery and an essential step forward, and quickly became popular among jurists.

There are two further facts ordinarily ignored by legal theoreticians and not mentioned in "general legal doctrines" although they are of greatest importance with regard to the origin and development of law.

(1) In certain branches of jurisprudence — chiefly that of so-called comparative law, which is devoted to the study and comparison of the law of different nations including that of lower levels of culture — there is a conviction that it is necessary to study and explain "the laws of the development" of law, or — more accurately — to explain the

tendencies and the directions of legal development; for the time being, however, this yearning to discover these "laws" of legal "development" has not been crowned with success.

(2) The problem of the origin and development of law is considered and solved somehow not only by jurisprudence but also by sociology (the theory of society: of social processes and social development). In their attempts to reduce all social phenomena and their development to fundamental factors, forces, or processes, sociologists make corresponding assertions as well regarding the origin and development of law even when they are not speaking specifically about law as such, and the relevant doctrines are sometimes distinguished by greater depth, and possess a more serious character, than can be said as to doctrines of contemporary jurisprudence.

SECTION 44. *Toward a Scientific Theory of the Development of Law*

The problem of the origin and development of law and of the causal action of law is a psychological problem as to the origin of imperative-attributive impulsions and of impulsive-intellectual combinations or corresponding psychic dispositions (propensities to experience the corresponding impulsions), and as to the factors and processes defining their development. Between certain sociological theories (such as the Darwinian, the theory of historical materialism and the like) and the nature of law as special ethical experiences, there is no essential antagonism: one can, on the contrary, follow Darwinism or historical materialism in sociology, and the theory of law as imperative-attributive experiences at the same time. Moreover, the theory of law as imperative-attributive experiences and corresponding dispositions affords some support to both sociological theories. Thus if law is an individual-psychic experience based on corresponding dispositions, it seems from the point of view of the Darwinian theory analogous to various other elements and attributes of the psycho-physical apparatus (the organism), the origin and development of which is explained by this theory. From the point of view of economic materialism, reducing the law to special psychic phenomena is not unfavorable: legal phenomena appear to be psychic correlates — reflections of social material — and their content changes in history in accordance with changes of social material, as a function of the latter. Nonetheless, even if these sociological theories are correct, they do not suffice for the construction of an adequate theory of the origin and development of law.

Besides the establishment of the proper concept of law, the building of a scientific theory of its development requires preliminary knowledge or postulates of a twofold sort.

(1) The theory of the causal action of law — in particular of its motivational and pedagogic action. Law (together with the other factors of socio-psychic life, including morality, normative aesthetics, and others) influences the development of the human mind and changes human character in the direction of better adaptation to social life but is itself changed in conformity with these psychic changes and adapted thereto. This is the key to discovery of the historical tendencies of legal development. In general, the historical process of the formation and changing of law has been basically one of a gradual adaptation of legal motivation and pedagogy to the particular condition of the national mind. More exactly by means of the psychic action of the legal system, individual and mass conduct — and the national mind — have been directed toward general welfare. *Pari passu* with the adaptation of the human mind to social life goes a corresponding change in the law also — with, however, sundry complications, temporary delays, and so forth. The most recent legal systems require from the citizen more in the sense of socially rational conduct than did earlier systems of law which were adapted to a more primitive mentality, and attain the required conduct by acting upon the loftier sides of human character. They make use of results already attained, and rest on qualities of mass character on which earlier systems of legal motivation — adjusted to a more coarse and socially less fitting mentality — could not rest. This may be illustrated by the transition, in the production of material goods, from the system of slavery — from slave labor with its primitive and coarse motivation (the whip of overseers, the master's right to punish by death, and so forth) — to the system of free labor, economic freedom, and competition (independent free motivation). This is a symptom and a product of the cultural advance of human masses. The same is true as to the socialization of production now proceeding in various spheres, which presupposes for its success a certain degree not only of economic efficiency as such but also of the capacity and inclination to work energetically for the general good and not for oneself. In precisely the same way the substitution of a system of self-government for a despotic regime, and then the gradual democratization of the state, are symptoms and products of progress of the national mind. As human character grows better, less and less motivational pressure of the punitive-remunerative class is required in order to attain socially rational conduct. Punishments and rewards are lessened, and the collective responsibility of the whole group for violations — the intensifying motivational pressure — is re-

placed by individual responsibility. The earlier inexorable liability for evil caused (though undesignedly) is replaced by a system of punishment which admits various justifications and mitigations of responsibility and so forth. In the lower stages of culture, threats in the form of creditors cutting the delinquent debtor into pieces (the Twelve Tables), selling him into slavery, beating him in the public square until he paid, doubling the debt in case of delay, and other forms of cruelty applied in order to secure the precise and honorable fulfillment of a right resting on contract. The history of the law of contracts displays a progressive lessening of this pressure. Formerly the proper conduct of members of the household was attained by the threat of discipline by the head of the household (including the right to impose punishment of death) and his corresponding responsibility for acts of members of his household, but later history of family law displays a progressive lessening of the motivational pressures. In periods when smaller social organizations (which formerly exterminated each other) were unified to form larger groups — such as extensive states — that very fact caused greater insistence upon socially rational behavior and a demand for a coöperative attitude toward former aliens and foes. The menacing character of punishments and in general the coerciveness of the social regime was heightened, but only temporarily until the national mentality attained such development as made mitigation of the regime possible. Of course the relevant laws of the historical development of mankind and its institutions do not signify that clever people study and measure the progress of the human mind and devise law accordingly: the progress of socio-psychic adaptation is subconscious. The processes which evoke and direct it remain a mystery.

(2) Solution of this problem requires that a scientific theory of socio-psychic processes — scientific sociology — be created. The Darwinian theory (the only theory embracing the subconscious mechanism of adaptation) is in no state to explain the socio-psychic adaptation which is independent of the dying out of individuals and the breaking up of groups. It leaves out of view the special processes occurring on the basis of communication and, in general, of the psychic community between members of social groups. Psychic community is, so to speak, mutual psychic infection: not intellectual infection merely but emotional infection as well. Not only the relevant ideas, but also the emotions and impulsions connected therewith in the minds of those so communicating, are communicated and given currency. Against what caused the individual to suffer, negative impulsions — repulsions, antipathies — are developed in individual minds; while in favor of forces which had acted

in the opposite direction attractive impulsions — sympathies — are developed. The impulsive-intellectual *social* communion and psychic infection give rise to definite resultants (shared appraisals) in the life of a series of successive generations. With reference to such phenomena as falsehood, defamation, and the like, such resultants inevitably become negative impulsions, although advantages may enure to persons resorting to such actions. These impulsive resultants are communicated by impulsive-intellectual communion and infection to individuals while they are still in their childhood and beyond. On the basis of such impulsive-intellectual complexes, of whose origin the individual is unaware, inner discords, quarrels, and clashes — a battle of impulsions — may take place.

Representing the relatively uniform resultants of innumerable facts in the lives of persons (dead and living), the impulsive appraisals *supra* are proportional to the average values of the appraised objects, phenomena, rules and types of conduct — such as technical, economic, and educative methods, and methods of hygiene, and in general everything that can be conceived of and communicated, and the resulting processes are analogous to the struggle for existence and natural selection (although they are different in principle because they are produced by impulsions and not by the sickle of death). Such unconscious adaptation, improvement, and development takes place in all spheres of life: in the language itself (the chief instrument of the processes in which we are interested), in the classification of phenomena and objects, in the customs and rules of national hygiene, medicine, agronomy, education, morality, law, and so forth. Continuously these products — including the changing consciousness of mankind — alter and are adapted to the changing conditions of life.

In view of the fact that the relevant theory — the theory of impulsive choice and development — is adequate, not to law specially, but to an incomparably wider class of phenomena, and that the exposition, development, and demonstration thereof here would be inconsistent with the system of this treatise and would require a great deal of space, this chapter is limited to these brief and preliminary points, while a circumstantial proof and development of a general theory — and (on the basis thereof) of a special theory of the origin and development of law — must form the content of a special treatise.

INDEX

Bei Fragen zur Produktsicherheit wenden Sie sich bitte an:
If you have any questions regarding product safety, please contact:

Walter de Gruyter GmbH
Genthiner Straße 13
10785 Berlin
productsafety@degruyterbrill.com